MW00862137

GONE
to the
GRAVE

GONE
to the
GRAVE

Burial Customs of the Arkansas Ozarks, 1850–1950

Abby Burnett

University Press of Mississippi / Jackson

www.upress.state.ms.us

The University Press of Mississippi is a member
of the Association of American University Presses.

Copyright © 2014 by University Press of Mississippi
All rights reserved
Manufactured in the United States of America

First printing 2014
∞
Library of Congress Cataloging-in-Publication Data

Burnett, Abby.
Gone to the grave : burial customs of the Arkansas Ozarks,
1850–1950 / Abby Burnett.
pages cm
Includes bibliographical references and index.
ISBN 978-1-62846-111-4 (cloth : alk. paper) — ISBN 978-1-62846-112-1
(ebook) 1. Funeral rites and ceremonies—Arkansas—History. 2. Burial—
Social aspects—Arkansas—History. 3. Funeral rites and ceremonies—Ozark
Mountains—History. 4. Burial—Social aspects—Ozark Mountains—
History. 5. Arkansas—Social life and customs. 6. Ozark Mountains—
Social life and customs. I. Title.
GT3210.A75B87 2014
393'.9309767—dc23   2014010365

British Library Cataloging-in-Publication Data available

This book is dedicated to
Barbara Jaquish and Bill Flanagan,
whose idea got it started,
and to James Binns,
whose persistence got it finished.

Thou art gone to the grave
But we will not deplore thee
Since God was thy ransoming guide
He gave thee, He took thee
and He will restore thee
and death has no sting
since the Savior has died.

—**Lafayette Buchanan,** 1831–1849
Wesley Cemetery (Madison County)

Epitaph taken from "At A Funeral," by Reginald Heber (1783–1826), Bishop of Calcutta, India, for the Church of England. Heber wrote the poem following the death of his infant son, and several of its verses have been found on tombstones in the Arkansas Ozarks. The third line, as originally published, read, "Whose God was thy Ransom, thy Guardian, and Guide."

CONTENTS

PREFACE

The way in which society deals with death has undergone a radical change over a short period of time. Gone are the days when the sick were cared for in the home and, when they died, their bodies were washed, dressed, placed in locally made coffins, and lowered into hand-dug graves. While this was once the norm throughout the South, in the Arkansas Ozarks these traditions continued up almost to the present day, making the region a valuable source of material that elsewhere has been forgotten.

In the most remote and isolated areas of these mountains, it fell to members of the deceased's community to undertake each labor-intensive job necessary for burial. As more than one source has stated, "People were more caring back then." They had to be because, lacking an undertaker or the money with which to pay one, people relied on one another during times of sickness and death. The changeover from this way of life, and death, to today's customs began as undertakers set up shop across the Ozarks, first in the largest towns, where there were higher incomes and looser social ties. In rural communities the old ways continued until the end of World War II. Change, when it came, was brought about in part by the population shift that started during the drought years and the Depression in the 1930s, when people left the Ozarks to find work in other states. During World War II, men left to fight and not all survivors returned to their communities. By the 1950s the large labor force and the know-how needed for the home burial simply weren't available any longer. Traditions were changing in other ways as well, with both births and deaths now taking place in hospitals, rather than at home. With the advent of burial insurance, a growing acceptance of embalming, and improved roads giving undertakers egress into formerly inaccessible mountain communities, customs that had once governed life and death inevitably and irrevocably ceased.

Origins of the People and Their Customs

This book focuses on the Arkansas Ozarks, but the burial customs practiced there did not originate in those mountains, and in most instances are found

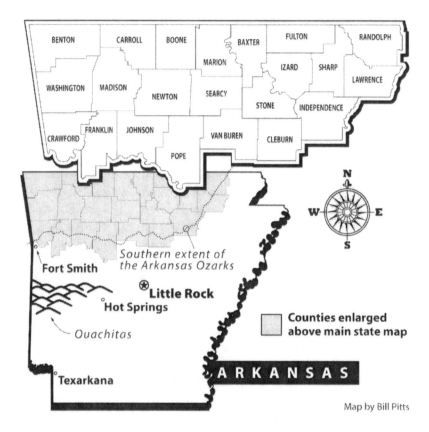

Map by Bill Pitts

throughout the South. Prior to the Civil War, two-thirds of settlers to the Arkansas Ozarks came from Tennessee and Missouri.[1] "The region's pioneer settlers possessed a homogeneity rarely witnessed west of the Mississippi," according to historian Brooks Blevins, noting that while Appalachia is credited with populating the Ozarks, in fact, settlers often arrived in Arkansas after migrating through other states, most notably Illinois, Alabama, Mississippi, and Kentucky.[2] Based on census records in 1870 and 1880, Missouri, followed by Tennessee, were the primary states of origin of white settlers to Arkansas, with Texas and Mississippi in third and fourth places, respectively.[3]

The Ozark Mountains lie, both geographically and culturally, within a region known as the Upland South. Though its exact boundaries have been debated, one book on the subject defines this territory as "the inner margin of the Atlantic coastal plain, through southern Appalachia, across the Ohio River into southern Indiana and Illinois, where it is very nearly severed in two at the 'isthmus' of the Shawnee Hill, and then southwestward through the Ozarks,

Ouachitas, and the Hill Country of Texas."[4] Settlers felt at home in the Ozarks because of the mountains' similarity to the landscape they had left behind.

Naturally, these families brought their culture with them, including such things as burial traditions, superstitions, and the use of medicinal plants, documented by folklore collectors in other states. While it is not feasible to trace every custom back to a point of origin, even a cursory examination of these collections reveals nearly identical practices, everything from delayed funerals to Decoration Day ceremonies. Frank C. Brown, compiling North Carolina folklore in 1964, provided one of the most compact comparisons of superstitions found throughout the South. Brown's collection of death and funereal customs is lavishly footnoted, and nearly every item recorded in North Carolina was found elsewhere, notably in Tennessee, Texas, Kentucky, and Missouri—all states of origin of Ozark pioneers. Time and again Brown links North Carolina customs with those collected by Arkansas's Vance Randolph and Charles Morrow Wilson.[5] There are so many parallels that it is interesting to note the few customs that *aren't* replicated in Arkansas. To give just two examples, superstitions concerning yeast-raised bread do not apply, as cornbread was an Ozark dietary staple. Nor does North Carolina's cow-lore translate (such as a lowing or bawling cow foretelling death) because hogs, not cattle, were the primary livestock in the Ozarks.

Research Methodology

The span of this book, 1850 to 1950, encompasses the Civil War through World War II. The earliest time period is documented through family histories, diaries, newspapers, Works Progress Administration (WPA) interviews, and the writings of historian-storytellers such as Silas Turnbo. Research into the late 1800s to early 1900s comes from published reminiscences, historical quarterlies, and obituaries. For the period of the 1920s to the 1950s I have been fortunate to interview Ozark residents about the old customs, and to draw on others' folklore collections, oral histories, and *Foxfire*-inspired interviews with elderly citizens.

Both the U.S. Census mortality schedules (1850–1880) and the billing records kept by storekeepers and early undertakers proved to be rich sources of information. Lest the latter sound like dull reading, consider the ledger entry from Fort Smith's Birnie Brothers undertaking firm. On 22 April 1897, Maude Allen's burial expenses were paid by Fagan Bourland, later mayor of Fort Smith, surely because Allen's cause of death was "Killed by Mrs. Fagan Bourland."

Graveyards were another valuable resource, as many of the oldest ones contain grave coverings more commonly found in other southern states, brought to Arkansas by early settlers. In addition, every burial custom discussed in this book can be documented through the tombstone record, its symbolism, inscriptions, and poetry. In studying epitaphs I have been greatly aided by historical society volunteers who transcribed and published entire inscriptions, not just names and dates.

When it seemed relevant I have included stories that took place just outside the book's 1850–1950 time period or that were gathered outside the Arkansas Ozarks. In addition to a few stories from the Missouri Ozarks or whose exact location relative to the state line could not be determined, I have used material from the entirety of the Arkansas Ozarks' twenty-two counties, even though portions of nine of these counties lie just outside the Ozarks' boundaries. Other exceptions include material from Fort Smith (Sebastian County), which has excellent early undertaking records and an African American–owned funeral home and which was the headquarters of a large coffin company; Hot Springs (Garland County), a spa town with a well-documented history; and Little Rock, home to the state's capitol, medical school, and insane asylum. I have made multiple visits to all twenty-two counties in order to do research but, because I live in northwest Arkansas, this book contains an abundance of material from the six counties in the northwest corner of the state.

There has been some debate over the value and accuracy of oral histories. Certainly stories can include errors, given the fallibility of human memory, or be sanitized by later generations. (One family upgraded their ancestor's profession, overseer of a county poor farm, to "He ran a hotel.") Such things have not deterred me from conducting interviews, however, as I found that descriptions of funerals do not vary much between speakers or counties, and are consistent with older published accounts from across the Ozarks. Folklore does not have to be collected from the area's oldest residents, perhaps, but since it has been possible to interview people who remembered seeing or even participating in these customs, I felt privileged to record their stories.

Naturally, there were many people I wish I had interviewed. My greatest regret is that I never discussed this subject with my neighbors, Dennis and Ruth Bowen Eoff, the first people my husband, Ron, and I met when we moved to the Boston Mountains in 1986. This couple was born and raised in the vicinity, as were many generations of their families. Over the years the Eoffs often shared bits of folk wisdom, such as that a March snow, melted and bottled, has the power to soothe a burn throughout the coming year. Ruth showed me how to recognize an inconspicuous plant called Poor John, used by her midwife mother-in-law to make a fever-reducing tea; Dennis shared a thermos of spicewood tea and pointed out sassafras, the two plants used in alternate seasons to make teas to either thin or thicken the blood.

Dennis was clearly troubled when he saw my husband transplanting a row of small cedar trees along our driveway. "When they're tall enough to shade your grave, you'll die," he prophesied. Whether as a result of violating this taboo or countless others my husband did, in fact, die when the trees reached approximately his height. But by then Ron had also added a room onto the north side of our log house while we were living there, and he had turned a window into a door, all taboos that Mary Celestia Parler's folklore students collected as things sure to cause a death. Such prohibitions—found also in Brown's North Carolina folklore collection—may explain why so many older homes in the Ozarks have two front doors.

Several subjects related to death and burial have not been covered here, or at least not in any depth. Because their residency falls outside of the book's time period I have omitted Native American burial customs, as well as ones unique to Catholics and Jews, given these faiths' small numbers in the Ozarks. Furthermore, I have had to omit the subject of writing wills, in part because so many early courthouses burned down (some multiple times), while the role played by religion, faith-healing, and prayer were also outside the scope of this book.

Throughout the research and writing I have been generously blessed with friends who have acted as research assistants, and by both paid and volunteer staff at historical societies, libraries, and museums, some of whom set up interviews for me with their own elderly relatives. I am deeply grateful to the more than sixty people who agreed to be interviewed (listed in the Bibliography), as well as to everyone who entrusted me with personal family photographs, funeral memorabilia, and stories that vividly dramatize the pain of losing loved ones. Given this generosity and the wealth of material it was hard to stop researching and begin writing. I suspect that I will never again work with a subject that interests and teaches me as much. Still, if one truism sums up a book on the subject of death, it's that sooner or later, everything must end.

—**Abby Burnett**
Kingston, Arkansas

ACKNOWLEDGMENTS

I wish to express my deep gratitude to everyone who has helped, in any way, with the creation of this book. In particular, I would like to thank Tommie Mooney and Bruce Vaughan, who graciously put up with my numerous requests for help, advice, and information throughout this project. In addition, I give grateful thanks to the following volunteers and staff at historical societies, museums, genealogy rooms, and libraries across the Ozarks for their help, as well as to friends and family who assisted me:

Jerry Akins, Desmond Walls Allen, Jane Andrewson, Gail Ashbrook, Jon Austin, Donald B. Ball, Judy Bancerowski, Cecilia Bankhead, Jim Barnett, Nola Barnett, Lee Bean, Bob and Patty Besom, Jim Binns, Judy Blackwell, Jerry Boen, Charles and Mary Boewe, Phil Bolinger, Andrea Cantrell, Billie Ruth (Smith) Clark, Mickey Clements, Cheri Coley, Ellen Compton, Wilma Jones Cowan, Gail Cowart, Hope Hodgdon Creek, John Cross, Bob Curry, Judy Davis, Ann Skelton Deemer, Marie Demeroukas, Donna Dodson, Vernon Eaton, Loucille Edwards, Al Einert, Lucille Brown Elder, Tina Farmer, Pat Halstead, Mildred Hamby, Tricia Hearn, Scott Hensley, Randy High, Jerry Hogan, Marlene Jackson, James Johnston, Mary Kelly, Liz Lester, Geraldine Littleton, Allyn Lord, Renee Lucy, Pat Lynch, Toinette Madison, Daniel Martin, Mollie McAllister, Lois McCutcheon, Kathleen McMurrin, Jason Meyers, Martha Milburn, Leighann C. Neilson, Liz and Wendel Norton, Shelley Ott-Bellopede, Max Parnell, George C. Phillips, Bill Plack, Anne Prichard, Vickie Pruetzel, Jerry L. Puryear, Jeremy Pye, Shirley Pyron, Carolyn Reno, Mark Reynolds, Liz Robbins, Dolores Rush, Joy Russell, Amanda E. F. Saar, Ethel Simpson, Pete Sims Jr., Marilyn Smith, Randy Smith, Geoffery Stark, Jana Stephens, Larry Stroud, Rhonda Teeter, Virginia Threet, Su Tipple, Raymond W. Toler Jr., Debbie Upton, John C. Waggoner Jr., Carl Wallian, Ann Webb, June Westphal, Cindy Wilson, Twyla Gill Wright, Susan Young, Vineta Terherst Wingate, Thomas Wonderly, Geneva Worley, Mary Wright, and David Zimmerman.

GONE
to the
GRAVE

CHAPTER ONE

Keeping Death at Bay

Death rides on
    every passing
breeze, and lurks
    in every flower.

—**Infant Harrison,** born and died 1889
Wesley Cemetery (Madison County)

There are so many ways to die.

Consider the fate of Rich McDonald, decapitated by a flying grindstone when his gristmill blew up (Washington County, 1900),[1] or Zoni Harvey (Carroll County, 1900), who heated her curling iron in the chimney of an oil lamp, which exploded, burning her to death.[2] Otis Hoskins's end was almost as unusual. Found hanging upside down in the reins beneath a horse-drawn mowing machine, the boy's death was ruled accidental because he was too well liked for it to have been foul play.[3]

Any number of people died from being crushed between or beneath railroad cars, swept away by swollen creeks, or struck by lightning while gathering crops. Miners died in cave-ins, well diggers from ill-timed dynamite charges, and timber workers from carelessness around axes and sawmill blades. Diverse fatal injuries plagued farmers: kicked or dragged to death by horses and mules, or caught and mangled in farm machinery. Children's deaths were especially inventive: drowning in rain barrels, shot by hunters who mistook them for game, killed by toys of their own devising, or eaten by hogs.

These deaths sound almost improbable but they all were culled from obituaries published up through the early 1900s, an age unencumbered by safety regulations, basic sanitation, and pure food and drug laws. Prior to the discovery of antibiotics and other drugs, people died from diseases we

Figure 1.1 The cause of death given on young Lilly V. Howerton's tombstone, in Rock Springs Cemetery (Carroll County), was surprisingly common in the late 1800s and early 1900s. *Photo by Abby Burnett.*

rarely encounter (tuberculosis, rabies) or would hardly consider fatal if we did (measles, whooping cough, infections, rashes). The least dramatic and certainly most commonplace way to leave this world was via sickness, either a chronic disease or during an epidemic of smallpox, typhoid, cholera, or yellow fever or in the great influenza epidemic of 1918.

One cause—burning to death—would seem freakish today, but was once surprisingly commonplace and primarily affected women and children. It happened because open fires were used outdoors during butchering, doing laundry and making soap, and women and toddlers (both boys and girls) wore long dresses. The newspaper account of a Miss Graham suffering fatal burns (Washington County, 1876) is striking for its concluding remark, that two other women in her community had received serious burns when their clothing caught fire—*on the same day.*[4] Benton County newspapers reported at least ten deaths from this cause in 1910 (including ones outside the county), having reported twenty-one deaths from burning over the preceding five years; more than one obituary for a child who burned to death includes mention that another sibling had previously died from the same cause. It's no wonder the State Department of Health, listing possible causes of death in its biennial report (1926–1928), included "conflagrations, burns and scalds."[5]

Newspapers treated readers to a steady diet of articles about bizarre deaths, some reprinted from other papers, such as the three separate events where fishermen were dragged underwater and drowned by immense catfish (Benton County, 1885, 1901, 1908).[6] While it's hard to nominate just one story as the most outrageous, the death of circus snake-handler Lee Meltwood (Fayetteville, Washington County, 1894) is a contender. During his performance Meltwood was repeatedly struck in the face by the large diamondback rattler but managed to grab up all of his poisonous reptiles as they slithered into the terrified, stampeding audience. Only then did he seek medical attention, dying in agony a day later.[7]

Such accounts make for interesting reading, but they do not provide a complete record of the numbers, and causes, of Arkansans' deaths, because many early newspapers did not include obituaries; those that did eulogized only the most notable deaths. Nor can deaths be ascertained from cemeteries, as professionally carved tombstones were almost unknown in rural parts of the Ozarks until well after the Civil War, and an untold number of graves are marked with nothing but fieldstones—if marked at all. Though the state established a Bureau of Vital Statistics in 1914, the Arkansas Medical Society had to spend the next decade cajoling doctors to report births and deaths, and not until 1927 was there sufficient compliance for Arkansas's vital statistics to be included in the U.S. Census Bureau's registration area.[8] By the 1940s, however, reporting was steadily improving, attributed in part to "promotional campaigns" and the fact that county newspapers published lists of births.[9]

Such laxness in reporting is understandable, given that almost all births and deaths occurred in the home. Anyone dying in a small town or on an isolated homestead often did so without a doctor present. The deceased's body would have remained in the home while the coffin and grave were created by neighbors, without any record keeping involved. Nor do burial records exist, as cemeteries were often on private land and even church and town cemeteries neither charged for graves nor kept records of them.

The U.S. Census mortality schedules for the years 1850, 1860, 1870, and 1880 provide a glimpse at what people died from. In these years census takers inquired at each household for the name, age, and sex and for the cause and month of death of each person who had died during the preceding twelve months. On the 1880 census local doctors were asked to corroborate these and any additional deaths, but not all complied. This record merely shows what people were believed to have died from during these one-year windows, but is neither a complete nor an accurate record. Furthermore, the 1850 and 1860 schedules made little attempt to count deaths of African Americans, who as "slave inhabitants" are listed only by first names.

Mortality schedules make fascinating reading, but the causes of death recorded there are almost impossible to tabulate, given how misleading certain antiquated medical terms can be. For example, while it's easy enough to translate "consumption" into the modern "tuberculosis," this disease—or variations on it—went by a long list of names. These include scrofula (tuberculosis of the neck's lymph glands), marasmus (a term now applied to an ailment in children), King's evil, phthisis, miner's consumption, quick consumption, tubercular pneumonia, white plague, white swelling (tuberculosis of the bone), and tuberculosis of the spine and various organs. Terms such as "catarrh of lungs," "congestion of lungs," "lung sickness," and "lung hemorrhage" are usually synonymous with tuberculosis, but lung fever and winter fever, though sounding like a match, refer to pneumonia.

According to several estimates, the 1850–1870 mortality schedules may have been underreported, nationally, by as much as 40 percent.[10] The deaths of infants and the elderly were often overlooked, and not all families willingly divulged murders, suicides, abortions, and cancers. One exasperated census-taker working in north-central Arkansas, just outside the Ozarks (Conway County, 1880), gave vent to his feeling in the "Remarks" portion of the form. "It is allmost [*sic*] a matter of impossibility to find out from families what caused a death."[11] Sixty years later a WPA worker gathering information for the Historical Records Survey (Lawrence County, 1940) discovered that no birth records were on file at the courthouse, and only those deaths between 10 February 1914 and 18 December 1917 were recorded, nor did anyone know whether such records had *ever* been kept.[12]

Doctors' Medicine

Friends nor physicians could not save
This mortal body from the grave,
Neither shall the grave confine it here
When the Lord our savior does appear.

—**N. A. Baker,** 1847–1889
Hindsville/Smith Cemetery (Madison County)

Families tried any number of folk therapies in an attempt to save or prolong life, many of them based on little more than faith, false hope, or fresh air.

As one man put it (Benton County, 1920s), "Except for accidents, Doc wasn't called until all the home remedies failed."[13] According to Ray Martin, whenever his grandfather noticed a neighbor heading out to fetch the doctor (Fulton County, late 1800s to mid-1900s) he would stop what he was doing and start building a casket. That was because "by the time they got a doctor it was too late."[14] Though Martin may have exaggerated somewhat, summoning the doctor generally *was* done as a last resort. It's easy to see how a vicious cycle quickly developed: doctors who could not save their patients reinforced mistrust in their services, causing families to wait even longer the next time they needed medical help. Doctors argued that they could have cured more patients if they'd been called sooner, but their case wasn't helped by the many stories in which a doctor pronounced a patient's condition terminal, only to have that person's life saved by an older family member applying a folk remedy.

During the Civil War, women nursed the sick in their communities, as there were few professional doctors. Robert W. Mecklin kept a diary of his family's struggles during the war (Washington County, 1863–1864), in which he praised the abilities of his widowed daughter. "While the hospital was here she was much with the sick," Mecklin wrote of the Mount Comfort community, "and having read the books of practice left here by the surgeons of the hospital when they stampeded, she is really better qualified to administer medicine than some of our quacks." When one man was stricken with typhoid pneumonia, the woman, "though known to be a Rebel's widow," made the dangerous, eight-mile round trip to Fayetteville to get medicine from the Federal surgeon. She spent the next week sitting up with this man, then with her own children, before becoming ill herself.[15]

Mistrust of doctors was often justified. Physicians had made an unsuccessful effort in 1831 to regulate their profession, but the state didn't pass medical licensing legislation for another fifty years. This "Quack Law" permitted all doctors who had been five-year residents of the state to merely appear before a board and register with their county clerk, without taking any tests. In 1895 the law was changed to require that each county's board be made up of at least two doctors who had graduated from a recognized medical school. Nonetheless, the Arkansas Medical Society deemed the new law "a disgrace."[16]

Prior to the establishment of the state's School of Medicine in Little Rock (Pulaski County, 1879), an aspiring doctor could learn medicine in one of three ways: by serving an apprenticeship with an established doctor, who would then write a letter attesting to his pupil's competence; by attending a for-profit school run by doctors who charged for each lecture and where students received no hands-on training, or by attending a university medical school out of state.[17] African American physicians organized a medical association in the early 1880s. In 1893 its name officially became the Arkansas Medical, Dental, and Pharmaceutical Association, an organization still in existence.[18]

Families who wanted medical attention often had difficulty paying for it. As a result, doctors accepted everything from mittens to melons in lieu of cash, as well as firewood, livestock, and physical labor such as butchering or hoeing cotton. Despite this, some doctors were never able to collect what they were owed. Dr. Leonidas Kirby (Boone County, started practice in 1871) wrote off debts for relatives, fellow professionals, Presbyterian preachers, and widows, and other doctors often did the same. After making fifteen visits to a man dying of tuberculosis, for which he was owed $15.50 (1878), Kirby added a note in the margin of his billing ledger, saying the patient had paid his debt to his creator, but "I hope he has made a balance in full as for me he left nothing with which to balance except Charity."[19]

Some unscrupulous doctors preyed on the invalids who traveled to springs and spa towns, which caused the state to pass an act in 1903, forbidding such behavior. The act imposed fines of $25 to $200 on doctors who "for the purpose of procuring patients, employ any solicitor, capper or drummer, or shall subsidize or employ any hotel or boarding house, or advertise his business or remedies by untruthful or improbable statements . . . or who shall obtain any fee or compensation from any one by any assurance or promise that a manifestly incurable disease is curable." Doctors could now lose their licenses for such acts as performing surgery while drunk.[20]

Homemade Medicine

Medical information and advice on nursing the sick were available to the public in early, popular self-help books, such as *Gunn's Domestic Medicine* or *The People's Common Sense Medical Adviser in Plain English*,[21] known to have been used in Arkansas. In addition, women who planned ahead, like Marian Tebbetts Banes (Washington County, 1850s), prepared for emergencies by stocking a special shelf in a closet with supplies and patent medicines.

> There were always bandages for stumped toes. . . . Then there was a bottle of hive syrup for Lillian, who had a bad habit of bringing both Father and Mother to their feet in the middle of the night with a cough that portended croup. Then there were boxes of mustard and flour, and suitable cloths for making mustard plasters, and a lump of mutton tallow for chapped hands, and cherry pectoral and Ayer's expectorant, and carminative balsam and a big root of Turkish

rhubarb and, in a concealed place somewhere, a pill box of blue mass pills, and a lot of other things.[22]

Medicine also grew wild, in nature. A good account of home medicine is found in John Quincy Wolf's account of his boyhood (Izard, later part of Stone County, after 1876), describing a way of life that had been unchanged for decades:

> The housewives were the doctors, and the majority of them were medical-minded and economy-wise. They had by rote a hundred or two old remedies, handed down by tradition from past generations or learned from the Indians, and they used these remedies with great confidence, supplementing them with patent medicines. For their drugs they depended mainly upon the "yarb" (herb) garden and the forest. My aunt took great pride in her yarbs, and with reason, for she had a wide variety of them.

Wolf gave a catalog of medicinal plants, everything from such familiar herbs as peppermint, catnip, sage, thyme, and basil to the more potent-sounding wormwood, golden seal, Virginia snakeroot, and calamus. In addition, his aunt gathered portions of the following wild plants, trees, and shrubs:

> Slippery elm, wild cherry, wild plum, wahoo, spicewood, white oak, mullein, sumac, sassafrack (sassafras), ginseng, yellow dock, burdock, plantain, Jerusalem oak, tansy, May apple, rattlesnake master, yellow puccoon, and prickly pear. Against such an array of medical yarbs, barks, and roots, the ordinary ailment did not have a sporting chance.[23]

One plant in Wolf's catalog, calamus root, is also known as Sweet Flag, a swamp-growing plant with the botanic name *Acorus calamus*. Dr. Joe Hall, who trained in St. Louis, was unfamiliar with calamus when he started practicing medicine in the Ozarks (Washington County, pre-1950). According to Dr. Hall, older people chewed the root to relieve indigestion, but the fibers weren't digestible and, if swallowed, could form a dense blockage, called a calamus root obstruction, at the stomach's outlet into the small intestine. "The old doctors knew the people were chewing it, if it was the right time of the year and if they happened to have the usual symptoms for that disorder," said Hall, who observed one operation to remove a fibrous root ball. "The older doctors are the only ones who knew anything about it—you don't study that in school."

Samuel Robert Coger, reminiscing about his childhood (Madison County, born 1905), recalled the plant growing in a large sinkhole in a back pasture, a place children were forbidden to go. Despite this, "we used to sneak up there and chew on calamus roots for hours. It had a rather pleasing sweetish taste."[24] According to other accounts, calamus had the ability to expel worms in children, calm colicky babies, and ease labor pain.

Patent Medicine

Those with money and access to stores could dose themselves with ready-made patent medicines, so-called because the government supposedly protected their formulas and ingredients. (In actuality, very few were patented.)[25] These cure-alls often contained small amounts of dangerous drugs and large amounts of alcohol and were advertised with such wildly extravagant claims that one wit joked they were guaranteed to cure all disease *and* resurrect the dead.[26] The term "snake oil" has become a shorthand for such dubious claims, but this product actually existed: Miller's Antiseptic Oil, "Known as Snake Oil," made in Jackson, Tennessee, and touted in Arkansas newspapers. Though the product's name was later changed to Miller's Oil, the package bore the reminder, "does not contain snake oil."[27] Among the grandiosely named products whose ads take up so much space in early Arkansas newspapers are Dr. Clark Johnson's Indian Blood Syrup, Kirkwood's Famous Malarion ("It is little, lively and loud"), Samaritan Nervine (cures epileptic fits, St. Vitis dance, opium eating, et cetera), J. & C. Maguire's Cundurango ("removes fecal matter from the stomach"), Dr. Crook's Wine of Tar, and Dill's Balm, a liniment that could also be taken internally for stomach upsets.

Dr. King's New Discovery was one of the state's most widely advertised nostrums. "A Scrap of Paper Saves Her Life" ran one of its headlines (1890), and it makes compelling reading.

> It was just an ordinary scrap of wrapping paper, but it saved her life. She was in the last stages of consumption, told by her physicians that she was incurable and could live only a short time; she weighed less than seventy pounds. On a piece of wrapping paper she read of Dr. King's New Discovery, and got a sample bottle; it helped her, she bought a large bottle, it helped her more, bought another and grew better fast, continued its use and is now strong, healthy, rosy, plump, weighing 140 pounds.[28]

Six-year-old Maudie Eldridge (Benton County, 1895) pinned her hopes on this product. The child had a premonition that she would not live long, and started saving her money for Dr. King's New Discovery, which cost fifty cents for a small bottle. On the night she became ill, Maudie told her siblings that she had saved only half the money she needed, sadly concluding, "it would be of no use for I will never get well," and she gave the money to her mother before she died.[29]

Because even the smallest towns had general stores that sold these medicines, it was easy for people to self-diagnose and self-prescribe rather than pay a doctor's fee. Families could also concoct their own versions of brandname elixirs from recipes found in at least one household manual, *The People's Home Library*. Whether or not the homemade version of Lydia Pinkham's Vegetable Compound ("for female troubles") was as good as the original, both versions were certainly alcoholic.[30]

The Arkansas Association of Pharmacists, founded in 1882, began work the following year to get the state legislature to regulate patent medicines. Over the next four legislative sessions, all model bills that the association presented were rejected on the grounds that new laws would hurt pharmacists and doctors. Also, between 1881 and 1907 numerous attempts were made, with little result, to regulate the sale of poisons or medicines containing poison (as many did), to require that patent medicine labels list ingredients including poisons, and to regulate the doctors who made and sold medicine.

In 1903 the Little Rock press applauded the defeat of such regulations as the Holland Bill (requiring medicine with a measurable amount of poison to be labeled "This medicine contains poison"), claiming it would have been nothing more than "an act to deprive the people of Arkansas of the right to buy remedies without first paying a doctor for the privilege."[31] Other writers scoffed at the notion that anyone had been killed by these medicines, but in 1906 the *Journal of the Arkansas Medical Society* published the names of forty-eight people who had died from taking patent medicines,[32] hardly a complete list. Finally, in 1907, the state legislature passed the Greenhaw Law, modeled on Congress's Pure Food and Drug Act of 1906. Watered down from a stricter bill, this one required that medicine labels state the product's drug and alcohol content (though not the presence of poisons), contained numerous exceptions, and was not seen as wholly effective.[33]

General stores sold a variety of medicines over the counter. One early store inventory, that of merchant W. H. Rhea (Washington County, 1859), includes "flour of sulphur, Jayne's Sanative Pills, Brown's liniment, Comstock's Pills, Bateman's Drops, Eye water, W & M Syrup, Turkish Balm, British Oil, Quinine, Calomel, Vermifuge, Stephens Lye Salve, Cholera Mixture, Ear oil, and Cordial."[34] It's unclear what some of these brand-name products claimed to cure, but the account ledgers of other stores show customers charging generic drugs: bitters, paregoric, liver pills, laudanum, painkillers, liniment, and quinine—especially quinine. This was an important purchase wherever malaria was present, as it was nearly everywhere.

Early diaries describe the need for medicine to combat the aches and "chilling" of malarial fevers. Isaac A. Clarke's diary (Carroll County, 1866) names the antimalarial remedies he took in a single year: an unspecified medicine for ague, R's Ready Relief when ague medicine was unavailable, liquor of Iodine of Iron, bitters, brand-name quinine, and Ayer's Ague Cure.[35] He also treated his enlarged spleen (called "ague cake") with a homemade concoction of lard and red-pepper liniment. Such purchases were not cheap; diarist John Guin Bledsoe (Pope and Conway counties, 1867) paid $2 for a bottle of quinine in January and $3.50 for one in November; by way of comparison, he paid $1.87 for twenty-five pounds of flour that same year.[36]

Quinine is intensely bitter and causes unpleasant and sometimes permanent side effects, such as ringing of the ears. The standard dose, "the amount that would lie on a dime," was often diluted in black coffee in an attempt to mask the taste. Various patent medicines, such as Grove's Tasteless Chill Tonic (described by users as anything *but* tasteless), Kress' Fever Tonic, and Cheatnam's Chill Tonic,[37] all contained quinine but promised not to impair the patient's nerves, digestion, or hearing. Then there was the descriptive Schaap's Shake No More[38] and the locally produced "Arkansas Fever Tonic . . . warranted to cure all fever whether contagious or of miasmatic origins" in under twenty hours.[39] Nationally, efforts to eradicate malaria began after World War II with federally funded projects to drain swamps and spray mosquito habitats with DDT.

Laxatives are another drug found in abundance in store inventories. In the words of one humor writer (outside the Ozarks, White County, born 1908), "our grandcestors were afflicted with bad bowels. They had lazy bowels and it seems they were forever and eternally trying to get their bowels in good working order and keep them that way."[40] This explains why so many laxative brands were charged by customers at Pettigrew's Mooney Barker drugstore (Madison County, 1925), including Carter's Liver Pills (which treated constipation), Foley's Cathartic Pills ("wholesome and cleansing"), Electric Laxative, A.G. Tablets, Goff's Laxative Pills, Beecham's Pills, Cascarets, King's Pills, and Dr. Morse's Indian Root Pills, as well as Doan's Pills (a diuretic) and other unnamed concoctions intended for children,[41] very likely the ever-popular Black Draught.

With so many foul-tasting, potentially harmful elixirs available, Silas Turnbo may have been making a subtle point when describing his father-in-law, who stayed healthy right up to his death at age 103. Mr. Steel, Turnbo wrote, "took but a small quantity of medicine"[42] over the course of his long life.

The Medicine Show

Traveling medicine shows were another popular source of cure-alls. Though free shows competed with doctors and pharmacists, who sometimes tried to shut them down, these provided much-appreciated entertainment in small towns up through the Depression. In addition to touting a particular medicine and providing services such as pulling teeth, some shows included vaudeville acts, magicians, both black minstrels and "black face comedians" (white men using makeup and dialect to impersonate blacks), and such exotic livestock as elephants, bears, and monkeys.[43]

E. H. Abington was one of the state's successful showmen. Abington, a doctor and registered pharmacist, sold the patent medicine "To-Ho-Ya" (Sebastian and Crawford counties, 1911). He and partner J. J. McRae at one time employed ten medicine men who, accompanied by black minstrel entertainers, traveled a circuit throughout Arkansas, Oklahoma, Kansas, and Texas, shipping five hundred bottles of the elixir into towns ahead of their shows.[44] At the other end of the spectrum there was the show that visited Zinc (Boone County, 1920s), with nothing more than a banjo player and a "medicine man" selling a cure-all from the back of a covered wagon.[45] Some shows were small enough to travel in a single buggy.

During the Depression these free entertainments drew large crowds. Bruce Vaughan described one, the O'Quaka Indian herb show that came to Huntsville (Madison County, 1930s) every summer. This featured musical acts, exhortations to buy bottles of O'Quaka, and sales of boxes of candy supposedly containing valuable prizes. Though anonymous audience members delightedly displayed expensive watches found in their boxes, local people tended to receive cheap whistles, puzzles, or key rings in their purchases.

O'Quaka's aid to digestion was demonstrated by means of a "glass stomach." This was merely a giant bottle into which the show's "doctor" dropped a variety of foods before capping the neck of the bottle with a balloon. The balloon filled with gas and exploded, as did a second balloon. Then a spoonful of O'Quaka was added to the jug, and a third balloon put in place, which first expanded with gas then deflated slowly as the mixture presumably took effect. "Sounds of amazement swept through the assembled audience," Vaughan wrote. "As the doctor expected, sales of O'Quaka were very good that evening."[46]

These showmen used a patter, or sales pitch, to sway the audience. As an adult, James C. Hefley could still imitate the one used by the "high-hatted medicine man" who visited Mount Judy (Newton County, 1930s) in his youth. "This healing potion which I hold before you good people is good for arthritis, kidney stones, backaches, hangnail, dandruff and has even been known to cure TB. Hit's available fer only one dollar, folks, that's jist one dollar. Less than whut a drunkard would spend for a gallon of whiskey. But ye'd better not wait too long fer the supplies air strictly limited. That's right, folks, only one dollar fer the healin' of yer arthritis, kidney stones, and backaches. Step right up, folks. Don't be shy. Only a dollar."[47]

Faith and Fresh Air

Consumption (now called pulmonary tuberculosis) accounted for one-fifth of deaths in the United States between 1800 and 1870,[48] and by 1900 was the country's second leading cause of death after pneumonia. Despite Arkansas's incomplete statistics, there is no reason to suppose these numbers were any lower in the Ozarks, where this cause of death predominates on mortality schedules and in obituaries. "The strong hold of consumption laid its unreleasing grasp upon the lungs of our dear daughter and sister until she could breathe no more," was the graphic language used in Martha Mills's obituary (Benton County, 1900).[49]

The onset of certain ominous symptoms, such as coughing up blood, was tantamount to a death sentence, and there was little hope beyond putting one's faith in one of the few therapies of the day. The earliest treatment for TB involved keeping the patient in bed in a warm room, away from drafts. John Quincy Wolf wrote that in his youth patients were bundled up in their heaviest clothes, in wintertime, and "kept in the warmest and most nearly air-tight room on the place lest a blast of fresh, cold air strike him and give him a chill or a fresh cold. He was never permitted to go out of doors, but was kept close to a warm fire, day and night. In late spring and summer, he was encouraged to take plenty of exercise and chop wood, hoe cotton, and walk as far and as often as his strength permitted."[50]

Early patent medicine ads, masquerading as newspaper articles, also issued dire warnings against fresh air. Dr. J. H. Schenck wrote a full column of advice in a Little Rock paper (Pulaski County, 1871) urging patients to avoid cold, damp weather and night air,[51] while the ad for Hostetter's Stomach Bitters (Washington County, 1872) warned that air "is the source of diseases of which millions die" and called fog and mist an "aerial virus" that "holds in solution its portion of miasmatic poison."[52] It's no wonder some people nailed their windows shut.

These attitudes changed over time. In 1880 an advertisement for Dr. Pierce's Golden Medical Discovery and Pleasant Purgative Pellets gave the following advice to consumptives: "A party which occupies a room for hours breathing the same air, might be compared to a party of bathers drinking the water in which they bathe. The patient must keep the window of his bedroom open. Night air is fresh air without daylight."[53] Makers of the popular and heavily advertised Scott's Emulsion put their product at the top of a list of consumption cures (ahead of fresh air, rest, and eating large meals),[54] while Ayer's Cherry Pectoral remarked, "Your doctor will tell you that fresh air and good food are the real cures for consumption," while also urging readers to use their product.[55] Some counties attempted to educate the public on the value of fresh air. "School children were shown glaring slogans and exhibits of magnified germs and pieces of lungs," recalled Margaret Montague (Crawford County, early 1900s). "One poster read, 'Every nail you drive in your window is a nail driven in your coffin.'"[56]

The belief in the healing efficacy of fresh air originated with German doctor Hermann Brehmer, who founded the first TB sanitarium, in the Silesian mountains, in 1859. The idea caught on in this country a quarter-century later, when the first sanitarium was built in the Adirondack Mountains in 1884. In Arkansas some cities had small sanitariums, established by local doctors specializing in tuberculosis treatments, but the State Tuberculosis Sanatorium, located near Booneville (Logan County), did not accept its first patient until 1910. The first such facility for African Americans, the McRae Memorial Tuberculosis Sanatorium near Little Rock (having just thirty-two beds), was not founded until 1931, and not until 1966 were blacks treated at the Booneville facility.[57] Despite these hospitals, Arkansas's mortality rate from TB was one of the country's highest prior to new treatment discoveries in the 1960s. In all, the Booneville sanatorium would treat over seventy thousand patients from across the state before closing in 1973.

The belief that clean air—or colder, warmer, or drier air than the sufferer was currently inhaling—could cure TB became deeply entrenched. Obituaries show people coming to Arkansas in the hope of a cure (especially to the spa towns, discussed below), while just as many Arkansans sought relief outside the state. Indeed, there must have been a steady stream of consumptives passing one another as invalids from Missouri, Nebraska, Oregon, and Minnesota came to Arkansas, while afflicted Arkansans headed to California, Colorado, Kansas, Oklahoma, Texas, and New Mexico, all hoping to benefit their diseased lungs. (Arizona was both a source of invalids and a destination for them.) Even moves of a short distance within the Arkansas Ozarks were tried in the hope of receiving a health benefit, with the sufferers living outdoors in tents.

Such therapeutic camping was the homemade version of another therapy, the Burr Cottage. These were little buildings, screened on the sides to permit airflow, which a county could temporarily and cheaply erect on a patient's own property. These structures were the invention of Mississippi doctor William J. Burr in the 1920s to solve the problem of providing care when medical facilities were overcrowded. Somewhat contradictorily, these buildings were intended to provide a patient with excellent nursing by his family while, at the same time, keeping them from becoming infected. Though there was a social stigma to such isolation, the fact that the building was temporary in nature "may be a factor in providing hope and the will to get well."[58]

Burr Cottages were in use in Arkansas in the 1930s, either in response to overcrowding at the sanatorium or in counties that could not afford to send their residents there. The contract signed by one recipient (Crawford County, 1937) spelled out that the building was a temporary, removable structure and not part of the landowner's real estate.[59]

Taking the Waters

"Let those, drink now who never drank before,
And those who always drank, now drink the more."[60]

"Of all the States in the Union, Arkansas stands at the head, both for the number of its springs and for their great curative powers," asserted the *Arkansas State Gazetteer and Business Directory* (1884–1885).[61] This was the heyday of the health resort. Visitors flocked to the popular Ozarks spa towns of Eureka Springs (Carroll County), Sulphur Springs, Siloam Springs (both in Benton County), and Heber Springs (Cleburne County) to bathe in and drink from the therapeutic waters, billed as curing a long list of ailments, predominately those of the kidneys and bladder. Faith in the curative power of spring water was bolstered by testimonials from those who were healed. The largest and most famous of Arkansas's spa towns is Hot Springs (Garland County), in the Ouachita Mountains. The town, part of the Hot Springs National Park (established 1832), was up and running by 1888, having numerous bathhouses that treated diseases of the wealthy and poor alike.

Eureka Springs is the oldest spa town in the Arkansas Ozarks. Founded in 1879, by the 1880 census Eureka Springs contained three thousand permanent residents[62] and, depending on whose account is to be believed, as many as fifteen thousand visiting invalids. Entrepreneur, doctor, and "quack medicine man" Alvah Jackson discovered the springs in 1854, later marketing the water as "Dr. Jackson's Eye Water"[63] and treating invalids from both armies there during the Civil War. After spring water cured a prominent county

Figure 1.2 Health seekers, in the 1880s, sampling water from one of Eureka Springs's numerous medicinal springs. An early guidebook advised visitors to equip themselves with walking sticks and to carry drinking cups at all times. *Bank of Eureka Springs Historic Museum Photo Collection.*

judge of a skin disease, other sufferers rushed to Eureka in the hope of similar healing. The town quickly grew from a rudimentary tent and shack city with mud streets to a full-fledged resort complete with hotels, bathhouses, an opera house and, by the 1890s, electric lighting and a trolley. Mary Baker Eddy, founder of Christian Science, was available for consultations during her visit there in August 1889.[64]

It didn't hurt matters that Eureka's water was free from foul tastes and odors, something local newspapers promoted heavily. Invalids were advised to drink liberally from all of the town's springs, but it may have been the exercise occasioned by long walks to outlying springs and other natural wonders, as well as being thoroughly hydrated, that did the sick more good than anything else. Promoters liked to say it was easier to list the ailments the springs *didn't* cure than to enumerate all the ones they did, but in some instances the water caused disease instead of curing it. In Eureka Springs in 1920, following two summers plagued by outbreaks of typhoid and gastrointestinal illness, the state's chief sanitary engineer tested the water. Though no source for the contamination was found, seven of the town's largest and most popular springs were deemed unsafe for drinking.[65]

Spa towns wishing to attract visitors—especially wealthy invalids and vacationers—needed to be within reach of a railroad. Eureka Springs got its railroad in 1883, connecting it to Seligman, Missouri, and in 1900 was also joined to Harrison (Boone County) by rail. Towns in other parts of the Ozarks having natural springs were often platted with an eye to an approaching railroad line, and in all cases these towns' heydays arrived with the railroad. Towns with medicinal springs drew the most visitors, but across the Ozarks many towns tried to attract health seekers. Among these were Marble City (Newton County, 1890s), Ravenden Springs (Randolph County, established 1883), Elixir Springs (Boone County, 1883),[66] and Sulphur Rock (Independence County, 1903),[67] but there were many others. Mammoth Spring (Fulton County, 1880s) was a tourist destination, but no medicinal properties were assigned to the water that gushed from its single, immense spring that was too cold to be used for therapeutic bathing.

Though invalids appreciated fresh-tasting water, sulfur water, which gives off a strong odor of rotten eggs, was thought to be especially potent. This explains a joke made by the editor of a Harrison newspaper (Boone County, 1882): "The water in the Court House well is either developing remarkable medicinal qualities, or else there is a dead cat in it,"[68] while the Purdy Spring near Fayetteville (Washington County, about 1900) was described as tasting "like water from a hog-wallerin' mud hole." Despite or because of this, the spring's owner sold water for ten cents per gallon.[69]

Some towns posted signs at each of their springs listing the ailments and conditions the water supposedly cured. Heber Springs's red sulfur water was billed as a stimulant, laxative, and "promoter of gland action," while its white sulfur cured indigestion, headaches, and sleeplessness and was especially recommended for "nervous females." The black sulfur was touted as removing both urine and sweat from patients, while the town's Arsenius, chalybeate, and "eye water" springs had equally specific properties. Patients were advised to first have their medical histories evaluated in order to ascertain the right water to drink, in the proper quantity, at the correct time of day.[70]

These spa towns enjoyed growth and prosperity well into the 1900s, but when the fad for "taking the waters" was over, all suffered a similar decline. Improved drugs and new medical therapies also contributed to the spas' downfalls as, simultaneously, doctors stopped prescribing a change of scene for their patients. The Depression, followed by World War I, curtailed tourism, after which more Americans purchased automobiles and were no longer dependent on railroads to get them to fixed destinations.

Staunching Bleeding

Faith in one's local doctor made little difference if he couldn't be reached in time. This was especially true in cases of profuse bleeding, where something as simple as a nosebleed—as found on two mortality schedules—could result in death.[71] When someone was hemorrhaging, the fastest course of action was to get word to a "blood-stopper." This was someone who got results, usually by reciting a certain passage from the Bible. Given how secretive some sources were about their ability to stop blood, it's surprising how well documented the use of this verse was. Still, in some communities it was believed that only certain people could work this magic or that revealing the source robbed it of its power.

The all-important verse is Ezekiel 16:6, "And when I passed by thee, and saw thee polluted in thine own blood, I said unto thee *when thou wast* in thy blood, Live; yeah, I said unto thee *when thou wast* in thy blood, Live." Emma Bessie Phillips (Newton County, born 1913) suffered a nosebleed so severe that her mother got on the party line and begged healer Adeline Meadows to help her child. "Adeline silently repeated the verse to herself, and ere long the bleeding stopped."[72] This charm was also used to help women who bled excessively during childbirth, and the healer did not have to be physically present for it to work. Folklorist Otto Rayburn recounted his son's experience when the family was living at Caddo Gap (Montgomery County, Missouri, 1940). "We told our neighbor and he asked the boy's full name, then went out into the yard and repeated a few words—we couldn't hear them. And lo and behold, the bleeding stopped!"[73]

Folklorist Vance Randolph collected variations on the process, such as that the verse is repeated while walking toward the east, that a man could share this knowledge with three women and a woman with three men (usually someone not related to the teller), but also the conflicting belief that the charm would cease to work if shared a third time.[74] He was also told that the verse must never be written down and, according to one informant, that it had to be recited while walking east after calling the sufferer and the wound "by name."[75] Pope County folklore includes the variation that the seventh son of a seventh son can stop bleeding.[76]

It was also believed that placing a silver coin in the mouth would stop blood loss in people and animals. Silver coins were sometimes used inside the "belly bands" of newborn babies (a tight strip of material that held the navel cord against the body and supposedly prevented a rupture), although in this instance the coin's purpose is unclear. Mary Parler's folklore students collected the information that rubbing a baby's gums with a silver dollar, or silver thimble, would help the teeth break through.[77] Other blood-stopping techniques included using fireplace soot and tight bandaging, applying turpentine and sugar to an injury, and holding the wound in the smoke of smoldering wool rags or sugar.

Among African Americans, spiderwebs and soot were sometimes used, as witnessed by Margaret Mullen (Washington County, 1920s) after "yard man" Will Carr gashed himself with a sickle. Carr refused medical aid and asked instead to be helped to the family's smokehouse, where he retrieved handfuls of sooty cobwebs. He "made a poultice of the fearsome stuff, patting it over the wound, pulling the flesh together, building up a heavy pad to staunch the flow of blood."[78]

Rabies Treatments

Snode Smith, investigating a disturbance among his hogs one night, did not see the rabid dog that bit his finger (Washington County, 1890). But, availing himself of the standard therapy at the time, he had several madstones applied to the bite, and believed himself to be out of danger. Eighteen months later, however, he exhibited signs of the dreaded disease hydrophobia, or rabies. "For several days he could swallow no water and later even the sight of it caused violent convulsions," reported the newspaper. After a week of suffering Smith "died a most horrible death, it requiring several strong men to prevent deeds of violence."[79]

Rabies was the most feared of all the incurable diseases, for it guaranteed an agonizing death. Victims sometimes alternated between trying to injure their caregivers and begging to be killed, and their plight was so horrifying to witness that even a doctor, William Sherman Rogers (Van Buren County, after 1905), wept openly when recalling one child's death from this cause.[80] Rabies is a viral disease that attacks the body's central nervous system, and its incubation period varies, meaning that someone bitten by a rabid animal never knew when the hallucinations and convulsions might strike. One telltale symptom was the patient's horror of water and an inability to swallow it, hence the original name hydrophobia—literally "fear of water." Sufferers were sometimes tied

Figure 1.3 A madstone, once the standard folk remedy for treating bites from rabid animals by applying the surface of the stone to the bite to draw out infectious matter. Somewhat unusually, this stone has been sawed in half, and its exterior surface protected by a coating of sealing wax. *In the collection of the Heritage Center Museum, Berryville, Carroll County Historical Society. Photo by Abby Burnett.*

to their beds (or, in one account, chained to a tree) to protect onlookers, though doctors tried to subdue these patients with large doses of morphine.

In 1885 Frenchman Louis Pasteur successfully used a vaccine to treat rabies in humans, and the news of his discovery spread rapidly. By 1890 Pasteur treatment centers had been established in New York City and Chicago, Illinois, with others up and running in other major cities shortly thereafter.[81] However, it would be almost thirty years before Arkansas had a facility, a short-lived one at that (Little Rock, 1912–1914). Instead, Arkansans at risk, who could afford it, journeyed to New York or St. Louis, Missouri, for a series of injections of Pasteur's serum. Prior to Pasteur's discovery, and in Arkansas for decades after it, anyone suspected of having contracted rabies had two treatment options. One was cauterizing the wound with a red-hot iron or a caustic chemical such as carbolic acid. Cauterization was considered most effective when administered within hours of the bite,[82] but some patients died of rabies despite undergoing this painful procedure.

The most popular folk treatment was applying a madstone to the bite to draw out the poison. Accounts vary, but in most the stone is a type of calcium deposit found inside a deer, often an all-white or albino deer, and retrieved from the animal's stomach or its entrails.[83] Randolph, who saw several such stones, described them as porous and resembling "volcanic ash," though another account likened one to a leach that filled with poison when stuck to a wound.[84]

Josiah Abner Smith had two such stones (Van Buren County, acquired early 1900s) that he used on patients. His grandson, Watson Smith, described the technique, noting that it would not work on snakebites. First, a madstone would be placed in a pan of milk and the liquid brought to a boil. Next, using a sharp object, Smith would "scratch or ruffle up the place where the fangs or teeth of the animal had bitten the person." The stone would be removed from the milk, dried, applied to the bite, and held in place until it stuck there on its own. Smith noted that the treatment took longer for some people and that it always worked—with one exception, a child bitten on the nose by a rabid dog, a failure he attributed to the stone not being "properly positioned."[85]

Other doctors also owned and used such stones, including Civil War doctor Jas. McAdams (White County, 1890s), who supposedly paid one thousand dollars for a madstone credited with forty-one cures by 1891.[86] This stone had such a reputation that people traveled great distances to use it. Willis Taylor Inman (Independence County, 1897) sought out this madstone and described its use in a letter home, the stone adhering to him as he wrote. He described how the stone had stuck for twenty-four hours the first time, then for three separate twelve-hour periods, then for ten, six, and another ten hours. The treatment was surely worth the wait; Inman lived another twenty years.[87]

Madstones were so valuable that they were never loaned out; instead, patients were brought to the stone for treatment. According to one family legend (Pope County, early 1900s?), two brothers sawed their madstone in half so one could take a piece when he moved out of state.[88] Other stones were brought to Arkansas. A newspaper article described a two-hundred-year-old madstone (Johnson County, 1893) that had come from England, which, if true, means that this object was in use at the end of the 1600s.[89] The concept of a stone capable of extracting poison is much older, however, and has been found in both Europe and India in the 1300s. Its closest relative, the bezoar (Arabic for "antidote") used in Europe in the 1500s, was a stone found in the digestive tracts of deer and applied in the same manner as the madstone—a word, incidentally, coined in this country around 1864.[90]

Madstones were used in the Arkansas and Missouri Ozarks into the 1930s though newspapers occasionally warned against them and the Arkansas Medical Society (1906) had condemned their use.[91] From an early date people were told to seek Pasteur treatment, which was easier said than done. After a rabid dog bit several children (central Arkansas, Conway County, 1890) their physician appealed to Little Rock doctors for information about Pasteur injections, apparently without receiving a response. This prompted the *Arkansas Gazette* to ask, "If Pasteur, of France, has a remedy by inoculation, why do not the physicians of Little Rock move to investigate and apply their methods?" and urged the State Medical Association to act.[92]

Eventually someone did, a Dr. Loyd O. Thompson, who established a Pasteur Institute (Little Rock, 1912)[93] and a few months later received a government license to manufacture and sell rabies vaccine.[94] Less than two years later, however, Dr. Thompson relocated to Hot Springs (Garland County, 1914), where he treated venereal disease,[95] a far more lucrative specialty. Still, by this date a specialized treatment center was no longer necessary, because the University of Arkansas School of Medicine in Little Rock could test the heads of animals suspected of being rabid. If the virus was found, the patient could then undergo rabies injections at home, administered by a pharmacist or family doctor. In 1912, Michigan-based pharmaceutical company Parke, Davis & Co. advertised that upon receipt of a telegram they would immediately send a package of seven pre-filled syringes, each containing a single dose of antirabic vaccine, directly to the doctor. Two more packages, containing seven doses apiece, would follow at intervals.[96] By the 1930s county health units routinely kept doses of such vaccine on hand.

Despite the Pasteur vaccine's publicity (even small-town papers carried stories of its success), the public did not relinquish its faith in madstones and other folk remedies. Ten-year-old Elmer Hinkle, the first Arkansan known to have received the Pasteur treatment (Independence County, 1891), was taken first to Searcy (White County) to have a madstone applied, then on to New York for Pasteur treatment. Hinkle survived the bite and the therapies,[97] but not everyone did. Four-year-old Jennie Carnahan was treated locally after she was mauled by a rabid dog in Fort Smith (Sebastian County, 1907). Then, when the family doctor decided the child needed the Pasteur treatment, he and her father took Jennie to the Pasteur Institute in New York. Six days had elapsed between the attack and the girl's departure, but Jennie died of rabies while at the institute.[98] One man did everything right but died anyway. Austin Collier (Carroll County, 1924) took the head of the dog that bit him to Little Rock for testing, and despite no evidence of rabies being found he underwent the shots both in Little Rock and back home in Carrollton. Even so, he died of rabies.[99]

Children were given unimaginably foolish advice to avoid being bitten, to stand still and hold their breath ("all odor from the body ceases").[100] Folklorists even recorded that doing so would cause a dog to be physically unable to bite.[101] The more prudent course of action was to remove the source of the disease by killing all dogs in town once rabies was evident. After numerous dogs were bitten at Hardy (Sharp County, 1901), the town passed an ordinance "requiring the killing of every dog running at large," a job undertaken by the town marshal and the dogs' owners. Even pets and valuable hunting dogs were destroyed. The newspaper warned visitors to leave their dogs at home or keep them tied to their wagons while in town.[102] In the 1920s some towns required that dogs be muzzled, and impounded those that weren't,[103] but by this time the practice of vaccinating dogs had all but ended the threat from rabies.

CHAPTER TWO

Sitting up with the Sick and Dying

She has fallen asleep / She is resting at last
The pulse has grown still / And the fever is past;
She suffers no longer / In heart or in brain,
And the pain that so / Racked her shall
Not come again. / She has fallen asleep
O Lord, 'tis now past, / Thank God, as we weep,
She is resting at last.

—**Mrs. Ollie Cline,** 1887–1909
Russell Cemetery (Johnson County)

Deaths caused by a bolt of lightning or a tornado, from drowning or a misstep around machinery, came without warning and often without witnesses. But in the Arkansas Ozarks someone suffering from a chronic illness or the gradual decline of old age died surrounded by family and neighbors, all of whom had been in attendance throughout the days and nights leading up to the death. Members of the community stepped in to do whatever was needed. As William Erwin Halbrook wrote, describing the customs of his boyhood (Van Buren County, 1880s), "Neighbors were readily at one another's services in need. If a member of a family was sick we took it in turn about sitting up of nights and administering the medicine and other nursing chores. We would make a trip for one to the nearest town for a doctor. If his cotton needed picking or any other farm emergency because of some misfortune all the neighbors joined in and came to his need."[1]

Of all these jobs, sitting up all night was possibly the most important, as doing so allowed the family to get a night's rest. It brought comfort to the invalid, too, knowing someone was awake, or easily wakened if the need arose. "Sometimes there would be a large crowd all night in the sick room," wrote Wayman Hogue (Van Buren County, born 1870). "This, however, was never objectionable. The number of people coming in to set up registered the patient's popularity. A man or any member of his family, when in the first throes of typhoid fever or pneumonia, felt highly complimented when a large crowd was in his room setting up, although it was at a time when silence and quietude should prevail."[2]

This practice, which took place both in rural and urban communities, was a form of insurance. In a time when hospitals were few, distant and expensive, and long before there were social services and visiting nurses, one helped one's neighbors and they, in turn, reciprocated when needed. In the words of the Marble City Chamber of Commerce (Newton County, 1889), "If the people of the work shops in the east that live from day to day without knowing from what source their day's supplies would come in case of sickness . . . could only see and realize with what ease, and [one] might say luxuries the people of our rural districts are blest, they surely would be willing to give up their dirty, smoky attics for a pleasant home of their own here among we Newton County people."[3]

The Logistics of Sitting Up

In general, men sat up with men and women with women, though there was no absolute rule about this. In some communities women or older people were the ones who most commonly performed this role, which, to be strictly accurate, was known as "setting up." Still, there are accounts of adult men sitting up with a neighbor's sick child, of women sitting up with men, and of men sitting up with elderly women. Parents took their children with them on these occasions, and occasionally the children also had to help, as happened to Evadean Phillips Sloan when she was no older than twelve (Izard County, 1935). "I stood up over [Aunt Belle Haynes] all night long one night when I was just a kid, and held her ears; one hand on one ear and one hand on the other ear," Sloan recalled of an eccentric relative. "She was sick and she said she could feel more electric coming through my hands than anybody else's."[4]

Sometimes a particular person would be, in the vernacular, "a good hand to sit with the sick." One such man was described by Nellie Terherst (Boone/Carroll counties, 1930s–1940s). "Uncle Pete, he took care of the sick. I guess he had a lot of faults or sorryness, or not doing, but now he *would* do that—sit up night after night with sick people." Husbands and wives would sometimes go together to sit up, to be relieved around midnight by another couple. Organizing this rotation, in communities without telephones, was done informally as everyone knew who was sick and would come without being asked.

"I knew when I saw Dad filling the lantern with coal oil what I was in for," Lou Ann Clough Ott said of her childhood at Rush (Marion County, early 1930s). "Someone was either bad sick, or had passed on. They would take me and go." Burr Fancher (Madison County, born 1926) recalled how, after dark, "You could see the lanterns going up the mountain, as people went to be with the sick."

Even sitters who changed off with one another had difficulty getting enough rest. Gladys McChristian's mother described how she coped when having to sit up from midnight to daylight during a relative's long illness (Madison County, early 1900s). "After everything got quiet and all the others were in bed, grandma would get over to the back side of the bed and say, 'Now daughter come lie down by me and if I need anything I'll wake you.' Mother said she didn't know how she could ever have stood it if grandma hadn't been so thoughtful and made it possible for her to sleep more."[5] Men, especially, took pride in keeping a night watch then putting in a full day's labor. Kendall Bohlen (Madison County, 1930s) said, "I'd sit up all night long with sick people and go home and work in the fields, then sleep, then go back again,"[6] while Mack Gibson walked four miles night after night for weeks to sit up with a sick man (Madison County, 1930s).[7]

Initially, family members would do the nursing, but as an invalid's illness progressed it would become clear when the family needed additional help. Herron Thompson Whitfield (Izard County, 1929) recalled sleeping in the same room as his elderly, arthritic aunt and getting up many times each night to reposition her in bed. "That went on till finally mother said, 'We'll just have to go to setting up with her,'" recalled Whitfield, who was fifteen at the time. Neighbors began to take turns sitting up with her, though the woman lived only a few weeks after this was initiated.[8] Still, no matter how lengthy the illness, neighbors were prepared for the long haul, as happened to one family (Marion County, 1930s) where neighbors came and sat up for an entire winter and spring with an older woman until she died.[9]

This help was appreciated, but families did the nursing for as long as possible before requesting help. When Peter Mankins Sr. "took a chill" (Washington County, 1882), he was sick for just two days, during which his son sat watch beside his bed. In the night, Mankins requested a drink of water after which "it was noticed that he was breathing shorter than usual and in five minutes he was dead," according to his obituary. It's possible the illness was of such short duration the family hadn't yet asked neighbors to sit up. Or perhaps Peter Jr. kept watch over his frail father for another reason: Peter Mankins Sr.

was 111 years old when he died.[10] Rev. James A. Walden wrote several diary entries about "waiting on" his wife and small children through the night in order to give them medicine (Washington County, 1879 and 1881), and on various occasions he, not his wife, sat up all night with their sick children.[11]

According to stories handed down by whites, blacks also provided nursing care. Silas Turnbo tells of "River Bill" Coker taking two male slaves with him when he sat up with a neighbor with pneumonia (Marion County, 1849–1850). It was the slaves' job to chop wood and keep a hot fire going,[12] as houses were not insulated and normally fires were banked at night and rekindled in the morning; keeping an invalid warm meant staying awake and feeding the fire. Post–Civil War accounts mention blacks and whites nursing one another. The obituary of Della Black, an African American woman who provided childcare (Benton County, 1902), noted how she had been "especially kind and attentive to the sick, always offering her services in times of need."[13] James Franks (Izard County, born 1928) described a black family that once lived near him. "If somebody got sick in the country, I don't care who it was, they was the best people you ever seen for sickness," Franks recalled. "They'd go to anybody's house and they'd stay if you needed 'em, and they'd just take care of you."[14] Among whites, Jennie Gunter's obituary (Washington County, 1901) mentioned that, "Her ministrations to the sick or needy were not restricted by race or station. She would watch through the long hours of the night by the bedside of a sick negro as willingly as she would attend her dearest friend."[15]

Mistaken Medicine

Among the subjects that nineteen-year-old Elvena Maxfield recorded in her diary were the deaths that occurred in her town of Batesville (Independence County, 1861). She continued this diary through the Civil War where, in addition to war casualties, she listed deaths of friends and relatives from both natural and accidental causes. Throughout, she mentions sitting up with the sick and dying.

"I feel very sad setting all alone by the perhaps dying bed of Fannie," she wrote at midnight, taking her turn watching a friend's infant daughter for whom the doctor had predicted recovery. "I am afraid she is worse." One week later Maxfield was proven right. "Poor little thing she suffered a great deal before she died."[16] Several times, often correctly, Maxfield wrote that she did not expect someone to live long. (Though she made this pronouncement repeatedly concerning her grandma Engles, by the time the diary ceased in 1866 there had been no mention of this lady's death.)

Maxfield did not describe her nursing duties other than mentioning one very important task. On 4 September, she wrote of her sister Lucretia's long illness, "Lute is still no better. I am setting up to give her medicine."[17] There was an excellent reason for doing so. Many medicines doctors prescribed contained dangerous ingredients, ones that were easily fatal in the wrong dosage. Furthermore, because these drugs were dispensed in a variety of non-standardized, unlabeled bottles and packages, it was prudent for the sick to have their medications doled out to them.

Early doctors concocted their own remedies from ingredients they carried with them on house calls.[18] Etta McColloch (Washington County, born early 1870s) described how one Cane Hill doctor dispensed drugs to her family. "He opened his pill bags, with many little bottles fitted into cases, took out his pocket knife and measured powder on the tip of the blade, put it on squares of white paper and folded it. Or, he might measure powder out of two or three bottles and mix it together."[19] Doctors left verbal instructions for how and when the drugs were to be taken, and well into the 1920s some doctors were still dispensing medicine in this manner.

Doctors' medical satchels and saddlebags usually contained strychnine (a stimulant, in small quantities), digitalis (for heart conditions), quinine (for malaria), paregoric (containing opium, used to treat diarrhea), castor oil, salts, calomel, and blue mass. Some inventories also include turpentine and antidotes for poisons. Though stores sold all of these items to the public, it was preferred for a doctor to dispense blue mass, due to its dangerous side effects. This substance, bulked out with blue chalk or a blue dye, contained mercury, the same ingredient used in calomel (mercurous chloride).

Mercury is a poison, and an overdose could result in a painful, unpleasant, and sometimes fatal condition known as "salivation." Hiram Abiff Whittington, a Massachusetts native living in Little Rock (Pulaski County, 1832), wrote a graphic description to his family after doctors overdosed him. "In plain terms, it is giving a fellow calomel until he drools at the mouth like a mad-dog. Your gums become so sore that you cannot eat, and your teeth all become loose so that you can take hold of them with your fingers and pull them out; in this fix, you have to lay after you get over the fever, with mouth open and the saliva running from it like the matter from a horse's nose when he has the distemper."[20] Other symptoms included a swollen face and the tongue protruding from the mouth, with saliva "flowing out at a rate of from a pint to a quart in twenty-four hours."[21]

During the Civil War, Dr. William Alexander Hammond, surgeon general to the U.S. Army, had calomel and tarter emetic (also containing mercury) removed from the list of drugs available to military surgeons, on the

grounds that these were overused and caused salivation and mercurial gan-
grene. Army doctors refused to comply, and Hammond's edict earned him
enemies and led, ultimately, to his being relieved of duty in 1864.[22] Doctors
continued to use mercury-based medicines to treat a long list of ailments that
included constipation, dysentery, malaria, syphilis, tuberculosis, and worms
in children. As late as the 1920s records kept by doctors show that they were
still dispensing calomel.

Well into the 1900s it was so commonplace for doctors to own drugstores and to dispense medicine that one who *didn't* merited mention in the
local newspaper: "Dr. Love is the first doctor to give us a prescription and
would not fill it himself" (Johnson County, 1912). Around this time the same
newspaper carried advertisements for five other Johnson County doctors, all
having addresses above or in various drugstores.[23] According to one humorist,
doctors sometimes used up odds and ends of medicine by combining them in
one large jug. "When they had a case they could not diagnose, they gave them
a dose out of the 'blue jug' and with good results—sometimes."[24]

When doctors concocted liquid medicines they did so in glass bottles
that were used over and over again, ones they did not necessarily label. As
noted earlier, Arkansas law eventually required that poisons (including arsenic, strychnine, and opium, used medicinally) had to be labeled, but this did
nothing to stop the reuse of bottles, which led to accidental poisoning.

A description of Dr. I. Harmon Pavatt's Damascus office (Van Buren
County, prior to 1940) shows how the process worked. "The middle room was
the examining room and in it were lots of bottles thrown on top of each other
in a box. They had been collected by children and were to be used as containers for liquid medicine. They did not look too clean and were not sterilized."
The doctor would rinse out a bottle, using a bucket of water kept on hand for
this purpose, add some drugs, fill the bottle with water, stopper it, and give
the patient oral instructions for its use.[25] Children weren't the only ones in the
bottle business; one medical bill (Van Buren County, 1922) was offset by a box
of bottles brought in by the patient's wife.[26] The practice of refilling containers
was so common that when gelatin capsules first made their appearance some
patients emptied them, swallowed the drugs they contained, and returned the
"little cups" to their doctor.[27]

Such accounts took place decades after Maxfield kept her diary, but she
herself had a "close call" in 1861, "caused by drinking a portion of medicine out
of a bottle." From later entries it appears that she dosed herself for a malarial
chill and probably took either the wrong medicine or too much of the correct
one. The situation was serious enough that a doctor was summoned to give her
an emetic, and she required bed rest for several days following the episode.[28]

Quinine was widely used to offset malarial symptoms, and while a common side effect was a ringing in the ears, an overdose was dangerous. (On the 1880 census of the blind, deaf, and senile of Washington County, A. J. Armstrong was listed as semi-mute and semi-deaf, the result of taking large doses of quinine at age two.)[29] Estimating the correct amount was tricky, as according to one memoir (Lawrence County, 1930s), "a dose was what one could hold on the end of a knife blade."[30]

That the sick required help with their medications is understandable, since it was not uncommon for even healthy people to mistake one medicine for another. Newspaper articles tell of parents reaching for the wrong bottle when dosing their children, and of pharmacists mistaking and mislabeling various drugs, with fatal results. Given the bitterness of many medicines, it's no wonder people didn't question the taste when mistaking strychnine for some other equally bitter drug, as happened to a mentally impaired man (Benton County, 1893), found dead beside an empty strychnine bottle. His obituary surmised, "there is but little doubt but that the poor boy got out the poison and took a dose not knowing but what it was quinine as he had taken a great deal of that medicine in his life."[31]

Causes of death gleaned from obituaries include accidental overdoses from oil of chenopodium (used to expel worms), headache powder, patent medicine, quinine, liver tablets, laudanum, opium, and morphine, all of which were sold over the counter a century ago. Conversely, persons committing suicide rarely did so by overdosing on drugs; instead, they tended to swallow carbolic acid or brand-name poisons such as Rough on Rats and the attractively packaged Daisy Fly Killer.

Doctors weren't immune to making mistakes, either. The 1870 Mortality Schedule lists one cause of death as "accidentally poisoned by physician" but such errors also occurred within their own households, such as a young man living with a doctor (Randolph County, 1885), who died after mistaking aconite (a narcotic poison used as a sedative) for cough syrup.[32] Doctors were sometimes the victims of their own remedies, as in the case of Dr. Graham (Searcy County, 1893), who wrote himself a prescription for chloroform and laudanum to ease his rheumatism and died as a result. The fact that Dr. Graham was in jail at the time suggests that this might not have been accidental.[33]

Those who sat up all night with the sick had the responsibility of giving medicine from the correct bottle, in the right amount, at the proper time, a job made all the more difficult by a lack of light. Nursing was done by candlelight, by oil lamp, or by kerosene lantern until the Rural Electrification Act of 1936 led to the establishment of electric cooperatives in Arkansas. However, most reminiscences from rural areas state that electric lines arrived in the mid- to late 1940s, so lanterns would have been in use for most of the time period covered here.

Other Nursing Duties

Nursing involved more than merely "smoothing the dying pillow." This exhausting work is illustrated by the care Sophia Sawyer gave to the young women, both Cherokee and white, who attended her Fayetteville Female Seminary (Washington County, 1839 to 1854). Though she was often debilitated by tuberculosis, Sawyer nursed her students herself. "People who boarded her girls dreaded her arrival under these circumstances as she subordinated the entire household to the care of her patient. First the room was thoroughly cleaned, then clean bed clothes and sleeping garments. Miss Sawyer personally supervised the preparation of good nourishing food and throughout the illness ruled the house with an iron hand that was not always kept in a velvet glove."[34]

Doctors, exposed to the maladies of their patients, sometimes also required care. When a typhoid epidemic hit Huntsville (Madison County, about 1926), the town's physician, Dr. Beeby, became ill. His wife, LaVera—newly married and a stranger to the area—couldn't find another doctor to attend her husband at the hotel where they were living. "Then a wagon pulled by a team of mules drove up to the door of the hotel," she reminisced in later years. "Thirteen men from Whorton Creek got out of that wagon and said they had come to 'hope me,' which meant to help. Big Jim Bowerman walked right in and began bathing my husband. He went to the drugstore and bought some medicine for malaria. These thirteen men cared for my husband and by the next day, we could already see improvement."[35]

Keeping a patient cool in hot weather was another chore requiring constant attention. Since houses did not have screens, keeping air circulating both cooled the patient and waved away insects. During one man's dying, in an August drought (Van Buren County, 1936), helpers hung wet sheets in the bedroom windows, hoping to cool whatever breeze might waft through. In rural communities up through the Depression, people simply did not have access to paper with which to create hand fans, as it was not uncommon for an entire neighborhood to share a single subscription to the newspaper, and paper grocery bags and other sources of free paper were unknown. Undertakers often distributed cardboard fans at funerals, but even these were not always widely available.

Sitting up belongs to the era before hospitals and nursing homes, but as this professional care came into being there was a transition period, during which people would sit up all night at the bedsides of hospitalized friends. Though in a hospital setting, care was taken to observe the numerous superstitions concerning invalids and their beds. A sick man was never to be shaved; patients were never supposed to be moved from one bed to another, and "a person never changed ends of a bed of a sick person,"[36] that is, reversed the patient's direction so that he now lay toward the foot of the bed. Whether at home or in the hospital, it was bad luck to sweep under a patient's bed, as doing so implied that the person wasn't expected to live.

There were also injunctions against placing the head of the bed in a particular direction. Folklore sources disagree on whether a north, west, or eastward orientation is lucky or unlucky for the patient, but they agree that the bed must parallel the direction of the floorboards. This superstition dates back to at least the middle of the 1800s in England. There, orienting the patient's bed with the floorboards, roof beam, or joists made for an easier death. A patient whose bed formed a right angle to any of these things might not be able to die. A related superstition forbade placing a bed so the sleeper's feet faced the door, as that is the way a corpse is carried out of the room.[37] In the Ozarks, tradition dictated that once the person died it was imperative for the body to be carried out feet first; to do otherwise might enable the spirit to look back.[38]

Farm Chores

It has been a long-standing tradition in rural Ozark communities for people to help their neighbors complete large projects, such as building houses and barns, shocking and threshing grain, making molasses, killing hogs, and doing quilting. Such shared labor extended to times of trouble as well. When a man fell ill his neighbors harvested his crops, cultivated his garden, worked livestock, and cut firewood for the family. Aid came from another quarter, as well. Men who were members of fraternal organizations such as the Masons, International Order of Odd Fellows, Woodmen of the World—even the Klan— made it a point to assist fellow lodge members in need. "One time daddy got sick for part of the summer and the neighbors helped with the crops and the Odd Fellows gave him seventeen dollars," reminisced Chloe Phillips Strode Baker (Madison County, born 1928). "He joined the lodge when he was eighteen years old."[39]

All fraternal organizations helped their members, but the Odd Fellows made this part of their creed: "to visit the sick, relieve the distressed, bury the dead and educate the orphan." Lodge members who fell ill when traveling were assured of care—provided someone knew they were members in good standing (discussed in the Conclusion). Still, a man didn't have to join a lodge to receive help from other men in his community, nor does there appear to have been any accounting kept of work or materials given to one another. John Quincy Wolf, writing of the period immediately after the Civil War in what was then Izard County (today part of Stone), described his grandfather's willingness to donate labor, disputing the claim that work was traded equally. "At least in our neighborhood, settlers who had lived on farms where all the land had long since been cleared and all the needed houses built were just as active in the gatherings as were the newcomers. Of course there was a very practical side to the work, but the claims of neighborliness were strong, and the pleasures of a community get-together were genuine."[40]

During outbreaks of contagious illnesses, taking on the heavier jobs around a farm might be the only way to lend support. In such cases family members were often left to nurse one another, with neighbors leaving food, water, and firewood—or a coffin, if needed—on a front porch, but venturing no closer. Typhoid, smallpox, diphtheria, measles, scarlet fever, and whooping cough were all valid reasons to keep a safe distance. During the 1918 influenza epidemic the custom of nursing neighbors appears to have been completely abandoned, out of fear of contagion but also because there simply were not enough able-bodied people left to help others. Still, even during epidemics so severe that quarantines were imposed and public gatherings (including funerals) forbidden, there are accounts of neighbors nursing the sick and taking orphaned children into their homes for care.

The Stigma of Dying Alone

The taboo against leaving a dead body unattended is well documented, but little has been written about the stigma of dying alone, perhaps because it happened so rarely. "Mrs. Reed was with her husband for a day before he died," according to one newspaper's correction (Benton County, 1898). "We repeat these last mentioned facts at the request of the family who wish to correct the statements as given in a local paper last week," presumably that he died alone.[41] This family's indignation at the newspaper report was nothing compared to the ire of a Mrs. Martin's survivors, however (Benton County, 1891). Martin's son-in-law, "W. W. Barney . . . took occasion to feel offended at the notice we gave of the death because he said it was misleading—causing the people to believe the lady was neglected." The rest of the "apology" could hardly have mollified Barney. "Because a person dies suddenly and alone it does not follow that the person was mistreated. We know of many such cases where the best of care was given the one who died thus."[42]

Dying unattended was unthinkable, but it was also unfortunate when someone died far from family, even if in the presence of others. This sentiment is poetically expressed on the tombstone of Pennsylvania-born John Acheson (Randolph County, 1833), whose epitaph says he was without family and, "in a strange land strangers wept / Strangers to him who guessed not / Half his worth."[43]

While it was sad when someone died far from home, with neither "loving hands nor pitying hearts" to minister to the person,[44] deaths of the insane were even more tragic. The writer who attended Mary E. Gordon's funeral (Pope County, 1888) found it sadder than any other he'd witnessed, including those for victims of suicide, lynching, and drunkenness. The fact that she'd had no one to "close her frenzied eyes"[45] and had died "deserted and disowned" was as horrible to this writer as John Mauger's death in a Kansas insane asylum (Carroll County resident, 1898). According to the newspaper, "He died with not a friend or relative near him in the last moments and the probability is that his end was hastened by a realization that he was . . . abandoned by all whom he had known and befriended during his busy life."[46] The person's dying words were highly prized, which is why Richard Morris's death, alone in his barn (Benton County, 1909), was deemed especially sad, because "he died with no one to receive a parting message. We cannot know what his last thoughts were nor what he might have said if one had been near."[47]

It was customary for obituaries to list the names of all family members present at the deathbed, and to explain why others were not. As Sarah Nash died (Madison County, 1911), her lengthy soliloquy was written down and carved in its entirety along one side of her tombstone. Nash was considerate enough to say, "All has been done for me that can be done. You have left nothing undone. I have this written for fear the other children will not get here in time, and this will be such a comfort for them to read."[48]

In cases where a patient's life ebbed slowly there was the likelihood that a great many people would be in attendance, if only to offer moral support to the family. Bruce Vaughan remembered how neighbors flocked to the home of his great-grandmother, Matilda Catherine Hartley ("Ma") Kelly, as she neared death, following a stroke (Washington County, 1934). "Soon neighbors started dropping by. The men dressed in starched white shirts and clean blue denim overalls gathered in small groups on the porch and under the shade trees in the yard. The women sat in straight-backed chairs in the living room, which also served as Ma's bedroom. Mostly they were quiet, but occasionally someone would say, 'She was a good Christian woman,' or 'She's going to a far better place.' The women would nod in agreement and say, 'Yes, a far better place."'[49]

Last Words and Requests

I hear a voice you cannot hear
Which says I must not stay,
I see a hand you cannot see
Which beckons me away.

—**S. N. Lyle**, 1875–1932
Lowes Creek Cemetery (Franklin County)

Sometimes the dying used their diminishing time on earth in practical ways. It was not uncommon for someone to request burial in a certain cemetery, plan the funeral service right down to the selection of hymns and Bible verses, and pick out a burial outfit. Franklin and Charity Wright (Franklin County, early 1900s) left nothing to chance. This couple stored "two coffin patterns cut from black walnut lumber, ready to be nailed together when the time came," their burial clothing, and a tombstone, bearing their names and birth dates, in a spare bedroom. These items caused their young great-granddaughter to dislike spending the night there.[50]

Even some children got their affairs in order. Judging from their obituaries, little girls most often gave away their possessions, requested a particular burial dress, or specified that a certain doll be placed in their coffins. One child, seven-year-old Cora Belle Brinson (Washington County, 1885), after informing her parents that she would not get well, proceeded to instruct them on where to bury her—and them—when the time came.[51]

Children's last words have been found carved on tombstones, especially on boys' stones. Several died telling their mothers not to cry, including three-year-old Charles Boles (Washington County, 1886), who also said, "I must go to Heaven and see my Father." (Charles was born two months after Thomas Boles's death, suggesting that the boy was anxious to meet his earthly father in heaven, rather than his heavenly Father.)[52] "Mama get me well, the Dr. won't," said five-year-old J. H. Williams (Franklin County, 1899),[53] while fifteen-year-old Ronald Crockett's tombstone quotes him saying, "Cover my head Mama and let me go to sleep never to wake any more," followed by, "Let me die never to die any more" (Carroll County, 1904).[54] If such inscriptions are to be believed, the dying occasionally spoke in rhymed verse, as did Sarah Kelly

(Benton, 1890). Her husband, Marcus, a tombstone carver, inscribed these words on her stone, headed "A Request."

My darling little children,
Take heed to what I say,
As I am on my dying bed,
And soon must pass away.
I have loved you in your infancy,
And you've loved me quite well,
If you by acts in future years,
Your love for me would tell,
Always be industrious,
And do your duty well.[55]

Those who sat up had the opportunity to fulfill last requests, offer comfort, and be comforted in turn by evidence that heaven awaited. Though Otto Rayburn collected the belief that the dying could foretell the future, no evidence of this has been found in memoirs or letters. However, obituaries do give examples of the dying, in Rayburn's words, "glimpsing the land of no return that they are about to enter."[56] Some people reportedly heard music or singing, or saw dazzlingly bright celestial mansions, or angelic visions of paradise. Mary Elizabeth Marrs (Madison County, 1888) experienced visions of heaven that were "so bright that she shouted glory to God on high and was, as it were, permitted to see God while in her flesh." She even described her launch across the River Jordan: "I am now passing over, I can see its waters. Tell people to meet me in Heaven. Angels are around me now."[57] As Emma Lee Featherstone lay on her deathbed (Benton County, 1906), she offered to take messages from her sisters to their mother, who had died three years earlier,[58] while others reported the ability to converse with previously deceased family members.

Though such visions comforted the living, last words could also be heartbreaking, as when the person died agonizing over salvation. Some utterances were unvarnished statements of a physical condition: "I feel awful bad," "I'm fainting," "I'm going to die." Some of the oddest last words are those giving advice, such as those of a Mr. Axton before he committed suicide (Benton County, 1896): "Beware of wine and women,"[59] or Mary Borland's tombstone inscription (Franklin County, 1910), advising her husband to take care of their home because "you do not want to live with young folks."[60] Margaret Lake's tombstone gave her last request: "Bury me in Tennessee by the side of my little children," which, since she was buried in Van Buren's Fairview Cemetery (Crawford County, 1869), means her dying wish was not granted.[61]

Figure 2.1 Tombstone of Sarah Mayes (died 1903), Evergreen Cemetery, Fayetteville (Washington County), containing the deceased's last words. *Photo by Abby Burnett.*

The deathbed confession, an attempt to clear a troubled conscience, was especially important. A good example of this comes from Turnbo, who, in addition to collecting Ozark stories, practiced medicine under the auspices of a licensed doctor. He described a visit to a very sick patient (Marion County, 1879) who, on being informed he had no hope of recovering, asked Turnbo to hear a secret he had kept for over twenty years. The man then confessed to having killed a man who had wronged him—only to discover that he'd murdered the wrong person.

"I committed a foul deed," the dying man told Turnbo. "My sin was deep dark and unbearable. . . . I do not know the man's name nor where he lived but from the moment I fled from the presence of that dying man to this minute I see his form as he lay in the throes of death at the side of the road as plain as I did when I looked down on him as he lay in his death struggles." The patient, who gave Turnbo permission to tell his story, died a week later.[62] Another deathbed confession was made by Joe Vaughn (Newton County, 1926), who told his family that he was really the famed outlaw Frank James—a revelation so convincing they put both names on his tombstone.[63] "A dying man's testimony is admissible in courts of law in every nation because of the known fact that a dying man has no reason to lie and will tell the truth if he knows himself to be dying," according to one collector of Ozark oddities.[64]

Some people sensed when they were about to die, and many last words are similar to those of Celia Shipp (Madison County, 1916), who called her young granddaughter to her bedside and told her, "Honey, I'm leavin', I'll see you over yonder."[65] The most common last request the dying made, however, was for loved ones to live good lives so they could all be reunited in heaven, which prompted a few families to seek immediate baptism. This request shows up time and again in memoirs, obituaries, and on tombstones; a good example comes from the letter, written just hours before his death, by sixteen-year-old Johnnie Chism (Searcy County, 1898) to his two brothers. "I have no hope of ever seeing you any more on earth, but be prepared to meet me in heaven, for heaven is my home. Good-by, brothers, and if I never meet you again meet me in heaven. . . . Give yourselves to God for the sake of your dying brother. Meet me in Heaven, where parting is no more."[66]

Death Superstitions

A sudden death could cause families to berate themselves for not having correctly interpreted the ways in which the natural world had tried to alert them. Folklore collected throughout the South contains numerous signs believed to foretell death, but one predominates: the bird as harbinger, especially whip-poor-wills, doves, roosters, crows, and screech owls. First, there were taboos against birds getting into the house, as a bird flying indoors was believed to foretell a coming death. It was also considered bad luck for a bird to fly inside after dark, to be caught indoors, to light on a bedstead or someone's head, to fly against a mirror, or even to flutter outside a window. This superstition has roots in England at least as far back as the 1700s.[67]

Then there are cases where just seeing a bird foretold a death. After several members of the Risley family suffered the effects of lightning striking their house, killing young Ada Risley (Ozark County, Missouri, year unknown), her father later recalled an odd incident. "On the day before the death of his little child a small bird lit on his shoulder then on his head and chirped a little song," the father told a friend, adding that he'd tried to scare it away, to no avail. "Mr. Risley would repeat the story of the bird and shed tears for he seemed to incline to the belief that it was a warning of the sudden taking away of his beloved child."[68]

Another man was more attuned to a bird's meaning. Benjamin Moses Tolbert Wilson was on his way to work when a bird landed on his hat. Wilson immediately informed his boss that his mother was dying, and he left for his old homeplace. Since he lived in Texarkana, in the far southwest corner of the state (Miller County, 1906), it took him a week to reach her in Randolph County (in the north-east corner of the state) and he arrived a few hours before her funeral. He did not know how he knew she was dying, nor did his wife know where Wilson was until she spoke with his foreman.[69]

Those in attendance in the home would have known the traditions to observe as soon as the patient died. The oft-repeated superstitions of stopping the clock (easily accomplished by removing the pendulum's weighted end) and covering all mirrors immediately after a death were not unique to the Ozarks, though certainly found there. Sometimes clocks were stopped to ensure that they did not accidentally stop by themselves, which would herald another death within the family. This was almost as dire as having a previously stopped clock start up on its own; other accounts state that clocks will stop of their own accord when a family member dies, but with no dire consequences.[70]

Another task was covering the mirrors, using either white or black fabric, so mourners wouldn't accidentally view themselves, the corpse, or the casket in the mirror, any one of which could bring about another death. Having a mirror—or a portrait—fall from the wall was another bad omen,[71] and either for this reason or out of a belief in the power of a spirit to enter the living through that person's photograph, in some households all photos were immediately turned downward or placed in drawers after a death. As late as 1957 Kevin Hatfield (Madison County) recalled seeing the photographs in his grandfather's bedroom put away after his death—even though his grandfather had died in a hospital and not in this room.

Death

The tint of health has left her cheek
And cold is her fair brow.
Her eyes are closed, her pulse is still,
She is an angel now.

—Otus J. Huggins, 1877–1895
Duncan Cemetery (Franklin County)

Now comes the moment that all of the sitting up, nursing, watching, and listening have led to: death. Folk remedies and doctors' medicines, prayer, strict adherence to taboos and superstitions—all of them, ultimately, must fail. The body is mortal. It dies.

What happens at this moment is the least-documented part of the complicated process, perhaps because it is so personal and so laden with emotion. Despite this, dying was not a private act, and the deathbed scene was usually attended by as many family members, friends, neighbors, relatives, and small children as could crowd into the bedroom. Though this final scene was widely witnessed, it was rarely recorded in any detail. One account, however, comes from a diary entry written by John Guin Bledsoe, a teacher and Baptist minister (Pope and Conway counties, 1867). He and his wife, Susan Bernice Hurst, were among family members keeping a vigil at the bedside of Susan's father until the man's death five days later. This is Bledsoe's account of what he witnessed.

Symptoms worse—breathing hard, pulse low, utterance indistinct. As the day advanced he seemed to be steadily sinking and at 4 o'clock he had not the power of speech, his eyes were almost set, the cold sweat was issuing from his extremities, and clear indications of approaching death were visible.

Even the little boys and girls were solemn and thoughtful. Sons and daughters were now and then weeping over a kind father as he neared the shores of death while the bitter moanings of the agonized mother and companion were being borne in plaintive accents on the evening air. Oh! Death wilt thou not cease to affrat? Wilt thou not relent over the bitter agonies of the affectionate children and the heart-rending cries of the confiding wife? No.

The bosom of the afflicted one heaves as the mighty throes of death agitate it. Sympathizing friends watch in silence the steady progress of the ruthless destroyer death. The struggles of nature grow more and more feeble. The death glare glimmers in the sunken eyes and the breathing becomes slow and faint. The excited family gather around to witness the last struggle of their husband and father and as their wailings were borne away on the passing breeze the body ceased to move and the spirit winged its way to the place of disembodied spirits there to remain until the resurrection morn.[72]

CHAPTER THREE

Laying out the Body

Softly smooth the quiet breast
Gently fold her hands to rest
Think what work those hands have done
What marks they left beneath the sun
Over the cold and lifeless feet
Spread the snowey winding sheet
Then look back when all is o'er
Think what thornes they felt before.

—**Martha Ashing,** 1841–1876
Kersey Cemetery (Franklin County)[1]

As the dying body released its final breath it would be reasonable to assume that friends and neighbors, so long in attendance at the deathbed, were heaving sighs of their own—ones of relief. However, the minute death occurred those same members of the community now had to begin work on a variety of jobs that demanded their labor, materials, skill, and speed.

Burial within twenty-four hours is frequently cited as the norm, but even when delayed it was imperative to wash, dress, and position the body immediately, tasks collectively known as "laying out." Those doing this job had to work quickly because rigor mortis, the process that causes the body's muscles to become rigid, can begin in as little as two hours and last for several days. Given the number of variables that impact rigor (such as ambient temperature, certain causes of death, and the deceased's physical condition), it's no wonder that even modern sources disagree on the factors that hasten it. As undertaker Tom Olmstead expressed it, "We're none of us alike before or after death."[2] Embalming (discussed in chapter 12) would eventually make it possible to delay burial

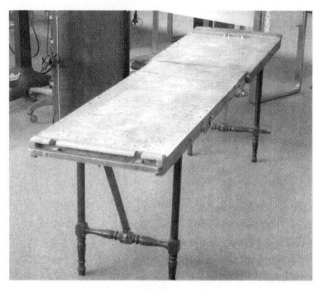

Figure 3.1 Perforated cooling board, patented by Gleason Board Co., Rochester, New York, in 1881 and 1886, on which bodies were laid when preparing them for burial. *In the collection of the Boone County Heritage Museum, Harrison; photo by Abby Burnett.*

for several days, but some communities traditionally held bodies for an average of three days without embalming, even in hot weather.

Laying out began by placing the corpse on a flat surface. This could be a couple of boards or a door resting on chairs or sawhorses, or a piece of perforated wood, called a cooling board. (Children's bodies were sometimes laid out on an ironing board or sewing machine.) Such a platform enabled several people to work at once, but more importantly it ensured that the supine body would rigidify in a completely flat position. Prior to a government program (late 1930s–1940) that enabled families to make their own cotton-stuffed mattresses, people slept atop large fabric bags, called "ticks," filled with straw, corn shuck strips, or feathers, that rested on the bed frame's slats or interlaced ropes. A body left on such a sagging mattress would conform to its shape, and given the narrow confines of the coffin it was imperative to lay the body out flat and straight.

Washing the Body

Though there is no obvious need to wash and re-dress a body before burial, this act was rarely omitted. "The hillfolk have a veritable mania for washing dead bodies; the moment a death occurs the neighbors strip the corpse and begin to scrub it vigorously," wrote Vance Randolph. "A man may be dirty all his life, and in his last illness his body and bedding may be so foul that one can hardly stay in the cabin, but he goes to his grave clean, so far as soap and water can cleanse him." Randolph noted further that family members never washed the body, which was done by members of the community, "except in case of the direst necessity."[3]

"It was considered unethical for a loved one to be used to bathe and dress a close relative," columnist Rex Harral wrote of his mother's death (Cleburne County, 1928).[4] Still, there were exceptions. No one came forward to assist Gussy Brown's family after he died from what was thought to be diphtheria (Boone County, 1930), so his six brothers divvied up the jobs, including bathing and shaving the body. Neighbors did not visit the home for several more weeks, fearing contagion.[5] Though possibly apocryphal, one Ozark writer (Missouri, 1956) described a scene where two men stripped, washed, positioned, and covered the body of an elderly woman, stating that "it wouldn't be right" for the woman's granddaughter to do this job.[6] This prohibition was also observed in African American communities.

Though most accounts mention men laying out men and women laying out women, this was not strictly adhered to. Women certainly laid out men's bodies during the Civil War, burying men killed by bushwhackers but working in such haste and stealth that it was impossible for them to wash and re-dress a body. In some communities midwives assisted with laying out the dead of both sexes. Race was not necessarily a factor. Though not all white undertakers would handle black bodies, there are instances where the races helped one another lay out their dead. Mary Alice Mason, her husband, and teenaged son were the only African American family in the county, staying on after all blacks had been ordered to leave the previous year. When Mary Alice died at Cotter (Baxter County, 1908), at age fifty-three, "There being no negro people in town, the white ladies went in to prepare the body for burial," according to a front-page newspaper account. "There was no hesitancy on the part of the white ladies, several prominent, too, in doing all they could do in rendering assistance."[7]

No matter who did the job, the community's barber was usually called in to shave a male corpse, and barbers also sometimes laid out the dead. Doing so landed barber Bert Poland in jail (Baxter County, 1928) after the body of "Buck" Toney, whom Poland had dressed for burial, was exhumed and found to have died from a fractured skull, a detail Poland apparently never noticed. The amount of blood found in various parts of the Toney house, and the fact that the family operated a still, may explain why a hired barber—and not neighbors—laid out his body. Charges were eventually dropped against Poland and the man's relatives.[8]

Not everyone could stomach handling the dead, but only pregnant women were expressly forbidden to do so. Nor were they supposed to look at bodies or attend burials, lest they "mark" or disfigure the unborn child. Orphea Wyatt was pregnant when her great-grandmother died (Newton County, 1949), and though she was not allowed to go to the funeral, she *was* asked to trim the coffin, which was brought to her for this purpose. "I couldn't think of nothing worse," she recalled. Addie Adkisson, nevertheless, attended a funeral while she was pregnant (Izard County, late 1920s or early 1930s) but took precautions. "I didn't look at the corpse, nor I didn't touch it," she said.[9]

Using dishpans full of warm, soapy water, the body would be washed then dried. Iva Gross (Madison County, born 1900) described the two times she helped lay out bodies, the first being that of an elderly neighbor. "I'd set up with her night after night, and when she died her face drawed, and I had to rub her face, hold it sort of, until it looked natural. And me and an old woman, we washed her and dressed her. The next one I remember was a baby. I guess it was [old enough to be] walkin'. . . . Well, I was young then, and I begun to wash its little feet, and the woman with me said, 'Don't do that, bathe its face first.'"[10]

Dead bodies have been called ceremonially unclean but sometimes the corpse was truly dirty. One interview subject, speaking on condition of anonymity, described how men in the community got a deceased neighbor ready for burial (Boone County, 1940s). "The man never would take a bath. He'd put on a pair of unions [whole body, one-piece underwear] in the wintertime, and they were on there until spring. . . . So Dad and Mr. Murphy and Mr. Adams laid that man out on a board, and he was so dirty they had to just scrape him. I remember my daddy saying, 'That was the nastiest damn man I ever seen.'" Though clearly an extreme case, in this man's defense there was a tradition elsewhere (Pope County, early 1900s) of men being sewn into their undergarments in the fall and not removing them until spring.[11]

Another step was combing the hair. Otto Rayburn recorded the belief that "a native Hillman never parts his hair with a comb that has touched the head of a corpse" as this brought bad luck,[12] and certainly women's decorative combs have been found in graves when cemeteries were relocated. In one account, at least, the deceased's comb became a treasured memento. When Catharine Stirman laid out her friend, Sophia Sawyer (Washington County, 1854), she placed her own decorative tortoiseshell comb in Sawyer's hair. Some time in the next thirty years, when Sawyer's coffin was exhumed for reburial in another cemetery, Will Stirman happened to pass by, saw his aunt's comb in Sawyer's coffin, and removed it so his aunt could have it for a keepsake. It is not known whether Mrs. Stirman wore it again or simply kept it out of sentiment.[13]

Positioning the Body

"Gently close the sweet bright eyes, / Fold her hands upon her breast" begins a poem written in memory of eighteen-year-old Anna Shibley (Crawford County, 1882).[14] The job of closing the deceased's eyes was always done first, either because open, staring eyes were disturbing to the living, or more logically because rigor mortis begins with the eye and facial muscles before spreading downward through the body. (It relaxes in reverse order, from feet to face, as decomposition begins.)[15]

It wasn't enough just to close the eyes; they had to be made to stay closed, and it was traditional to weight them with coins. Randolph repeated a story told to him by a public health nurse in Arkansas, who placed little pieces of paper under her deceased patient's eyelids to anchor them. She told him, "the family objected, saying: 'We may be on relief, but we still got our corpse money!' They brought out two old silver dollars and laid them on the dead man's eyes. It appears that some families keep these same coins, set aside for this purpose only, for several generations."[16] (On one occasion Randolph also saw a body buried with a silver dollar in its mouth, a custom family members declined to explain to him.)[17] Among whites it was customary to remove and save these coins. Though silver coins were preferred as copper could turn the skin green, every denomination of coin has been mentioned in this connection: pennies, Buffalo nickels, dimes, silver dollars, and half-dollar coins. This explains the old expression about a person who would "steal the nickels off a dead man's eyes" to denote the lowest of the low.

It was not necessary to leave these coins in place, and within African American communities there was no rule about preserving them. In 1983, archaeologists relocating Cedar Grove Cemetery, an African American burying ground in the southwestern corner of the state (Lafayette County, established post–Civil War), found coins in some of the exhumed coffins. While a few coins had been sewn onto clothing and others were perhaps worn around the neck,[18] one grave contained two coins, a nickel and a dime, one of them found in the eye socket of the skull.[19] This is one of the few times the custom can be documented in Arkansas, but a 1936 excavation in Flushing, New York, turned up "rare pennies . . . that had covered the eyes of the dead" in what had been the town's "Colored Cemetery" throughout the 1800s.[20]

Figure 3.2 The grave of Mary C. Watkins (died 1878), Little Rock's Mount Holly Cemetery (Pulaski County), has a sculpture of an angel lifting Mary from her grave. Her arms are crossed on her chest, in the traditional posture of a laid-out body. *Photo by Abby Burnett.*

Another part of the process was tying the corpse's jaw shut so the mouth did not gape open, using a strip of fabric, napkin, or diaper for this purpose. It, too, would be removed once rigor mortis set in, as the jaw and hands do not relax, even after rigor passes. Lydia Moser Rider (Izard County, born 1916) was a young girl when a neighbor died, and she was asked to do the family's wash. "They'd tied a rag around his head to hold his mouth closed, and when I was taking the sheets and things off the bed, that rag come tumbling out, and I like to a'died! But I had to take that out, and untie it, and put it in the laundry."[21] Diapers were used for this purpose, as well as in a more intimate way, to keep fluids from leaking from bodily orifices. Izola Strong Taylor handed down the story of how, as a teenager (Johnson County, mid-1920s), she was taught by older women in her family to lay out the dead. Many years later she told a friend that the corpse was diapered with a piece of fabric filled with salt, to absorb any leakage.[22]

Another requirement was straightening the body's legs and positioning the arms. In later years undertakers used a metal device to keep the hands

Figure 3.3 Double doves, representing the death of a mother and child, on the tombstone of Flemone Hanna and her infant (died 1873), White House Cemetery (Washington County). *Photo by Abby Burnett.*

in place, but families had to be creative. Mary Jane Hough (rural Missouri Ozarks, early 1900s) described positioning an infant's body. "We got a straight board and laid the baby flat. Then we shaped it and put a towel where we wanted its arms," a technique probably used to position adult bodies as well.[23] Generally, the arms were folded over the breast, but in some instances a particular object was placed in the deceased's hands. Children often cradled toys, while men were sometimes interred with their hats, walking sticks, or even guns. The most common item for anyone, male or female, to be buried with was a Bible, remnants of which have been found in older graves when cemeteries are relocated.

One of the saddest sights for funeral goers was the double death of a mother and infant. Even when the deaths occurred several days apart, the mother might be positioned holding her baby, as was done with Rose Budd (Washington County, 1915). Budd gave birth to her first child, a boy who died soon after. Four days later she, too, succumbed and the baby's body was placed in its mother's arms for viewing and burial.[24] Tombstone inscriptions mention these double burials: "And by her side our baby rests" (Washington County, 1895) or even "Mary's sweet little infant babe lies sleeping at her feet" (Newton County, 1901).

Sewing for the Dead

Randolph wrote that strips of torn fabric wrapped around a body, called a winding sheet, predated other burial garments,[25] but in the Arkansas Ozarks this term and the shroud are usually used interchangeably. Whether or not torn fabric was used, people were aware of the practice because a vision of a coil of paper or fabric rising in the air, or hearing the sound of tearing fabric, foretold a death. Winding sheets were not used after the mid-1800s in the northeastern United States,[26] but in Arkansas bodies were buried either in shrouds or conventional clothing. However, photographs taken of bodies in coffins in the 1930s occasionally show a large piece of fabric wrapping a clothed body, leaving only the face exposed. This may be a holdover of the winding sheet and is an example of yet another type of fabric used in burial.

In Arkansas a shroud was a plain, loose-fitting garment, similar to a choir robe, worn by either men or women. In the early years of the funeral industry undertakers advertised such things as "ladies' and gents' burial robes,"[27] although some merchants made a distinction between shrouds and burial robes, offering both for sale. Eventually, however, it was only older people who requested this garment. The obituary of ninety-year-old James Byler (Benton County, 1915) noted, "At his request he was robed in the old fashioned robe and laid to rest,"[28] though records kept by Dunn Funeral Home in Sulphur Springs (Benton County) reveal adults still being buried in robes when that business closed in 1942.

Vera Ann Cypert Jacobs described the shroud local women made for her mother (Clark County, outside the Ozarks, 1929). "It was made out of satin black crepe with full sleeves that came down to her hands. . . . I am sure that they must have put quite a bit of underwear on her because Mother had always talked about when they buried her mother they didn't put enough underwear on her and she just thought it was awful. You know women used to wear several slips."[29]

It was once traditional to bury the dead in a new outfit. According to an undertaker's textbook on funeral psychology (1945), "We still array our dead in his or her best clothing, a custom survival of the finery with which early man clothed his dead."[30] Somehow that "best clothing" became "new clothing." In some communities a man's family would buy him a new suit for burial, but

Figure 3.4 Clasping hands symbolize the farewell between the dead and the living. In this example, on the stone of Florence Peel (1858–1922), the dead hand (*on the left*) wears a loose shroud sleeve. Clinton Cemetery (Van Buren). *Photo by Abby Burnett.*

itemized funeral home records also list charges for cleaning or pressing men's suits, indicating that men could be buried in previously worn garments. Especially during the Depression, men living in farming communities were usually buried in their newest or least-patched pair of bib overalls, but women often set aside special clothing. One older woman showed social worker Mary Marquess her "grave clothes" that she stored in a box under her bed (Benton County, early 1960s). This lady, who had worked as a female attendant at a local funeral home in the 1940s, set aside handmade white cotton underwear, a slip, stockings, and a dress (but not shoes) to be buried in. This was the second set she had prepared, having given away her first set so a friend could be buried in new garments.

Older people were more likely to make and set aside burial garments. Geraldine Hatfield (Madison County, born 1934) wrote, "I recall visiting in one home where this was the case, the caskets were under a bed and had the burial clothes inside."[31] One woman, Nancy Warren (Benton County, born 1829), used to pack a certain black silk dress whenever she visited relatives to ensure burial in this garment in case she died during the visit. She discussed her desire so often that just the words, "black silk dress," would cause

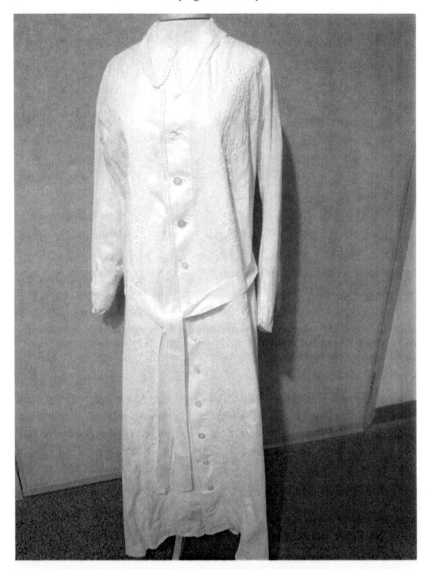

Figure 3.5 Burial shroud made by Mrs. Joe Elizabeth Wilkinson when she was a teenager, in the late 1860s, for her own burial. Wilkinson believed she was dying but later survived an amputation and went on to live a long life. This shroud is not a typical, loosely fitting garment, but instead is made like a conventional dress, with crocheted trim, white embroidery, cut-work, and pearl buttons down the front. The shroud was later donated to the Old Independence Regional Museum, Batesville, by her granddaughters. *Courtesy of Old Independence Regional Museum, Barnes/Simmons Collection.*

young relatives to be overcome with laughter.[32] Another couple was even more thorough. "In a drawer of the bureau Grandmother kept ready his and her burial clothes. Every few years these would be used for best and carefully replaced. Grandfather's shirt she made by hand from cloth she bleached herself," according to an account of John Thaddeus and Mary Rebekah Skelton (Washington County, late 1800s).[33]

This emphasis on new garments explains the prohibition against making new clothing for anyone who was sick, lest that garment become his or her burial outfit. Other superstitions prohibit any sewing on a garment, such as fixing a hem or tightening a button, while the person is wearing it, and clothing sewn while still on the living might have been too reminiscent of altering a garment already on a corpse. (This contradicts the Pope County custom of sewing undergarments on in the fall, mentioned above.) The living were also prohibited from wearing new garments to a funeral, lest that cause the death of the wearer or a family member.[34]

When a woman or child died, women in the community gathered to make both a garment and, usually, the coffin's fabric lining. Viola Williams (Boone County, born 1927) speculated that dresses were sewn for adult women because the shrouds sold by funeral homes looked too much like nightgowns, but sometimes such a gown was necessary. The logbook of Dunn Funeral Home contains an entry that Sarah Cathrina Wilson would be buried in a homemade robe (Benton County, 1926), possibly due to the fact that she weighed 350 pounds.[35]

Within black communities the same rule applied: the deceased was dressed in the newest clothing owned or in a specially made garment. However, according to one folklore source, not specific to the Ozarks (Pine Bluff, Jefferson County, after 1895), the body must have on "some purple article of clothing."[36] During the Depression, when money was scarce, members of Fayetteville's African American community (Washington County, 1930s) used the deceased's best clothing for burial. This could be anything from overalls to a Sunday dress or suit, but it was not bought for the occasion and was usually black in color. The body might be wrapped in the person's favorite quilt, too. As a child, Ethel Tompkins watched her mother and other ladies lay out the body of an older member of their church (Jackson County, outside the Ozarks, 1950). "It was a white dress—most of them were put in white dresses," she recalled. "She was considered a 'mother of the church' and I think it was a regular dress. It might have been one she wore on Sunday," as all of these women dressed in white every Sunday. Men, she said of this sharecropping community, were always laid out by the church deacons and buried wearing overalls.

Children, even stillborn babies, also got new clothing. Opal Arnold Taylor, describing her little brother's death (Searcy County, 1917), recalled that neighbors came to the family's home to sew, using fabric bought especially for the occasion. "New cloth! New cloth! And the grown-ups were buried the same way, they always had new cloth."[37] One explanation for this is that babies and children routinely wore hand-me-downs. Given the many superstitions that attempt to stave off death, it was hardly likely that burying one child in another's clothing, would have been tolerated.

The bodies of children and young women were usually dressed in white; older adults wore black unless they had requested otherwise or if it was a community tradition, as noted above. Mayme Collier Graham (Carroll County, 1919) was probably typical of other older women in the way she was dressed for her funeral: "The burial clothes were a long black dress, with a long black apron over it; the apron being edged with a wide ruffle of the same black material."[38] Older women who had followed the tradition of keeping their heads covered were usually dressed in a cap of some kind.

In several instances bridal outfits were used in lieu of shrouds. When twenty-year-old Mary Ann (no last name), a former slave, died (Washington County, 1874), the weather was too icy to procure a burial robe in Durham, the nearest town. She died in the home of the Lewis family, where she worked, and Matilda Lewis gave her wedding attire for Mary Ann to be buried in.[39] Drowning victim Ruth Holland (Madison County, 1930) was buried in a shroud made from yards of white satin, fulfilling the prediction Holland had made when announcing her engagement to her little sister Ruby, "The next new dress I have will be satin."

Men were most often dressed in the style of clothing they'd worn in life, generally their Sunday best. Bernice Mhoon (Washington County, born 1923) recalled seeing her uncle in his coffin: "He had on one of these old, long black coats and a pair of dark trousers, and the best I can remember, his shirt was white with a little black pinstripe; he had no tie—he was a Pentecost man and wouldn't have had a tie on, under no circumstances."

Funeral homes sold conventional burial clothing in current styles. The Brashears undertaking family (Madison County, 1936 to the present) once carried "box suits." These were men's suits, shirts, and ties basted into cardboard boxes that could be set upright for display. There was also, briefly, a line of women's dresses in boxes, though these garments were later sold on hangers. The men's suits were full-piece garments, but a cheaper version was also available, made like a loose-fitting hospital gown. Though knee-length and open, it looked like a suit from the waist up, the only portion of the body visible in the casket. "They never looked very good," admits Sumner Brashears.

Ray and Orphea Wyatt (Newton County, 1943) recalled the first time they purchased such a garment from a funeral home and, believing they had bought a complete suit, thought they had been cheated. Art Stepp described the same experience when buying a suit of clothing from a Clarksville funeral home for a relative who owned nothing nice enough to be buried in (Johnson County, 1930s). "When they got home and went to put them on him, they found they'd got a shirt out that had no back on it, and didn't know what to do—whether to tell the family or not. We decided to keep our mouths shut. The coat had no back on it. The shirt didn't have sleeves, just cuffs."

Garments that looked like conventional fitted dresses were available for women and children. Of the nearly 750 bodies the Dunn family buried (Benton County, 1893–1942), 161 of these, all adults, went to their graves in purchased burial robes, suits, and dresses. There were usually additional charges for a union suit and either socks or hose when men and women were buried in robes.[40] Veterans were often buried in their uniforms—especially those who had fought in the Civil War. "While memories of his life hold sway / He sleeps in uniform of gray" is carved on Hugh Routh's tombstone (Boone County, 1919).[41] Veterans were also buried wearing their medals, which is why G.A.R. ribbons and insignia are scarce today. A member of the Masons would be laid out wearing his apron—the badge of a Mason, and in Arkansas this fraternal lodge lays another apron atop the casket before burial, as well.

It was not always possible to practice the niceties of laying out in cases of suicide, murder, or drowning where the body was found long after death. But for all other deaths it would be hard to overstate the importance of having a special burial garment. This is seen in the account of a shooting in Oaks (Indian Territory, 1895, adjudicated in Benton County, Arkansas), which left the murdered man surrounded by people unwilling to dress his body. Youtsler Carson, who had shot Nathaniel Williams for allegedly stealing his team of horses, "gave the corpse his own best clothes" before being led away by authorities.[42]

Shoes and Stockings

It might seem unnecessary to mention that dressing a body for burial included putting on shoes, but there is some controversy over whether the dead were shod. It has been stated that African Americans buried their dead without shoes,[43] yet the archaeologists who excavated and relocated Cedar Grove Cemetery, mentioned above, found that "shoes appear to be associated with individuals of most age groups."[44] A single item in the Mary Parler folklore collection states, "They used to believe that you should never bury anyone with shoes on" (Washington County, 1958),[45] but this contradicts both anecdotal and archaeological evidence, including the Arkansas Archeological Survey's excavation of Eddy Cemetery (Crawford County, used by whites from the 1870s to about 1900), which found evidence of shoes in seven out of sixteen burials.[46] Tom Olmstead, who learned the funeral director's trade from his father (Cleburne County, 1930s), is adamant that the dead were always buried wearing shoes.

Though it would seem logical for the poorest Ozark residents to reuse the deceased's shoes, the earliest burials took place in an era when coffins had one-piece lids. The corpse's feet would have been exposed when the lid was set to one side while the body was being viewed. Still, descriptions of later burials, at the time when caskets hid the lower body, also mention the presence of shoes.

> When Brother Landon Bain's wife died in February . . . some neighbors went to the Bain home to "sit up with the dead" while the grieving husband slept. Bro. Bain was of necessity a frugal man. . . . The next morning . . . Elsie [Johnson] and Gola [Burge] had a hard time convincing Mr. Bain to wait until Mrs. Epperson arrived to dress his wife for burial. He wanted to put a pair of worn-out high-topped shoes on his wife's feet. The entire group was very relieved when Mrs. Epperson arrived, as she convinced Mr. Bain not to use those shoes. (Sharp County, 1924)[47]

It's unclear whether Mrs. Epperson wanted to dress Mrs. Bain in a better pair of shoes or if the delay of so many hours made it impossible to get any shoes—let alone high-topped ones—onto the wife's feet.

Additional evidence for the presence of shoes comes from undertakers' advertisements for burial supplies, such as James Bozarth's ad (Washington County, 1896) for burial goods, including both robes and shoes.[48] The first reference to burial shoes found in the Dunn Funeral Home's records (Benton County, 1909) is a $1 charge; their charges for slippers and burial shoes continued well into the 1930s at prices ranging from $1.50 to $3.50, always for women's burials. The most expensive burial slippers were those sold by undertaker H. F. Morton of Eureka Springs (Carroll County, 1924), because using Morton's pricing code the shoes he sold for $5 had cost the undertaker $2.50.[49] Such slippers were conventional-looking shoes made with elastic or fabric behind the heel to facilitate sliding them onto stiff, unyielding feet. According to Betty Crumrine Rahm, her family's business, Arkansas Funeral Home (Johnson County, after 1933), sold a gray satin burial dress with matching

Figure 3.6 Edmund Thomas Caudle sitting with his deceased wife, Martha M. Courtney Caudle, Springdale (Washington County), March 1911. *Courtesy Shiloh Museum of Ozark History/George Caudle Collection (S-82-89-1).*

satin shoes that laced up the back, to simplify getting them onto the feet.[50] One family found a creative solution following a grandmother's death (Carroll County, 1919), wrapping her feet and ankles in wide black ribbon to create "burial shoes."[51]

Placing Salt on the Stomach

Of all of the burial customs and superstitions originating outside the Ozarks, one of the oddest and most ancient is the custom of placing a bowl of salt (or a mixture of salt and earth) on the corpse's abdomen, symbolizing the spirit and the flesh. The practice came to this country from northern England in the 1700s and migrated with settlers to Appalachia, where it continued unabated and was eventually brought to the Ozarks.[52] This practice is mentioned in folklore collections but has not been found in eyewitness accounts of funerals.

The custom has often been attributed to African American burials. In these accounts a bowl of salt is placed on the corpse's stomach, usually in cases where the person died by drowning. Parler's students collected two versions, though neither from the Ozarks. In one (Hempstead County, 1959), a man helped bury an African American where a bowl of salt was placed on the stomach until the body was buried to "keep out the evil spirits." A variation on this was to put an unbroken egg surrounded by a ring of salt on the body's chest. Another account, collected in Gurdon (Clark County, 1958), stated that following the retrieval of a drowning victim, other blacks followed the egg-and-salt ritual.[53] One suggestion is that it was believed to keep the body's abdomen from bloating.[54] A Fort Smith mortician (Sebastian County, date unknown) told Randolph about the dish of salt, claiming to have seen this done by "country people in his territory" to keep the stomach from bloating, although Randolph also recorded an old saying, "The Devil hates salt," and the belief that bewitched cattle would not eat salt.[55]

The archaeologists relocating Cedar Grove Cemetery found a ceramic saucer under the pelvis of one burial (estimated between 1900 and 1927), but it is not clear whether this was a remnant of the salt ritual or part of a completely separate tradition, placing objects used by the deceased during his final illness atop the grave "to keep the deceased from returning."[56]

Waiting Too Long

Flossie Cook Smith, a friend of schoolteacher Kate Fancher, recalled one extremely cold winter when a woman died near Kingston (Madison County, 1920s or 1930s). Fancher was known to be the "best hand" at laying out a body, and Cook assisted her on this and other occasions. "It was the coldest time there ever was . . . it was so cold you just couldn't stay warm and with just a wood stove in the house. When this woman died, well, they brought her bed in the room where the stove was. . . . This daughter, Sarah, wouldn't let them take her back in one of the cold rooms." Severe winter weather and deep snow kept Fancher and Smith from reaching the family until two or three days after the death, by which time "she was just deteriorating," Smith said. "That woman was smelling so bad when we took her out of there, it was worse than anything."[57]

Imodell Price Burnett recalled that during the Depression bodies were often kept in the home until decomposition had begun. "It would get pretty bad," she recalled. In another account, summer graveside services were held with the coffin downwind of the mourners due to the bodily fluids that were leaking from it.

Once the body was washed, dressed, and positioned, there was nothing left to do except cover it with a sheet to protect it until the coffin could be made and delivered, usually the following day. The body, still resting on the boards on which it had been laid out, would normally be placed in the house's

coolest room (or occasionally on a bed) to remain until the burial. Some folklore states that the dead were not to be touched again once they'd been laid
out, but this contradicts the African American belief, collected outside the
Ozarks, that touching the dead confers special benefits. "If you put your hand
on the head of a dead man, you will never worry about him; he will never
haunt you, and you will never fear death," according to Casie Jones Brown, a
former slave (Greene County, born 1840s).[58] Furthermore, the clasping hands
motif found on numerous tombstones across the Ozarks appears to depict
the very real custom of taking the deceased's hand one last time, in farewell.

Depending on a family's traditions, the sheet that covered the body was
later used to wrap it in the coffin or else was saved and reused. "All genteel
families owned a choice hand-woven linen sheet to cover their dead while
they waited for the coffin to be made," according to an account of the Blackburn family (Benton County, mid- to late 1800s). This dates back to a time
when a large and prosperous family might have a "loom room" set aside just
for weaving such things as coverlets, linen, and the "laying-out sheet."[59] In 1971
descendant Vera Key exhibited "a burial sheet of linen" made by the Blackburn women that "was spread tenderly over the one what had died, until the
coffin could be made."[60]

Laying out accounts generally follow a predictable set of steps, but
occasionally a story includes unusual details. When Gladys Ball and her six-
month-old child died from influenza (Madison County, 1918), Gladys Counts
described her mother's experience attending the death.

> It was in December and a lot of snow and ice was on the ground . . . and the
> night she died mother and Aunt Rhoda Rogers were the only ones there. They
> had to wash her, dress her and lay her out on a board like they used to do and
> mother said the next morning when they looked out the door there on a rose
> bush she had planted in the front yard was a beautiful yellow rose, two green
> leaves and a bud.

This event would have been especially meaningful to onlookers at the time,
because tombstone iconography often used a rose to symbolize an adult life.
A bud—or a bud on a broken stalk—represented the life of a baby that, in the
words of a widely popular epitaph, had been "budded on earth to bloom in
heaven."

> They were all shocked to see it. Mom went out and cut it and pinned it on her
> [Gladys Ball's] dress for burial that day and mother said it made her think of the
> scripture which says, "the bud on earth shall bloom in glory."[61]

CHAPTER FOUR

Sitting up with the Body

Calm on the bosom of thy God,
Fair Spirit rest thee now!
E'en while with ours thy footsteps trod
His seal was on thy brow.
Dust, to its narrow house beneath
Soul, to its place on high!
They that have seen his look in death
No more may fear to die.

—**Thomas Irby Hicks,** 1827–1893
Mountain Home Cemetery (Baxter County)

The morning after a neighbor died in Spring Valley (Washington County, 1931) Matilda Kelly saw something from her front porch that troubled her. "Isn't that a shame," Kelly remarked to great-grandson Bruce Vaughan, "Addie Holmesley has done a washing, and Tom Means is waiting to be buried." Holmesley's laundry, flapping on the clothesline, provided visible proof that she had put her own needs ahead of those of the deceased's family.

According to Vaughan, "When a neighbor died, you stopped whatever you were doing. You didn't do a washing, or celebrate or have a party or go to work. You honored it."[1] The one place where laundry and housework *were* permissible, even mandated, was in the home of the deceased. There, a number of household tasks had to be completed in advance of a very important part of the burial ritual: sitting up all night with the body.

Washing and Scrubbing

Scrubbing the bedstead was the first order of business, once the body had been lifted off it. Vaughan, recalling his great-grandmother's death following a stroke (Washington County, 1934), described the scene. While neighbors laid out Kelly's body in one room, "other neighbor women knocked down her bed, then scrubbed the bed and entire room with Lysol. After the scrubbing, the bed was 'put out to sun' in the backyard. One of the ladies gathered up all the bedclothes, along with Ma's nightgowns, then tied them up in a sheet" to do later with her own laundry.[2]

Vaughan's account took place in relatively recent times, but this practice was an old one. Silas Turnbo gives one description from Missouri (Ozark County, 1872) in which a wife attempted to sterilize the bed and bedding on which her husband had died. She submerged the bed in "a hole of water" and weighted it with rocks, leaving it in place for ten to twelve days. "The woman supposed in doing this that the germs of the disease would be soaked out of the bed clothes."[3]

Because both warmth and sunshine were believed to be purifiers, the deceased's sheets and clothing could also be hung outdoors to air. One newspaper article (Crawford County, 1874) advised that no matter how foul fabric might have become from the "essence" of such things as decomposing animals, decaying plants, and outdoor toilets, "heat alone—dry heat—will remove the odors, which are thus sent off in a volatile state. . . . The bed clothing may be used, and body garments worn longer, by ventilating with heated air."[4] Some families attempted to safeguard against contagion by boiling the deceased's bedding, including featherbeds. The neighbors of two teenaged brothers who died from tuberculosis (Madison County, early 1900s) were especially vigilant. These neighbors "burned the bedding, cleaned the house and iron beds with lye water, and begged the neighbors for quilts, sheets, pillowcases, pillows. The merchants gave them straw mattresses."[5]

It was common for doctors to spend the night in the homes of critically ill patients or women in labor. The next morning the doctor might go on to visit other patients in the neighborhood, but "he always dreaded returning the next day, for there was no way for him to have had word of his [first] patient since leaving," according to one witness (Washington County, 1890). "The first things he began watching for as he neared the house were an empty bedstead and bedding airing in the yard. If he saw them, he knew that his patient had died since he had been gone."[6] Clothing was another give-away. Vance Randolph recorded the expression, "Poor Jim's britches will be a-hangin' out most any day now!" meaning the person was close to death.[7]

Feather Crowns—Angel Wreaths

The subject of washing bedding—especially feather pillows—dovetails nicely with another custom: searching for evidence that the deceased was in heaven.

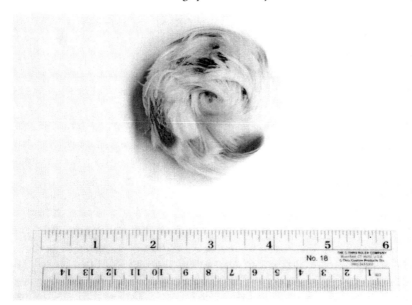

Figure 4.1 A feather crown found in a pillow after a death, taken to be a sign that the deceased's soul was safely in heaven. It was believed that human hands could not have made such a crown. *In the collection of the Heritage Center Museum, Berryville, Carroll County Historical Society. Photo by Abby Burnett.*

Proof of this came from finding a feather crown (also called by any combination of the words "heavenly" and "angel" with "wreath" or "crown") inside the deceased's pillow or featherbed. One Missouri folklorist described this crown, or tightly packed ball of feathers, as having the quill ends of the feathers pointing inward. "It was made in a perfect spiral shape similar to a snail shell . . . and was by far too complicated and perfect in construction to have been made by the hands of those simple folk."[8] In rare instances, the feathers supposedly formed the shape of a cross.

"Back then, after someone died, you took the bedding out and everything, and mama wanted to wash the pillow ticking," recounted Norma Jean Wilson Tomlinson (Izard County, mid-1940s) of her grandfather's death. Tomlinson's mother dearly wanted to find a crown, but a thorough search of the feathers yielded nothing. "Well, she washed the ticking and it hung on the clothesline many weeks, and she didn't think any more about it. When she went to put the feathers back in, she found two crowns of feathers . . . and they were woven in a way that no earthly human being could ever have done it." Tomlinson's mother showed the crowns to other family members and her daughter, a former skeptic, and all agreed that "a miracle" had occurred to relieve their minds.[9] According to another source, "the telling of finding an angel wreath in a pillow of the deceased was read along with the obituary."[10]

Though most folklore agrees that the deceased's pillow is searched immediately after a death, finding a crown before the person died was taken as evidence that he would die soon[11] and, at least according to Randolph, destroying
this crown might prolong the person's life. (Burning a sick person's pillow
could also remove such a "hex" and aid his recovery.)[12] Randolph also records
how, in cases where a person's life had been less than exemplary, the discovery
of a crown both shocked and relieved the relatives.[13] Sylvia Hill (Missouri,
date unknown) recalled that when she was five years old she questioned her
mother about the whereabouts of her father's feather crown. Her mother,
"turned white and said—'Honey, I was afraid to look!'"[14]

Pillows of the elderly and the devout, who were unlikely to have jeop-
ardized their chances of getting into heaven, were a sure source of feather
crowns, but any discovery of a crown elicited interest and sometimes made
the newspapers. "Mrs. Mary Leach died at her rooms in the old Eagle hotel
last Saturday. She was quite an elderly lady and there was considerable interest
over the crowns of feathers taken from the pillow on which she died. It is said
that a crown of feathers forms in the pillow under the head of the righteous"
(Benton County, 1906).[15]

Randolph collected many theories concerning how the feather balls were
created, everything from moth larvae cementing the feathers in formation to
crowns occurring in feathers that had not been scalded. Other suggestions
were that the feathers' barbs hooked onto one another in the direction of the
feathers' curved shapes, or that the shapes formed around loose threads or
other fabric from the pillow ticking.[16]

Most families preserved the crowns carefully and treated them with rev-
erence, in one instance even requesting to be buried with a loved one's feather
crown. Still, not everyone found these strange objects comforting. "I do think
people should know that these feathers are not works of art but of the evil
one, in plain English, just a way of escaping punishment for murder," a Missouri woman told one folklore collector. "If you'll take a fool's advice you'll get
rid of the specimens you have at once."[17]

Saving Other Mementoes

Death prompted families to save and treasure all sorts of objects. In addition
to the coins used to weight the eyes, some people saved swatches of fabric
from the burial garment and coffin liner. One mother (Hot Springs, Garland
County, 1915) even kept the linen fabric in which the navy had wrapped her
son's body, after he was killed while serving in the Philippines. Either despite

or because of the fact that David Birnbaum's name was stenciled in black ink on one side, Charity Birnbaum decorated the reverse side with hand-crocheted lace and used the fabric as a tablecloth.[18]

Though it was a common practice to save locks of hair cut from the deceased's head, having this hair made into jewelry does not seem to have been popular in the Ozarks, perhaps due to the expense. Though the 1897 Sears, Roebuck catalog offered mourning jewelry made from hair mailed to the company, to be woven into an intricate design inside a brooch, locket, ring, or watch fob, and books gave instructions for turning hair into flowers for memorial wreaths, collectors of such pieces say it is rare to find examples made in the Ozarks.

Of particular significance was the clothing worn by someone who died a violent death. There are accounts of bloody garments being rolled up and placed in the coffin beside the body, either to dispose of them or to hide evidence of murder. As a child, Charlene Cook Grigg saw bloody garments rolled up and placed in the coffin of a relative who was said to have committed suicide but whom her parents believed to have been murdered (Madison County, 1942), a practice also documented by archaeologists excavating a grave (Crawford County, death date unknown).[19] The coffin was also a place to dispose of other unwanted items, such as the gun with which someone committed suicide.

It was not unheard of for families to save the clothing in which a relative died a violent death. During the Civil War necessity dictated burying people in the clothing in which they were killed, but at other times families managed to preserve such garments. The military uniform Archibald Yell was wearing when killed at the Battle of Buena Vista (Mexico, 1847), "so badly cut in pieces that it barely hangs together, 14 holes and splits by the lances of the Mexicans," was displayed in the front hallway of his home (Washington County, 1847).[20] This was an especially gruesome keepsake because Yell's body had been buried in Mexico for five months before being exhumed and shipped back for reburial in Fayetteville.[21] Another such garment was the shirt worn by Nancy Rand Kerley's son, who was stabbed to death (Izard County, 1922). Kerley kept this shirt for over fifty years, and displayed the slashed, bloodstained garment to her granddaughter, asking, "Would you like to see the clothes your daddy got killed in?"[22]

One popular act of remembrance was taking a postmortem photograph of the body in its coffin, which in some instances was the only picture the family had of the deceased. These photos were an acceptable part of mourning and the practice of taking them has, in some communities, continued up to the present day.

Figure 4.2 A postmortem photo of Caldonia Bolinger (1876–1940), in her casket outside her home on Whorton Creek. *Courtesy of the Madison County Historical and Genealogical Society, Huntsville, and Phil Bolinger.*

Other customs included taking a photograph with all of the relatives grouped around a family member's coffin or taking a group shot in which someone held a portrait of the deceased. The Vaughn family even had what might be termed a "pre-mortem" taken on the day before Samuel Vaughn was to be hanged for murder (Washington County, 1894). Vaughn was permitted to leave jail with his wife, their grown children, and other assorted relatives in order to have a "group picture" taken at one of Fayetteville's photo studios.[23]

Memorial cards were another type of memento, these being printed by out-of-state companies with gilt lettering on heavy black cardstock. These cards included the deceased's name and dates, a memorial poem, and sometimes a photo. Though a few examples are found in Ozark museums, the practice does not seem to have been common in rural areas. H. F. Wendell & Co., of Leipsic, Ohio, was one such business that sold cards via mail order throughout the Midwest. This company, which offered to print a single memorial card or two hundred of them, issued a catalog that contained a large selection of verses from which to choose. Many of these verses have been used as epitaphs on tombstones across the Ozarks, indicating that such catalogs were widely circulated.[24] Among Catholics, prayer cards are handed out to mourners at the saying of the rosary before the funeral, and these are another type of memento saved by the family, as is the personalized cross placed on the coffin during the funeral.

Figure 4.3 Lafayette Gregg's memorial card, 1891, Fayetteville. These cards, printed on heavy cardstock and sometimes containing photos of the deceased, were given away as mementoes. *Courtesy Shiloh Museum of Ozark History/Martha Audrain Collection (S-98-17-5).*

Wearing Mourning Clothing

Though numerous accounts describe sewing new garments in which to clothe the dead, these never mention sewing mourning outfits for the living to wear. All the same, mourning garments were worn in some cities from a very early date. Hiram Abiff Whittington, writing from Little Rock (Pulaski County, 1831) to his brother in Massachusetts, mentioned that there had been over twenty deaths in the previous three months. "There is not a family in this

Figure 4.4 Mary Jane Johnson Chastain, likely in mourning for her second husband, Lewis L. Chastain, Bentonville (Benton County), 1910s. *Courtesy Shiloh Museum of Ozark History/Benton County History Book Collection (S-92-49-94).*

town but what are in weeds," he wrote, using an archaic term for black mourning garments.[25] This custom, less likely to take place in rural communities, appears to have ended completely by the Depression, a time when many other funeral customs were also on their way out.

Mourning clothing is not mentioned in connection with funerals because it took time to make these garments, and with burial proceeding so rapidly it would have been impossible to do this sewing in time. In England in the mid-1800s, prior to the establishment of warehouses that stocked ready-made mourning clothes, the bereaved were given an eight-day grace period before being expected to don black garments, a custom that did not end in that country until World War I.[26]

In the Ozarks there are a few early accounts of women wearing mourning. Archibald Yell's youngest daughter attended her father's funeral (Washington County, 1847) "dressed in deep mourning," while her schoolmates acknowledged the loss by wearing black sashes and hair bows.[27] (The five-month delay in returning Yell's body gave his family ample time to have mourning garments made.) Because Mrs. Gunter Berry's dying request was to be buried in a white shroud (Madison County, 1911), "in sympathy with this wish the choir and friends wore white, the pulpit was draped in white, the church in black."[28]

A treatise on Tennessee mourning customs states that widows were expected to wear black for two and a half years, less for other family deaths, rules set down in etiquette books of the day.[29] Arkansas widows may have followed similar guidelines, but the wearing of mourning is never mentioned in connection with men. Those who joined fraternal lodges and military organizations participated in the custom to the extent of draping their meeting rooms, and sometimes their flags, in black when one of their members died. The men then donned tokens of mourning, usually black armbands. Some fraternal societies issued each member with a special bar pin, from which hung a ribbon emblazoned with the name and logo of the organization. The reverse side of the ribbon was black and could be worn facing outward as a tribute following a death.

Food for the Watchers

Just as they had during the deceased's final illness, neighbors brought food to the family following the death, although in some communities women came to the home and did the cooking. Women prepared whatever was in season, but cooked cabbage was prohibited, presumably because its odor was too reminiscent of the smell of death and decomposition, and might be mistaken for such. The practice of taking food to a bereaved family continues to the present day, and is intended to feed the family and the visitors making condolence calls.

In the past, however, the food was intended primarily for those who sat up all night with the body and for feeding mourners who returned to the house following graveside services. Floyd Foster Copeland (Izard County, born 1933) recalled that his mother once took a jar of home-canned peaches to an impoverished family where someone was critically ill, only to learn that the person had died. "The family then asked mother if they could still keep the jar of peaches. That story just broke my heart."[30]

There are few accounts of exactly what was brought, but contributions depended on the time of year and each cook's specialties. In an era before refrigerators, spoilage probably wasn't even considered, but foods such as the sliced cucumbers and sweet onions marinated in vinegar, water, and sugar, which Rella Lee Cooper (Benton County, late 1800s) traditionally took to families, had the advantage of not needing to be kept cold.[31] Some accounts mention fried chicken, yeast-raised bread, pie, and other desserts—in other words, special foods normally reserved for company meals. Phillip W. Steele (Washington County, born 1934) remembered the fried chicken, vegetables, rolls, apple butter, and desserts that were served to those who came to one house to pay their respects. However, "As a child, I found it extremely difficult to sit in the same room with the open casket and enjoy such a meal," he wrote.[32]

Sitting up All Night

In the Ozarks, the dead were never left unattended. Whether the deceased was an infant or an octogenarian, African American or white, a beloved member of the community or an anonymous stranger, that body was never left alone for so much as a minute. "You didn't leave the family there with the dead by themselves" is how James C. Scott Jr. (Pope County, 1923) explained the custom. Others have stressed that sitting up is a way of showing respect. "This was the last thing that I could do for that person," Dale Haskins said (Sharp County, pre-1960).[33]

Many people were in the home during and immediately following a death, but once all preparations were complete there came an interval, usually overnight, before the coffin was delivered. Now members of the community were needed to sit up all night beside, or near, the body. Although occasionally a single person spent all night, this watching—again known as sitting or "setting" up—was usually done by groups of people, taken in shifts. The term *wake* is rarely found and was more likely to be used in Catholic communities or in accounts written in modern times. It was never a wake in the manner portrayed in fiction, with music, dancing, drinking, and rowdy behavior. Though alcohol might be consumed, and there are a few accounts of practical jokes played on watchers who fell asleep, sitting up was a solemn occasion.

It was also one in which watchers had various duties to perform throughout the night, ones requiring their wakefulness, and for this reason coffee was always provided for the gathering. "It was the custom for neighboring women or relatives to stay up until 10 or 11 o'clock, when two or three couples of the young people would wait out the remainder of the night," Herbert Jones said of his youth in Plumerville (just outside the Ozarks in Conway County, early 1900s). "We would make candy in the forepart of the night, and sandwiches and coffee toward morning."[34] In some Izard County communities "a singing" would be held that night in the family's home.[35]

If the deceased had joined a fraternal lodge, fellow lodge brothers would oversee the business of sitting up. When Daniel J. Chapman died (Independence County, 1857), Judge Beaufort Neely sent the following message to lodge member Col. Henry Neill, informing him of Chapman's death. "His corpse arrived at Batesville but a few minutes since. . . . Dr. Chapman's corpse is at my house and if it be in your power we would be glad to have your company tonight. We will certainly expect you."[36]

Though it was traditional for friends to sit up with the body, there was no taboo against family or relatives being present, as occasionally happened. During the transition period (between the world wars), as professional undertakers assumed more of the community's tasks, it was common for an undertaker to return the embalmed body to the home, where the sitting up would be done. In some places, such as Batesville (Independence County), only men sat up, according to James Rutherford, recalling Depression-era funerals. He said that the body, in a closed casket, would be in the parlor while the men sat in another room discussing farming and business. "It was not a novelty, it was the expected thing," he said. In some counties men sat up with male bodies, women sat with female ones, or with children, but in the majority of accounts there was no such segregation, and men and women watched together.

As a child, Kathryn Horton (Searcy County, born 1929) was taken with her parents when they went to sit up. "The deceased was laid out on his bed, the one he slept in during his life, and people would come and sit around the bed. They'd discuss the person, talk about his life, and they kept a lamp lit all night. Mostly it was sitting in quiet conversation of the deceased, or in celebration of his life," she said, noting that children slept when their parents sat up. One newspaper columnist recreated a conversation between three men as they sat up with a body. The men began by discussing the deceased's good qualities but as time passed their thoughts turned to topics that concerned the living. "Some of the shrewdest hoss trading I ever witnessed and some of the rankest off-color jokes I ever heard were part and [parcel] to sitting up with the dead—after the hour of Twelve."[37]

Where Sitting up Occurred

A family affluent enough to have a formal parlor would place the body in this room. In small, rural homes, however, families had to make do with any available space. When a family simply had no room, others volunteered their homes for the sitting up. Veda McElhaney Tassey (Madison County, born 1915) recalled how people often brought bodies to her family's home, to be both laid out and kept overnight. "We'd have one room and we had a cot, and we'd fix that cot and lay them out in the front room. People would come in and help us set up with them," she recalled. Tassey's father, the town of Witter's storekeeper, postmaster, and (unofficial) doctor, kept caskets on hand and often preached funerals over the bodies that had spent the night in his home. Though sitting up traditionally took place in the home, a church might be used during winter weather or when roads were bad.

Jessie Bryant, recalling the African American burial traditions of her youth in Fayetteville (Washington County, 1930s), said, "In the homes there was always this one room that was completely cleaned and that was where the body was laid, and there was always someone sitting with the body . . . day or night. . . . Up until the burial there was always people in and out, working in that house. . . . Everyone converged on that house."

One family reserved its finest possessions for funerals, in keeping with the southern tradition of giving the deceased the best that one has to offer. Mildred Smith, as a child, caught glimpses of this mysterious room in the home of Susie, Martha, and Charlie Bohannan, her unmarried aunts and uncle who lived near Hindsville (Madison County, late 1930s to early 1940s). Though the unpainted house was primitive in all other respects, "one room just off Uncle Charlie's room . . . was always kept shut and locked, but an aunt would sometimes unlock it and go in to retrieve photographs or other family keepsakes to show us. If I were in just the right spot at the time she opened the door, I could get a quick glimpse of a dim, amazingly pretty (to me) room," which had flowered wallpaper, lace curtains, a carpet, a large bed covered with a counterpane, and a gas light chandelier hanging from the ceiling. "I instinctively knew better than to ask too many questions about that strange place. All Aunt Susie would explain about the taboo subject was that the room was 'where the dead people go,'" which gave the impressionable child the notion that this room was somehow an anteroom of heaven.

Smith's mother later explained that because Hindsville had no funeral home, the Bohannans reserved this room for sitting up with family members after they died. "Proper respect for the deceased would be shown by using the best furnishing the house had to offer," which meant that the room was used solely on this occasion. Smith said the body would be laid out on the bed, and transferred to a casket prior to the funeral, and that only male relatives sat up.[38]

Keeping Animals at Bay

Those who sat up all night did not do so in the dark, as there are accounts of candles and, later, of other lights left burning through the night when there was a body in residence. After all, the watchers had to be able to see clearly in order to perform certain jobs.

Arkansans, when asked why people once sat up all night with the dead, usually answer, "Out of respect." Farther back the response would have been

"Cats." It was once believed that cats, attracted by the smell of death, were compelled to lick or chew on the corpse's cartilaginous ears and nose. Such disfiguration would have upset the mourners and rendered the remains unviewable. "The belief that cats will mutilate a dead body is widespread in the Ozarks and throughout the Southland, but this has never been substantiated," wrote Otto Rayburn. "Like most of cat lore, it is probably pure superstition."[39] Despite Rayburn's dismissive attitude, sources are adamant that cats were, indeed, a real threat to the corpse.

"There was quite a strange feeling in the South regarding cats—as they were said to haunt a dead person—and often strange cats would be found wandering through a house where a dead person lay," according to a folklore report on black superstitions delivered in Little Rock (Pulaski County, 1919). "Even the white people were imbued with a kind of superstition regarding cats at this time."[40] This prohibition against allowing cats near a corpse is a very old one, found in print in the 1700s in England and Scotland. There, both dogs and cats were killed if they jumped over a body, believed to be very bad luck, and cats were locked up in a house as soon as there was a local death, perhaps to prevent their loss. Charles Dickens mentioned this custom in *Bleak House* (published 1852), where a surgeon reminds his patient's family to get the cat out of the room following the death.[41] Randolph also recorded that "some unspeakable calamity" would occur if a cat so much as came near a body.[42]

University of Arkansas students amassed quite a collection of stories concerning cats mutilating corpses. "During the Civil War my roommate's grandfather went with eleven other fellows on a burial party," recounted Charles E. Brinkley of Marked Tree (Poinsett County, 1955), the location of the story unknown. "While ten of them dug graves for their fallen buddies, two of them had to stand over the bodies and fight off thousands of cats which were trying to carry off the bodies. His grandfather never did like cats after that."[43] Another student, Wesley M. Parker of Little Rock, described his mother's experience (Pulaski County, "many years ago") attending a closed-coffin funeral, necessitated by a cat who "was eating the man's face when it was discovered by watchers in the next room."[44] A more recent story belongs to Wayne Martin (Madison County, born 1935), who told how a relative wielded a broom to remove a cat from a wake. "The cat got up under the sheet with the corpse and the corpse got a worse beating than the cat did."[45]

"Cats were certainly an issue, prior to embalming," concurred Kevin Hatfield, quoting his mother's childhood experiences (Madison County, late 1930s). "The watchers tried to keep the room pretty well ventilated, and by the 1930s they had screens in the windows. My mother said the worst part

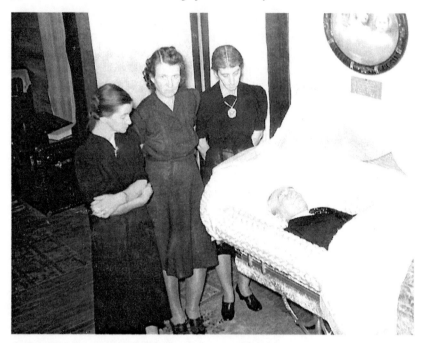

Figure 4.5 Jim Burk (1873–1941) laid out in his home. Daughters Mattie, Tilda, and Maudie (likely the same three girls in the portrait above the casket) view their father. Note the mesh veil draped over the upper lid of the casket, used to protect the body. *Courtesy of the Madison County Historical and Genealogical Society, Huntsville, and Phil Bolinger.*

was how the cats would howl, and make a horrible screeching noise and even be jumping at the screens [trying to get in], and how much it scared her." If cats were a threat, dogs near a death scene served a purpose, according to Rayburn, as "during a crisis in the home, the faithful dog is a barometer of conditions." Normal canine behavior was an indication that the patient would recover; cringing behavior and/or howling was a sign that "all that the doctor can do will be of little or no avail."[46]

Those sitting up in unscreened houses, where doors and windows stood open in warm weather, were mindful of other things that could harm the body, such as rats, mice, and flies. The idea of flies crawling on the deceased's face was so unsettling that undertakers began providing a drape to put over the open casket. This was a large piece of fine net, sometimes lace trimmed, that formed a protective screen but allowed a view of the body underneath. In cases where the body's appearance might upset viewers (such as after a drowning), a thicker net was used that was harder to see through. Families, however, would remove this veil when taking their final look at the deceased.

The Use of Wet Cloths

The watchers had another important task to perform, keeping wet cloths on the deceased's hands and face. This was intended to ensure that the skin looked natural, without darkening. No one substance was used, but reminiscences mention baking soda and water, vinegar, camphor, some type of alcohol, or a preservative (but not embalming) fluid, sold by funeral homes. Randolph recorded that an early preservative liquid was a weak tea made from the bark of the wahoo bush (*Euonymus*), also used to make a remedy for chills and fever.[47] One account (Pope County, about 1920) mentions using both "a sweet smelling stuff" and a cloth soaked in soda and water, interchangeably, but these were acknowledged to be of no real benefit if burial was delayed too long.[48] Even undertakers were advised to "use a bleacher frequently over the face and hands of the deceased" in cases where neither embalming nor ice were used.[49]

Such cloths had to be changed regularly to keep them moist. LaVera Beeby (Madison County, 1926) called this job "her first introduction to death." Beeby and her husband were living in a Huntsville hotel when the proprietor's mother-in-law died. "The dead woman's casket was placed in a room at the end of a long hallway . . . LaVera was asked to sit in the lobby with the Home Ec. teacher who was making a dress for the deceased. Every hour she [LaVera] was to go down the hall and change the cloth, soaked in a special solution, on the dead woman's face. Every hour she got up, walked down the hall, only to return with her task uncompleted. Much to her relief, she was saved by three students . . . who came by and offered to stay the rest of the night."[50]

Ice

The availability of ice was a big factor in prolonging preservation of a body during hot weather. Little Rock had a commercial ice company as early as 1897,[51] but elsewhere the only supply came from someone who had an ice-house in which to store blocks cut during the winter. The affluent Peel family had one (Benton County, 1875),[52] and there are accounts of others, such as Phillip W. Steele's description of the one his grandparents maintained (Washington County, date unknown). "Neighboring farmers all got together and sawed ice from the river with a horse and special plow with an ice cutting blade attached," he wrote. Blocks of this ice, packed in sawdust, would be stacked in the barn. "Apparently, the sawdust insulation provided protection from thawing, and the ice lasted even throughout those hot Ozark summers.

Grandad also recalled that it was not uncommon to find a fish, turtle, frog, or critter frozen in an ice block."[53]

Once towns established power plants, generally in the early 1900s, commercial ice production was possible. This was the era when housewives placed signs in their windows so the ice deliveryman knew how much to bring. Though this ice was primarily used to fill home iceboxes (the forerunner of the refrigerator), there are accounts of other uses. When sixteen-year-old W. O. Sears died during an especially hot July (Izard County, 1933), his family procured one-hundred-pound blocks of ice from the locker plant at Calico Rock. "The men got great big tubs, and put them in our living room," recalled Goldie Marie Sears Estes. "Then they packed the tubs with the huge blocks of ice . . . and put him in the casket, and put the casket on top of the tubs of ice."[54]

Sometimes glass canning jars were filled with ice and placed directly against and around the body. The use of ice, which rural families almost always had to travel some distance to obtain, seems to have been a feature of delayed funerals in hot weather, or as in the case of W. O. Sears, who died after a fall from a bluff, where the body was deteriorating. Even jars of well water might be tried, in an attempt to buy time.

Keeping the corpse cool would have been made easier with an ice casket, a device in which a body could be placed either above or below blocks of ice, then viewed through a window in the casket's lid. (The body would later be placed in a conventional casket for burial.) According to the U.S. Patent Office, between 1846 and 1884 twenty-three patents were issued for such devices, or improvements to them, including two applied for by the aptly named Mary Ann Frost (Barnesville, Ohio, 1879).[55] It's unknown whether this invention was used in Arkansas, but one enigmatic reference has been found, an entry in the Dunn Funeral Home's records (Benton County, 1896) for the August funeral of W. B. Crossman. Under a column headed "Coffin or Casket and Size" is the notation: "Ice box, $4.00."[56] If the Dunns were trying out an ice casket—or something similar—they used it only this once. Four years later, in 1900, they began embalming bodies.

Burying in Haste

With the rare exception of a dying person requesting that a coffin be procured in advance, every one of the many labor-intensive jobs needed for burial were begun after the death occurred. It's a wonder anyone was buried the same day he or she died, yet this happened surprisingly often.

Though same-day burials sound like a logical practice during extremely hot summers, when risks of decomposition, vermin, and contagion would be greatest, such was not the case. An examination of obituaries from Benton, Searcy, and Washington county newspapers, 1882 to 1920 (used because they have been collected and published in their entirety), and funeral notices from Van Buren (Crawford County, 1872–1914)[57] and Pocahontas (Randolph County, 1911–1920),[58] yields a total of 124 same-day deaths and burials. (Mentions of same-day burials have also been found in Ozark newspapers as early as 1860 and as recently as the 1930s.) Of these, 63 burials occurred during the cold months of October through April, while 61 burials took place from May through September, traditionally the warmest months.

Undertakers' records routinely show a delay between death and burial, which embalming made possible. Still, even these records show some burials on the same day as the death. Morton Mortuary, one of several funeral homes in business in Eureka Springs (Carroll County, 1924–1938), lists nine such burials between 1927 and 1934, six of them in the cold months and three of them in summer, out of a total of 129 bodies processed during those years.[59] Such burials made up as much as a quarter of the Dunn Funeral Home's business (Benton County, 1893–1942); the numbers compiled for both of these firms exclude bodies being shipped out of state. The Dunns did not offer embalming until 1900, and between 1894 and 1930 they handled sixty-seven same-day deaths and burials, evenly divided between cold and hot months of the year (thirty-three and thirty-four, respectively). Only one of these bodies was embalmed, a woman who died of consumption in 1909.[60]

To summarize, hot weather was not necessarily a factor when death and burial took place on the same day. And, it should be noted, the causes of death given in these obituaries range from sudden deaths to lingering ones, and include accidents, illnesses, and suicides, while the ages of the deceased range from stillborns through the elderly. Occasionally, it is possible to guess why the burial proceeded so quickly, such as deaths from violence or the deaths of indigents, where there was unlikely to be a funeral. Some are less obvious, as when two-year-old William Craig died at 8 A.M. in August (Washington County, 1906) and was buried that evening. Later that night, his mother gave birth, suggesting that her labor and delivery may have expedited William's burial.[61]

Only one obituary for a same-day death and burial was that of an African American—seventeen-year-old Esma Schrimsey (Benton County, 1895), who died of consumption. While blacks certainly had obituaries in even the earliest newspapers, as a demographic they were vastly underrepresented, which may explain why only one example has been found for this practice. Or perhaps Schrimsey's cause of death mandated a rapid burial, because when Hillory Finney, "one of Bentonville's native colored citizens," died of "quick consumption" on a Tuesday morning in October (Benton County, 1906), he was buried the next day,[62] even though it was standard practice among African Americans to delay burial for a week or more.

Another need for haste may have been due to the belief that a body stretched after death. "I have heard them say many times, let's hurry and get back and get the burial over tomorrow. He or she is stretching and if we wait longer we can't get the body in the coffin," according to "Old Timer," who claimed to have made many trips to town with a measuring stick to purchase a coffin in a hurry (unspecified location in the Ozarks, 1956).[63] Judging from obituaries, burials took place in rain, extreme cold, snow, after dark, and on major holidays, including Christmas Day. Same-day burial allowed members of the community—who had already devoted so much of their time and energy to the deceased—to get back to their own families and farms.

There is a different case to be made for burying quickly in winter. That there were so many same-day burials in cold weather is explained by the following story, told by Erma Rhea Williams Moore (Izard County, about 1937).

> When my Grandpa Guffey died there was the biggest snow on . . . it started snowing about dark and it snowed so hard all night long. And he died that night that it was snowing and the next day snow was just getting deeper and deeper. And John Gifford . . . told mom, "you'd better bury him this evening because there's no telling how many days it'll be before you can get him buried." And late in the evening they buried him.
>
> Mom said that during World War I this Warren [family] had a boy to be killed in the war. . . . They sent him back from wherever he was and the weather got so bad they could not bury him for one month. . . . They said they had him laying on a bed in the bedroom and people would just go every night and set up with them. And that's why mom buried my grandpa so early. Course it had been a lot of hours; he was definitely gone. But she wouldn't have buried him that quick if the weather hadn't been so bad.[64]

The Fear of Premature Burial

A scant amount of time elapsed between the death and burial, and most people went to their graves without a doctor or coroner having pronounced them dead. It's no wonder there was a fear of premature burial; that is, of being buried alive. Lacking visible and olfactory evidence that decomposition had begun, it was feared that certain medical conditions—what was once termed "cata-lepsy" but which today is called a coma or a persistent vegetative state—might mimic death. In this condition, when a patient's breathing and pulse could not be detected, there was no test to conclusively prove that death had occurred.

The fear of premature burial originated in the 1700s, when doctors debated but could not agree on infallible signs of death; well into the 1800s doctors still admitted they could not know for sure.[65] Arkansas doctors weren't sure, either. In 1908 the *Journal of the Arkansas Medical Association* reprinted an article from a Belgian journal that described how to hold a flame to a patient's arm to create a blister; if it filled with air, rather than fluid, this supposedly proved the patient had expired.[66]

Newspapers in the Ozarks fed readers a steady diet of stories, usually from out of state, about persons who were revived just in time to avoid being buried alive. The most sensational of these accounts came from a Kansas newspaper and was picked up and reprinted by others, including the *Springdale News* (Washington County, 1901). This supposedly true tale concerned the death of the five-year-old daughter of Mr. and Mrs. Samuel McPreas of Hanston, Kansas, whose body was placed in a metal casket and conveyed to the cemetery in an open wagon. The sky suddenly changed color and, despite the absence of any storm clouds, a bolt of lightning struck the metal casket, splitting it open. "Thereupon to the amazement and consternation of the funeral party, the child sat up and called for her mother," who went into hysterics and was reportedly in danger of losing her sanity over her child's close call.[67]

This account was horrifying, but nearly every community had a story of someone who was revived after having been declared dead or, worse, of someone buried despite a suspicion that they were alive. The *Arkansas Gazette* even ran a story about a black man, hanged for murder and pronounced dead by two doctors, who came back to life in his coffin and had to be executed a second time (Pulaski County, 1892).[68] Some thirty years later another condemned criminal—this one electrocuted—revived and had to be returned to the chair and dispatched a second time.[69]

Despite such tales, this worry was never given as the reason for sitting up all night with a body. Yet it is easy to find examples of near-premature burials throughout the Ozarks, such as Turnbo's casual mention of how a daughter of the Coker family (Marion County, early 1800s) after a long illness, "sank so low that the family supposed that life was extinct and they laid her out for dead but to their great joy she revived."[70] Or Robert Arnold's obituary (Randolph County, 1914), which remarked on "a peculiar incident" that happened to him during the Civil War when he was wounded in battle, pronounced dead, but was "roused just in time to escape burial."[71]

Sometimes these "dead" were aware of their state. Art Stepp grew up hearing stories of the death of his great-uncle, Oscar Acord (Johnson County, 1937), and how men came to sit with the body. "He could hear what they were saying, where to bury him, what clothes to put on him, but he couldn't move. There was a bottle of whiskey on a shelf and they noticed that his eyes were open, and that he was looking at the whiskey. They gave him some whiskey— that brought him to." According to Addie Adkisson (Izard County, born 1907) the standard diagnostic tool was a feather, held under the patient's nose. "If that feather moved they'd know they was getting a little air . . ." she said. "A feather will tell you."[72]

Those who have exhumed caskets during cemetery relocations believe they have seen proof of premature burial. They cite such evidence as the body within the coffin turned face down or sideways, or of finding the lid's lining in tatters, as though from being clawed at. Before funeral homes acquired mechanical devices to do the job, men used ropes to lower coffins into their graves, and the least bit of tilting would cause the body to roll onto its side. The most logical explanation for a contorted skeleton, however, is the fact that muscles contract as body tissues break down during decomposition.[73]

Nationally, there were patented "life detectors" on the market that could be buried in the casket, sending up a signal if the person revived. Some of these devices included an electrical alarm and air tube (1871), a mechanism that raised a flag and opened a vent (both 1882), or provided a combination of air-intake and alarm system.[74] The best known of these inventions was the Bateson Revival Device, known colloquially as "Bateson's Belfry." This was a bell that was mounted above ground, near the head of the casket. The bell was connected to a long cord whose end was attached to the corpse's hand or feet so that any movement within the coffin would cause the bell to ring. It is not known whether such devices were used in the Ozarks. In the late 1990s an elderly woman visiting Fayetteville's Evergreen Cemetery told the sexton that, as a child, she'd seen bells suspended over some of the graves. However, this would put their use no earlier than about 1920, long after the practice had been discontinued.[75]

Given such widespread accounts of premature burial, it's no wonder some people begged their relatives to take certain precautions when the time came. The simplest method, though a trial to the living, was to delay burial until decomposition was advanced. Turnbo records that Sam Magness's dying request was that his family wait four days before burying him (Marion County, 1859), although he gave no reason for this. His family complied, waiting from Sunday until Thursday, in February, before proceeding.[76] Ella Johnson, a former slave interviewed by the WPA (Little Rock, Pulaski County,

1930s), told the story of Reuban White, a Baptist pastor who was almost buried prematurely. Johnson was present as White's coffin was lowered into the grave, and heard him knocking from inside—the only thing that saved him. The next time he died his body was kept in the First Baptist Church for an entire week and, "Reuben White didn't come back when they buried him the second time," Johnson noted dryly.[77]

Annie Acord Eubanks revived without anyone's help after lapsing into a coma when she was twelve years old (Johnson County, 1860). All that had prevented her burial was the fact that she'd "died" on a Sunday, a day her family was unable to purchase coffin materials. For the rest of her long life she feared another such episode and had her husband construct a special coffin that could be opened from the inside. "When it was completed . . . she told her family that, if she died, she was to be placed in her special coffin, and that it was to be put high up in one of the magnolia trees in front of the house so that animals could not disturb it. Then, after a week, if she had not come out, they could bury her." Eubanks died in 1936, while living with an adult daughter, and there is no record that her last request was honored or whether the special coffin was used.[78] This is one of two stories found of dead bodies being placed in trees prior to burial. The other concerns an infant's death (Newton County, likely between 1910 and 1915), where the body was placed in a metal bucket and put high in a tree overnight, possibly to keep dogs from getting it. This story was told by a witness to the event, not because of he considered it unusual but because the family was so poor they had to use the same basin, in which they'd washed the baby's body, to prepare food to feed mourners after the funeral.[79]

Bodies, as they begin to deteriorate, sometimes do unexpected things. Watchers have been startled to see a corpse suddenly sit up or to hear one emit sounds, sometimes mistaken for signs of life. Lou Ann Clough Ott's mother-in-law both sewed for and laid out the dead (Marion County, 1930s), and once helped bath the body of a woman who had died in childbirth. "She said when they washed her, or bathed her, they turned her over and she groaned. She often wondered, now, if they might have buried her alive. She [the deceased] never got cold. I bet she went into a coma. Back then, you had no way of knowing."

Such stories belong to the era when people just didn't know for sure—and they wondered. One of the oddest of these events was witnessed by John Quincy Wolf (then Izard County, 1876) after his mother died when he was twelve years old. "When the lid of the coffin was moved, I saw drops of perspiration all over Mother's forehead, and I heard people at the graveside question whether she was really dead or in a state of suspended animation. The burial proceeded, however, and she was duly interred."[80]

Coffins and Caskets

Shed not for her the bitter tear,
Nor give the heart to vain regret
'Tis but the casket that lies here
The gem that fills it sparkles yet.

—**Philadelphia Tunstill**, 1842–1907
Evergreen Cemetery (Washington County)

Deep in a remote hollow in the mountains, far from the nearest dwelling, young Columbus Vaughn sat alone, his back to a big, empty wooden coffin (Newton County, 1930s). The light was fading, owls and animals had begun to stir, but what terrified the boy was his memory of the relative for whom the coffin was intended, "gasping for her last breath." Vaughn and his uncle had walked a long way into the woods to where a stack of rough-sawn sweet gum lumber was stored. Using rudimentary tools, they constructed the big, hexagonal box and solid lid, then discovered that it was too heavy for them to carry. Vaughn's uncle went to get help and the boy was left to wait, his imagination conjuring up, in equal measure, visions of wild animals and "haunts."

"A coffin, the sounds, the isolation, the loneliness along with the revisualizing of those last gasping moments of one struggling to ward away the grim reaper and losing the battle wrought in us fears almost too esoteric to be endured by mortals," Vaughn later wrote of his experience. He acknowledged that he would have been quite safe inside the coffin, but at the time was too frightened even to look at it. Finally, long after dark, the boy heard men returning to retrieve the box.[1]

Such a container was a true coffin, though "coffin" and "casket" are often used interchangeably. There are distinct differences, however. The coffin, which is the older of the two styles, is six-sided, widest where it accommodates the

Figure 5.1 Graves of David Tucker "Tuck" Smith, wife, Elizabeth Trollinger Smith, and two of their daughters, death dates spanning 1859–1909, Tuck Smith Cemetery (Washington County). These graves have coffin-shaped false crypt coverings and necked discoid headstones. Both of these styles, used singly and in combination, were brought to Arkansas by settlers from the Carolinas, Kentucky, and Tennessee. *Photo by Abby Burnett.*

body's shoulders, and tapers toward the feet. Sometimes irreverently called a "toe pincher," the coffin has a separate, one-piece lid, which must be lifted off when mourners view the body. This style, with variations, is seen above ground in the Ozarks' oldest graveyards. Known as false crypts, these stone "coffins," though made to the same scale as the one below ground, do not contain a body; instead, they serve as a *memento mori*, reminding viewers of their own mortality.

The word *casket* originally meant a jewel box or a container for something precious, and is the more recent of the two container styles, still in use today. These are rectangular boxes, or rectangles with beveled corners, whose lids are attached with a hinge along the box's longest side. Casket lids are usually divided slightly below the midsection, allowing the body to be viewed from the waist up when the upper half of the lid is raised. Caskets usually had handles and other decorative hardware and cost more than coffins. For example, between 1893 and 1900, Benton County undertakers W. W. Dunn and Son charged $8 to $25 for an adult's coffin and $40 to $80 for an adult's casket.[2]

American colonists did not bury their dead in containers, and it wasn't until the 1700s that coffins came into use. Caskets didn't make an appearance

until at least 1849, the term found for the first time in a Boston, Massachusetts, undertaker's ad, but was likely being made by more than one person.[3]
By the end of World War I caskets had replaced coffins in cities,[4] but rural
residents went on using both. For that reason the Arkansas Coffin Company
in Fort Smith produced the two styles well into the 1930s,[5] with carpenters
in small communities continuing to build the traditional coffin shape for at
least a decade after that.[6] Bud Phillips, attending Ewing Baughman's funeral
(Newton County, 1948), commented, "His was the last home made, black cloth
covered coffin that I have seen."[7]

The Men Who Made Them

Though most men living in rural areas stated their profession as "farmer" on
the various censuses, many worked at a variety of jobs. This makes it difficult to document such part-time occupations as preaching funerals, carving tombstones, or making coffins. One man, James Willis Phillips (Searcy
County, 1868–1934), listed as a farmer on four censuses, is credited with having made 135 caskets for neighbors in his Pleasant Grove community, work he
did not charge for.[8] The practice of working at multiple trades also took place
in cities, where furniture dealers and cabinetmakers made coffins and caskets
and sold burial goods. There was, after all, little difference between constructing a coffin and a bureau, bedstead, table, wardrobe, or washstand—all objects
the Fayetteville Cabinet Shop listed in its advertising (Washington County,
1854).[9]

In rural communities blacksmiths were the ones who most often built
coffins and wooden vaults, boxes that protected the coffin in the grave. After
all, in addition to working with metal, blacksmiths also made and repaired
farming implements and wagons, which had wooden components, so they
had to be good carpenters. (Occasionally one also dabbled in dentistry, as the
pinchers and pliers used in blacksmithing could also be used to pull teeth.)[10]
Blacksmith James Oates (Washington County, 1900) "branched into" running
a wagon yard, manufacturing wagons, buggies, farm tools, and caskets,[11] while
Weyman and Reeves (Independence County, 1903), besides having "one of
the largest and best equipped blacksmith shops in the county," had a sideline
business in undertaking and the sale of coffins, caskets, shrouds, and undertaking supplies.[12]

One blacksmith, Jesse Elmer Moody (Madison County, 1893–1974), was
the coffin builder, undertaker, and keeper of birth and death records for the
town of St. Paul. Moody opened his blacksmith shop around 1920 and kept

Figure 5.2 Blacksmith Jesse Moody with a coffin he built, St. Paul (Madison County), prior to 1965. Moody built coffins, laid out the dead, arranged for graves to be dug, and kept the birth and death records for his community. *Courtesy Shiloh Museum of Ozark History/Wayne Martin Collection (S-96-2-248), and Dan Martin.*

the town's birth and death records from 1930 to 1954,[13] during which time he reportedly also made over two hundred coffins.[14] "I've worked up enough lumber for coffins and coffin boxes during my life to build a building no telling how long and wide," he told an interviewer in 1968.[15] When the occasion demanded, Moody also laid out bodies and arranged to have graves dug. Coffin sales declined through the years and ended in 1942; he made just one coffin after that, in 1965. The boxes he built were plain and utilitarian, lined inside with white fabric and covered on the exterior with either black or white fabric depending on whether the deceased was male or female.[16]

Moody sometimes had help from his brother Al, who had a penchant for taking naps inside the padded, satin-lined caskets. This practice ended after Jesse announced his intention of nailing the lid down on his brother because, he joked, "It will save us a lot of trouble later on."[17] It is surprising that no taboo forbade the living from lying in a coffin. Van Buren County coffin builder Coy Roten asked his brother Roby to do this to "see if it fit"; the next coffin he built was Roby's.[18]

By the 1970s life had changed so radically that blacksmiths and their myriad skills were no longer needed. Wayne Martin (Madison County, born 1935) credits the time he spent hanging out in Moody's shop, as a boy, with teaching him "much of what I really needed to survive in life." He recalled a secret the blacksmith once shared. "He told me that if he could come back and do life over, that he would be an undertaker," Martin said. That way, "he would never be able to work himself out of a job."[19]

Moody's sturdy workmanship was valued by the living, and at least one person ordered a casket "pre-need," but caskets purchased in advance had a way of not getting used. Some were inadvertently destroyed; other times descendants opted to buy something fancier. Men stood a better chance of being buried in a particular coffin if they or a relative made it themselves. Such was the case with Craven Wilson, a farmer, minister, and Civil War veteran (Randolph County, born 1846). A year before his death, Wilson bought walnut planks and hired a carpenter to build his coffin, but the job was never completed. This unfinished box was left behind when Wilson, severely disabled, moved into his son's home in Texarkana (Miller County, 1930). There the son and another man built a coffin to Wilson's specifications out of white pine, which pleased the old man so much he wanted to keep it in his bedroom. "When a fellow buys an overcoat, he wants to see it doesn't he?" a local newspaper quoted him as saying. "It's mine and I want to see it. And see it I did." An undertaker argued long and hard before persuading Wilson to let him store the coffin at his place of business until needed,[20] but just a few months later Wilson was, indeed, buried in this box.

Construction Techniques

When circumstances demanded greater haste than usual, neighbors would head to the nearest large town to purchase a ready-made coffin. Otherwise, it was customary for coffin construction to begin immediately after the death occurred. There were practical reasons for not stockpiling such things: they took up a lot of space, tied up planed lumber that might be needed for other projects, and were usually decorated with fabric colors specific to the age and sex of the deceased.

Folklorists have collected tales of the coffin stick, a hickory or hazel "measuring pole" as long as the body, plus an extra six inches to accommodate postmortem stretching. This stick would be brought to the coffin builder to determine the correct length to build, then taken to the cemetery to give grave diggers an idea what size hole to dig. This folklore was collected throughout the Missouri Ozarks, but Arkansas death stories do not mention it except in fiction. Benson Fox (Searcy County, 1914–2008) wrote a fictionalized account of a coffin stick being taken to the cemetery but, contradictorily, Fox also insisted, "the story is a fact, I saw it with my own eyes," so perhaps such sticks *were* used on occasion.[21]

Coffin builders needed very little help with measurements and rarely used patterns. Most had known the deceased, and according to blacksmith Rex Harral, who assisted with building half a dozen coffins (Cleburne County, mid-1930s), the builders made adjustments based on the deceased's size. Ulis Morrison recalled that while "a lot of guesswork" went into making one, "I never made one too small." One builder nearly did, however. A carpenter constructed a newborn's coffin without seeing the child, and as a result, "they just had to stuff her down in that" (Izard County, 1945). This was unfortunate but understandable, as the baby weighed fourteen pounds at birth.[22]

Almost any type of wood might be used, though pine was preferred because it was cheap, readily available, easy to work with, and lightweight—of importance to the pallbearers. Despite the custom of giving the dead the best materials one had, people made their living cutting timber in the Ozarks, where hardwoods were a cash crop. Black gum wood, which had little market value, was sometimes used in coffin construction. The chinquapin, once common across the Ozarks, began dying out from chestnut blight in the 1940s and was not used because it made noise when burned. "I've heard guys joking they wanted their coffins made out of chinquapin so they could go through hell a poppin'," said Wayne Martin, but folklore collected outside the Ozarks claims that it was unlucky to use *any* wood that popped and cracked when burned as a heat source.

Quick access to lumber, either rough boards or smoothly planed ones, was crucial. As one writer summed it up, "In the old days everything was not so easily obtained as it is today. The old pioneer was aware of that fact, and most of them kept a sufficient supply of good workable lumber on hand at all times to make a coffin or two, in case they were needed. . . . In the early days lumber was one of the scarcest articles of any."[23] Some sawmills kept a pile of planks reserved solely for this use, for builders to help themselves to when the need arose. According to Gladys Counts (Madison County, born 1910), whose father built coffins, "They would hold a pie supper to buy coffin timber and they stacked it in back of the school house. All of us kids would really shy away from that lumber. . . . I guess we were superstitious of it some way."[24] Not all children were so reserved. According to Art Stepp (Madison County, born 1927), "Old timers would have lumber sawed, special wood, and put it upstairs in the attic. One grandson, mean as could be, he'd go up and dance a jig on that lumber."

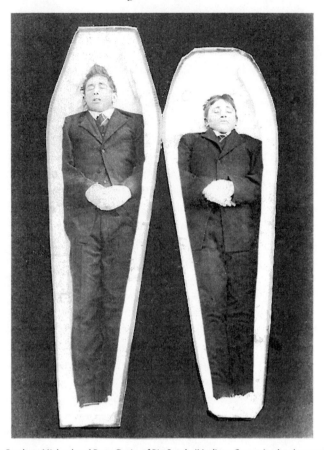

Figure 5.3 Brothers Michael and Peter Derie, of Big Sandy (Madison County), who drowned in January 1901 in the White River. The boys' coffins, while not identical, both have rounded edges made by bending, not mitering, the wood. *Courtesy Madison County Historical and Genealogical Society, Huntsville.*

When lumber was not available, or there was no money with which to buy any, builders turned creative—and generous. Erma Rhea Williams Moore remembered her father tearing broad ceiling planks out of a rental house he owned to get coffin material during a severe winter (Izard County, 1937),[25] and Morrison also tore lumber out of an old house for this purpose and once ripped out baseboards to make a child's casket. Accounts tell of people tearing out house and barn floors, pulling off siding and, when nothing else was available, using oak and pine lumber that was still green.

Builders wanted to work with the widest boards they could get. After a 1926 tornado uprooted several virgin pine trees at the Harral home, Rex

Figure 5.4 Interior view of a hand-made coffin used for initiation rituals by the Odd Fellows, Kingston lodge, in the 1920s. Closely spaced rough cuts, known as kerfing, allowed wood to be bent at the corners. *Coffin courtesy Grandpa's Flea Market, Kingston; photo by Abby Burnett.*

Harral's father had the trees planed into boards one inch thick and fourteen inches wide, solely for use in casket building. Two years later some of those boards were fashioned into his wife's casket, and four months after that, his own.[26] Wider planks meant less work joining them together for the lids, and yielded a stronger product.

Two methods were used to create the angles at the wide "shoulders" of a coffin. One was cutting boards at the correct angles and mitering them. The other method, known as kerfing, involved making a series of closely spaced cuts along—but not through—the inside of the boards where they were to form the angle. Next the boards were steamed, boiled, or soaked in water to make them pliable, then bent and nailed into position.[27] This gave the outermost corners of a hexagonal coffin a slightly rounded appearance, enhancing the box's human silhouette.

Coffin Padding, Lining, and Colors

It was customary to use fabric to line and cover the boxes and their lids. In communities where cotton was grown, people used carded cotton to pad the inside of the box and even the interior of the lid; elsewhere, quilt batting or even a finished bed quilt might be used for this purpose. Infants' coffins were sometimes padded with feather pillows, while a regular pillow would be made and placed under an adult's head in the coffin. In the 1930s, when flour and animal feed were sold in colorful cloth bags, this fabric would be used for clothing and bedding—and coffin pillows.

Covering and lining the coffin took a lot of fabric, as shown in the letter James Logan sent to a store at Ozark (Franklin County, 1841). Logan ordered "eight yards of fine cambrick, eight yards of bleached domestic and a sufficient quantity of suitable stuff to line the outside, and a pair of white gloves. Also, a paper of Sadlers tacks and one pound of eight penny nails."[28]

Because the body was waiting to be buried, a coffin was used as soon as it was finished, which meant there was no time for paint or varnish to dry. Instead, the coffin's exterior would be covered with fabric, held in place with tacks or decorative brads. (Such coverings also hid rough or inferior wood.) Owners of general stores who sold ready-made coffins usually lined the interiors, but no matter who built the box, women usually did the fabric work. There was a technique to fitting the lining. The ends of the interior fabric liner were tacked to the box's upper edge, the tacks then covered with a strip of lace or other trim. Upholstering the casket lid appears to have been a fad in some communities, as the Putnam Funeral Home (Fort Smith, Sebastian County, early 1900s) added a $3.50 fee for this service.[29]

Generally, adult coffins were covered in black and infants' and children's coffins in white, with white linings. As one obituary (Benton County, 1906) reminded readers, "death . . . comes for the little white casket or the sable six foot coffin."[30] However, the choice of color and type of fabric varied according to local traditions and available materials. One account (Carroll County, approximately 1900) states that "the covering was usually of velvet and [the] lining over cotton padding was off-white silk or satin," with a "frill" of lace or fringe around the top edge of the box.[31] Other accounts mention velvet and velour, black linings and pillows, and children being buried in black coffins. Young women—especially young mothers who died in childbirth—were usually buried in white coffins and caskets.[32] Other colors were used on occasion. Eul Dean Clark recalled that, in Boxley Valley (Newton County, mid-1930s), children's caskets were either pink or blue, inside and out, though in this community homemade adult coffins were not covered in fabric.

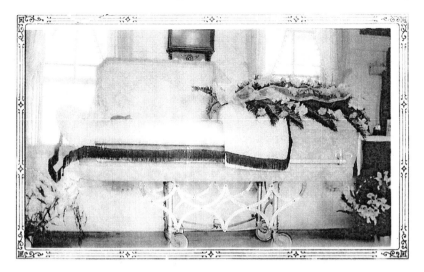

Figure 5.5 Caldonia Bolinger's casket, showing patterned or embossed fabric on the exterior, photographed at her home on Whorton Creek, 1940. *Courtesy of the Madison County Historical and Genealogical Society, Huntsville, and Phil Bolinger.*

While somber hues were the norm, occasionally brighter colors were used. Addie Adkisson (Izard County, born 1907) said of locally made coffins, "Most of 'em was lined with white lace. And on the outside of it you'd put green cloth . . . or gray cloth. We finally got to where we got this embossed gray cloth."[33] Though gray was popular by the 1920s, in some communities it was considered very unlucky. "My Gawd . . . they used grey agin . . . they'll be another death in this family afore the year is out," says a father upon seeing his infant's coffin, in an undated account of an Ozarks "backwoods buryin."[34]

Jessie Bryant (Washington County, 1930s) recalled that Fayetteville's African American community always purchased gray caskets, but this wasn't true everywhere. P. O. Wren (Izard County, born 1920) said, "When I was a kid, they'd always be a bunch go to the Colored Church. I've gone to their funerals. I went to Rudolph's [Allison] funeral. They buried him in a bright, red casket."[35] Funeral director Rev. A. J. Parish, owner of the Rowell-Parish Mortuary in Fort Smith (Sebastian County, established 1966, purchased by Parish in 1985), said caskets chosen by the African American community during his early years in business were predominantly white, pink, or blue. However, "I was at a casket company in Guthrie, Oklahoma, and saw this red one. The manager said, 'We're going to send it to you, and if it doesn't sell we'll pick it up.' The very next week it sold. So we had them send another one, same thing, it didn't sit there a week. Then we got cold feet, and didn't order any more [red ones]." Parish took a chance on a green casket, but it didn't sell and had to be returned.

Proceeding with Speed

Due to the labor involved, builders and their helpers often had to work through the night to finish the job. "I can hear my father, building caskets right now, way into the night, all night long that old hammer would go, building a coffin. Maybe some of the neighbors would come and help but it was always done at Rufe's barn," recalled Nina Zoe Davis Blair (Izard County, probably 1920s) of her father, Rufus Davis.[36] The women who made the lining for the coffin were also prepared to work through the night and, as noted earlier, they usually had the added job of sewing a new outfit for the deceased. Such work went on nonstop at times, such as during the influenza pandemic; Rob Simpson (Randolph County, 1918) "made coffins for six others, and at last needed one for himself."[37]

Even when there was lumber at hand, other supplies had to be purchased from the nearest store. A neighbor would make this trip, chosen either for his skill in selecting the best materials or merely because he had the fastest horse. Ted Larimer, a teenager when he lived with his grandmother, was once pressed into service for this job (Carroll County, 1936). "Aunt Rosie Bunch died. She lived a mile from us. Someone came from her house in the wee hours to get me out of bed. I rode this old bony horse—it was pouring rain—holding a note in my hand, trying to keep it dry, all the way to town, six miles. Masey Sites had Sites Mercantile. I got Masey up—it was nearly four in the morning."

Sites got dressed, unlocked his store, climbed a tall, rolling ladder to reach the stock on the highest shelves, and awaited instructions. Larimer, however, could barely make out his grandmother's list. "I'm having a heck of a time reading the printing anyhow, and it had got wet despite my efforts. I told him how much cotton I wanted, and how much damask. I can still see him, looking down at me from that ladder. He said, 'Boy, put that in your pocket. I 'spect I've outfitted more coffins than you've ever seen.'"

Some storekeepers gave builders carte blanche to help themselves to materials at any hour of the day or night, giving them keys to the store and trusting them to write down, and later pay for, the needed items. This practice had one drawback. When the Stewarts' general store at Cave Springs was robbed one night (Benton County, between 1910 and 1920), those who saw lights on inside the building didn't sound an alarm because they assumed there had been a death and someone was inside getting items required for the burial.[38]

The need for speed explains another custom, though one that does not appear to have been widespread: covering the coffin's exterior with crepe paper. There are two accounts of dampened black crepe paper applied to coffins or caskets, that of Jackson Abraham Creek (Madison County, 1932)[39] and Isaac Newton Keeling (Searcy County, 1933), both occurring at a time when this paper was cheap, readily available, and popular for making Decoration Day flowers.

Casket Sets and Coffin Hardware

While not all general stores sold caskets, most stocked the special hardware used to decorate a finished one. These pieces were known collectively as a "casket set" and were made up of six handles and the decorative screws that attached the lid to the box; sometimes a plaque or coffin plate was included. The screws, called thumbscrews, were topped with decorative finials, usually in a stylized design. (Intricate three-dimensional urns, lambs, or doves sitting on nests are found in catalogs of mortuary hardware.)

The plaque, which was attached to the coffin's lid, was often sold separately. Though in other states silver-plated plaques were engraved with the name and dates of the deceased and then removed and kept by the family,[40] Ozark burials proceeded too quickly for such a refinement except in cities, where undertakers charged for engraving. Most plates were purchased already inscribed "At Rest," "Rest in Peace," or "Beloved Mother" and were buried with the coffin. This hardware usually had a dull pewter or silver-colored finish, though one Madison County grave digger told of uncovering a golden coffin handle when digging too close to an earlier burial.

During the Depression funeral homes also sold this hardware. The pieces, organized into paper bags inside a cardboard box, included everything needed to trim a casket at home: hinges, decorative coffin screws with escutcheon plates, interior corner braces, handles, screws, and perhaps a bag of tacks for attaching the lining. It is important to note that the exterior items were merely decorative, not functional. None of the handles was strong enough to support the weight of a loaded coffin, which pallbearers carried by its bottom edge. The thumbscrews, while pretty, were useful only during the drive to the cemetery. Once there, the lid of the box was removed for a final viewing, after which these screws would be replaced, supplemented with long nails driven into the lid.

These are the basic components of the casket set, but other pieces of metal were also available for purchase. Coffin screws could be set into small

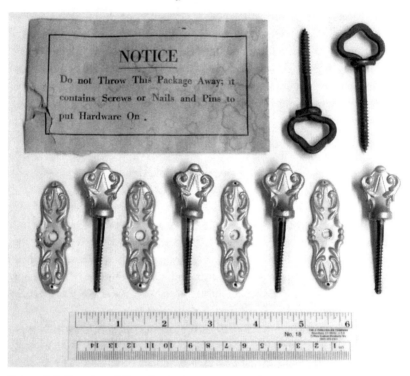

Figure 5.6 Coffin screws sold by Nelson Funeral Home, Berryville. General stores and funeral homes sold "coffin sets" containing all hardware needed to trim a homemade coffin. *In the collection of the Heritage Center Museum, Berryville, Carroll County Historical Society; photo by Abby Burnett.*

escutcheons or screw plates, decorative pieces of metal resting flush with the coffin lid, into which the screw was inserted. There were also small metal brads that decorated the lid or delineated the edges of the box, as well as metal pieces that protected the corners of the box and helped anchor the fabric covering. Individual pieces of coffin hardware often show up in the billing records kept by general stores. Edmiston's store, which did not sell coffins (Washington County, 1882), lists coffin handles at $3.75 to $4.50 for three pair, or $2.00 for just two sets, likely for a child; coffin screws were twenty cents per dozen. Customers also charged coffin tacks, "cut tacks," wood screws, and nails.

When it came to fabric, these records contain charges for yards of cotton cloth ("domestic"), fabric specifically called coffin lining, fringe (five yards was the standard amount), ribbon, and lace. Sixteen such entries were made in 1882, half of which were made by one person charging hardware to another's account, evidence of a neighbor getting the supplies needed by the deceased's family.[41] Though labor was almost always free, one early account (Marion

County, pre–Civil War) states that families usually paid for the shroud and coffin trimmings and occasionally for the lumber used to build the coffin.[42]

Long after city dwellers had begun purchasing factory-made caskets from undertakers, merchants in the larger towns were still catering to the needs of a rural clientele. An ad in the *Winslow American* (Washington County, 1937) offered "hardware trimmings for handmade coffins" but by the 1940s such hardware was becoming scarce. Nellie Terherst recalled her grandfather's dying wish to be buried in a handmade casket (Carroll County/Stone County, Missouri line, 1943). "They had such a hard time ever finding the hardware, the handles and things, for him," she said, "but they hunted until they finally found them, and his casket was made." Four years later her grandmother, nearing death, wanted a casket similar to her husband's, but told her family to buy a ready-made one to spare them another difficult search.

The most elaborate piece of hardware was the window or viewing pane embedded in the coffin's lid, directly above the deceased's face. Special hardware that attached and protected this glass was in use starting around 1860,[43] generally a feature of mass-produced coffins and caskets. Two Crawford County cemeteries excavated by the Arkansas Archeological Survey held five burials with windows,[44] but except for ones used in metal burial cases (discussed below) this feature is rarely mentioned in written accounts.

Vaults and Outer Boxes

Some builders had the added task of making a wooden box vault and lid to protect the coffin in the grave. (The older practice of digging a vault in the grave's floor is discussed in chapter 7.) Factory-made coffins and caskets were shipped in wooden boxes, and storekeepers and undertakers sometimes gave these to families to use as vaults, though graves fell in despite their use. The cast concrete vault came later, but during the Depression most people declined this added expense, while metal vaults were unavailable during World War II when metal was needed for the war effort.

Commercially made metal vaults could be purchased from early funeral homes. Prices, culled from itemized funeral bills, show charges for steel vaults ranging from a low of $59 (Izard County, 1927)[45] to a high of $150 (Crawford County, 1938).[46] One advertisement, for the Baker Vault (Washington County, 1905) ominously suggested that its vault protected burials from burglars, burrowing animals, air, water, and vermin. Capitalizing on the public's fear of grave robbing, this ad guaranteed that the vault "furnishes absolute protection against the ravages of the human ghoul" (Washington County, 1905), adding the unverifiable claim: "60,000 bodies mutilated annually on dissecting tables."[47]

Residents of the Ozarks were far removed, geographically, from Little Rock and its medical school where student doctors were in constant need of cadavers to dissect. One of the few people to worry about grave robbers was Owen Standridge (Pope County, date unknown), who believed he had swallowed a small snake while drinking out of a creek, which had grown inside his body. After refusing his doctors permission to operate, Standridge became convinced they planned to solve the mystery by digging him up and cutting him open after he died. At his request his family buried him under several loads of creek gravel to protect the grave.[48] (The delusion of a "stomach snake" or other reptile or amphibian living inside the body was once remarkably common and enduring, having been documented in ancient Egypt up through the present.)[49]

The only people who had to worry about ending up on a dissecting table were convicted criminals. In 1873, six years before the state established a medical school, doctors got the legislature to pass an act making dissection legal. This legislation allowed for bodies, which would have been buried at public expense, to be given to "regular" physicians or medical students working under the supervision of one. Such corpses were "to be used . . . for the advancement of anatomical science." Exceptions were made for any person who had requested burial, or if the person's friends or family made the same request within twenty-four hours of the death. Nor would someone be dissected who died "before making himself known."[50] (Two condemned men in Fort Smith, in 1886 and 1887, made last requests that doctors refrain from cutting up their bodies.)[51]

Prisoners had reason to worry. When the state penitentiary's cemetery was relocated (Little Rock, Pulaski County, 1894), one coffin was found to be empty. This was the grave of Jim Burrows, a train robber who had died in prison of natural causes six years earlier. An investigation concluded, "the only plausible theory is that Burrows' body was stolen by medical students for dissection purposes."[52] Nor was the prohibition against dissecting strangers ever honored, as the cadavers used by the medical school were "almost entirely those unknown transients whose passages through town by river or land were interrupted by a timely demise from age, or an untimely demise by some of the violent crowd found in most river towns."[53]

Medical students were expected to pay the school "a mere nominal cost" for their legally obtained cadavers, but those who were not financially well off almost certainly resorted to grave robbing.[54] Little Rock's African American population suspected the worst, since the state's first official dissection "and most thereafter" used black cadavers (Little Rock, 1874).[55] Within a few years a rumor circulated that whites used various ruses to trap blacks in order to kill and dissect them, and a newspaper's response to this urban legend could hardly have reassured them. "The colored should have sense enough to know that such suspicion is groundless," the writer chided. "Medical colleges, rather than drawing subjects from the streets, chosen from the living, snatch them from the graveyards."[56]

Unconventional Coffins

Even a child's small coffin was time-consuming to make. Flossie Cook Smith's husband, Orden, a skilled woodworker, labored through the night to build his first coffin and wooden vault for nephew Dwain Smith (Madison County, 1934). Smith put two large handles on each side, and postmortem photos of other children show adult-sized hardware on their coffins.[57] Some stores did sell hardware for children's coffins,[58] but John Bowen, another woodworker living near Kingston at about the same time (Madison County, after 1920), made his own. For a baby girl's coffin, Bowen made "handles" of pink ribbon decorated with ribbon rosettes and tacked them on the sides. "'Course, they couldn't carry it that way," recalled his daughter, Gladys Bowen Bradshaw. "They picked it up in their arms and carried it." Infants, being so small, were sometimes buried in any handy container. When a traveler suffered a miscarriage (Van Buren County, 1889), local women "prepared a wooden soda box as a casket."[59] Coy Ford's premature brother was buried in a shoebox (Newton County, late 1940s) with a specially made miniature pillow and covered in a white handkerchief; a small wooden box was used as a vault.

Adult bodies were occasionally buried in unconventional containers, or coffins modified to fit a need. Addie Adkisson told how her father's crippled knee made it impossible for him to fully straighten his leg. He died at midnight on a Saturday from an accidental gunshot (Izard County, 1913), and because he had once expressed a desire to be buried on Sunday, the family hurried to make arrangements. They purchased a varnished oak casket, but the man's bent leg kept the lid from closing. "They had to put a strip around it just like the casket, then they put the lid on it," his daughter recalled.[60] The parents of "Hutch" Duggins faced a similar problem after their son's rheumatism caused him to die in a contorted position (Marion County, date unknown). The disease "contracted his body and limbs in such form that the family were compelled to bury him in a square box."[61]

Figure 5.7 Sog and Easter Eubanks sharing one coffin, October 14, 1937 (Madison County). Easter died of malaria in the morning and her husband, after praying to follow her, died later the same day. *Courtesy of the Madison County Historical and Genealogical Society, Huntsville.*

An oversized corpse presented a different problem, as happened when 350-pound T. D. Cain died on a visit to Pocahontas (Randolph County, 1916). The town's undertaker had to have a casket made to order by a St. Louis firm so Cain's body could be shipped home to Missouri.[62] The Arkansas Coffin Company in Fort Smith (Sebastian County, early 1900s to 1989) occasionally made oversized caskets, reinforcing them with metal straps and bolts. The largest one they ever made (date unknown), for a man so heavy a backhoe, not pallbearers, conveyed him to the grave, easily accommodated three employees who were photographed standing in it.[63]

Oversized containers were occasionally built to accommodate multiple family members killed in a tornado, or a mother and child burial. Though extremely rare, a double casket could be made to hold two adult bodies. The best documented of these double burials was that of Easter Eubanks, who died at nine in the morning, probably from malaria (Madison County, 1937).

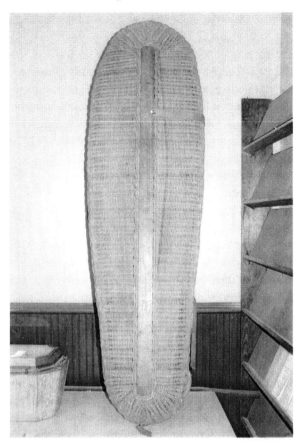

Figure 5.8 Wicker ambulance basket used by undertakers to transport bodies, often mistaken for a burial container. *In the collection of the Heritage Center Museum, Berryville, Carroll County Historical Society; photo by Vineta Wingate.*

Easter's eighty-two-year-old husband, Sog, then lay down on his bed and began praying to die. "I'm going now, daughter," he announced, and died soon after of a heart attack. Local blacksmith George Harriman, assisted by three other men, made the couple's immense double coffin—a first for him.

One style of "coffin" whose use has been misunderstood is the coffin-shaped wicker basket, with separate lid and leather carrying straps, whose woven shape resembles the stylized human form. Though often mislabeled a coffin or traveling coffin, the correct name for this container is an ambulance basket. Supply catalogs published from the late 1800s to the 1930s sold these baskets in a range of lengths, including child-sized, which undertakers used to transport but not bury bodies,[64] making them an early version of the body bag.

Prices

Rural builders tended not to charge their neighbors, but in urban areas people expected to pay for caskets. Though prices show up in everything from undertakers' ads to itemized city expenditures, the amounts are misleading. Without knowing whether hardwood or pine was used, the amount of fabric and coffin hardware that went into the construction, the size or length of the person being buried, and whether a vault was included, it is impossible to compare these figures.

Sometimes these purchases weren't made with cash. General stores accepted eggs, feathers, beeswax, manual labor, and the use of teams for hauling freight in payment, and those who built coffins also accepted barter. Cabinetmaker Orren Reiff (Washington County, 1844) built two coffins at $2 apiece for Ezekiel Venable, who paid for them by cutting oats, giving one day's labor and two bushels of wheat, and by his wife sewing for Reiff. Three years later Reiff was paid in pork for an adult's $3.50 coffin.[65]

Cities had to foot the bill when paupers died. Such was the case in Russellville (Pope County, 1891), where the town council appropriated $2 for a coffin, presumably for an indigent burial.[66] This was considerably lower than the $5 fees billed to both the Fort Smith's pauper commissioner and the U.S. marshal's office, the latter being for coffins for men Judge Isaac Parker sentenced to hang (Sebastian County, 1882–1896).[67]

If any amount can be said to be the standard fee in the mid-1800s, $5 may come the closest. Prosperous Thomas Ivy, whose estate was valued at $3,400 (Independence County, 1858), was buried in a $5 coffin,[68] still the going rate fifteen years later. Even in 1902 a furniture company could advertise "a full line of Caskets and Coffins" at prices from $5 to $150 (Benton County).[69] Stores and undertakers charged a lot more than local builders. The records of Bart Atkinson, Berryville furniture dealer and undertaker (Carroll County, 1911–1914), lists $20 and $25 charges for low-end adult coffins, on up to $125 for a copper-lined casket.[70] According to a former employee of the Arkansas Coffin Company, $35 bought "a pretty good casket" in the 1920s (Fort Smith, Sebastian County).[71]

If these prices reflect the norm, no wonder wealthy Manuel Davis's funeral was considered shockingly ostentatious (Stone County, 1917). "Mr. Davis was a product of our mammon-worshipping Christian civilization, so-called, and made a success of life, according to its idea of success," sneered the *Batesville Record*, acknowledging that Davis had started life poor and saved what he made. "He was buried in a casket said to have cost $800."[72] This sounds exorbitant for the time, yet was hardly the most expensive casket on the national

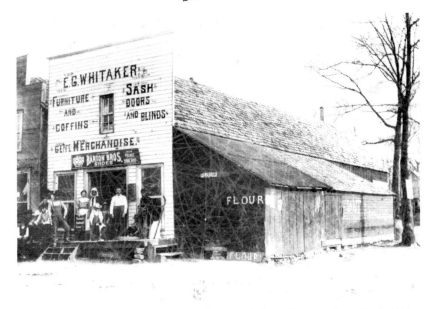

Figure 5.9 General stores sold a wide variety of goods, including coffins, as evidenced by the E. G. Whitaker store in Alpena (Carroll County), about 1900. Whitaker, wearing a white shirt, stands in the doorway. *Courtesy of Boone County Library, Harrison.*

market. Pennsylvania-based Boyertown Burial Casket Company's 1926 price list offered two styles of "solid cast bronze" caskets for $3,700 and $4,000,[73] which online calculators translate as roughly equal to $48,000 and $52,000 in today's money.

Local "Factories"

Storekeepers understood the need for haste, and offered burial containers "on short notice, any time, day or night" (Izard County, 1905),[74] or with the reassurance, "Not necessary to 'phone ahead. We have a complete stock. *Come on!*" (Madison County, 1927).[75] Another way to obtain a coffin in a hurry was from someone who built and stockpiled a small selection. According to records kept by blacksmiths Charles "Jack" Grubb and his son Thomas "Lee" Grubbs (Madison County, late 1800s through 1913), the family kept a half dozen finished caskets on hand at all times, with prices ranging from $2 (likely an infant's coffin) to $16. A small pulley, suspended under the eave of the roof, was used to hoist the finished caskets up to the second story for storage.[76] They also attached an "at rest" escutcheon to their work but, unlike conventional coffin hardware, this "plate" was made of heavy paper, similar to the papier-mâché fiber in an egg carton, painted silver.[77]

Locally made was always preferable to factory-produced. According to Gladys McChristian (Madison County, born 1910), "At first, people were skeptical of the store bought caskets. They said the bottom was liable to fall out en route to the grave."[78] Nellie Terherst (Carroll County, 1919) voiced a similar belief. "It's that they don't hold up, they're going to cave in, in a few weeks; that wood's not going to last." It did not go unnoticed that the grave of Charles Grubb, buried in the cherry wood casket he'd made for his own use (Madison County, 1913), did not sink until long after that of his wife, buried thirteen years later in a purchased metal casket inside a pine vault (Madison County, 1929).[79]

Factory-Made Merchandise

There have been a number of coffin factories in Arkansas over the years, the best-documented and longest lived being the Arkansas Coffin Company in Fort Smith (Sebastian County). Founded about 1906,[80] the business changed "coffin" to "casket" in its name in the 1950s. Jesse David Matlock Sr. started working for the factory as its bookkeeper in 1907; he later bought the company, which stayed in the Matlock family until it closed in 1989. Matlock's grandson, David Matlock, who started working for the business in the late 1940s when he was still in high school, served as its salesman, and ultimately worked in every part of the factory except the sewing room. During his fifty-year career he witnessed numerous changes to the industry.

Fabric played a big part in construction. Coffins were lined with fabric tacked over "cotton sweepings," fibers too short to be woven into cloth. The men who fitted linings into the caskets would fill one side of their mouths with tacks, spitting them out one at a time and using a magnetized tack hammer to pick up and nail each one in place. "Some of the guys could chew tobacco and spit tacks and never get any soil on the material," Matlock marveled. "It was unbelievable how fast those guys could . . . handle a tack hammer and the tacks and keep the tobacco juice separate."[81]

Cloth-covered caskets were a staple of the business through the Depression. Matlock said that plain or embossed gray fabric was used to cover the cheaper adult caskets; more expensive ones were covered with felt or wool broadcloth, the wood underneath being neither primed nor painted. Children's caskets were covered in white, pink, or blue material, the company also serving as a distributor for a line of gingham-covered caskets made in Oklahoma. "There was always a need for caskets," Matlock said. "At that time, you could get a casket without any hardware [which would be placed inside] . . . it was kind of like a do-it-yourself kit. My dad said they did that an awful lot during the Depression" to save money and to make them easier to ship.

During its early years the company bent or steamed wood to create the angled sides of the traditional hexagonal coffin, but by the time Matlock started work, precut wooden casket pieces were assembled when an order came in. (As late as the 1980s they still got the occasional order for a traditional hexagonal coffin.) The company bought cypress from El Dorado, Arkansas, as well as using hardwoods, and they shipped the caskets in lightweight spruce or pine boxes, chosen to save freight costs. The company also sold concrete vaults.

The factory milled its own wood on the ground floor; fabric and sewing rooms, where linings were made and where the caskets were assembled, were located on the second floor. When metal caskets became popular, the company purchased the components and assembled them, spraying them with paint and clear lacquer. (There was even a brief fad for paint sprayed through a piece of lace.) The third floor, where painting and spraying was done (so fumes could escape through the roof), was also where a few finished products were kept on display. "Some of the black funeral homes, they didn't have show rooms, so they'd bring the families up there" to look at various models, Matlock said. And just like storekeepers in previous decades, Matlock occasionally got late-night phone calls from customers needing to make an immediate purchase.

In addition to the oversized container mentioned above, custom orders included caskets made without any metal components for Orthodox Hebrew and Greek Orthodox burials, simple wooden caskets covered in black fabric for the local Catholic sisters' home, and metal caskets for a federal prison in Colorado. Another custom order was constructing slightly smaller caskets to fit into older, narrow mausoleum spaces built to house coffins. The business made several modifications to its product line over the years but finally, in 1989, they finished off everything that was in production and sold the remaining casket hardware to small companies in Missouri and Oklahoma. Then the last casket maker in Arkansas, which had outlasted competing factories around the state in Texarkana, Fordyce, Little Rock, Pine Bluff, Van Buren, and West Memphis, closed its doors for good.[82]

Metal Burial Cases

The tale of the military officer killed in battle and shipped home in an alcohol-filled coffin has been told of former Arkansas governor Archibald Yell and Batesville's Capt. Andrew Porter. Both men fought in the Mexican War; both were killed at the Battle of Buena Vista (Mexico, 1847). This sepulchral urban legend may have originated in the practice of burying officers' bodies in tin coffins to facilitate their eventual exhumations. Yell was initially buried in a tin coffin placed inside a wooden one, in the belief that his family would want his body shipped home, which proved to be the case. Four months after the battle, when members of the Arkansas Mounted Volunteers were about to leave Mexico, they exhumed the bodies of Yell, Porter, and a Private Pelham for transport home to Arkansas, filling these coffins with charcoal to prevent seepage and odors.[83]

Though it sounds improbable, the alcohol-filled coffin has a basis in reality. Beginning in 1940, writers working for the Works Progress Administration interviewed their counties' oldest residents using a set list of questions. One of these prompted George Meriwether (Independence County, born 1852) to tell the following story about a Mrs. Tunstall: "She was buried in a malic with [a] glass top[,] she was preserved in alcohol and during the Civil War the glass was broken and the jewelry was stolen. They thought the soldiers had done this. After the air struck her she had to be buried."[84]

It isn't clear what Meriwether meant by a "malic." The interviewer wrote legibly but spelled poorly, so perhaps the word was a corruption of "metallic," as numerous metallic burial cases were on the market by this time. Whatever the container, such a thing violates the taboo against leaving a body unattended while above ground, yet the same story has been handed down in the Tunstall family. The woman placed in this container was Elizabeth Magness Tunstall (1816–1856), second wife of wealthy landowner Capt. Thomas Todd Tunstall. Elizabeth loved horses, and after she died the capsule containing her body was situated in the family graveyard, overlooking her husband's racetrack. According to her tombstone she died in October at Jacksonport, Arkansas, a distance of roughly twenty miles; conceivably alcohol preserved her body on its transport home.[85] Today her grave has a white marble marker, with no evidence of a capsule or the bier that supported one.

Tunstall's capsule, while unusual, had a precedent. Eccentric St. Louis physician Joseph Nash McDowell also used an alcohol-filled capsule (described as being similar to a diploma case) to house the body of his fourteen-year-old daughter inside a cave he owned (Hannibal, Missouri, about 1847). The body was later buried in the McDowells' cemetery plot in St. Louis, but not before numerous townspeople had broken into the cave to take a look at the dead girl floating in liquid.[86] It's unknown why McDowell preserved her in this manner; perhaps he planned to autopsy her body.

These examples document an extremely rare type of burial container, but patented, mass-produced, molded metal coffins were quite common. The earliest American patent for such a device was granted to James A. Gray, a Virginian, in 1836; by 1860 others had applied for patents for coffins made from iron, zinc, and glass in combination with such materials as stone, clay, wood, and cement. The best known and most widely distributed model was the Fisk Burial Case, a patented metal coffin molded in the shape of a supine body with an oval viewing window set directly above the corpse's face.

The Fisk Metallic Coffin was patented and exhibited in 1848[87] by its inventor, Almond D. Fisk,[88] who made his first iron burial case in 1849 at his New York foundry and died a year later. His patents were licensed to a number of other companies and the cases became popular after various celebrities either endorsed their use or were buried in them. By the Civil War they were in such demand that seventeen models were available to choose from. The Cincinnati, Ohio, firm of Crane and Breed trace their company's origins to the Fisk patents they acquired when Martin Crane purchased a casket business and foundry in 1853.[89] By 1858 the company was selling both the Fisk case and its own designs, discontinuing production of Fisk's original design in 1867.[90]

Such coffins were used in Arkansas during the Civil War, especially by the military in instances where the family might wish to eventually have the body exhumed for reburial. Their popularity continued after the war. Eureka Springs's undertaker and coffin-dealer J. W. Willett (Carroll County, 1881) advertised that he carried Fisk's metallic burial cases, "without question the most beautiful and finely finished in the market." Because Willett also embalmed the bodies of visiting invalids who were unsuccessful in their quest for healing, these air and watertight coffins were needed when shipping bodies back home.[91]

An early Fisk catalog issued the reminder that "care must be taken to see that the glass frame over the face is cemented properly after the body is in the case."[92] This was an important step, as the metal case sealed out air and thus inhibited decomposition. It made possible the following story, found in the obituary of Mary Stewart Battles, who died near Eureka Springs (Carroll County, 1911). Forty-nine years earlier her husband, Nelson Battles, a Civil War soldier stationed at Camp Wickliffe, Kentucky, died of the measles at age thirty-two. His brother brought the body back to Arkansas, where it was buried in a Mayfield cemetery (Washington County, 1862), but upon his wife's death Nelson's airtight metal coffin was exhumed so the two could be interred together.

When the body was removed Thursday, Tracy Battles, aged fifty-four, of Chardon, expressed a desire to see his father, whom he had never known. The top of the casket was removed and through the glass Mr. Battles gazed for the first time upon this father's face in a perfect state of preservation. The venerable Edwin Battles, the last of the family, viewed his brother's face Thursday and said: "He looks just as he did the day we buried him." Mrs. Melissa Richmond, the daughter, now fifty years old, also saw her father Thursday for the first time in her life. She had no childish memory of his face. The remains were apparently those of a person who had been dead for two days. The soldier's blanket was just as white as when wrapped around the body nearly a half century ago. The skin, flesh, and hair were perfect[ly] natural, the hair showing comb marks plainly. At the cemetery many gazed upon the remarkable sight.[93]

CHAPTER SIX

Notification, Transportation, and Farewell

Thou art gone dear boy, where only bliss is known.
Gone where love and joy are one—
yet take these tears mortality's relief,
and until we share thy joy forgive our grief.
These little rites, a stone, a hearse receive.
Tis all a father or a mother dear can give.

—William Thomas Hurst, 1899–1900
Evergreen Cemetery (Washington County)

Farmer A. V. Hicks's sons had to think up an excuse to give their father the morning he asked them to do some plowing. Hicks had forgotten that the day was his seventy-second birthday, but his boys had not, and they had planned a celebration. Soon friends and neighbors, laden with baskets of food, began arriving and at noon a meal was served to fifty guests (Washington County, 1906). The surprised honoree was delighted. His front yard, filled with people, attracted the notice of a passing stranger, who drew the obvious conclusion. He asked who had died.[1]

The stranger's mistake was understandable, because a large gathering of people in front of a house often signified a death within. This was just one way in which news spread. Often, those returning home from sitting up at a death-bed would notify neighbors as they passed and, in the era of party-line telephones, everyone listened in on others' calls without scruple. Each residence was assigned its own combination of long and short rings, which sounded in every house on the line when there was an incoming call, meaning everyone knew who was getting a call. A single, continuous ring signaled an emergency.

Then "everyone was to listen in to see what was wrong, and what could be done about it" (Baxter County, 1903).[2] The downside, besides a lack of privacy, was the occasional dissemination of misinformation. "A call came through on the party line (probably before daylight) stating that the funeral would be tomorrow," Bud Phillips wrote of his great-aunt's death one Saturday morning (Pope County, 1940). "Many, including our family, went to the cemetery and waited all thru that Saturday until finally more word came through indicating that the service was to be on Sunday."[3]

Bells and Wreaths

A century or so ago people routinely took orders, or received news, from whistles and bells. In addition to such obvious examples as school, church, and fire bells, some factories blew a five-minute warning whistle so employees would be on time, and during World War II town canneries sometimes used a whistle or siren to announced the arrival of trainloads of produce in need of immediate processing. Coalmines (Johnson County, late 1920s) blew three blasts on their steam-powered whistles to notify miners when there was work. Though movies depict such whistles shrilling to alert families of a mine cave-in, one miner's wife never mentioned this use in her diary (Johnson County, 1923–1930). Lola Brown recorded the names of miners who died from natural causes, falling down dead, being run over by a train and, yes, from a mining injury, but the only time she mentioned a whistle was when noting the days when the mines would "blow for work."[4] According to Virgil Phillips (Johnson County, born 1920), mine operators also used one long blast of the whistle to signify that there was *no* work, usually from such causes as cave-ins, union strikes, or dangerous fumes in the mineshafts.

Not all churches, schools, fraternal lodges, and community buildings (often one and the same structure) had steeples containing bells, but when they did have one with a carrying tone it was used to announce deaths. This custom differed from place to place, tolling out the deceased's age, announcing the start of a funeral or notifying grave diggers that it was time to start work. According to one very early account, the Cane Hill college bell—salvaged from a steamboat that sank in the Arkansas River—was tolled the entire time it took a funeral procession to travel from church to cemetery (Washington County, some time after 1852).[5]

Ulis Morrison (Searcy County, born 1901), who grew up near a church, rang many a death announcement, something he described as "clapping" the bell one time for each year of the deceased's age. "You'd clap and pause and give another clap. It wasn't just a steady ring. . . . You wouldn't turn the bell up high enough [in its holder] for it to go over, it would go just high enough for it to clap." Truman Gurley (Madison County, born 1911) acquired the bell, cast in 1888, that was used near Kingston. "When people heard it they knowed something was wrong. If you rang it, and let it ring, neighbors would come running." Families owning a dinner bell would use that, in a crisis, to alert their neighbors.

In Catholic communities the church bell rang for a dual purpose. "It was to alert people," said Mary Vaughan of Tontitown's St. Joseph's Church (Washington County, mid-1930s). "If we'd be in a field two miles away, we could hear it ring. If you were doing something when you heard it, you stopped and said a prayer. You didn't always know who the person was until you came out of the fields, but you might have a general idea." In the earliest days of this community, founded by Italian Catholic immigrants in 1889, the church bell was rung at 6:00 A.M. each day and tolled when there was a death, "the number of tolls dependent on whether the deceased was a man or a woman."[6]

By the 1930s, most homes in rural Arkansas towns were connected via party-line telephones. Placing a call involved first ringing "Central," the town switchboard. "Fires, sickness, death, births—all were relayed to Central even before other family members were notified," according to William Maddox (Van Buren County, 1930s). "If the worst happened, Central was a clearing house for all the details pertinent to the funeral arrangements, such as the hour of the service, pallbearers, minister and choir members."[7] This operator also kept track of the doctor's whereabouts, which was important in emergencies.

One early method of notification involved hanging black draperies on a building or a black wreath on the door. Emma Maguire's obituary (Washington County, 1875) mentioned that "her home is draped in deepest mourning," as was Peter Van Winkle's hotel (Washington County, 1882), following their deaths.[8] Because all businesses closed during funerals, the Olmstead funeral home gave away specially printed notices for merchants to post, stating the time their stores would reopen (Heber Springs, Cleburne County, 1940s).[9] Most citizens hardly needed this reminder, however, because funeral attendance was all but mandatory, and schools closed so the children could attend en masse.

When brakeman and assistant conductor Jefferson Adams was killed on the job (Benton County, 1917), the trains of the Kansas City and Missouri Railroad were "annulled" for his funeral.[10] Even courts adjourned, and when William Spears, a lawyer and former judge, died (Newton County, 1945), the county fairgrounds emptied out when his funeral started. "Everybody

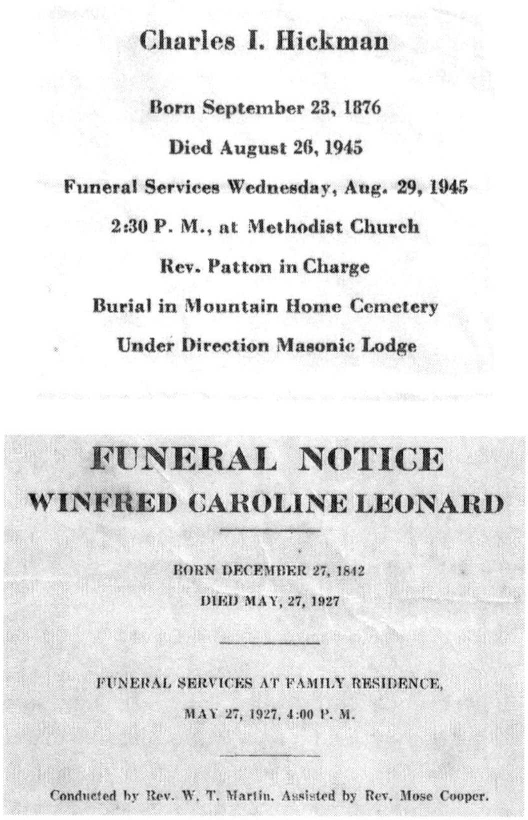

Charles I. Hickman

Born September 23, 1876

Died August 26, 1945

Funeral Services Wednesday, Aug. 29, 1945

2:30 P. M., at Methodist Church

Rev. Patton in Charge

Burial in Mountain Home Cemetery

Under Direction Masonic Lodge

FUNERAL NOTICE
WINFRED CAROLINE LEONARD

BORN DECEMBER 27, 1842

DIED MAY, 27, 1927

FUNERAL SERVICES AT FAMILY RESIDENCE,

MAY 27, 1927, 4:00 P. M.

Conducted by Rev. W. T. Martin. Assisted by Rev. Mose Cooper.

Figure 6.1 Printed notices were handed out, or left in stores, to publicize funerals. *Courtesy Baxter County Historical and Genealogical Society/Mrs. Nellie Mitchell and Garvin Carroll collection.*

abandoned the fair, and everybody accompanied the body to the cemetery for the last sad rites. And then they all came back, and the foot races began."[11] Such respect extended even to some persons having very little connection to Arkansas. H. M. Byllesby died in his dentist's office in Chicago, Illinois, but because he had owned over six hundred utilities across the country, including Ozark's power company (Franklin County, 1924), the local office sported a large floral wreath on its door and remained closed for a day.[12]

Funeral Notices

Only rarely did a death take place in time for publications in a weekly newspaper; in most cases the funeral was over by the time a paper went to press. Even a death notice in a daily paper provided scant time to publicize a

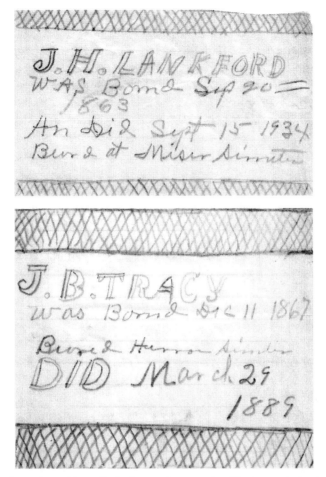

Figure 6.2 Those who could not afford to have notices printed could make ones by hand to distribute to the public. Here "born'd" was correct usage, while "died" was spelled "did." *Courtesy Baxter County Historical and Genealogical Society/Mrs. Nellie Mitchell and Garvin Carroll collection.*

funeral's time and location. A better way to get the word out was through a funeral notice, also called a funeral invitation. These small cards or rectangles of paper, printed in the newspaper office's print shop, gave all pertinent information: the name and age of the deceased, and the date, time, and place of the funeral and burial. These notices were distributed throughout residential areas, left in stores for people to pick up, or tacked up like small posters for anyone to read.[13] The small notices, set off with heavy black borders to denote mourning, resembled somber party invitations both in appearance and language used, as they often began, "Friends and acquaintances of the family are respectfully invited to attend."

A grandchild of James T. Tracy, reminiscing about Tracy's general store in Mountain Home (Baxter County, 1898–1940), recalled his habit of saving these bits of paper. "At that time, when someone died, hand distributed notices was the custom. Grandpa always filed his on the spindle, and there was a thick stack of them. Usually, he did not attend funerals, but when the hearse drove past his store from church to cemetery, Grandpa stood respectfully in his doorway as his deceased fellow citizen took his final ride down Main Street."[14] Daughter Nellie Tracy Mitchell saved these notices. These were either professionally printed cards or ones scrawled in pencil on small squares of lined tablet paper, and the handwritten notices are likely to read like this one: "Sary Jane Grant was Bornd [sic] 20 June 1869 and Did [sic] July 26, 1925."[15]

Professionally printed notices, found across the Ozarks, have death dates from the early 1870s through the 1920s, and sometimes include the exact time of death ("9:45 p.m." and "5:35 a.m."). In examples from Crawford County, most funerals were held at the family residence, giving the time as "today" and leaving it up to friends to know where and when this was. Three notices mention an early morning death with the funeral later the same day, showing the speed with which both printers and families had to work.

Obituaries: "We drop the sympathetic tear"[16]

Early obituaries contained biographical, medical, spiritual, and personal information unimaginable today. Because they were published long after the funeral, some accounts included the funeral text, memorial poetry, a summation of the deceased's virtues and, following the loss of a child, advice and comfort to grieving parents.

English ship captain Andrew Shilling was the first person to have a published obituary, written in 1622—fifty years before the word *newspaper* was coined. His death, fighting the Portuguese in the Persian Gulf, was written about in one of London's one-page journals (the forerunner of the newspaper), but even earlier than this, in the 1580s, deaths were described in published pamphlets. Shilling's write-up broke new ground and is billed as the first obituary because it described the deceased's life and character. The first obituary published in the United States was that of Jane Treat, killed by lightning in her home in Medord, Massachusetts, in 1704.[17] (Her tombstone, rather disappointingly, does not mention this event.)

Treat's obituary gave a detailed description of the damage done to her body by the jolt of electricity; two centuries later Ozark writers were equally forthcoming when eulogizing violent deaths. Women and children whose clothing caught fire were usually described as "nearly roasted" or "burned to a crisp." A man who committed suicide with a gun had his "brains scattered to the four winds" (Benton County, 1888),[18] poetic language when contrasted with that of W. C. Stone, who died from the same cause (Washington County, 1898): "the brains were scattered on the rafters above and in every direction."[19] Worse yet was the exploding boiler that killed three men (Pope County, 1886), the body of one, "completely torn to shreds, a portion of which could not be found,"[20] or the appearance of seven-year-old Charlie Champion, struck by a train, "so horrifying that men and women had to be helped away from the scene."[21] (Not all train deaths were accidents. Placing a murder victim's body on the tracks was a good way to obliterate evidence of the crime.)

Of all the violent deaths, the careless handling of firearms provoked newspaper writers to their greatest heights of editorializing, blaming both victims and their parents. When Tom Moore, a student at the University of Arkansas, was shot while "scuffling" with a friend (Washington County, 1904), a writer railed against playing with revolvers, stressing how "only the participants are to blame."[22] The obituary of John Walker, killed by two boys playing with guns, contained even stronger language (Washington County, 1886). The event "brings forcibly to mind the utter inexcusable and culpable conduct of parents who permit thoughtless and careless children to carry guns."[23]

The obituaries of suicides tend to read like how-to manuals, giving explicit instructions on positioning a rifle or shotgun while simultaneously pulling the trigger. Similarly, when the final exit involved poison, the product used would be named. Stories about hangings included practical tips on what to stand on, the number of strands of binder twine needed, as well as cautionary tales about ropes that turned out to be too long—or that stretched.

Accidental deaths, especially those of children, spurred writers to issue public service announcements. The death of Hezekiah Gregg, age thirteen, who was run over by the Frisco train at Winslow (Washington County, 1899), was seen as "another warning to the small boys of the land who are daily tempting death by their efforts to ride on trains where they have no business."[24] Other obituaries warned against the dangers of rivers ("Persons who cannot swim will do well to exercise great care when in the river"),[25] indulging in card playing and carrying weapons, and drunkenness. Some obituaries warned belatedly against innocuous objects, as when a baby died after sucking on a pencil. "Our people cannot be too careful how they handle the purple lead of these pencils; it is rank poison" (Boone County, 1883).[26] The parents of the three-year-old child who drank Daisy Fly Killer (Boone County, 1911) were reminded how "great care should be used" in keeping poisons out of children's reach,[27] though in this case the product's colorful, enticing package was really to blame.

Writers thought nothing of mentioning if the deceased stuttered, was feeble minded, or was obese, such as Kate Kell, "the heaviest woman in Arkansas," who weighed 350 to 400 pounds (Washington County, 1899).[28] The deceased's personal foibles also came under scrutiny, as happened to murder victim John Cox, known for his habit of carrying large amounts of money on his person (Searcy County, 1917). The writer saw this as "another great object lesson to teach us that the only safe place for money is to place it where one cannot lose it, and that is in a sound bank, backed by insurance from robbery or fire." (The robbers did not find Cox's money and checks, hidden in his shoes.)[29]

Lives of the disadvantaged and difficult would be summed up using blunt and often caustic language. "He was an old bachelor and as stingy as they make 'em" was said of one man (Washington County, 1917) estimated to be worth as much as $500,000,[30] while another writer (Searcy County, 1906) pulled no punches when describing indigent, ninety-year-old "Uncle John," found dead in the woods. "His peculiarities and don't-care disposition made him almost a pest on the community. He had recently been placed on the pauper list—but the assistance was too late. This is one pauper that has landed at the end of his journey without expense." Despite this damning summation the writer urged others to "speak kindly" to those who were similarly impoverished and alone in the world.[31]

Though obituary writers relished grisly details, they were circumspect when describing deaths from illness. (Rabies deaths were the exception.) If only Lillie McCasland's obituary writer had been more forthcoming (Searcy County, 1924). McCasland died after suffering for a full year, "stricken with a most baffling malady which literally broke her poor body asunder."[32] Still, occasionally a medical detail or two slips through, as in the obituary of L. D. Phillips (Sharp County, 1917). After being lauded for his business acumen, many personal friendships, and willingness to help those in need, it was mentioned that Phillips had died from a nervous breakdown following an operation for hemorrhoids.[33]

These are just a few examples of the language used by newspaper writers. Obituaries written by ministers are gentler in tone, more spiritual in nature, and contain a rather obvious religious agenda. Here may be found the deceased's state of spiritual preparedness (or lack thereof), whether he or she was baptized or had joined a church, and whether the person "was a great sufferer," enduring illness without complaint. Often these tracts ended with a reminder to the living to seek God. Few writers, be they ministers, friends, or newspaper editors, could resist the urge to sermonize. The obituary of Thomas Sweeden (Pope County, 1884) concluded with these remarks: "Mr.

Sweeden's motto was the golden rule and he believed in a moral life. This is good as far as it goes, but we believe in religion in our hearts and in our feet, heads, and even in our pockets."[34]

Over the past century, both the obituary's language and its content have changed dramatically. At one time, writers thought nothing of referring to the deceased's body as a corpse, ashes, or "lifeless clay." Nor were finances off-limits, giving the dollar amount of an insurance settlement, describing a dependent as a "penniless widow," or revealing how the deceased had been buried at the town's expense. These little gems of biography, while expressing the community's sympathy, also provided readers with all pertinent information, including a dying person's last words or the full text of a suicide note. Sometimes, the details paint an especially vivid picture, as in the following (Carroll County, 1908):

> Randal Emmet, the blind, one-armed man who has been a familiar figure in this country for the past twenty years, has passed to his reward.... Mr. Emmet was horribly mangled by the premature explosion of a blast in a well near Zion Hill on Dec. 9, 1887, both eye balls were blown out, his skull fractured and an arm so badly lacerated that amputation was necessary. From this horrible condition he recovered to the extent that he groped through a miserable existence for more than twenty years to finally die of consumption. His wife preceded him in death three years ago. He was the father of ten children, eight of whom were born after the accident happened.[35]

African American Obituaries

Far fewer obituaries were published for African Americans than for whites, though when it came to violent deaths, blacks had their remains described as graphically as anyone else's. While some newspapers undoubtedly excluded blacks, all members of the working class—black and white—were underrepresented on the obituary pages, perhaps for financial reasons. Though some editors published obituaries for free, an Evening Shade newspaper (Sharp County, 1890) announced a charge of five cents per line for all "lengthy" death notices, obituaries, and resolutions of respect by fraternal lodges. The explanation was that "when they are printed free of charge it is simply a tribute from the publisher, and not from friends."[36] Such fees likely kept all but the wealthiest families from publishing tributes.

There are numerous differences between the obituaries of blacks and whites. One is that the race of those attending funerals is often mentioned.

Take, for instance, the funeral of Reece B. Hogins, a colonel in the Confederacy and, much later, mayor of Russellville (Pope County, 1909). According to his obituary, Frank (no last name given), "the faithful old negro who cared for 'Marse Hogins' in his youth," was accorded a place of honor near the coffin at Hogins's funeral. "No tear was more sincere than those which dampened the ebony cheeks of this faithful old servant."[37]

Another difference is that African Americans' obituaries were segregated in the two statewide papers published in Little Rock. The *Arkansas Democrat* was still running blacks' obituaries under the headline "Deaths of Negroes" (which, unlike those of whites, ran without individual headings) in the late 1950s, while the *Arkansas Gazette* segregated its obituaries until September 1964. Many decades after the Civil War and emancipation, the name of a slave owner would be included in the former slave's obituary; in some cases, so was the price once paid to purchase him.[38]

Those who had been born slaves and without recorded birth dates were frequently believed to have died at advanced ages, usually well into the triple digits. (In contrast, a white man dying in 1850, at age fifty-three, had his cause of death listed as "old age.")[39] One man, Wiley Sloan (Lawrence County, 1917), who believed himself to be 114 years old, "decided that he would never die as long as he resided in Imboden, [and] has emigrated to what he thinks is a more propitious climate for shuffling off this mortal coil."[40]

Presumably it was white writers who summarized African American lives and deaths, and they did so in language that today can only be read as racist. Upon his death, "Uncle" Milt Sanford (Bentonville, 1901), age sixty-four, received a standard write-up that included his time of death, its cause, and his virtues ("faithful, honest and industrious"), but the writer added that Sanford "had never given the police officers one moment's trouble," a statement not made about whites.[41] This condescending tone is seen in the obituary of Josephine Crenshaw (Randolph County, 1912), who was described as "well respected among the white people, being of good character and harmless in every way."[42] Though the use of "aunt" and "uncle" before the names of elderly blacks sounds racist, these terms, along with "grandpa" and "grandma," were also bestowed on elderly whites and were used out of respect for the person's advanced age. In some instances, the condescension was intended as praise, as in the case of Charley May, a Russellville barber (Pope County, 1905). "Charley had a colored skin, but when it came to his dealings with his fellow men he was all white."[43]

There was no lack of outright racism, however. Consider Caesar Bean's obituary (Crawford County, 1904): "He knew his place and was always polite and attentive. It is a pity his class of colored people is becoming so rare."[44] Still worse is the initial write-up of former slave Kimsey Lambert's death (Benton County, 1909). The *Benton County Democrat* got the man's name wrong, and though Lambert had lived in the community for over fifty years and was well known, the writer had nothing to say about him beyond calling him an "old slave darky" and an "old-time darky," and then, to cement this point, ended the brief obituary with, "In fact he was a good darky." One week later local Presbyterian minister Peter Carnahan (who was white) set the record straight with a long and sensitively written piece in the same newspaper. In it, he described Lambert's goodness and strength of character, and his "Christian submission and resignation" that renewed the minister's own faith.[45]

Perhaps because whites were writing for a predominantly white readership, blacks were often described according to their relation to white families, such as noting that Annie Dickson's husband (Washington County, 1882) "has the sympathy of his white friends in his sad loss and bereavement."[46] Della Black (Benton County, 1902) was remembered for nursing numerous white children and caring for the sick.[47] One long and personal obituary was written for Hannah Burnsides (Washington County, 1883), whose age at death was unknown but, typically, was estimated at past the century mark. The writer stated that he had known Burnsides for thirty-one years, and told where she'd lived, her various owners' names, and the families for whom she had worked, then mentioned her most noted eccentricity. In addition to being a "welcome visitor" in the homes of white ladies, "Aunt Hannah had a particular fondness for old shoes and would frequently ask the ladies . . . to give her a pair of their 'old shoes;' she would carry them home and lay them away in a box . . . for 'hard times.'"[48]

Obituary Parodies

Obituaries were entertaining in their own right, but newspapers also treated their readers to parodies. Farewell tributes to beloved animals have been found for dogs, cats, milk cows, hogs, and mules, all of whom had names and several of whom had their ages spelled out in years, months, and days, as was done with human deaths. Fayetteville's Van Hoose family enjoyed these parodies so much they masterminded at least two of their own, one a tribute to a favorite cow (Washington County, 1892).[49] Fifteen years earlier the *Fayetteville Democrat* published a lengthy obituary for Colonel Van Hoose's dog Ponto, which included a short, laudatory verse signed by "A Friend to the Dog." It included lines commenting on national politics, "He had lived to see the dog made free. / Hayes put in where Tilden ought to be."[50]

When describing deaths of pets, writers used language identical to that found in human obituaries. Dollie, a fifteen-year-old monkey owned by Capt. George Richards (Fort Smith, Sebastian County, 1909), had two doctors in attendance during her final illness. "The end came when Richards asked her for a hug and the small animal folded her arms around his neck and expired," a detail found in children's obituaries. Local undertaker J. G. Putnam embalmed the body so Richards could take Dollie home to St. Louis for burial.[51] In another example, the death of the Johnson brothers' prized Duroc hog (Madison County, 1924) was regretted by both the owners and by "a great number of friends he had made."[52] One mule, "Old Jim" (Sharp County, 1897), inspired three lengthy tributes, one of which estimated that he'd hauled logging wagons a total of 1,860,000 feet over his lifetime. The editor of the *Sharp County Record* lauded this mule and called the tributes he inspired "charming to all lovers of the bright and spicy side of life."[53]

Transporting the Coffin

The next part of the burial ritual involves transporting the deceased to the cemetery. This subject, rather than the funeral, comes next in the sequence of events because funerals did not necessarily precede the trip to the cemetery or even take place on the day of the burial. Transporting a coffined body was a job that, again, required help from the community. By the late 1800s city dwellers could hire a horse-drawn hearse from an undertaking establishment or a livery stable. In rural communities, in the late 1920s and early 1930s coffins were likely be conveyed in the bed of someone's pickup truck or, once undertaking businesses were well established, in a motorized hearse.

During the transition from horse-drawn to motorized hearses, funeral processions were likely to be made up of both types of vehicles. First came the hearse, then cars, "and then came the slower moving horses and buggies with the indignant occupants choking and sputtering because of the churned-up dust they had to take" (Benton County, about 1913 to 1920, after which streets were paved).[54] Up into the Depression it was the norm in rural communities to transport coffins in wagons, and one with rubber tires was preferable to one with iron wheels, both for the comfort of any passengers and to ensure less jostling of the corpse.

There are also stories of reaching a cemetery via boat, but this could be perilous. The funeral procession of Scott Page (Pope County, 1927) had to ford Moccasin Creek multiple times after heavy rains, when the creek was out of its banks. Mid-stream while making the final crossing, "the water on the up-stream

Figure 6.3 Undertaker Bart H. Atkinson (*right*) driving his glass-sided hearse with matched team of black horses, Berryville (Carroll County), about 1915. *Courtesy of the Heritage Center Museum, Berryville, Carroll County Historical Society.*

Figure 6.4 Funeral of Viola Hawkins, 1932. The coffin was delivered to the Kingston Cemetery (Madison County) in the back of Marvin Little's truck. Little, *at right,* is in white shirt and cap. Hawkins's daughter, Myrtle, *seated beside coffin,* is comforted by other women. *Courtesy of the Madison County Historical and Genealogical Society, Huntsville, and John D. Little.*

side poured over the top of the bottom section of the wagon bed. The coffin floated and had to be held against the lower side."[55] Coffins floated out of pickup trucks, too. One reason given for the founding of certain cemeteries is that families were unwilling to risk crossing high water to get to their customary burying ground, and simply started new graveyards on the opposite side.

The taboo against leaving the dead unattended sounds like a logical explanation for men riding in the wagon bed with the coffin or walking directly behind it en route to the cemetery. However, the custom of establishing cemeteries on high elevations, reached by steep, rough roads, meant that the coffin was in danger of sliding off the back of the vehicle, hence the need for additional manpower. One of the first sights to greet a Mrs. M. E. Jeter, recently moved to St. Paul (Madison County, 1887), was that of "a funeral cavalcade wending past the inn in a driving rainstorm as it traversed the rocky road up to old Riverside Cemetery. The pallbearers were seated on the yellow pine casket, their feet braced against the wagon bed to prevent its sliding," so depressing a sight that Mrs. Jeter regretted having left Missouri.[56]

"I remember walking behind the wagon that held Aunt Cat Williams' coffin," recalled Burr Fancher (Madison County, 1930s). "A steep hill came up, and this team was just struggling and the coffin started drifting toward the back of the wagon, and the men ran alongside and held the coffin until they got to a level spot." Sometimes the worst happened anyway. As the funeral procession of Mrs. Elisha Clark (Searcy County, 1892) was in transit, "on turning from the main road the wagon carrying the corpse turned over throwing the corpse out on the ground."[57] Still, most accounts sound festive, rather than harrowing. When "Old Grandma Anderson" died (Carroll County, approx. 1924), "all who went along just piled in the wagon with her" in order to have a ride to the burial.[58]

A wagon and team were not the best way to transport a coffin over mountainous terrain. Well into the twentieth century some mountain roads merely "followed the creek bed—that is, people drove their wagons on streambeds when there was no water in them[59]—while another account (Madison County, 1919) described rural roads as nothing more than "two wheel ruts winding through the woods."[60] Those living in isolated locations required extra help. Orphea Wyatt remembered men using a ladder to carry her grandfather's body off the property via a shortcut (Buffalo River area, 1930s), as going by the nearest road would have necessitated a full day's travel, while another account mentions suspending a coffin from poles, carried on neighbors' shoulders.[61]

One story in particular illustrates people's ingenuity in mountainous terrain. A child died at a time when Piney Creek had flooded the only available wagon road (Pope County, date unknown) and, after debating burying the body on the family's property, neighbors brought two teams of horses to the home. "The bed was removed from the Felkins' wagon, and the back and front wheels uncoupled. The coffin, with the body inside, was lashed to the front-wheel section. One of the teams was hooked to the two-wheel cart and they began the journey to Leonard's Valley" and the cemetery. "It was a mountain that had on its face tiers of bluffs and was covered by a heavy virgin forest. The teams were swapped when those pulling tired, and at times both teams had to be hooked to the two-wheel section of the running gear and its precious load." Men went ahead to move rocks and chop down trees, the family bringing up the rear, and in all it took a full day to reach the valley for the burial.[62]

Such journeys brought forth heroism, others elicited humor. Elizabeth Phillips Montgomery (Madison County, born 1835) witnessed one such incident, later recorded by one of her descendants.

> Some young men brought an ox cart with a coffin containing their grandmother's body. . . . It was a hot day and the ox balked at the first steep spot they came to. They could not get the ox to move and she heard one boy say, "I don't know why Grandma had to die in August, she ought to know that the oxen won't pull when it's hot!" They kept trying to get the ox to move and finally decided to light a fire under it. Then the ox moved alright, but just enough to put the wooden coffin over the fire! Grandma Betty would laugh and laugh about how they really had to scramble to get the whole thing off the fire.[63]

As the coffin-laden wagon passed by, people stood and men uncovered their heads; some fell into step and followed. The primary superstition concerning this passage is that a funeral procession must never halt, something of greater concern in cities than in the countryside. If the line of vehicles came upon a train on the tracks the procession was supposed to circle the block as many times as necessary until mourners could continue on, rather than stop. Anyone meeting a funeral head-on was expected to pull over and stop, while yet another superstition forbade counting the number of cars or wagons as they passed.[64]

Pulling one's car to the side of the road and stopping is still practiced in Arkansas, even on paved, multilane roads, and people now believe that this is done to show respect. However, in the 1970s the Arkansas Funeral Directors Association and the state police joined forces to try to convince motorists to abandon the practice, on the grounds that it caused accidents. Despite making the argument that "if the approaching motorist would slow their speed upon the approach of a funeral procession this would indicate the desired respect for the deceased," the altered custom did not catch on.[65]

Taking a Last Look

When my friends stand around my casket,
Taking the last view on earth,
Just think about the happiness in heaven,
Where my soul is at rest.

—**Beckie York,** 1877–1937
Rule Cemetery (Carroll County)

In times of sickness family members who were unable to attend the burial had to take their farewell look at the deceased at home. When the entire George Pryor family became ill (Marion County, 1845) and the wife and oldest child died, neighbors laid out the bodies in individual coffins. "Before placing the lids on them, they lifted up each coffin and placed them side by side at the bedside of the husband and father and raised the man up to take a farewell view of his dead wife and child. Then they lifted up the two sick children to see their departed mother and brother. The scene was one of sorrow and grief."[66] Some bodies, en route to the cemetery, made a stop at the homes of friends or relatives who were physically unable to attend the burial.

Once everyone had assembled at the cemetery, the coffin was placed on two chairs or sawhorses, brought along for this purpose. Whether there was to be a funeral or merely a short graveside service, a prayer, or some hymns, the final and most important step was viewing the remains. The rigid body, transported in a farm wagon without springs over rough roads, would have been jostled in its box, clothing become disarranged, and there was the added possibility that the eyes might have come open or that bodily fluids seeped out. Before family and friends took their final look, someone had to make the body presentable. Otho Tackett (Russellville area, Pope County, late 1920s) left an account of this rarely documented process.

"When the time came to view the body the cover was moved down and Rev. Marley Conley's wife would prepare the body for viewing, as travel over rough roads often caused the body to shift in the casket. I can remember her leaving with her hands stretched out holding soap and wash cloth in her hands on her way to the spring which was several yards from the cemetery, to wash her hands"[67] after she finished. Judy Bancerowski, Tackett's daughter, recalled her father's graphic miming of how a body might look on arrival, with contorted limbs and mouth agape. In her recollection of her father's account, the minister's wife "would walk slowly with her elbows extended forward, and lower hands and arms at a right angle, pointing up as you would see a surgeon preparing for surgery" as she left to wash her hands.[68]

Figure 6.5 The crowd takes a last look at Viola Hawkins, 1932. Daughter Myrtle, in black dress, leans over to say good-bye to her mother. *Courtesy of the Madison County Historical and Genealogical Society, Huntsville, and John D. Little.*

Even after these ministrations, the deceased was not always an appealing sight. As Columbus Vaughn reminded his readers (Newton County, born 1914), "no cosmetics were used on the departed leaving the corpse looking just as death had rendered it: pallid, ashen, wan and livid."[69] The undertaker's mesh veil, mentioned earlier, helped hide signs of decomposition, but prior to the use of this veil, or in communities lacking access to one, it was the custom to place a piece of fabric over the corpse's face, separate from the practice of placing a wet cloth there overnight. This square would be moved aside when taking the last look and, unlike the mesh veil, was buried with the body. In the case of one drowning, where the body was not found for twelve days, mourners left the fabric in place.

Mollie Williams, following an Austrian custom, gave her daughter Emma a poem pinned to a linen handkerchief on the girl's wedding day (Searcy County, 1890). The poem, titled "The Tear Handkerchief," was read aloud at the girl's wedding and again at her funeral just nine years later, when both were placed in the coffin as Emma had requested. Doing so fulfilled one of her mother's prophetic verses:

When the tender eyes are forever shut
And the loving lips are forever mute.
Then ere the face they loved is hid,
From mortal sight 'neath the coffin lid,

The kerchief, stained with the young bride's tears,
So carefully guarded for many years,
Is gently laid over the features pale
At death's cold bridal—a bridal veil—
And the kerchief laid so long away,
Hides the calm, still face on the burial day.[70]

Placing fabric over the corpse's face was also described by Opal Arnold Taylor, who wrote that a silk handkerchief was used when her two-year-old brother died (Searcy County, 1917). One of her father's farmworkers rode to Marshall to buy the requisite handkerchief to cover little Johnnie Luther's face. "Daddy kneeled down by the little coffin, and put his arm around me and my brother Ruff. . . . He lifted the handkerchief . . . and laid it back on his hair, and he said, 'Now look at your little brother for the last time on earth. You'll never see him again until Heaven.'"[71]

This leave-taking was generally accompanied by unrestrained expressions of grief. "In those days people hadn't learned to accept death philosophically and went into hysterics," recalled Nora Davis Standlee (Carroll County, born about 1895). She added, "Children not old enough to understand the situation would weep because their elders wept."[72] Jessie Bryant (Washington County, 1930s) described the expressions of grief that upset her as a child, growing up in Fayetteville's African American community. "Everybody viewed the body, then the families screamed and screamed and screamed. That was acceptable," she recalled. "We had professional mourners in the community," said Burr Fancher (Madison County, 1930s) of whites, noting that one woman in particular attended every funeral. "She'd try to bring comfort to the family, but yet she would cry and carry on, on their behalf I guess."

A Desire to See Death in All Its Forms

Not everyone who showed up at a death scene came to help. Some came to gawk at accidents, violent deaths, and decomposition; in fact, there was a positive relish for such sights. The doctor who arrived after Martha Swaney was shot (Washington County, 1889) could hardly enter her house as it was packed with "the most eager and excited collection of men and women ever seen together in Springdale,"[73] and such behavior was not unusual. Suicides (who had to be left untouched until a coroner's jury could convene to examine the scene), and those who died of horrible injuries, were viewed by scores of people. When Curtis Graham was murdered in the heat of August (Madison

County, 1922), "a big crowd watched as he was brought out" of the cave where he was found several days later.[74]

As if people didn't get enough exposure to bodies at funerals, the public also desired to look at famous—or infamous—corpses, so undertakers thoughtfully displayed the bodies of criminals, killed while committing a crime, in their show windows. Public hangings (discussed in chapter 11) attracted large crowds of spectators, with the executed body displayed afterward. For those who missed A. J. Hudspeth's hanging (Boone County, 1892), a reporter for the *Mountain Wave* (Searcy County) thoughtfully provided a description of the remains. "The features were not distorted as I expected; but retained a calm, quiet expression, in contrast to the sharp rigid expression that characterized the countenance before the black cap was adjusted."[75]

Finally, there was the business of viewing exhumed bodies, as happened when graves were moved. When the family of Sarah Whitlock decided to move their child's body a dozen or more years after her death (Marion County, 1869 or 1870) her sister later described what she saw. "My sister's face with the exception of the flesh being dried on the bones presented a natural appearance. All the features showed distinctly. A few locks of hair had become detached from the head but with the exceptions of that the hair and its dressing had retained its shape and color. The ear rings had dropped from the ears and lay in the bottom of the coffin."[76] Lest it appear that a fascination with bodily deterioration was unique to the Ozarks, Boston, Massachusetts, sexton L. M. Sargent published a memoir in 1856. Women, he observed, had an especially strong desire to "descend into the damp and dreary tomb—to lift the lid—and look upon the changing, softening, corrupting features of a parent or a child—to gaze upon the mouldering bones."[77]

Even a hardened sexton might have been shocked by the treatment given to two girls' remains (Washington County, 1901 and 1903). Sometime before 1901, Maud Dunlap Duncan's eighteen-month-old daughter Virginia died from dysentery. Her other child, six-year-old Helen, was so traumatized by her sister's burial that the girl made her grandmother promise she would never permit an in-ground burial for her. In 1903 Helen died of brain fever and the girls' grandmother—who, by then, had legally adopted Helen—kept her promise. She had Helen's body embalmed and placed in a casket with a glass top, and exhumed the coffin containing the baby, now merely a diapered skeleton. Both bodies were placed in a spare room of the grandparents' home until a mausoleum could be built. Two years later this structure developed a leak, and the soaked caskets were returned to the home until a new mausoleum could be constructed.

Figure 6.6 Men lift the lid onto the coffin of Viola Hawkins, 1932. The lid contains both decorative coffin hardware and nails, partially driven into the lid in advance and ready to be hammered into place. *Courtesy of the Madison County Historical and Genealogical Society, Huntsville, and John D. Little.*

Edna Page, the family's housekeeper, described seeing these children. "The skeleton of the baby was not disturbed, but the body of the older child was still intact. In spite of the fact that the face was covered with mold and the flesh beginning to slough from the bones, the mother and grandmother wiped away the mold. The body was too decomposed to enable them to put a fresh dress on it; the mother combed the hair and replaced the wet, faded ribbons with fresh ones." Page also heard the mortician warn the family not to touch Helen's body because of the embalming fluid (which likely contained arsenic) that had been used.[78]

Some time after this the family moved out, leaving the two bodies behind. The house was turned into a girls' school—named for Helen—and one of the students who attended classes there later recalled that "school was held in other rooms of the house while the bodies were still in the room reserved for that purpose," which the children called "the ghost room."[79] Despite the new mausoleum having been finished, the city of Winslow finally had to take legal action to get the family to place these bodies in it.[80]

Closing the Coffin

The final step before burial was placing the lid on the coffin or, in the case of a casket, closing the upper, hinged half. Not all families used decorative coffin hardware and, as mentioned earlier, these items served no practical purpose. So though coffin screws may have been used to fasten down the lid, long nails (driven partway into the lid in advance) would then be hammered into place. Wooden box vaults were also nailed shut. One boy, listening to men nail down his father's coffin lid (Madison County, 1920s), was heard to say, "I sure do hate to hear them driving them nails."[81]

A baby's death was, of course, an occasion for grief, but an undated newspaper article on Ozark folklore, titled "A Backwoods Buryin,'" described an unusually grim scene. A local schoolteacher and his sister built the baby's coffin, its lid having "big spikes" driven partway into it to save time at the graveside. Once the baby's body had been placed inside, two men carried the box to the cemetery, followed by family and friends.

> They placed two flat stones at the mouth of the yawning grave and deposited the casket on those. Four old crones dolorously began to quaver out the old hymn, "Nearer My God to Thee." Not a prayer was said, nor a scripture read. The coffin was opened, the folk filed past to look for the last time at the baby, then the teacher picked up a hammer, nailed the lid on securely, the sharp ringing blows of the hammer reverberating in a hundred tones as the hills caught up the echoes and tossed them back and forth.[82]

CHAPTER SEVEN

Creating Graves and Graveyards

The leaves cross over our graveyards
    When the cold wind blows and raves
They whirl and scatter on the frozen ground
    Then settle on the sunken graves.

They put me to mind of the children of the earth
    The mournful condition of us all
We are fresh and green in the spring of the year
    And are blown in the grave in the fall.

—Florence Elizabeth Rutherford, 1873–1889
Rutherford Cemetery (Independence County)

One evening, not long after dark, a man stopped at one of the stores in Kingston to ask what was going on in the town's cemetery (Madison County, 1968). As he was passing by he'd noticed lights shining in a far corner of the graveyard, beyond the oldest burials. None of the men present knew what was happening, so they all went to investigate. There they discovered two men digging a grave by the light of their car's headlights. These were the brothers of Sidney Ray ("Bud") Henson, a relative newcomer to the small town, who had arrived after their brother's death and thought they had to get the grave dug in time for his funeral the following day.

"Of course, graves were always dug on the day of the funeral because they didn't want to leave them overnight, it was a superstition," said Phillip Cain, who witnessed the scene. "They didn't know the custom—and they didn't realize people would have dug it the next morning." The local men pitched in, and though Cain helped create any number of graves in that cemetery over the years, "It's the only time I ever dug by lantern."

This story illustrates two important points. Traditionally, Ozark graves were dug by members of the community where, in some towns, it was considered an honor to be asked to dig someone's grave. Second, this work was done *only* on the day of the burial. Men would show up early that morning to begin digging; in fact, far more workers would be on hand than were needed, given that an adult's grave is not long enough to hold more than two men wielding picks and shovels.

Even when a death was clearly imminent, the grave was never dug in advance. To do so invited bad luck or another death in the family or, in some accounts, permitted an evil spirit to enter the grave. According to Orphea Wyatt (Newton County, born 1930), the taboo was taken seriously. "If you'd dug it the day before, they wouldn't put their folks in it," she said of the custom, practiced by many African Americans as well.

This superstition was widespread and flexible. When it was absolutely necessary to dig in advance, workers could leave a token amount of loose dirt in the bottom of the grave, to be removed on the morning of burial. Graves left standing overnight were usually covered with boards, for protection. The boards, and the taboo against digging in advance, both served a purpose in the days of free-ranging livestock, when animals could easily have fallen into an open grave, been injured or killed, and then been difficult to remove.

Logistics

Grave diggers never knew what they would encounter once they started work. Often an older resident who remembered the locations of unmarked graves would oversee the process but even with such help it was not unheard of to dig into an earlier burial. When this happened or if the men ran onto a rock too big to break, they simply filled in the partially dug grave and started over at a new location. Dirt, as it was dug from the grave, was thrown nearby. As the pile rose, wooden rails, like those in a split rail fence, were interlaced to create a pen to keep the dirt in place. Unlike today's burials, this pile was not covered and gave a visual reminder that the body was being returned to the earth.

Ray Wyatt (Newton County, born 1922) helped dig many a grave, and described the process that usually took half a day. "You had to start early of a morning, just with a hoe and a shovel and a pick. You'd hit some rocks, just maybe have a crowbar or something to drive through them. At Kapark Cemetery it was awfully rocky. One time, they had to get dynamite and shoot it out." Old-timers knew enough not to immediately get into the resulting hole,

Figure 7.1 Surrelda Edwards's coffin, covered in black fabric, in Reeves Mt. Cemetery (Madison County), 1941. Dirt from Edwards's grave is piled beside the grave, held in place with split rails that were removed as the grave was filled in. *Courtesy of Loucille Edwards.*

but to first light a sheet of newspaper and drop it into the grave to burn off fumes caused by the explosion.

Clay soil posed a special problem. Cain well remembered the difficulty men had digging one grave on a hot July morning (Madison County, 1950s or earlier). "We started at daylight, as soon as we could see. At three foot deep we hit clay-like stuff, you'd dig with a pick and pull out [soil] just the width of the pick. We worked like fightin' fire." This grave was not finished when the funeral procession arrived, and the casket had to be placed beside the hole during the service, then removed so men could continue digging.

This explains why the oldest cemeteries lack straight rows of graves or, as in the description of an older Pope County cemetery, have graves "laid out helter skelter among the trees."[1] Furthermore, some rural cemeteries followed the practice of burying bodies sequentially as deaths occurred, not in family plots, or buried paupers and the affluent side by side.[2] In later years funeral homes oversaw burials, often hiring just one man to do the digging; in some accounts former convicts were the preferred laborers as it was assumed prison time had acquainted them with hard manual labor. Today backhoes are used to dig graves, although a few older city cemeteries require that graves be dug by hand.

Tradition demands that graves face east. According to Christian belief, Christ will appear in the east at the Resurrection, thus bodies were buried so as to rise facing him, although pagan burials were also oriented toward sunrise.[3] Despite almost all burials facing east, somewhat confusingly the headstones' inscriptions may be turned toward either the east or the west. It helps to use the analogy of the grave as a bed and the tombstone as its headboard; the writing on this headboard can be placed directly above the body, or behind it, facing away, though the burial direction remains the same. Generally speaking, inscriptions on the oldest tombstones face west, enabling visitors to read the writing without walking on the grave (another taboo). In recent times, however, the writing has been positioned directly above the burials, so that both bodies and inscriptions face east. Modern granite markers' large lettering and simple inscriptions are easily read without walking on the grave.

There are exceptions to this rule, such as Catholic cemeteries, which often make use of all available burial space without regard to grave orientation. Then there is the occasional north-south burial in a cemetery where all other graves are oriented to east-west. No single explanation has been found for this, though folklore maintains that murderers are buried facing north.[4] During the Civil War the body of a man, shot in the town of Yellville (Marion County), lay where it fell for three days. Finally local women dug a grave, but "the ladies were not allowed to bury the dead man east and west according [to] burial rites and customs but [Union troops] made them dig the grave north and south or crossways as they termed it,"[5] perhaps as a means of dishonoring the corpse. Other suggestions are that these are the graves of suicides, non-Christians, or foreigners. In the case of an Irish railroad worker, most likely a Catholic (Madison County, 1887), it was thought that the family might someday want to move the remains—the north-south position thus making the grave easier to find, as it was marked only with fieldstones.[6] However, Oak Hill, a family cemetery (Carroll County), contains an entire row of burials oriented north-south, the meaning for this practice long since forgotten.

To be "six feet deep" is a jocular reference to death, but it was rarely feasible to dig so deep a grave by hand. Archaeologists, using ground-penetrating radar to locate older burials, have found many at depths of only three feet. Civil War burials were often, of necessity, even shallower. Still, the deeper the grave, the greater the protection it afforded from animals. According to a story collected just outside the Arkansas Ozarks, Peggy Barnett (White County, born 1868), living near a cemetery, was startled by what she thought were hysterical cries the night of a child's funeral. "People are screaming at the baby's grave. I am going to see if I can help them," she told neighbors, who persuaded her to stay home. "The next morning they found that the panthers had dug down to the box of the child that had been buried the day before."[7]

Vaulted Grave Shafts

Long before vaults were available, vaulted grave shafts were used to protect coffins. A conventional, rectangular grave shaft would be dug, with a level floor; into this floor would be dug a second grave, one in the exact shape of the coffin. Once the coffin had been placed in this cavity it would be covered over with boards, and the grave filled in.

According to the Arkansas Archeological Survey the origins of the practice are not well understood, but could be related to a British practice of placing a board over the top of the coffin prior to burial. This piece of wood, called a "coffin board," protected the burial container from dirt, from future digging (should a second coffin be interred above it), and spared mourners the sound of dirt being shoveled directly onto the lid. Though the custom was described in England in 1890, it was in use in America about a century before that, the earliest example coming from a Jamestown, Virginia, excavation of a burial having a death date between 1750 and 1780.[8]

Silas Turnbo gave descriptions of two Civil War burials where bodies were placed in vaulted graves without coffins,[9] while a very late account comes from John Harvell (Izard County, 1912). As a child he witnessed his mother's burial and, "I remember that a vault like place was in the bottom of the grave in the shape of a casket."[10] Ulis Morrison discovered that his family once used this burial method when he oversaw the exhumation and relocation of his great-grandfather's remains (Stone or Searcy County, burial late 1860s). Morrison watched while three feet of soil was excavated before the diggers hit a floor of solid rock, into which a hexagonal coffin shape had been carefully chiseled. "The sides of the walls were just as smooth as could be," Morrison marveled. "Someone took a lot of pains smoothing up the sides of the vault that they buried him in."

Frozen Ground, Watery Graves

"On Tuesday, notwithstanding the fact that the earth was sheathed with a heavy sheet of ice . . . the beautiful white casket that contained the deceased was placed in the hearse, protected from the sleet and rain and was followed by the family," according to Julia May Mason's obituary (Benton County, 1910).[11] City cemeteries in the northern United States, where winters are long and severe, had buildings known as holding vaults, where casketed bodies were held until graves could be dug in the spring, but this practice was unnecessary in the temperate Ozarks. Graves were dug even during cold winters, though diggers sometimes had to dynamite the frozen ground,[12] or light a fire to thaw the soil.[13] In extremely cold weather only the grave diggers would be at the gravesite; family members stayed home.

"Happy is the bride that the sun shines on; / Blessed are the dead that the rain falls on," goes the saying that, according to Vance Randolph, all Ozark residents once knew by heart. Rain at a funeral, he wrote, "is the best possible omen, since it means that the dead man's soul is at rest, and even a few drops of rain at this time go further to comfort the bereaved family than anything the 'preacher man' can do or say."[14] Though a good omen, a prolonged downpour could put the living at risk from rising streams. Country roads had few bridges spanning creeks, which could rise rapidly and dangerously—as numerous obituaries attest. Then, too, according to some folklore, allowing rain to get into an open grave invited another death in the family within the year.[15] This explains Lydia Moser Rider's recollection that, "there was four men a'standing over there, a'holding a quilt over them caskets," when her mother and uncle were buried, during a light rain, on the same day (Izard County, 1920).[16]

A more serious concern was the problem caused by a high water table or waterlogged soil. Even when water rushed into an open grave as quickly as it could be bailed or pumped out, the body still had to be buried. Poor drainage led to the abandonment of some cemeteries, while others were established specifically to avoid high water tables. Lower Wharton Cemetery (Madison County) was established atop a hill because the area's older burying ground, nearby, had numerous underground springs of water. "When the last person was buried there, they had to stand on the coffin to hold it down until they got enough dirt on top of it, because there was so much water that the coffin kept floating up," according to Elizabeth Phillips Montgomery (prior to 1933), who witnessed this event.[17]

Despite numerous stories of coffins submerged in water, one of Mary Parler's folklore students (city of Van Buren, 1958) collected the superstition that "To bury a corpse in a grave that had water in it meant another death in the family would occur in a short time."[18] Among the black community of Pine Bluff (Jefferson County, outside the Ozarks), there was a special superstition to counteract this. According to Pearl St. Clair (born 1891), as soon as death occurred, all containers of water in the home would be emptied to ensure the grave would not be a wet one.[19]

Figure 7.2 Tommie Hoskins and family at Decoration Day in Pine Grove Cemetery (Madison County), 1940s. The practice of mounding graves with fresh dirt is evident throughout this cemetery. *Courtesy of Tommie L. Hoskins Mooney Collection.*

Scraped, Mounded Graves

The Upland South, which encompasses the Ozark Mountains, is defined by numerous cultural traits (speech patterns, log construction of houses and barns) including, most significantly, its cemeteries. These are characterized by scraped and mounded graves, east-west grave orientation, certain decorations on the burials, gravehouses, introduced vegetation, and traditions of respect, such as Decoration Day. In addition, these graveyards are almost always fenced,[20] something necessary to protect them from free-ranging livestock. All of these traits were in place in the South by the 1830s,[21] although some traditions are now extremely rare, and certain burial practices are extinct.

A scraped and mounded grave is one where loose earth—or, in recent times sand, gravel, or small stones—has been placed in a large pile atop the length of the burial. If the grave should sink, due to the collapse of the coffin, additional dirt is added to maintain the pile. Grass is never permitted to grow on these mounds. The practice has been explained as keeping each grave looking like a recent one, which both respects the deceased's memory and serves as a *memento mori* for the living. Mounding kept fresh burials from being dug into by animals and may have been a safeguard against the southern superstition that "When a grave sinks early, another will follow soon."[22]

Such graves are found across the Ozarks, both in isolated cemeteries or, where not practiced by all members of a community, within some family plots. One trade publication for monument dealers (published 1934) somewhat self-servingly tried to end the practice, writing that a mounded grave "serves no purpose save to indicate the grave below" and was not needed once tombstones became available.[23] However, mounds are always used in addition to, and not in place of, tombstones.

Siting Cemeteries

"We truly hope that it is not the intention of anyone to disturb a cemetery because the pioneer settlers seen fit to select the best plots of ground in which to put away their dead friends and relatives," wrote Turnbo, decrying a farmer's cultivation of land that had been a family cemetery as early as 1822.[24] This highlights an important point: graveyards are situated on some of the finest— and most scenic—land in the Ozarks, in keeping with the custom of the living giving the best they have to offer to the dead.

One important characteristic of Upland South graveyards is that they are usually situated on high ground.[25] Historian Alan Jabbour gives four reasons for choosing an elevation: a desire to reserve fertile bottomland for crops, to avoid digging into underground water sources, to avoid erosion by using relatively level land (at the top of a ridge), and to place loved ones "closer to heaven."[26] However, Jeremy Pye, studying cemetery placement patterns in Crawford County, analyzed slope, elevation, proximity to water, and soil type without finding a correlation between these factors and cemetery locations. After studying 171 graveyards, Pye concluded, "the cemeteries that fall within the Boston Mountains occurred on every directional aspect, and showed no tendencies for any particular view." Overall, the most "productive variable" seemed to be the cemetery's proximity to an existing community.[27]

Lacking additional studies, it's hard to say whether these findings hold true for the rest of the Arkansas Ozarks. There are, however, numerous anecdotal accounts to explain why and where certain cemeteries were founded. First, ones located on high elevations were memorable and visible from a distance. Travelers, en route to Texas, buried bodies in McKinney Cemetery, near Ozark (Franklin County), and the cemetery's location atop a steep, unusually shaped hill was a visual mnemonic for those who wanted to find it again.[28] It was always preferable for travelers to bury in an established cemetery, something one-year-old Fannie Lex Bynum's mother worried about, when her daughter became deathly ill during the family's travels from Alabama to Arkansas (1868). "I knew she was going to die, there wasn't any way," Nina Zoe Davis Blair quoted her grandmother as saying. The family was passing a cemetery and decided to camp there while they waited for the child to die. Blair remembered the rationale: "If we have to leave Lex I'd rather leave her in a cemetery. If we get out on the road, we'd just have to leave her on the road somewhere."²⁹ The Bynum baby recovered, but not all traveling families were so fortunate; some had to bury their dead beside the road.

Another explanation is that cemeteries were situated in locations that had meaning for, or gave pleasure to, the living. One was established on the site where a man killed his last buck deer (Madison County, 1852),³⁰ another in the pasture where a stockman kept his prized horses and cattle (Marion County, some time before 1929).³¹ Five-year-old John Ingram (Randolph County, 1849) told his nursemaid, "When I die, I want to be buried here, where the wind blows a cool breeze and there's lots of shade," and a short time later his grave started the Ingram family's cemetery.³²

One of the earliest accounts of a cemetery's founding is that of Prairie Grove (Washington County, 1831), after Percilla Inman, visiting from Tennessee, died at nearby Cane Hill. "On her death bed she requested to be carried back to the prairie and buried among the flowers." Men at work building a combined school and church saw horsemen riding across the prairie carrying picks and spades and, after investigating this, Rev. Andrew Buchanan chose a gravesite northwest of the new building; later that afternoon he performed Inman's funeral.³³

Individual families, even those living in cities, established burying grounds on their own land long before there were public cemeteries. Given how laborious and time-consuming it was to transport a body any distance, it's easy to see how these private cemeteries came to be used by other members of the community. As cities grew, town fathers, or various fraternal lodges, established cemeteries for the use of the citizens, often with a potter's field in which to bury indigents, located in the least desirable portion of the grounds. In some cases families chose to forbid burials, as when Jane and George Washington Miser deeded a portion of their land, containing a spring, to trustees of the Methodist Episcopal South Church (Benton County, 1853). The deed included a provision, that "for the purpose of keeping the water pure and healthy, the above-mentioned men entered into the contract and agreed . . . that no dead body of any human being shall be entered on said tract of land given."³⁴

Batesville (Independence County) claims the distinction of having the state's earliest public graveyard, now called the Memorial Park Cemetery. The earliest legible tombstone there, for Jane Kinman ("Consort of Billy Kinman"), has a death date of 1816—two decades before Arkansas became a state. The town's first plat map, drawn in 1821, shows this cemetery lying well outside of town but by the mid-1860s this space was so full that "it was not uncommon when digging a new grave, to dig into the remains of another." Today the small graveyard is completely encircled by downtown city streets and buildings.[35]

None of the cemeteries in the Ozarks that were formally laid out was done in the popular style of the "garden" or "rural" cemetery typified by Boston's Mt. Auburn, established in 1831 and widely copied. Characteristics of this style include rolling, landscaped grounds, winding roadways, lush vegetation, ponds or fountains, and ornate, massive grave markers. Though this style did not reach the Ozarks, Arkansans visited these tourist attractions when they traveled and sent back glowing descriptions in letters.

Moving Graves

A desire to own land prompted Americans to leave settled communities and move westward. While Arkansans were hardly cut off from the relatives they had left behind, their tombstones still reflect the separation brought about by distance and death. "Asleep in Jesus far from me, / My kindred and their graves may be," begins one popular 1800s epitaph. Though death tore the family unit asunder, relatives went to extraordinary lengths to keep it intact within the confines of the cemetery. One man, Catlett Fitch, traveled to Little Rock to retrieve his father's body and bring it home to Madison County (1870s), which reportedly took three months and involved fording the Arkansas River.[36] Catholics also transported bodies great distances by wagon, in order to bury their dead in the consecrated ground of a church cemetery (Randolph County, starting in 1869).[37]

Others solved the problem by returning home to die. When the Thompson family, living in California, learned their twelve-year-old daughter had less than a month to live, the mother brought her child back to Marshall, Arkansas, by train, to be sure of burying her in their family plot (Searcy County, 1906). One month later Bessie died of complications from measles.[38] Nannie Richardson, despite having lived in Oklahoma for ten years, realized she was near death and returned to her former home of Ozark (Franklin County, 1909) so she could be buried in the town cemetery.[39]

It was also possible to exhume and move any person who died far from home. Though both English and Ozark folklore collections state that it is bad luck to move a grave, sextons' and funeral homes' records show a veritable parade of bodies being dug up and moved in the early 1900s. Disinterment cost far more than the original burial. Itemized records of Fayetteville's Evergreen Cemetery (Washington County, 1904–1919) list charges of $2.50 to dig an infant's grave and, at the start of the ledger, $5 to dig an adult's grave, but by the time the ledger ends, adult burials cost from $8 to $18 (children's burials remained about the same). The fees to exhume a grave during this time period do not follow any particular pattern. "Taking Miss Hannah up" cost $62 in 1906 (which included a $30 vault), but a few years later three graves (one for a baby) were moved at $25 apiece, and by 1919 adult exhumations cost from $35 to $50. At the other end of the scale, grave digger J. F. Moore charged just fifty cents to bury an amputated arm in 1912.[40]

The practice of exhuming and moving bodies ended with the advent of affordable embalming, which made it possible to ship remains by train. According to funeral director Tom Olmstead (Cleburne County), lots of bodies were shipped back from California at the end of World War II. "The people in Arkansas were notorious for going to California for work in the Defense plants, to make better money," he explained. "They established a residency, but when they died they wanted to be shipped back here for burial in the family plot."[41]

Shipping bodies was such an everyday occurrence there was even a song on the subject, titled "The Express Office." In it, an elderly father arrives at a train station and says to the clerk, "I'm lookin' for my boy, sir, / He's comin' home today," only to be told that he's come to the freight office, and should go to the depot. No, the father informs the clerk, his son will be among the freight, not the passengers because, "He's comin' home in a casket, sir, / He's comin' to us dead."[42]

Some bodies were buried and exhumed repeatedly, something more likely to happen to famous corpses,[43] such as Archibald Yell, who was interred in a Mexican War battlefield graveyard, the yard of his Fayetteville home (both in 1847) and, in 1872, in Evergreen Cemetery. It is the non-famous dead, however, who make better stories, such as traveler E. G. Axtell, who died from natural causes in the back of a wagon (Washington County, 1907). Upon the discovery that Axtell was from La Harpe, Kansas, a telegram was sent to notify his wife. No reply was forthcoming, and due to the August heat the body was buried in Springdale's city cemetery. Three days later Mrs. Axtell arrived on the train, accompanied by her undertaker. The body was exhumed but deemed too deteriorated to embalm. A plan to place it in a metal-lined box for the trip back to Kansas also failed when, en route to the train, someone noticed that the box was leaking, so Axtell's body was reburied in Bluff Cemetery. There is no record of him there now, so presumably his widow oversaw the third exhumation and reburial of her husband, as she had intended.[44]

History repeated itself just three years later when Frank Cochran's badly damaged body was found near the Winslow railroad tracks (Washington

County, 1910). Cochran's widow, in St. Louis, telegraphed that the body should be sent to Kansas for burial but did not remit funds for embalming and shipping. Cochran was buried locally but the money must have arrived, as he was later exhumed, embalmed, and sent to Kansas, perhaps made possible because he had died in early March.[45]

One wonders if local undertakers were familiar with claims made by the Egyptian Chemical Co., manufacturer of the "Oriental" embalming fluid. In an 1885 testimonial a St. Louis morgue superintendent said he'd embalmed a man "whose remains were found packed in a trunk in the Southern Hotel" using their product, thereby undoing the worst case of decomposition the superintendent had ever dealt with.[46]

African American Cemeteries

According to historian D. Gregory Jeane, writing about southern culture, while African American cemeteries shared some cultural traditions with white ones, a major difference was that they were not as well maintained.[47] While there may be clear differences between blacks' burials and well-funded city cemeteries, up through the Depression most small, rural white cemeteries (including those in towns) were not kept mowed, either, except just prior to Decoration Day, and even some city cemeteries did not receive professional upkeep until the 1950s.

Practically every county that once had slave inhabitants is said to have abandoned slave cemeteries, their locations now lost. But even some whites' overgrown burying grounds have disappeared. "North of the old log barn about one hundred feet there was a row of graves, mostly infants. It was a dark scary place to me, overgrown with brambles, persimmons and big thick cedars. . . . I was too afraid to push my way into the brambles," wrote Jewell Willey Phillips, describing her family's original burying grounds (Johnson County, writing in 1977). The writer's great-grandmother had, decades earlier, found the place so depressing that she requested burial in a "lovely wooded glade" she'd discovered, and her burial there (1874) established this white family's new cemetery.[48] The overgrown condition of the original burials would not have been considered disrespectful—or uncommon—among either blacks or whites.

There were no absolutes concerning where blacks were buried. African Americans, first as slaves, then freedmen and -women, have been interred in all-black cemeteries, in segregated sections within white cemeteries or, more rarely, in ones that were thoroughly integrated. There are also accounts of slave owners burying slaves alongside their own family members. And, as so often happened with white bodies, a single black burial could lead to the establishment of a cemetery for both blacks and whites.[49]

Eureka Springs's cemetery (Carroll County, founded 1889) was integrated from the beginning. There, blacks could buy plots anywhere within the grounds, lie side by side with whites in the potters' field, or share plots with them. Henry Jones was the minister of the African Methodist Episcopal Church (which he helped found in the 1890s), and though the spot is unmarked he and his wife were buried in the family plot of Jones's white counterpart, the minister of the town's Methodist Episcopal Church South.[50]

Some blacks were buried in white cemeteries but kept at a remove. Former slave Mariah Fancher, first owned then employed by the Fancher family, was buried atop a hillside within the confines of the Fancher family's cemetery (Carroll County, 1901). Her grave commands the highest, driest ground with the best view, but the inclusion of the word "colored" on her tombstone, and its separation from the rest of the family, argues for intentional segregation. In other families, whites deemed it an honor for a faithful black servant to be buried beside them. Amanda Thornton, born a slave and later the "life time colored companion" of Mrs. J. L. Shinn, was buried in the Shinn family plot "at the foot of her mistress' grave" in Oakland Cemetery (Pope County, 1932).[51] The Blakeleys managed to bury Adeline Blakeley, a former slave of the family, in their plot in Evergreen Cemetery (Washington County, 1945) by keeping her casket closed and telling the groundskeeper of this whites-only cemetery that she was their aunt. They then added her name and dates to their communal marker.

Lowering the Coffin, Filling in the Grave

Once the coffin lid had been fastened, pallbearers carried the box to the open grave and lowered it down. The term *pallbearer* is related to "pall," a large piece of fabric spread over the coffin during the funeral. Few references to palls have been found in the Ozarks, although it was once popular to carve tombstones as though partially draped with fringed fabric. Child pallbearers sometimes conveyed deceased playmates, siblings, or Sunday School classmates to the grave, though the caskets of infants were usually transported in the arms or on the shoulder of a family member. A dying person occasionally requested that friends serve as pallbearers, but usually men in the community performed the role.

Figure 7.3 Viola Hawkins's coffin being carried to the grave, Kingston (Madison County), 1932. Handles, though present, were merely decorative and pallbearers carried coffins from the bottom edge. *Courtesy of the Madison County Historical and Genealogical Society, Huntsville, and John D. Little.*

It was so rare for family to do this job that, when it happened, obituaries made note. At the conclusion of R. S. Woods's funeral (Benton County, 1901), his minister, Peter Carnahan, did something out of the ordinary. "I asked these sons, who had been so often led by the hand of their father or carried by him in his arms to the sanctuary, to act as pallbearers and bear his body out of the church to the carriage that was to carry him to his last resting place," Carnahan wrote. The seven sons "cheerfully complied, leaving a deeply solemn and impressive influence upon the whole audience."[52]

Figure 7.4 Men use ropes to lower Dwain Cook's coffin into its grave, Kingston (Madison County), 1934. *Photo courtesy of Charlene Grigg.*

Long and sturdy ropes were needed to lower the coffin down into the grave. Though Turnbo described a Civil War burial where, lacking rope, pallbearers used three strips of hickory bark (Howell County, Missouri, 1865),[53] traditionally ropes, or the lines from a wagon harness (usually eighteen or twenty feet long), were used. A couple of small pieces of wood would be placed on the underside of the casket or the inside of a wooden vault to provide a gap that permitted the lines to be pulled out after use, though according to Coy Ford (Newton County, late 1950s and early 1960s), ropes used to lower the casket were never pulled back out but were buried with it. Undertakers, instead, used a mechanical lowering device for this job.

Children sometimes tossed sprigs of evergreen into their schoolmates' graves, perhaps in imitation of a Masonic tradition, and in some parts of the Ozarks the "rose and dust" rite was performed. "The minister, taking some rose petals or dust in his hand says, 'We therefore commend his soul to God

Figure 7.5 Millie Elizabeth Sharp's coffin, Goshen Cemetery (Washington County), 1941, covered in artificial turf, called funeral grass. Placing artificial grass over the coffin was done by the funeral industry to symbolize the burial, sparing mourners seeing the casket lowered and the grave refilled. *Courtesy Shiloh Museum of Ozark History/Geneva Worley Collection (S-97-2-336).*

and commit his body to the ground, earth to earth (here are dropped some rose petals or dirt), ashes to ashes (and again are dropped petals or dirt), dust to dust (dropping petals or dust again)."[54]

There was no rule concerning who filled in the grave. Sometimes family members helped, as happened in Fayetteville's African American community in the 1930s, while elsewhere the men who dug the grave also refilled it. James Rutherford, speaking of Batesville (Independence County, prior to 1960), said this job was left to the pallbearers, after family left the cemetery. "That's a hot job. Usually there were not enough shovels. I have never seen enough shovels, usually two or three. Pallbearers would take turns—the rest of us would sit by and encourage them!"[55]

Despite this account, Ozark folklore dictates that it was very bad luck for anyone to leave the cemetery before the final shovelful of earth had been placed on the grave. To do otherwise invited another death or bad luck. It was also unlucky to take anything out of a cemetery, so floral tributes and their containers were always left behind, which explains one description of an isolated Pope County graveyard, where "parts of antique water glasses, bowls, and vases remained near some of the graves."[56]

Today mourners no longer remain to see the grave filled in, but there was a transition period between the modern custom and the era when everyone stayed. During this transition, funeral directors devised a bit of graveside showmanship to help mourners acknowledge the reality of burial without actually witnessing it. This involved the green carpeting undertakers placed around the gravesite,[57] or, later, artificial turf called "funeral grass" that was used to cover any raw dirt and make walking easier. Though this ceremony is no longer performed, Tom Olmstead remembered it well. "Pallbearers would place the casket on the lowering device, trip the device and the casket would go down about ground level. You'd have a piece of the funeral grass, pick it up by the corner, and use it to cover the lowering device and all, like the grave was going to look in years to come." This sent the message, Olmstead said, that "Dad is underground, it's final. We'll not see the casket any more."[58]

Amputated Limbs

The Christian belief that the body will rise out of its grave at the Resurrection might seem to explain the careful burial of body parts following an accident or amputation. There was even an epitaph to this effect, taken from a hymn written by Isaac Watts (early 1700s), "Great God, I Own Thy Sentence Just," quoted here in its original language:

> Though greedy worms devour my skin,
> And gnaw my wasting flesh,
> When God shall build my bones again,
> He clothes them all afresh.[59]

Certainly this was the belief, and the only way to explain the actions of a mother whose son died following an appendectomy (Boone County, 1909). The woman had her son's body exhumed so his appendix could be placed in the coffin, on the grounds that "it should find a resting place with the body."[60]

Where superstition is concerned, all Randolph has to say is that if a severed limb is not buried, "the owner will return after death in a mutilated condition and be forced to search for the lost member through all eternity."[61] (Given that during the Civil War, "amputees from Pea Ridge were a dime a dozen,"[62] northwest Arkansas ought to be overrun with ghosts searching for their long-lost appendages.) Faith and folklore aside, there was one very practical reason for properly burying a severed limb: having access to it in the future. The only known cure for phantom limb pain—the uncomfortable burning, itching, or tingling in the missing limb, as though it were still present—was to dig up the body part and turn it over or straighten it out, so that it would "rest" more comfortably.

Figure 7.6 Tombstone for Alva Greer's arm, amputated in 1882, the stone signed by the tombstone carver. Greer lived another ten years following the amputation. Highland Cemetery, Ozark (Franklin County). *Photo by Abby Burnett.*

People went to great lengths to retrieve buried limbs for this purpose, illustrated by the story of Robert Anderson Walker, who had only a sharp ax with which to defend himself against four bushwhackers (Benton County, 1860s). He decapitated one robber and severed the arm of another before the men fled.

> The bushwhacker, whose arm was severed, escaped and made his way back to his home in Missouri. One day, some of his family members came to the Robert A. Walker home, saying that the one-armed man was suffering phantom pains from his armless joint. They asked if they might dig up the buried arm. The request was granted, and they found it being disturbed by bugs. The problem was remedied, and the family took the arm back to Missouri for reburial.[63]

As a child, Bruce Vaughan witnessed a similar attempt to ease phantom limb pain. After Melessia Pruner was injured in an accident and her leg amputated, the local coffin maker built a box to bury it in (Washington County, some time prior to 1951). Later, the site of the amputation began to hurt. A local woman "explained to Mrs. Pruner that the cause of the pain was that her buried leg was turned in the wrong position. She assured Mrs. Pruner that if she would dig up the leg and reposition it in the box, her pain would disappear." Though skeptical, Pruner had this done. "Her pain did seem to be much better—for a short time. As you might expect, the pain returned. Again she had the leg dug up and repositioned before re-burying."[64]

There are accounts (one as recent as the 1960s) of severed legs, arms, feet, and fingers being dug up—often repeatedly—to bring relief to their owners. Parler's folklore students recorded that a severed limb must not be buried in a crooked or bent position (otherwise the stump will hurt) and must be buried in a box or casket to keep ants from crawling on it.[65] This is logical, given that one type of phantom limb pain mimics the feeling of ants crawling and in another, the feeling is that the missing hand is in a painful, clenched position.

Not all limbs and their owners were reunited in death; there are accounts of a body part being buried in one cemetery and its owner interred in another. Still, efforts were made to keep such things organized. In Ozark's Highland Cemetery (Franklin County), the Greer family plot is filled with tombstones carved with clasping hands and pointing fingers. At one end of Alva Greer's grave is a tiny marker carved with clasping hands; on the back are the words: "Alva's arm/amputated Nov. 3, 1882." Alva lost his arm in a sawmill accident; over ten years later he was buried in the plot with it.

CHAPTER EIGHT

Marking the Graves

No pompous marble to thy name we raise,
This humble stone bespeaks thy praise.
Parental fondness did thy life attend—
A tender mother and a faithful friend.

—Rhoda H. Jordan, 1809–1872
Hindsville Cemetery (Madison County)

Picking out a loved one's tombstone was more involved than just giving the deceased's name and dates to a carver. It also meant choosing from among the popular mourning motifs of the day that included doves, lambs, flowers, anchors, draperies, and hands. Occasionally the family chose a motif that was both literal and redundant: a tiny representation of a tombstone carved *on* the tombstone. In one example a bearded man points at a tiny obelisk labeled "My wife," in another, a woman bows her head beside a little tablet inscribed "In Memory." Even some epitaphs, verses on a stone expressing loss or mourning, mention "this perishing stone" or note how the deceased's virtues "and not this stone shall be his monument."

These self-referential devices call attention to the fact that the grave is marked with an actual stone. Such a thing was a huge improvement over the wooden grave markers once the norm in Arkansas cemeteries before there were professional stone carvers. The origins of this custom are found in the wooden "coffin posts" or "coffin rails" that marked Puritan graves in the 1600s.[1]

Marking graves was scarcely possible during the Civil War, especially for civilians. Soldiers were buried in trenches, though officers were buried individually, their graves sometimes enclosed by rails to protect and identify the site. Only the winning side had the luxury of ensuring proper burials, and while the Battle of Prairie Grove (Washington County, 1862) was considered a tactical draw, the Union side was in possession of the battlefield when it ended. A Union soldier with the Nineteenth Iowa regiment, John M. Wyatt, described the burials in a poem, later set to music:

> Now the battle is all over and our soldiers rest from toil.
> So carefully we placed our dead beneath the Southern soil.
> We placed them all in order, as formed on dress parade,
> And placed a board at each man's head to mark where he was laid.[2]

Capt. Edward G. Miller, who oversaw these burials, wrote that every grave was marked with a headboard carved with the deceased's name and regiment.[3] These bodies would later be moved to Fayetteville's National Cemetery.

Wooden headboards made sense during wartime, but as late as 1875, more than three decades after it was founded and a quarter-century after a local monument dealer had established a business, Little Rock's Mount Holly Cemetery was still using them. During this time a number of wooden boards and plot markers were destroyed due to the groundskeeper's practice of removing grass and other vegetation by burning it off.[4] It is still possible to find remnants of wooden headboards in some of the Ozarks' oldest cemeteries.

Professional Carvers

The wide variety of markers and grave coverings, clustered in the oldest sections of the oldest cemeteries, would tend to suggest that graves were being marked from a very early period, but such was not usually the case. One source claimed that carved tombstones did not come into common usage until about 1890 (Searcy County),[5] and certainly there were few carvers, other than stonemasons with a sideline, working in the Ozarks prior to the Civil War. This means many of the oldest burials were marked decades after the deaths occurred, something known as backdating.

Contemporary grave diggers maintain that it was once the custom to mark graves with the largest rock found when digging the shaft, or with one whose shape made it memorable. The latter would aid families hoping to someday acquire a professionally carved stone. Wealthy residents of the Ozarks often ordered from Missouri carvers, and the firm of Rosebrough Sons (St. Louis, established 1842) sent more stones, across a wider area, than any of its competitors. The work of Little Rock's James and Renton Tunnah, however, rarely found its way north.

Figure 8.1 Tombstone carver's sample stone, made about 1890, covered front and back with the most popular symbols of the day for customers to choose from. *Photo by Abby Burnett.*

Carvers were so scarce immediately after the Civil War that when Berryville educator Isaac A. Clarke (Carroll County, 1868) wanted to mark a friend's grave he had a hard time finding anyone to make a stone. Clarke finally found a local marble source and corresponded with someone who had seen an engraver's sample. A year after agreeing to pay $25 the marker was still not in place, but someone finally completed the job because Eliza Berry's stone grave covering contains a portion of a professionally carved marble tablet built into one end.[6] Clarke hadn't skimped on the price, either, as $10 was the standard fee for a basic marker up through the 1890s.

Monument companies would eventually establish permanent businesses in the larger towns, but until about 1900 tombstone carvers were itinerants who moved from place to place, quarrying stone near where it was needed. Once all tombstone work was exhausted (including marking burials dating back several decades), a carver had to move on to find more work. Most men signed their creations, but few added a business location as this was subject to change.

Figure 8.2 Tombstone made and signed by carver Nick Miller, Bluff Cemetery (Washington County). Miller's stones have been found in at least eight counties in the Arkansas Ozarks, as well as in southern Missouri. *Photo by Abby Burnett.*

The life of Nick Miller, a German immigrant (1846?–1898), is a case in point. Miller's signed tombstones are found in eight Arkansas counties as well as in southern Missouri, he established marble yards at least five times, and he trained numerous apprentices. Most often, however, he merely passed through an area, staying long enough to fill all available tombstone orders. Miller was well liked and well thought of, but he followed through on his plan to commit suicide after an extended period of heavy drinking (Carroll County, 1898).[7] His suicide note, besides naming three former apprentices who might be willing to buy his equipment, explained why he was ending his life. "I . . . am simply tired of making so many new starts in life," he wrote. "My body and mind are both sick and tired."[8]

Successful monument makers had to possess an unusual and diverse skill set. In addition to physical strength needed to quarry, carve, haul, and erect heavy tombstones, carvers had to have sculpting and lettering ability, a good business sense, and the patience to deal with grieving families. Most

Figure 8.3 "Goddess of Liberty" statue carved by Lucy J. Daniel and given to the Civil War veterans at their reunion at Pea Ridge National Military Park (Benton County), 1889. The statue, called the first monument honoring the perpetual friendship between the two sides, incorporates traditional tombstone symbolism. *Photo by Abby Burnett.*

augmented their offerings by also making building stones, marble tabletops and mantels, fireplace lintels, vases, urns, and cemetery coping; some made stone slabs used by tanneries.

Some time after 1880 the *Monumental News*, a national trade journal, searched for female tombstone carvers but located just three. One of these was Lucy J. Daniel, who had learned to carve from her father, Isom Daniel. The two opened a business in Springdale (Washington County, 1883–1886), where Lucy managed the marble shop and lettered and polished tombstones. The family moved their business to Missouri, but Isom and Lucy returned to Arkansas for the reunion of Union and Confederate veterans at Pea Ridge Battlefield (Benton County, 1889), where Lucy carved a female statue titled the "Goddess of Liberty." The statue, unveiled by her father, a Union veteran, is embellished with symbols commonly found on tombstones: a wreath of lilies and roses, an upraised finger (pointing to the words, "Angel Aloft"), and

Figure 8.4 Monument business of N. L. Burkhardt, Eureka Springs (Carroll County), 1925. Permanent monument yards were established in larger towns starting around 1900; prior to that most carvers were itinerants who traveled from town to town seeking work. *Bank of Eureka Springs Historic Museum Photo Collection.*

clasping hands, their cuffs labeled "The Blue" and "The Gray" beneath the words, "A reunited soldiery."[9] Though disparaged by the press, the statue was called the nation's first memorial to reunification.

The *Monumental News* concluded that, while many women ran marble businesses, ones who carved were scarce. This was attributed to their practice of stopping work when they married. As the third woman in the profile hinted coyly, "I love my trade and expect to follow it as long as my name is Miss Pearl Sams."[10] Nor did Lucy, who eventually returned to Arkansas (Baxter County), list a profession on any census after her name became Mrs. Twig.[11]

By the early 1900s tremendous changes in the monument industry forced itinerant carvers out of business. The public no longer wanted simple, tablet-style tombstones, preferring instead massive granite monuments. These were shipped in by rail from quarries in Georgia, Tennessee, Alabama, Ohio, and Vermont. According to retired carver P. E. Stone (Independence County, 1979), "Granite's hard and you take a good marble cutter, he can't cut granite. And then you take a good granite cutter, they don't like to work marble. It's a trade of its own."[12]

Pneumatic tools were introduced at about the same time and they, too, changed the business; in 1908 Ernest Dorman (Washington County,

1859–1938) advertised that his "pneumatic machinery makes prices the lowest."[13] Arkansas carvers did not begin using the sandblaster until the early 1930s, though it had been advertised in industry publications starting in the early 1900s. Dorman, always eager to try the latest technology, learned that sandblasting was not the timesaver he'd hoped, given the added step of creating and attaching a rubber stencil to the stone.[14] Such changes led to the establishment of permanent monument shops hiring employees who no longer signed their work.

The earliest carvers used newspaper ads to promote imported marble; later advertising stressed speed, accuracy, and quality ("Only the best materials used unless otherwise ordered").[15] One ad even appealed to clients' self esteem in the afterlife: "When you enter the gates of the silent city . . . you could take pride in pointing to a substantial and well-lettered monument if you buy from McGuire, Huntsville" (Madison County, 1913).[16]

Quarries

Some of the Ozarks' oldest grave markers were made from sandstone. Given its name, this is often assumed to be a soft, easily carved rock but depending on the varying compositions of quartz particles and other minerals that make it up, this stone can be extremely hard. As a result, most sandstone markers have weathered better than marble and are still crisply legible today. Dorman told an interviewer that when he started business (1880 or earlier) sandstone was the preferred stone for markers but, because "fashions change in tombstones as in everything else," people later wanted marble and granite, "in spite of the fact that sandstone lasts much longer."[17]

Arkansas had an abundance of stone, but lacked the railroads needed to get it to market. It should be noted that the terms *marble* and *limestone* were once used interchangeably. The quarry industry referred to any limestone that could be polished as "marble," unlike present-day geologists who do not define limestone according to its polishing characteristics.[18] The state's 1890 annual report listed Searcy, Marion, Boone, and Newton counties as having the greatest concentrations of marble, with another six counties having quarries producing building stones.[19] This stone never brought in the revenues optimistically forecast for it, and even within the state the marbles "have had but a limited local use," state geologist John Banner acknowledged in 1890.

The state's most famous piece of stone was the block it contributed to the Washington Monument. In 1836, the same year Arkansas became a state, four Newton County men obtained the commission to quarry a six by four by two-foot rectangle of "marble" (actually variegated limestone) and ship it to Washington, D.C. It was not until 1849, however, that the men pried the massive block from a site now lost, but believed to have been covered over by state highway 7[20] near what later became the town of Marble Falls, named in honor of this stone.[21] The slab was hauled sixty miles over the Boston Mountains to the Arkansas River, sent by barge to New Orleans, then on to Washington, D.C., and eventually incorporated into the interior of the monument.[22] "It is said to be the finest of any [stone] in that monument," bragged one newspaper (Carroll County, 1883).[23]

Though many towns in the Ozarks claimed to have marble deposits, only one quarry was a large-scale success: Pfeiffer Stone Company (Independence County, founded 1836), whose limestone was used to construct numerous large buildings both in and outside the state. In 1899 the Arkansas legislature funded a new state capitol building and, after deciding to construct it from Batesville limestone, the business really took off.[24] One of the company's early brochures (about 1913) listed its products as "mill and dimension blocks, rubble, crushed stone, sawed stone, machine planed mouldings, turned columns and balusters, monumental stock, cut stone for buildings, monument and mausoleum work," beneath the slogan, "The Finest Building Stone Known."[25] This brochure also mentioned that Batesville's "oolitic marble" absorbed significantly less water in immersion tests than granite, marble, or limestone, making it ideal for use in switchboards and electrical devices as it was a good insulator and would not conduct electricity.[26] Despite these diverse products the business could not survive the Depression, and the quarry closed around 1930.[27]

Epitaphs

"A block of sordid marble, cold / Cannot express the warmth of love," begins one epitaph. Maybe a tombstone couldn't express this, but the poetry inscribed on it certainly tried to. These epitaphs came from stone companies' and carvers' books of poetry, hymnals and, as mentioned earlier, memorial card catalogs. Certain well-known poems were often excerpted—Henry Wadsworth Longfellow's "Resignation"[28] was a popular choice—and in later years mail-order companies' tombstone catalogs contained epitaphs that were copied by local carvers. One verse in particular gives today's cemetery visitors a thrill, but is found across the United States and supposedly originated during the Renaissance in Italy where it is found, in Latin, in Florence's Santa Maria Novella church.[29] One variation goes:

Trav'ler view me as I lie
As you are so once was I
As I am now you soon must be
So prepare yourselves to follow me.[30]

Some families adapted popular epitaphs to suit the occasion; others wrote their own verses. It would be safe to say that the parents of one-year-old Madge Garrison (Searcy County, 1901) wrote the couplet on their daughter's stone: "We long to wear Jehovah's badge / And meet our darling little Madge."[31] The mother of Independence Spiva (Newton County, 4–22 July 1885) surely composed these verses:

Like a bird within its sheltered
nest chiled [child] within my arms
was pressed and sipped lifes
blossom at my breast.

The bird to better shelter
flown the nest is empty
and I alone am left to
make my broken hearted
moan.[32]

In addition to poetry, some stones include personal information, such as the deceased's favorite hymn, Bible verse or expression, the exact time of death, a profession, military record, church affiliation, or date of conversion. Especially intriguing are the inexplicable one-liners: "Revenge is my motto" (Washington County, 1869), "Death is a great boon to the old and suffering" (Johnson County, 1883), and "A lying in his grave" (Newton County, 1884).[33] Mary Beller Russell's epitaph, "Never struck her children," has added meaning in light of the fact that she was a schoolteacher (Boone County, 1902).[34]

Tombstones with the Cause of Death

On rare occasions a tombstone reveals how the person died. Illness, other than influenza, is not mentioned, nor is suicide, but the words "drowned" or "killed" are not hard to come by. Families may have found solace having an unusual cause of death named on a stone, as happened to Pearl Oxford. The boy was just sixteen when, according to his tombstone, he was "killed by lightning while plowing corn" (Boone County, 1903), an occupational death for a farmworker.[35] William Lafayette Cecil's death was also work related (Newton County, 1905), as according to his stone Cecil was "killed by a live wire at Fayetteville, Ark.," and the superintendent of the electric light plant brought the body home for burial. Cecil, a sixteen-year-old apprentice electrician, grabbed a power line that was supposed to have been shut off,[36] falling dead at the feet of several young ladies who were watching him work.

Given how often obituaries reveal that railroad workers were killed in wrecks, boiler explosions, or carelessness around the cars, there should be a lot of tombstones mentioning these causes. Instead, the stone of J. R. Beaty, an engineer (Crawford County, 1896), contains one of the few examples found, and it only hints at what occurred:

> Silent—on the wings of the wind for home
> The last way-station is safely passed;
> The steam sings low from the round black dome
> Wind chimes with the rain-drops falling fast.[37]

The poem's refrain, "He was called before he got in!" offers a clue, and a brief newspaper account reveals that Beaty, an engineer, slipped on an icy gangway and fell under the wheels of the train.[38]

A few stones tell of Civil War incidents. Joseph Buchanan's marker (Newton County, 1864) says he was killed by Confederates, "whilst in the service of the national army as a recruiting officer."[39] Kimbrell Hill's stone (Franklin County, 1901) reads, "G.H. Davis of Co. Ky; my horse was killed and fell on me. Kimbrell Hill taken him off in Price's Raid New Toney in 1864." (This would be Newtonia, the battle following that of Wilson's Creek, in Springfield, Missouri.)[40]

Tombstones with the words "murdered," "killed," or "assassinated" in lieu of "died" are tantalizing, and occasionally a murderer's name is given, usually in instances where families felt that justice had not been done. This was the case when two cousins, Sylvanus and John Hinds, got into an argument while cradling wheat (Madison County, 1863) and John struck Sylvanus in the neck with the blade of his cradle, resulting in Sylvanus's death from blood loss two weeks later. His tombstone gives both dates, adding that he "came to his death by being willfully murdered on June 13 by his cousin John Hinds."[41] The distinction that his *cousin* did this was necessary because Sylvanus's father and brother were also named John. The murderer escaped to California and stayed there.[42] Women committed murder, too. Frankey Seel was visiting her friend Hattie Youngblood when she noticed an old pistol, "playfully" pointed it at her friend and pulled the trigger (Boone County, 1906). Youngblood died before medical help could arrive. According to local lore the girls were in love with the same boy, though a newspaper account insisted they were close friends and that both families were "prostrated on account of the awful tragedy." All the same, Seel's parents got their daughter out of town and kept her whereabouts a secret; she later married and lived in Kansas.[43] Youngblood's family had to content themselves with carving "Murdered by Frankey Seel" on their daughter's stone.[44]

The most informative tombstone of all is that of Deny Hill (Franklin County, 1871), who was raped and murdered by her father's two farmworkers. Deny was just three and a half years old when the men lured her away from home and, having done their deed, left her body in a stream. "Bill Chinouth & Joe Forbush murdered this lovely child and hid her in the creek to get the family out to look so they mite rob & steal," was the motive Deny's father had carved on her marker. Surprisingly, when the child's body was found the two men had not fled, but because evidence pointed to them an armed guard was formed to escort the two to jail. En route Forbush supposedly made a full confession of the "sickening details," implicating his partner. The two were shot and killed when they attempted to escape, their bodies left beside the road. One newspaper wrote, "simple shooting was too good for the hellish fiends." Deny's father probably agreed, and placed their names and motive on his daughter's stone as a way of getting justice for her.[45] (The Hill family favored informative inscriptions. The stone of Obed Hill, in a nearby cemetery, tells how he was killed during a Kansas bank robbery in 1918.)[46]

African American Gravestones

Long after the Civil War, near towns where blacks were employed but lived separately, their graves were often not marked or, at best, given only fieldstones. Even in cemeteries where both races were buried, black graves were marked far less often than those of whites. Of the six hundred grave markers sold by northwest Arkansas's Hankins Monument Company between 1949 and 1951, with prices starting at $30, only one was ordered for a grave in Oak, the "Fayetteville Colored Cemetery" (1951),[47] a place containing few markers but numerous burials.

Several things explain this. The primary cause was economic, as professionally made tombstones were out of reach for all but the most affluent. Though no evidence has been found that carvers—who were white—refused to make stones for blacks, this remains a possibility. Then, too, with the exodus of blacks, either voluntarily or spurred by race riots, their communities' cemeteries could not be maintained and over time vandalism and nature have obliterated them.

Whites purchasing tombstones for blacks sometimes chose inscriptions that reveal more about the donor than the deceased. For example, Brown Cemetery (Johnson County) contains the grave of Jennie Maden, whose stone was erected by Arkansas Simpson (1840–1924). Though this stone is covered in writing, nowhere on it does a single date appear. It reads, "Sacred to the memory of Aunt Jennie Maden, Colored, Who was my nurse and caretaker after my mother's death when I was 3 years old. Her age was about 88 years when death claimed her 23 years ago. She was faithful to the end of her life, a staunch friend. Mrs. J.H. Simpson." According to the census, Jenny Madden was born about 1815, in Missouri, putting her death date at around 1903.

Photoceramics

The practice of permanently attaching a photograph to the tombstone is still practiced today. One early promotion for these tablets suggested that they allowed visitors to "seek the 'living' among the 'dead.'" This article (California, 1857) commented, "If on every tombstone there could be seen the life-likeness of the sleeper, as with sparkling eye, and noble mien . . . how much more inviting would then be the last resting places of the departed."[48] The Montgomery Ward mail-order company also stressed the psychological benefits of such a photo. "With the familiar face looking out at you, it seems as though with your visit there you have indeed paid the intended homage of respect and remembrance to one who has gone," according to the company's 1929 monument catalog.[49]

Such tablets are known as photoceramics, a French invention, patented in 1854, which transfers a picture onto a ceramic disc.[50] Discs are breakable and thus vulnerable to vandalism, weather, and rocks flung up by lawnmowers; it can be difficult to find older intact examples. The photos were often chosen to show an important event in the deceased's life, such as military service, while casual photos often show couples posing with such cherished possessions as horses, mules, vehicles, guns and, of course, pets. Occasionally, the person in the photo is very clearly deceased, with the coffin's lid or pillow visible in the background. Elsewhere in the United States, and especially among immigrant populations, it was the norm to show brides in wedding dresses and children in confirmation finery.

Figure 8.5 Photoceramic portrait attached to the tombstone of Elizabeth Thomason Hudson (1844–1923), Georges Creek Cemetery (Marion County). *Photo by Abby Burnett.*

Tombstone Symbolism

Though a trade publication optimistically believed that "symbols convey a definite message for all time,"[51] some meanings have been lost, or vary according to where the symbol is found. For example, elsewhere in the United States anchors on tombstones in a seafaring community could have literal interpretation, rather than representing the soul's safe anchorage in heaven. Tombstones in the Ozarks do not always conform to standard definitions. Lambs, said to represent the purity and innocence of infants and children, in Arkansas also symbolize adults' faith in Christ as their shepherd. Three-dimensional tree stumps, often incorrectly called the exclusive symbol of the Woodmen of the World, mark both adults' and children's graves, denoting a life that was cut down too soon. The column or obelisk, broken to represent a life cut short, today is often mistaken for vandalism. Other, one-of-a-kind symbols had meaning only to the deceased's family or referred to the person's line of work, such as the well digger's bas-relief carving of a man at a well. His was an occupational death, as he died from an ill-timed dynamite charge.[52]

The most popular motifs of all involve human hands that symbolize death and the afterlife in a variety of ways. An upraised index finger reminds the viewer to think of heaven, or calls attention to an inscribed banner; a downward reaching hand belongs to God, either plucking some representation of the life (fruit, flowers, or a bud) or breaking a chain and slipping the broken link onto one finger.

Clasping hands are even more widely used. Though graveyard guides say this represents matrimony, these hands never sport wedding rings. In the Ozarks this symbol is found universally, including on the stones of children, unmarried adults, and the elderly, and represent the farewell between the living and the dead. In almost all cases the hand extending from the panel's left side has straight, unflexed fingers (the dead hand), while the hand reaching from the opposite side (the living hand) actively clasps the other.[53] Further proof is found in the ribbon atop the panel, often bearing the words "A Sad Farewell" or "We will meet again." This echoes a popular epitaph: "We'll join thee in that Heavenly land / No more to take the parting hand." Though the two hands often emerge from gender-specific cuffs—a gathered sleeve on one and a man's buttoned shirt or coat sleeve on the other—these motifs, which were made in advance as part of a carver's stock, do not necessarily coincide with the sex of the deceased.

Other Burial Markers

Ozark cemeteries contain more than just conventional tombstones. Older burials were protected by a variety of grave coverings, their styles having all been traced back to Tennessee. These include box tombs or false crypts, slot and tab grave covers where headstone and footstone fit in slots cut into a box tomb's lid, ledgers (large stone slabs), comb graves (inward leaning slabs, resembling pup tents), tomb-tables (looking like a conventional table and extremely rare), and gravehouses. Variations occur within most of these categories, such as where box graves take the form of full-size stone coffins. Some combine styles, such as a comb set atop a box grave, or two empty stone boxes stacked on top of each other, considered to be transitional or hybrid versions of the individual styles.

One of the Upland South's most distinctive and intriguing mortuary structures is the gravehouse, an empty building set atop single or multiple burials. These buildings are neither mausoleums (which house coffins above ground) nor crypts (a room below ground for the same purpose) and serve no function other than protecting the grave, similar to those coverings listed above, and possibly a variant on these styles. Donald Ball, an authority on Upland South burial customs, had this to say about the origins of gravehouses:

The inspiration for their construction appears to have been derived from stone-table and box-tomb coverings which gained a degree of popularity in England and Scotland in the eighteenth century and were subsequently introduced to America at least as early as 1765. The all important perceived functions of the British prototypes were rapidly modified into a wide array of regional expressions variously crafted in wood, brick, and/or stone and reflective of taste, whim, cost, expediency, and the availability of preferred material(s).[54]

All of the coverings mentioned here have been found in cemeteries scattered across the Ozarks but not, as might be expected, ones in close proximity. John Waggoner, who documents existing gravehouses, has found numerous examples in his home state of Tennessee as well as across most of the south. "I still do not understand why a shelter built in the mountains of Kentucky can look similar to an example on the shores of the Gulf of Mexico," he said.[55]

The argument that these houses protected graves from being dug into by animals is valid only if the buildings were constructed immediately after burial, which would have been unlikely. (In two instances where builders dated grave coverings they made, a false crypt and a protective rock pen, each required a full year to build.) Accounts of a dying person requesting a house always state that this was done to keep rain from falling on the grave. At least one African American family followed the custom. The Grisso Cemetery (Baxter County, date unknown) contains a small rock building with a pitched roof. Called "the most imposing monument in the cemetery," this structure was built by a slave mason to protect his brother's grave.[56]

Such structures also protected the living. According to Howard "Monk" Hefley, one of two houses in his family's cemetery was constructed over the grave of a sixteen-year-old cousin (Newton County, probably 1930s). "His dad would go up there and sleep overnight with him, it was big enough for one person to crawl inside and sleep in it," Hefley recalled, estimating that the house was five or six feet high, three feet wide, and about six feet in length. Justice of the Peace Daniel Kilgore was said to have slept in cemeteries when tracking criminals across country; gravehouses would have provided him with shelter, as well. Perhaps coincidentally, he built a small house over the grave of his wife, Mahalia Jane (Madison County, 1931).[57]

The best-documented structures are those of the Agee children (Newton County, infant's unknown death date and 1914). After losing their second child, two-year-old Guffrey Agee, grandfather William Newton Christian used simple tools to construct two little houses over the children's graves. The structures are elaborate, the older child's house having windows, a drop

Figure 8.6 The Agee family posing next to the gravehouses covering burials of an unnamed infant (*left*) and Guffrey Agee (*right,* died 1914 at age two). The houses were built by the children's grandfather, William Newton Christian, *seated at left,* a Civil War veteran. Photo taken between 1915–1916, Agee/Hasty Cemetery (Newton County). *Photo courtesy of Sonja Carroll Bolton.*

Figure 8.7 Primitive gravehouse built over the grave of Mahalia Jane ("Haley") Kilgore (1862–1931), Kilgore Cemetery (Madison County). Such structures were made in a variety of styles, and from wood, metal, brick, and stone. *Photo by Abby Burnett.*

Figure 8.8 Example of a necked discoid stone, one of many variations on this style, in Denning Cemetery (Boone County). This is one of several such stones carved by Jacob Forney for members of his family. *Photo by Abby Burnett.*

ceiling, and wood trim. Once finished, Christian stored a small chair inside Guffrey's house. "Every day he would walk the two miles up the hill to the cemetery, take out his chair, and sit and whittle and 'be with the babies' until evening."[58] Thanks to restorations by succeeding generations of the Agee family, these houses are still standing but elsewhere known gravehouses have vanished, due to the depredations of nature, gravity, and overzealous cemetery groundskeepers.

There is another rare burial marker whose meaning and origins are unclear. These are necked discoids, stone tablets carved as though representing the outline of a human being, having a head, narrow neck, and squared-off shoulders. Some variations include heads in the shape of a rectangle, an arrowhead, or—for want of better descriptions—mushroom and lampshade cross-sections. Such stones may be freestanding or built into one end of a comb or false crypt.

From a distance this shape resembles a human form sitting up in its grave, although they do not have facial features (in fact, it is rare to find any stones with carving on the head area). According to Mike McNerney, the authority on this style, the shape is a corruption of the classic Celtic cross, the outer ends of the cross having been dropped from the design over time, leaving only the round top element. The style died out some time after the Civil War, with the exception of stones in family plots that were presumably purchased pre-need in order to match those of other family members. McNerney has documented examples across a fourteen-state area, including numerous examples, and variations, within the Ozarks.

Of the many older styles of grave coverings mentioned here, the false crypt—being an empty stone box—does not always mark an actual grave. During the Civil War some were constructed for the purpose of hiding food, a prized sidesaddle or, in one instance, county records from marauding bands of bushwhackers or soldiers. Molly Finley, a former slave, described how her owner buried money in the family cemetery, mounding up the dirt to give the appearance of a recent burial (Arkansas County, 1860s).[59] Those hiding food and possessions counted on others' fear of the dead to protect their property; it didn't always work. Sally Deans's body had just been buried in her family cemetery (Benton County) when "a band of bushwhackers came and thinking that the family had buried their treasures, dug Sally up, and dumped her out of the casket. Finding nothing else, they left, leaving the family to bury her again."[60]

Folkart Versus Factory-Made

Some families created their own grave markers. The Nelson Funeral Home (Berryville, Carroll County) sold monuments, but they also owned a small kit for making markers. This consisted of a rectangular mold with flared sides and a collection of raised metal letters and numbers that could be pressed into the wet concrete, then removed, to print the name and dates. This kit would be loaned to families so they could make their own markers.[61]

Though primitive tombstones sometimes have backward-facing letters or inept attempts at carved symbols, "borned" in place of "born" in the inscription was correct usage for its day. The editor of the Evening Shade newspaper (Sharp County, 1901) took the editor of the *Viola Ledger* to task over this item: "Borned, on the 3rd of August, to Mr. and Mrs. Will Hodge, a pare of boys." It's unclear whether "borned" or "pare" caused the editor to suggest that his counterpart "should consult the dictionary more freely or get out of the newspaper business."[62] Inscriptions reflect the way people talked, and "I am goen home" and "Blessed air the ded that die in the lord" (Newton County, 1887 and 1882)[63] certainly sound like local speech.

Locally produced markers are at one end of the spectrum; cast metal is at the other. In 1874 the Monumental Bronze Company of Bridgeport, Connecticut, began production of markers made from a material it termed "white bronze" but which was actually pure zinc. These hollow, blue-gray monuments could be cast in every imaginable shape, including statuary, but most copied the popular tombstone styles of the day, mimicking rough granite boulders or rustic, raised-twig lettering. The deceased's name, dates, and a choice of mourning symbols—even a bas-relief likeness—could be cast on panels that were then bolted into openings in the monument.[64]

One newspaper ad for Monumental Bronze (Washington County, 1908) promised that its markers needed no maintenance, and that moss would not grow on them—which was true.[65] When oxidized, the metal develops a protective coating that is impervious to weather and plant growth. The only downside is that over time the metal's weight causes seams to pop apart at the corners. These markers are found in city and rural cemeteries alike, but they never caught on in a big way, either nationwide or in Arkansas. Perhaps prospective buyers were suspicious of such patently false claims as "Granite soon gets moss-grown, discolored, requires constant expense and care, and eventually crumbles back to mother nature." This ad contained an equally bogus claim: "Many granite dealers have bought White Bronze for their own burial plots."[66] The opposite was true, as the company's earliest agents weren't buried beneath the zinc markers they sold to others.[67]

The only way to purchase a zinc marker was through an agent. Customers made purchases from an agent's illustrated catalog, not actual samples, and they usually had to erect the markers themselves. During World War I the government took over Monumental Bronze's foundry to make munitions; by the time the war ended so, too, had the fad for metal markers. The company produced no new monuments though it continued to cast inscription panels to attach to existing ones; the business closed in 1939.[68]

The Monumental Bronze Company and its subsidiaries was the largest and most famous maker of white bronze, but it wasn't the only source for such monuments. Another company, W.Z.W., or Warsaw Zinc Works of Warsaw, Missouri, sold a few models in Arkansas; attached plates give patent dates of 1894, 1901, and 1902. W.Z.W.'s designs were plainer than those of its competitors, but it offered an unusual design innovation, as is found on Mary Ollie Whitlow's marker (Madison County, 1900). Her simple metal tablet has a decorative panel attached via an invisible hinge that, when lifted, reveals the girl's photograph and funeral program, preserved behind a glass pane.[69]

Across the Ozarks iron grave markers are much more common than zinc ones. James Shelton of Gaston, Alabama, patented this design, called a "monument or sign holder," in 1887. While the patent drawings show it in a variety of shapes and sizes, it was his round-top tablet-style marker that caught on. It features a rectangular inscription panel, within which the deceased's name and dates were painted or written on paper, then covered with a piece of glass. This glass did not hold up well, and today it is difficult to find markers having legible names and dates. Customers could choose from a variety of mourning motifs, cast at the top of the tablet: lambs, doves, angels, clasping hands, pointing fingers, or a broken bud. There was also a tiny foot-stone, a miniature version of the marker, rarely found today.[70]

The two largest mail-order businesses that sold tombstones were Sears, Roebuck and Company and Montgomery Ward. In 1900 Sears's fall catalog offered five different monument styles, in a variety of sizes, carved from blue Vermont granite;[71] these sold so well that in 1905 the company published its first specialty catalog, titled "Tombstones and Monuments." Stones retailed for $4.88 to $40.00 for Vermont and Italian marble, with lettering extra.[72] In 1908 this specialty catalog grew to nearly 150 pages of markers and items for the family plot[73] but by the 1960s Sears was out of the monument business.

From 1906 to 1939 Montgomery Ward also sold tombstones, and they, too, issued separate catalogs devoted to this product. Customers chose a particular monument style, lettering, epitaph, and footstone; this marker would be shipped to them by rail along with directions for setting the stone. By 1929 economic times were so tough that the company expressed sympathy for its customers' financial plight. "Even though the last illness and funeral expenses may have left you in straitened finances for the time being, there is no need to wait for months or to deny yourself the comfort of knowing that the last resting place is suitably marked." (An easy payment plan was offered.)[74] Both companies shipped markers to Arkansas, but local carvers also copied designs from their catalogs.

Woodmen of the World

Joseph Cullen Root—already a member of the Masons, Odd Fellows, and Knights of Pythias—founded the Modern Woodmen of America in 1883 and the Woodmen of the World in 1890 (Omaha, Nebraska), specifically to sell life insurance to those who joined. He conceived of another benefit as well: giving each member a distinctive, three-dimensional stone tree trunk marker on his grave when he died.[75]

The tree trunk or tree stump was already a popular mourning symbol, but the Woodmen added a distinctive seal bearing a tree stump and a banner

Figure 8.9 Huntsville's Woodmen of the World, Camp No. 34, unveils a distinctive tree trunk tombstone for Bradfield Howell (1846–1906) in the Huntsville Cemetery (Madison County). Many camps had brass bands that played at such events; here men are holding up their ceremonial axes to form the letters "W.O.W.," for Woodmen of the World. *Madison County Historical and Genealogical Society, Huntsville.*

reading "Dum Tacet Clamat" ("Though silent, he speaks"), adopted in 1899. Though redundant, the tree stump emblem attached to a three-dimensional stone tree trunk identifies such a marker as belonging to a W.O.W. member. In its early years the company provided local monument companies with designs, which some carvers further embellished with three-dimensional ivy, scrolls, coiled ropes, doves, and squirrels of their own devising. Over time other patterns were added, but by the 1920s the company no longer provided tombstones for its members and today exists solely as an insurance company.

Root designated June 6 as Woodmen Memorial Day. In Arkansas the local chapters, called camps, used any weekend on or near this date to unveil and dedicate tombstones of members who had died during the previous year. The ceremony included a procession of Woodmen who lined up in a wedge-shaped formation around the grave. (Wedges, axes, and splitting mauls, also part of the original emblem, were often carved on the tree trunk.) The program included hymns, songs, and a speech by the camp's leader, or Sovereign, as part of the unveiling ceremony. The ceremony for a deceased Sovereign included sprinkling the stone with salt.[76] In addition, members decorated all W.O.W. members' graves each year.

These unveilings drew huge crowds who enjoyed the speeches, pageantry, music, and noon picnic. When Sovereign Eugene Phillips's stone was unveiled (Marion County, 1910), the local newspaper provided extensive coverage, describing the day-long ceremony that included a cornet band playing "Nearer My God to Thee." After the stone was ceremonially uncovered Zena, Phillips's three-year-old daughter, was lifted to the podium so she could recite a poem in memory of her father:

> My papa was a Woodmen
> You really couldn't find
> In all this good old world
> A papa so good as mine.
> He joined the order to protect
> Mama and we little girls.
> He was a faithful member
> Of the Woodmen of The World.
> He was a faithful husband;
> He was my papa dear;
> He was a noble Woodman
> The one that's buried here.[77]

Part of the organization's creed was that its members' graves would be marked. This ought not to have mattered to Fred Morley (Washington County, died 1919), whose father owned the largest monument business in northwest Arkansas (Fayetteville, Washington County, founded about 1886). Furthermore, Fred was the "son" in the business name, "Morley & Son." But by the time he joined the Woodmen, Fred had outlived his mother, two brothers, and two infant siblings, and had seen that none of their graves was given a stone by his father. Despite the business's slogan, "Mark every grave," when the last Morley died (1961), the only tombstone in the family plot was—and is— Fred's large granite marker bearing the distinctive W.O.W. emblem, denoting that he was a member in good standing.[78]

CHAPTER NINE

Funerals and Decoration Day

Rest mother rest, in quiet sleep,
While friends in sorrow o'er thee weep,
And here their heart-felt offerings bring
And near thy grave their requiem sing.

—**Bashuby Pittard,** 1779–1862
Huntsville Cemetery (Madison County)

As he aged, "Uncle Fate" Firestone began to dwell on his impending death and to prepare for it. He had a casket specially built, storing it in a back room of the Hensleys' general store, in Marshall (Searcy County, 1940s), so he could sleep in it when he made overnight visits to town.[1] Once Firestone, an itinerant preacher, decided he wanted to be buried in Canaan Cemetery, he had a grave dug there, one lined with concrete and marked with a tombstone.[2] Then, at the next Decoration Day, he stood beside the empty grave and preached his own funeral.

"I remember that he led in singing a hymn or two," recalled Brooxie Karns, a teenager at the time. "It was a regular graveside service in all ways, and just as he planned," a tradition he repeated for the next several years.[3] Firestone died in 1947, at age ninety, having requested that there be no funeral since he had done the job so thoroughly. Despite all of his arrangements, he was neither buried in this grave nor, by one account, in his special casket but was instead interred in another county beside a daughter who had died in infancy.[4]

Firestone was not the only preacher to eulogize himself. Charles Booth Whiteley, a Baptist minister, "like many men, had certain peculiarities, one of which was his desire to preach his own funeral." According to this account, published decades after Whiteley left Arkansas, the minister had doubted he would reach age fifty and, when he did, treated his congregation to his funeral oration, followed by a celebratory dinner (Carroll County, 1850).[5] In actuality Whiteley, preparing to move to Texas at the start of the Civil War and knowing he would never return, preached his own funeral as a farewell sermon.[6]

Judging from obituaries, quite a few dying people *wanted* to preach their own funerals but had to content themselves with selecting the hymns, poems, and Bible verses they instructed their ministers to use. Members of the Womack family were especially thorough in this regard. William Womack (Benton County, 1904) made funeral arrangements, sent a farewell to his church, and requested the funeral text, "Therefore be ye also ready: for in such hour as ye think not the Son of man cometh" (Matt. 24:44).[7] Ten years later as his wife, Elizabeth Jane, lay dying (Benton County, 1915), she selected her pallbearers, chose a song and poem to be performed by her children, and secured the services of three local ministers. Her funeral, she informed her family, should be "a service of triumph like the closing of a revival meeting."[8]

The Delayed Funeral

Archibald Smith's last request (Washington County, 1888) was for a funeral "at some appropriate time,"[9] because while burials took place immediately, funerals often did not. Some services were delayed for weeks, months, or even years, usually because there was no minister to officiate. This was the era of the circuit rider, ministers assigned to dozens of churches inside immense territories that had to be covered on horseback, by mule, or on foot. Though the Methodist circuit rider is the best known, in the South the Presbyterians and Baptists used them, too.[10]

Rev. L. C. O'Barr, a Methodist circuit rider (Pope County, 1867–1872), "went through cold and heat, wet and dry, swam rivers, and lay out at nights" when covering his eighty-mile territory; later his circuit was reduced to sixty square miles. "I never passed through happier periods in my life," he later recalled.[11] Methodist minister James A. Walden was not nearly so sanguine. Walden, saddled with ill health, little money, and a growing family to provide for, still managed to cover 2,500 to 3,000 miles per year between 1869 and 1874, traveling a territory that, at various times, included Boone, Carroll, Independence, and Washington counties.[12]

Though a friend, church elder, or justice of the peace might pray or read a Bible verse at the burial, families wanted their minister to preach the actual funeral service. This meant waiting until his next scheduled visit, which could be further delayed by winter weather or heavy spring rains. Some funerals were held until distant relatives could be notified. Deaths in winter were usually given funerals in the spring, sometimes at the cemetery's annual Decoration Day. Spring and summer deaths might have fall funerals, or be commemorated at the next camp meeting. The number of intervening months was of no importance, nor was the day of the week, as circuit riders preached their sermons on whatever day they could be there.

A delay gave relatives time to write a lengthy obituary to read at the funeral, and waiting until good weather ensured a larger crowd at what was often an all-day service, with a basket dinner at noon (Newton and Carroll counties, early 1900s).[13] This custom was not unique to the Ozarks. According to folklore collected in Kentucky (early 1900s), delayed funerals often took place after the crops had been gathered, and "a husband's funeral sermon is postponed until his wife dies, or vice versa, though the interval may be many years."[14]

Folklorists found the custom intriguing. Vance Randolph wrote, "I have heard of one case in which the funeral of a man's first wife was attended by his second spouse, who sat beside her husband and wept with him for the loss of her predecessor."[15] A Little Rock folklorist (Pulaski County, 1919) noted that among blacks a delay of two or even three years was not uncommon, asserting that it was quite usual for the funeral to be attended by a new spouse and any children born to this union. It was explained that the delay gave the dead time to rest in peace before any questionable character traits were mentioned at the funeral.[16]

Whether or not the delay helped the deceased rest more easily, it benefited the living. The funeral of Ella Barham, murdered in late 1912, did not take place for six months (Boone County, 1913). Perhaps her family hoped to eulogize their daughter after her murderer had been hanged but, convicted of the crime in January and sentenced to die in March, Odus Davidson did not go to the gallows until August 1913.[17] Barham's funeral, held in late May in the cemetery near where her dismembered body had been found, attracted hundreds of people. "It is the custom in this section to have funeral services after all friends have been notified," one newspaper explained,[18] but given the crime's sensational nature and wide coverage it is unlikely that anyone needed notification.

The delayed funeral was not the custom everywhere in the Ozarks, which was unfortunate as it would have been of benefit during times of contagion. During a smallpox epidemic (Boone County, 1882) the newspaper reminded readers, "attendance at a funeral of those who died of small-pox is equally as dangerous as exposure to those afflicted with the disease."[19] In 1928 the state's board of health forbade church funerals for any deaths caused by various communicable diseases, allowing only adult relatives to take part in a brief service and requiring newspaper death notices to state the cause of death.[20]

The Funeral Sermon

Funerals took place in the home, at the local schoolhouse, at a church, in proximity to the grave or, in the case of W. N. Counts (Washington County, 1912), "in the beautiful yard at his home, of which he was so proud."[21] Home funerals, preached from the front porch, allowed an overflow crowd to stand in the yard. The service usually took place in the afternoon to allow grave diggers time to finish a job that, as noted earlier, they'd begun that morning.

Ozark funerals, past and present, include the reading of the deceased's obituary, which posed a problem for illiterate ministers. Undertaker Felix Brashears (Madison County, after 1950) solved this problem by reading aloud the obituaries with these ministers preaching sermons from portions of the Bible they had memorized. Such services routinely lasted an hour or more, with those of African Americans traditionally taking at least two hours. A lengthy funeral showed respect for the deceased. Sebern J. Davis's church service (Franklin County, 1929) included scriptural readings by three ministers and a lengthy funeral text, interspersed with hymns, choral numbers, solos, and music performed by a visiting quartet. These rites were then followed by a lengthy graveside service.[22]

Heber Springs funeral director Tom Olmstead (Cleburne County, early 1940s) knew the tendencies of one minister who would, if someone arrived late, begin his sermon over from the beginning, repeating it word for word for the benefit of the latecomer. On one broiling summer day Olmstead, waiting outside the church, saw a couple arrive forty minutes into the eulogy and, knowing what this meant for the mourners trapped inside the hot building, stopped the couple and persuaded them to wait outside.[23]

Ministers used the occasion to issue the reminder that "the old must die and the young *may* die" and that death comes for all, often when least expected. Elderly Civil War veterans attending the funeral of a fellow Union soldier (Carroll County, 1921) were pointedly reminded of their imminent departures. The minister's remarks "were very largely in their behalf, pointing them to the not far distant end of their journey on earth and admonishing them to be sure their names were written in the Lamb's Book of Life."[24] Nor could those in the prime of life afford complacency. When E. H. Phillips, "the very picture of robust health," was killed by lightning (Washington County, 1872), his obituary writer reminded readers, "This sad lesson should teach that we too are mortal and liable at any moment to pass through the gateway of death to immortality. Let it then impress upon us the divine mandate 'be ye also ready.'"[25]

Some ministers exhorted the living to become saved, stressing that they could not meet their loved ones in the afterlife without doing so. Bruce Vaughan quoted the preacher at his grandfather's funeral (Madison County,

1951) as saying repeatedly, "OHHH, what a pity that his children will never see him again because they do not belong to the only Church that can save them—the Church of Christ,"[26] a ploy still used today.

Mourners did not hold back from displays of emotion—on the contrary, this behavior was encouraged. Randolph described such outpourings as "gabbling and hollering" and claimed to have witnessed "the immediate relatives of the deceased fling themselves on the corpse with loud yells, roll groaning and kicking on the floor, and even try to leap after the coffin when it is lowered into the grave."[27] Some ministers encouraged this behavior. Vaughan, recalling the Baptist services he attended as a child, said, "I remember that most country preachers did not feel that they had preached a good sermon until they had the family in hysterics. Fainting was quite common, and added to the feeling that the funeral was 'well preached.'"[28]

Some accounts claim that "it was the custom in these hills to postpone a burying until somebody ... rose to heap praises on the dear departed," but such compliments were questionable. "There was the burying when it seemed nobody, but nobody could say a good word for the man to be interred. Finally in desperation, one neighbor rose and said, 'I can say this much for Bill; he wasn't as bad all the time as he was some of the time.'"[29] Other attempts supposedly included, "Well now, he's sure a good whistler" (Cleburne County, date some time before 1936),[30] and "He's got the best set of teeth I ever saw" (Missouri Ozarks, date unknown).[31]

Not all deaths were occasions for regret, especially those of the poor, the mentally impaired, the elderly, and the suffering. All the same, funerals were expected to be sad occasions, even when the deceased was not well known. Percilla Inman, described earlier, had died far from her home and Rev. Andrew Buchanan used that fact in her funeral oration (Washington County, 1830):

> The suppressed feelings of the little audience broke forth in sobs and tears when he came to speak of her family at home watching for her return, of eyes clouded with bitter sorrow in the desolation of spirit ... and where there were little hearts that had grown big and heavy in the darkened rooms, waiting and praying for footsteps ... which shall never wake again the echoes of that expectant house.[32]

Though any number of Bible verses are applicable to funerals, one was a staple: "I am the resurrection and the life: he that believeth in me, though he were dead, yet shall he live: and whosoever liveth and believeth in me, shall never die" (John 11:25–26). Funeral directors had to be ready to recite this one, on occasions when a minister did not show up, and they carried little books of verses and hymns for just such emergencies. One volume (published 1925) included texts for the burial of children, as well as Bible verses suitable for the funeral of "a Godly Woman," "a Person of Advanced Age," and "One in Public Life."[33]

In One Minister's Own Words

Funerals were delivered extemporaneously, but fortunately one minister, Rev. William Sherman, kept notes on some of the hundreds of funerals he preached over his long career as a Methodist minister (Washington and Benton counties, 1886–1959). He had known many of his subjects well, and included anecdotes and personal details in their funeral sermons. For example, when eulogizing William Hill (Franklin County, 1941), he confided, "Mr. Hill elected to live a bachelor's life, and when the Hotel Bristow was built in 1909 he selected his room #8 and has occupied it ever since and went to his reward from that room."[34]

Sherman often felt himself unequal to the task of summing up the life of an elderly person. "They have lived so devotedly, worked so hard, sacrificed so much that I feel my inability to pay a proper tribute to them," he said on more than one occasion.[35] Yet he tried, listing the many changes this person had witnessed over the course of a long lifetime, such as the invention of the telegraph, telephone, electric lights, and airplanes.[36] He also liked to quote from poems; one, admittedly a summation of "the philosophy of doubt, of despair," he discovered while browsing epitaphs in a cemetery:

> Man is born into this world all naked and bare
> With nothing to cheer him but trouble and care
> And when he dies he goes—
> No one knows where.[37]

Recalling the hundreds of funerals he had preached, Reverend Sherman wrote: "Some of them would have broken a heart of stone—no attendants, no tears, no flowers, no hope. Others have brought us [so] close to heaven we could almost hear the angels sing."[38] Not surprisingly, the minister picked out the Bible verses and hymns he wanted used at his own funeral.

African American Funerals

Green Kuykendall, born a slave, spent thirty-eight years as both a janitor in the Clarksville courthouse and a hauler of goods. When he died (Franklin

County, 1938), "his funeral was attended not only by the colored people of the town but also by a large number of his white friends, as well, including all of the present county officials whom he served so faithfully," stated his obituary.[39] It was not uncommon for African American funerals to have whites in attendance, where they took center stage.

"Whites and blacks . . . behaved in highly patterned ways reflecting racial segregation," according to a source about the South in general, but this was certainly true of Arkansas. "Blacks at white funerals sat or stood in the back of the room, but whites at black funerals sat on the front row and viewed the body before others attending did so."[40] At the funeral of former slave Aaron Van Winkle, held in Fayetteville's Colored Methodist Episcopal Church (Washington County, 1904), the white mourners were "requested to pass around first."[41] Kuykendall's obituary said that he "was the friend of all, of those who occupied not only the seats of honor but also of those who were forced to remain in the rear," and it's not hard to figure out which races occupied which positions.

White and black communities, though having many funeral customs in common, differ when it comes to the waiting period between death and burial. Rev. A. J. Parish, owner of Rowell-Parish Mortuary in Fort Smith (Sebastian County), serving the city's black and Muslim communities, said that traditionally there is a week's delay between death and burial. "Saturdays are a big day for us. We've had deaths on Thursday or Friday, and the service is held a week from that Saturday," to allow relatives living out of state to arrive. He recalled one burial, held just three days after a death, where he was asked why the family had rushed the process. (All of these bodies were embalmed.) Another difference, Parish said, is that graveside funeral services are very rare in the African American community; almost all funerals are held in a church, even if the deceased was not a member.

In Fayetteville (Washington County, 1930s), Sunday funerals were the norm. According to Jessie Bryant, "If it was Sunday, there was a funeral, they were not held through the week," as this was during the era when the town's black population was not allowed in the funeral homes.

Music and Flowers

Music was, and remains, an important part of the funeral service. "The best singers from other communities came, rain, snow or shine, to sing the hauntingly sweet and sad refrains from the old worn song books," recalled Opal Arnold Taylor, herself a member of one such musical group (Searcy County, born 1915).[42] "In the Sweet By and By," "Shall We Gather at the River," and "When the Roll Is Called Up Yonder"[43] were funeral staples.

Figure 9.1 Members of the Cox family pose in Farmer Cemetery (Carroll County), beside the grave of son Coy Cox (1888–1908). Family members wear mourning and were photographed beside Coy's portrait. *Courtesy of the Heritage Center Museum, Berryville, Carroll County Historical Society.*

Some families had particular favorites. The Dodsons (Newton County) always sang the hymn "Just a Rose Will Do,"[44] whose last verse goes, "Just have an old-fashioned preacher / To preach a sermon or two / Don't spend your money for flowers / Just a rose will do." It's unlikely that many people *did* spend money on flowers, at least not in rural communities, where floral offerings tended to be wildflowers or ones grown in home gardens. One flowering tree associated with funerals is the Sarvis, also known as Sarvisberry or Serviceberry (*Amelanchier arborea*), the first thing to produce blooms in the spring. It is supposedly named after its use in church services in the east; in Arkansas it was used at the first funerals preached in the spring.[45]

Flowers played an important role in the funeral—and not necessarily because they masked the odor of decomposition, as folklore would have it. Ministers liked to equate an abundance of blooms with the community's regard for the deceased. Some arrangements specifically symbolized the deceased's life, such as the ladder of tea roses, with a broken fifteenth rung, brought to the funeral of fifteen-year-old Claudia Tabor (Washington County, 1895).[46] An account of another funeral (Hot Springs, Garland County, 1893) mentions floral arrangements in the shape of a cross, star, anchor (symbolizing hope), open Bible—even a harp made of flowers, one string symbolically broken.[47]

In towns without a florist, or where there was no money to buy flowers, women created their own arrangements. "I can remember having great big tubs of roses and my sister and I would sit by my mother and the women who had gathered to make wreaths of all these different kinds of flowers that were going to be used at the funeral," Norma Conner said of Harrison funerals (Boone County, 1920s).[48] The casket of murder victim Bud Maynard (Baxter County, 1929) was covered with "wreaths of red, pink, and white roses and there were wreaths of daisies, all interwoven with wild fern. There were fan-shaped masses of roses with nasturtiums and here and there forget-me-nots woven in. A giant stalk of agave [yucca] with hundreds of snow-white blossoms placed near the head of the coffin completed the floral tribute."[49]

Daisies were a controversial choice, as the plant invasively takes over pastures and will not be eaten by cattle. Ruby and Ruth Holland's father eradicated the plant by paying his daughters by the bucket for the flower heads, causing Ruth to tell her sister, "When I die, I don't want any daisies on my grave!" That's exactly what someone brought to Ruth's funeral, however (Madison County, 1930), but Ruth's mother decided, "Someone put them on there with love and we're not taking them off."

Funerals of the Fraternal Lodges

Around the same time J. J. Barnett joined the Primitive Baptist Church he also became a Mason (Benton County, 1883), an act "distasteful" to the Baptists. Forced to choose between the two, Barnett withdrew his church membership and remained a Mason to the end of his life. When he died in 1890 this fraternal organization oversaw his funeral and burial, as was done for any member in good standing.[50] A Mason must ask the Master of the Lodge for these funeral rites, and even those who did so in suicide notes had their requests honored. Masons who died in wars were unable to make the request, but a special memorial service could be performed over their graves after the fact.

There is a prescribed Masonic funeral service, held privately in the lodge's meeting room, but when the funeral is held in a church the Masons serve as pallbearers and perform a graveside ritual.[51] These pallbearers wear their white aprons, white gloves, and a black armband and tuck a sprig of evergreen in their lapels, which is later thrown into the grave.[52] The Masonic graveside ritual of Sebern J. Davis, mentioned above, was described in the newspaper: opening of the lodge, invocation, exaltation, depositing an apron "as an emblem of the craft" along with a sprig of evergreen, followed by "the funeral ode and secret honors" before Davis's body was finally consigned to the grave.[53]

Other fraternal lodges had similar funeral and burial customs. Addie Adkisson remembered how, preceding her father's funeral (Izard County, 1913) as she, her mother, and sister came down the walkway in front of the church the Odd Fellows "stood on each side of us, and held them spears up with the tips touching. . . . We went in under them spears," and that later the men dropped cedar twigs into the grave.[54] Even children could join organizations that would oversee their burials. The Boy Scouts had a funeral rite presided over by the Scout Master, and when twelve-year-old Lowell Stevenson was killed by a car as he delivered the daily newspaper (Pope County, 1930), his active and honorary pallbearers were all paperboys.[55]

The Ku Klux Klan had a special funeral ritual as well, mentioned in obituaries in the 1920s (the Klan's second incarnation, lasting from 1915 into the 1930s). According to one obituary, six silent, robed Klansmen acted as pallbearers at one man's funeral (Franklin County, 1924),[56] while Floyd Wright's funeral (Searcy County, 1925) was conducted by his Masonic lodge, after which "a delegation from Bear Creek Klan No. 88, Knights of the Ku Klux Klan, in regalia . . . paid their respects to a departed brother with an impressive ceremony."[57] Just what these "respects" involved is unknown, but one woman, who witnessed a Klan funeral when she was a child, described men in white robes and hoods, each carrying a torch, marching around the grave (Searcy County, 1930s).[58]

Masons honored deceased members by publishing Resolutions of Respect in local newspapers, a practice copied by the Klan. "The Marshall Klan, through the providence of God, has lost a noble member, a faithful Christian and a pure American," began the tribute to W. H. Helm (Searcy County, 1924). It concluded with a poem, speaking to their Klansman brother in heaven:

> We are left to fight the battle,
>   Guided by the God we love,
> And when we have gained the victory,
>   Then we will join the Klan above.[59]

Decoration Day

One by one life robs us of
Our treasure.
Nothing is our own
    Except our dead.

—**W. H. Jennings**, 1856–1929
Canaan Cemetery (Searcy County)

Respect for the dead did not end with the funeral, it continued with the annual event known as Decoration Day, a time for the refurbishment and beautification of cemeteries. This was the day when families placed flowers on the graves, attended a special program or sermon, shared a bountiful meal, and socialized with friends and family, some of whom they saw only on this occasion. Of the many funeral customs once routinely observed, only Decoration Day is still practiced, though considerably reduced in scale.

This event outranked even Christmas in importance. Some have called it the most anticipated day on the calendar, a time when women got new dresses and hats and children got new clothes, something not necessarily true of Easter, Christmas, or the start of the school year. Memorial Day is now associated with visiting cemeteries, but in the past Decoration Days were held on weekends starting in April and running through September, scheduled so as to not conflict with those in adjacent communities. It was not uncommon for people to attend the events in every cemetery where they had family buried.

According to Alan Jabbour, an authority on Decoration Day in the southern Appalachian mountains, in the north the practice has its origins in Gen. John Alexander Logan's edict that 30 May 1868, "is designated for the purpose of strewing with flowers or otherwise decorating the graves of comrades who died in defense of their country during the late rebellion." Logan's wife later said that it was her description of seeing the decorated graves of Confederate soldiers (Petersburg, Virginia, 1868) that inspired her husband to order the Grand Army to do likewise.

Though this marks the start of the tradition in the north, it is unknown when the earlier, southern version originated, "yet it seems clear that the practice is southern, and its practice seems to be strongest in the countryside of a region often loosely described as the Upland South," according to Jabbour. Though one speculation is that it grew out of the practice of holding daylong, delayed funerals, the custom seems to have originated in the coastal and piedmont South, carried into the Appalachias and then to Arkansas as settlers migrated west.[60]

Cleaning the Graveyard

Keeping grass cut was a problem in an era before lawnmowers. Up through the 1930s the front yards of most rural homes were grass-free expanses of packed, swept dirt rigorously maintained; flowers occupied beds at the perimeter. The grounds of rural cemeteries, however, were cleared of brush, brambles, and grass just once a year, prior to Decoration Day. Except for burials taking place immediately after this cleanup, it was the norm for grave diggers to hack a path through head-high weeds when starting work on a grave. Roxie Cook described conditions in Kingston's cemetery the day they buried her son, Dwain (Madison County, 1934). "They was a mess," she said of local cemeteries, noting that conditions didn't change for another ten years. "They was briars, and Johnson grass, and logs, and what have you high as this ceiling in there. They took a brush hook and cut a trail out down to where they buried him."[61]

Even city cemeteries having a paid sexton easily became overgrown. The Ladies' Cemetery Association planned to beautify the Russellville city cemetery (Pope County, 1903), but first they asked everyone to come assist the sexton in the removing weeds and trash that had piled up since the previous autumn. "Women have peculiar qualifications for such work, and they take pride in it," the local paper noted.[62]

Given the amount of work involved, only the smallest family graveyards could hold a cleaning in the morning and a decoration that same afternoon. In larger cemeteries, cleanups (which also involved a potluck meal and visiting) and decorations were separate, daylong events. Families wore their oldest clothing because the work was dirty and physically demanding. Men used axes to chop away vines and brought grubbing hoes, briar hooks, rakes, shovels, and pitchforks to remove underbrush. Sometimes sheep were turned loose to graze away grass in a cemetery, while one Searcy County family cemetery was routinely burned over to remove brush. Still, most accounts describe men using cradles and shears to cut high grass, though when mowers became available, in the 1930s, people loaned their equipment for this purpose.

Graves covered by rock pens or cairns usually needed to have their stones restacked; fallen tombstones had to be righted. Scraped or mounded graves had to be raked and weeded and were usually given a fresh topping of dirt or sand. Graves that had sunk had to be top-filled with dirt to make them

Figure 9.2 Three-dimensional lamb carving on the grave of Kittie V. Weir (1874–1875), Bentonville City Cemetery (Benton County). Ozark cemeteries contain numerous examples of both professionally carved and folk art lambs, many of them resembling playthings. *Photo by Abby Burnett.*

level. Copperheads and rattlesnakes lurked in deep underbrush, workers were stung when they disturbed nests of yellow jackets or wasps, but nevertheless children participated in the cleanup. They also played together, after being cautioned not to walk on or step over a grave. According to Rena Bean Poteet (Johnson County, born 1916), "our elders had taught us that to do so would not only be the greatest disrespect but would also bring us grievous bad luck."[63]

Children liked to play among the tombstones. One child, accompanying her mother as she cleaned family graves, would play with the three-dimensional marble lambs atop infants' and children's burials (Madison County, 1930s). Having few toys of her own, these lamb carvings proved irresistible to the little girl. Though her mother tried to return them to the correct graves, no such sculptures are found there today.[64]

Decorating with Flowers

Fresh flowers weren't always available for funerals and burials, but by Decoration Day something would be in bloom. Some people gathered wildflowers from pastures and ditches, others brought blooms from flowering catalpa and black locust trees, their blossoms smelling of jasmine. One account, itemizing the "old homestead flowers" found in Sunset Cemetery (Washington County, 1940s?), mentioned tiger lilies, Confederate roses, princess feathers, dusty miller, and "flowers of thoughtfulness and flowers of forget-me-not."[65] Blooms were picked early on Decoration Day and wrapped in wet newspaper, or placed in tubs of water. "By the time you got down there in a wagon, you know how they looked," commented Flossie Cook Smith, adding that her family included wild ferns in their bouquets, which lasted longer.[66]

Perhaps because cemeteries weren't maintained year-round, it was not common to plant flowers on the graves or within family plots. Roses, however, were an exception, and isolated burying grounds are still good places to find the old varieties. According to Coy Ford (Newton County, born 1941), the small Crossroads Cemetery, near where Ford grew up, once had as many as fourteen trellises supporting climbing roses, none in existence today.

All graves were decorated, even those whose occupants were unknown. "There were always a few that nobody ever came to visit, but today they were covered in cut roses and seven sisters and wild flowers like all the rest," wrote Charldene Sparks (Newton County, born 1931).[67] Pauline Davis Steele recalled how her mother brought an abundance of flowers even though her family had no graves to mark (Washington County, early 1900s). "One grave stood out . . . it was off to one side and [had] no marker and no one knew who had been buried there. My mother would put extra flowers on this one. She would always say, 'Poor soul, poor soul.'"[68]

In the absence of inscribed tombstones even families sometimes forgot where their relatives were buried. "You just remembered the grave by the location and the shape of a native stone they picked up while filling the grave," according to Gladys McChristian (Madison County, born 1910). "Grandma Glenn didn't get to go [to Decoration Day] very often when her children were small, and when she did go, there had been so many more little graves [added] that she couldn't find her little Walter's grave. She never did seem to worry about it much that I could tell. Lots of other people lost their children's graves. Sometimes two people would both claim the same little grave and both would decorate it."[69]

Crepe Paper

Even when fresh flowers were available, some women also made ones out of crepe paper, "for backup." In the 1920s the Dennison Manufacturing Company, makers of this cheap, colorful paper, published a booklet of instructions for making flowers[70] and women also shared designs, cutting their patterns out of newspaper. Once again, roses were the most popular—and the most realistic. The stretchy paper could be curled to resemble open petals and leaves, glued to stems made by wrapping lengths of baling wire or cut coat hangers with green paper. Other designs included carnations, peonies, foxglove, tulips, daffodils, and lilies, assembled into bouquets, wreaths, and sprays. "Some of them were gaudy, some attractive, some cute, and a few looked unbelievably real. They all looked colorful at a distance and broke the desolate appearance of a bare mound of earth," according to a description from the Ouachita Mountains (Montgomery County, 1920s).[71]

Bernice Mhoon recalled how her mother set to work immediately after Decoration Day to begin making flowers for the following year. "She'd have one wall in the bedroom nearly covered with them. She made all that she could afford to buy paper for." Nellie Terherst remembered her grandmother's flowers. "She wasn't very good at it, but she was faithful at doing it!"

Crepe paper flowers didn't last all that much longer than fresh ones. "I can tell you this, it will sure rain on Memorial Day, or that night," Terherst said. "Aunt Della Glenn would work for days and days making flowers," recalled McChristian. "Then the first showers of rain laid them flat."[72] In an attempt to preserve them, some women dipped the flowers in melted paraffin, used to seal jelly jars, although this delayed deterioration only slightly. No matter what their condition, all flowers would be left in place until the following year's cleanup.

One other use for crepe paper was making clothing for little girls to wear at Decoration Day. At Ben's Branch Cemetery (Newton County, about 1920) young girls presented a program wearing matching paper dresses, presumably over their regular clothes.[73] Opal Arnold Taylor (Searcy County, born 1912) described making her six-year-old sister an entire outfit from white crepe paper. The dress was torn to create a fringe, and Taylor also used twisted wire and crepe paper to make a basket, filled with white paper roses, which the child wore to a Decoration Day.[74]

Other Grave Decorations

Wind chimes, solar-powered landscape lighting, and plastic knick-knacks that adorn contemporary graves are modern versions of what are termed grave goods, objects placed on a grave for decoration and remembrance. Two folklore students at the University of Arkansas described seeing grave goods

Figure 9.3 Bill Evans preaching beside the grave of his wife, Martha Jane Evans, in Old Evans Cemetery (Johnson County), Decoration Day, 1939. Daughter Mary Ellen Hamilton and her husband, Jode, look on. Martha (1866–1936) has a wooden frame surrounding her grave, similar to ones used to hold a decorative mixture of glass and crockery fragments, and a shadowbox protecting a picture of an angel. *Photo by Robert "Bob" Eaton, courtesy of Vernon L. Eaton.*

on African American burials near Russellville (Pope County, 1958) and on the graves of both blacks and whites in the southeastern part of the state (Ashley County), having death dates starting around 1900. They noted that only the graves of women and children were decorated this way, the children's burials having such toys as lead soldiers and parts of tea sets.[75] Another folklore collection described a child's grave (somewhere in the Arkansas Ozarks, 1941) as being outlined with upside-down canning jars, each one protecting a toy.[76]

The use of shells and household objects on African American graves was supposedly a holdover from West African traditions,[77] but such things were also placed on whites' graves. A study of the Upland South noted that "eyeglasses, eyecups, mugs, shaving articles, or other personal items" were common decorations on adult graves, though children's burials were more likely to have a wider variety of grave goods.[78]

One especially rare custom was creating a grave covering from bits of broken glass and china. Jane Evans (Madison County, pre-1931) would create a colorful mixture from pulverized dishes and bottles, combined with the previous year's mix, her grandchildren having the job of picking up and washing the bits and pieces found on the graves. Before Decoration Day this mixture would be spread atop newspapers inside the wooden frames that outlined each grave. India Evans Acord, Evans's granddaughter, later described Evans's rationale to her daughter-in-law, Peggy Harmon Stepp. "Granny Jane was half Indian," she said. "The broken glass is to keep evil spirits away. The broken dish is also a symbol of a broken family circle."[79]

Tommie Mooney grew up hearing about Evans. "She'd keep every broken jar, every old blue fruit jar, amethyst colored jars, any kind of glass that got broken during the year," Mooney recalled. "Anything the neighbors broke during the year, they saved it, knowing she'd come and pick it up." Some of this glassware is embedded in the ground there to this day. Whatever Evans's origins (she was born in Indiana, and is identified as white on all censuses), this tradition has African American roots. "Negro graves were always decorated with the last article used by the departed, and broken pitchers and broken bits of colored glass were considered even more appropriate than the white shells from the beach nearby," according to a source on slavery in Georgia;[80] another source states that broken dishes help the departing spirit break ties with the living.[81]

Elsewhere, opaque blue glass Vicks salve jars were used as grave ornaments, having been specially saved for this purpose.[82] Then there's Benjamin F. Red's reminiscence about finding an abandoned log house near which lay broken pieces of china (somewhere in Arkansas, story told in 1938). A graveyard in the vicinity contained the grave of a World War I soldier. "I saw pieces of the oddly patterned dishes decorating the side of the grave ... and a closer examination showed that they were parts of the broken dishes from the back door of the old ruined house."[83]

In a landlocked state like Arkansas, it comes as a surprise to find shells used as grave decorations, but the custom is an old one. For years, schoolchildren decorated the site where nine civilian men had been executed by Union troops (Madison County, 1863), placing wildflowers and mussel shells on the spot, though the victims had been buried elsewhere. Some of these shells were still there until recently, which helped researchers identify where the massacre occurred.[84] Traditionally, the scallop or cockleshell is a Christian emblem, symbolizing journeys, pilgrimages, and the baptism of Jesus.[85] Scallop shells sometimes form a decorative backdrop for motifs carved on tombstones and, while actual scallop shells are not found on graves, conch shells are. One speculation is that they "make mournful notes when blown"[86] but more likely they, too, were merely decorative. Both conches and other shells are listed among items sold by a Fort Smith undertaker in the late 1880s,[87] while one mail-order company sold conch shells, inscribed "At Rest," for graveyard decorations.

"I would love so much to have some of those large pretty sea shells to put on my children's graves," Clementine Watson Boles (Washington County, 1889) wrote to her aunt in Corpus Christi, Texas.[88] There are no conch shells in the Boles's plot today, but such shells are found in other cemeteries, often cemented to tombstones, bases, or plot curbing. Over time the exteriors have weathered to a shade of gray that, from a distance, make them appear to be made of stone or concrete.

Planting Cedars

The Eastern red cedar, called a "cemetery tree" by old-timers, has been used in southern burying grounds to delineate the corners of family plots, mark the heads of graves, flank entrances, or line avenues within the cemetery. According to Jabbour, cedars have a precedent in the yew trees found in English churchyards, some dating to pre-Christian times. "Yews are not native to the Upland South, but the native Eastern red cedar seems to have been adopted in Upland South cemeteries as a fitting cultural analog to the British churchyard yew," according to Jabbour.[89] There is no consensus on why the ancient English yews are so often found inside fenced cemeteries, whether from the need to protect cattle from the poisonous plant, to have wood handy for making longbows, or because the tree's evergreen color symbolizes the resurrection.

Though cedars are now found throughout the Ozarks, this was not always the case, and one Arkansan had to write home to Alabama to request seedlings to plant on her children's graves (1867).[90] In recent times, Dorsey Spurlock, an elderly man taking his first airplane ride (Madison County, 1991), expressed surprise at all of the cedars he saw from the air, as when he was a boy there was only one place, locally, to obtain these trees.

What is perplexing is that of all the superstitions concerning trees, by far the most widespread belief was that transplanting a cedar tree brings about the death of the person who does so. "When it gets big enough to shade your grave, you'll die" is how this is commonly expressed, the idea being that death will occur once the tree grows tall enough to cast a shadow the length of the person who transplanted it. Presumably this taboo did not apply to trees that were *intended* to shade a grave. This superstition is accompanied by the proviso that if a cedar absolutely must be transplanted then an elderly person should do the job.

Variations include a taboo against transplanting pines and weeping willow trees—significantly, these are also found in graveyards. Though brides and grooms in Randolph County once observed the custom planting cedars at either side of the walk leading to their home (called "beegee trees" or B-G, for "bride and groom"),[91] Randolph claimed the injunction against transplanting cedars was observed across the Ozarks.[92]

The Decoration Day Program

Unless the graveyard was adjacent to a church or schoolhouse, memorial services were held out in the open. Today, many cemeteries have permanent pavilions, open on the sides, that shelter pews or benches, modern versions of the brush or leaf arbors that were a standard feature of summer revival services.[93] When services were held indoors, "a 'runner' would be sent into the crowd to announce the event such as singing, public speaking, and the approximate time. Within minutes, the announcement would be spread through the crowd as effectively as if flashed on a television screen," according to John David Pile (Crawford County, 1930s).[94]

Decoration Day services were lengthy, their programs published in advance in town newspapers. Gar Creek Cemetery (Franklin County, 1911) announced there would be fourteen speeches, recitations, and declamations, in addition to a welcoming address and six songs.[95] Some events included sermons by one or more local ministers and, as noted above, this could be the occasion of an actual, delayed funeral, as well as a memorial to recent deaths. There might also be another attempt to save souls. "Some preacher from one of the community churches would preach a God-fearing sermon on death, hell, and damnation for the unsaved," wrote Sparks.[96] "It was about the resurrection, being ready to die," says Mooney, whose father was a Missionary Baptist minister (Madison County, late 1930s and early 1940s). "It was about always being prepared, and the possibility of being saved. I don't recall seeing anybody go up and be saved, but I'm sure it happened."

"Let's all feel that it is one of our duties to make this annual pilgrimage to the tombs of friends and loved ones," exhorted a community columnist (Madison County, 1930). After all, before another year was out, "we, ourselves, may have been laid to rest, and who are they that do not want the flowers as tokens of remembrance placed on their tombs?"[97]

Food

Those who reminisce about by-gone Decoration Days tend to wax especially nostalgic when describing the food, both its quantity and variety. At a time when luxuries were few and families lived on what they could raise, people brought their best foods to share at the noon meal, called "dinner on the ground." Food often *was* laid out on the ground, on tablecloths, but many cemeteries built long tables to hold this meal or laid planks atop pews brought from the nearest church. "If a preacher got carried away, they might not have lunch on time," conceded Mooney, and of course no one ate before a lengthy blessing was said.

"All persons are requested to come and bring a basket well filled with grub, so we can have a good time," the *Mountain Wave* urged its readers (Searcy County, 1898), adding the unnecessary reminder that these should be *loaded* picnic baskets.[98] Some women cooked for several days prior to the event; Terherst recalled her mother cooking fried chicken, fruit pies, corn-bread and biscuits, chicken and dumplings, garden produce, as well as bringing home-canned peaches and blackberries. Mhoon's mother would bake a couple of loaves of "light" bread (yeast-raised, not cornbread), as well as splurging on cans of mackerel for salmon cakes. One special, labor-intensive treat was the stack cake, made by baking numerous thin rounds of cake and layering them with cooked fruit or applesauce. The fruit softened and compacted the cake layers, which helped the towering construction stay together on the trip to the cemetery.

The same *Mountain Wave* article requesting plenty of "grub" also issued a few reminders. "All persons who come are expected to leave their prejudices and dogs at home and all young men are expected to leave their bottles and pistols at home."[99] The injunction against dogs was pointless—they arrived unbidden. "Every hound dog in the country showed up with the boys, to eat," said Burr Fancher (Madison County, 1930s). "We went to all of the Decoration Days, we went there to eat, not necessarily out of respect. We were hungry in the Depression. There were hundreds of people who showed up at these Decoration Days and the food was spread out for a quarter mile, all the food in the world," and it was there for all to share.

There was one downside to this. According to a Marion County history, "In an election year, most of the candidates for county offices attended all of these decorations and an aspiring candidate found himself duty-bound to eat a little from each table lest he offend some good lady and lose the vote of the family."[100] Besides the dangers of overeating, there was the threat of food poisoning. "Luckily nobody got ptomaine," recalled Fancher. "There was no

Figure 9.4 The Hoskins family helps ready the noon meal, served on long tables, known as "dinner on the ground," in Pine Grove Cemetery (Madison County), early 1940s. Addie Brandenburg Hoskins, *back to camera*, Tommie Hoskins, and her sister Geneva Hoskins, all wear dresses made from flour sacks by their mother, Addie. *Tommie L. Hoskins Mooney Collection.*

refrigeration for all those cream pies, with meringue, which is a recipe for food poisoning. They'd haul it in a wagon with mules for ten miles, but it was a tradition and a fine one."

Far from being depressing places, for one day of each year at least the cemetery was a vibrant, colorful place and the ritual that was practiced there was of comfort to the community. In the words of J. S. Helm (Izard County, born 1943), "I like to go to ol' graves cause you know your family gathered around that grave at one time, and you know you're walkin' in their tracks there."[101]

Childbirth, Children, and Death

The little crib is empty now
The little clothes laid by
A mother's hope, a father's joy
In death's cold arms doth lie.
Gone little May to thy home
On yonder blissful shore
We miss thee here but
Soon will come
Where thou hast gone before.

—May E. Cole, 1901–1901
Gaither Mountain Cemetery (Boone County)

Dwain Cook, just learning to walk, loved helping his grandfather do chores. "Daddy would cut stove wood out in the yard for Mother to cook with, little sticks. And that little old thing, he'd want to get that and carry it and lay it on the porch for Mother. . . . He was so sweet," Flossie Cook Smith said of her nephew.[1]

The toddler had barely passed his first birthday when whooping cough broke out in the Short Cove community where Dwain's mother, Roxie, had grown up (Madison County, 1934). Knowing this, she stayed away from a Mother's Day program at the school, only to have her relatives come visit her. Dwain caught whooping cough from a young cousin and suffered for two weeks before he died. Both custom and temperature dictated that burial take place the following day.

Dwain was the first grandchild in the family and, Smith said, "There hadn't been any deaths then to hurt us so bad."[2] Charlene Cook Grigg, born the following year, remembered seeing this brother's toys and the coins used

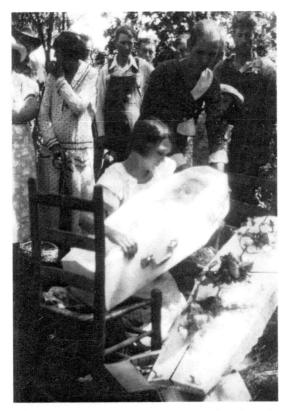

Figure 10.1 Roxie Cook holds son Dwain, in his coffin, Kingston (Madison County), 1934, with help from her mother, Myrtle May Mitchell. The coffin lid is covered in paper flowers, made by Kate Fancher. *Photo courtesy of Charlene Grigg.*

to weight his eyelids, and often witnessed her mother crying at his grave. "Mother didn't talk much about it, it was too hard," Grigg said, nor did her father ever speak of this son. According to her daughter, Roxie did, however, strongly urge one reluctant mother to have her children vaccinated, something that had not been available to Dwain. "If you went through the whooping cough like I did, you wouldn't slow down a minute to get those shots," she told the woman, who reluctantly acquiesced.

Giving Birth

Folk customs, medicinal plants, and patent medicines were believed to ease labor pain but nothing, and most certainly not the widespread superstition that placing an ax, knife, or scissors beneath the bed, would "cut" the pain or alleviate labor. Midwife Fanny Duck (Newton County, born 1869) administered her own remedy to the hundreds of women she helped with delivery. "I always kept some spicewood and black gum bark on hand," she told an interviewer when she was eighty-five, "and when I went to deliver a baby I always made and gave a cup full of black gum tea to start the misery and keep things going right for the baby to be born."[3] Teas concocted from eggshells, wasp nests, dirt dauber nests, and oil made from pigs' feet have all been mentioned in connection with bringing on or relieving labor pain,[4] along with black pepper tea, blackberry root tea, and gunpowder in water.

Doctors knew about this practice, and it gave them grounds for declaring midwives a public health problem. The fact that mortality from childbirth was higher in the South than in northern states was blamed on midwives, although mothers' poor nutrition was more likely the cause.

Midwives throughout the South—though not in the Ozarks—were predominantly African American,[5] but all midwives were labeled "a necessary evil" by Dr. C. W. Garrison, the state health officer, in 1930. Though he singled out black women as being "possessed of superstition and ignorance,"[6] both races practiced identical folk customs during deliveries. Many of these women learned their skills by helping their mothers deliver or through personal experience, as did midwife Florence Arnold (Sharp and Izard counties). Between 1884 and 1906 Arnold gave birth a total of sixteen times, with many of these births (none twins) separated by only one year.[7]

The state's attempts to regulate healthcare in 1881 and 1913 specifically exempted midwives, but after the United States Congress passed the Sheppard-Towner Maternity and Infancy Protection Act in 1921 Arkansas established its own Bureau of Child Hygiene. Now midwives and their practices came under scrutiny. By the mid-1920s individual county health units were teaching basic hygiene to some of the state's four thousand midwives,[8] while the state's board of health issued permits to those with established practices and forbade those it deemed "totally incompetent and incapable of improvement"[9] to deliver babies. It made no difference, and rates of maternal and infant deaths rose through 1928.[10]

Over the years, the board of health added to its list of requirements for midwives. By 1940 a first-time applicant had to submit letters of recommendation from two doctors, a nurse, and her county's health officer; undergo a physical examination that included a Wasserman test for venereal disease; and pass a home inspection. Among other things, her intelligence and ability to read were rated, her marital status recorded, and she was asked whether she was addicted to drugs or used snuff, and for the location of the nearest post office (presumably because of the need to file birth certificates). These licenses had to be renewed annually and, once in practice, women would be evaluated as to how faithfully they completed birth certificates, sought a doctor's help in difficult cases, and maintained their bags of equipment.[11] Midwives had to provide the items needed for a delivery, including sterile dressings and ampoules of silver nitrate (used in the newborn's eyes); some brought baby clothes and diapers with them to deliveries.

Ozark midwives often let their hard-won licenses lapse when the state made it increasingly difficult to renew them. In 1952 new regulations made practicing without a license a misdemeanor, punishable with a fine, jail time, or both,[12] prompting some women to stop practicing immediately, and others to do so only in emergencies. One Madison County woman, Marge Widdell Doty, delivered a number of babies without a license but, despite a local doctor's urging that she get one, refused in the belief that being licensed would require her to attend all labor cases, whether she wanted to or not.[13]

Statewide numbers of midwives, both licensed and not, declined steadily from 1940 on,[14] but the need for their services did not, as there was a chronic shortage of doctors and hospitals. "Even in these days of the miracle drugs, the 'granny midwife' is, of necessity, a strong health influence in rural sections of Arkansas," the *Arkansas Gazette* stated in 1950, and two years later the *Saturday Evening Post*, in a feature article about isolated Newton County, noted that there "children are born without medical assistance."[15]

Though many doctors disliked efforts to educate and thus legitimize midwives, not all were antagonistic toward them. "Although we have very few records . . . of how many babies Daddy delivered, we are sure it would be in the thousands—but he never ceased to be grateful to 'Granny' Franklin . . . for being present when he delivered his first baby," reminisced Reba Highfill Oakley of her father, Elisha Jay Highfill (Benton County, started practice in 1899). "He said if it had not been for her, he definitely would never have survived the ordeal."[16]

Not all families could afford a doctor's obstetrical fees. From the 1870s through the Depression, a regular house call was billed at $1 to $3.50, with charges of $5 and up to deliver babies. Dr. Leonidas Kirby (Boone County, 1878) charged one family the exorbitant fee of $34.50 for his mileage, an overnight house call, and "delivering wife with forceps," while some doctors added charges for postnatal visits and prescriptions.

In some cases the child's father or a neighbor delivered the baby, with local women almost always arriving before the doctor could. Dr. Kirby's records (1878–1910) have "born when I arrived" 48 times out of 709 births he logged,[17] but no matter when a doctor got there he would present the family with his bill. Midwives, though, did not charge for their services even though they, like doctors, were sometimes paid in produce. Their fee was first set at $5 by the state, the amount later increased to $35, although few either asked for or were offered money. This was especially unfair, as midwives stayed on in the home following the delivery, sometimes for days, caring for the mother and doing housework. They also acted as impromptu doctors during emergencies, and often laid out the dead in their communities.

The risks of pregnancy were exacerbated by the lack of prenatal care, something not provided by midwives and county health nurses until the 1930s. Other factors include early midwives' *and* doctors' inadequate knowledge of hygiene, and mothers' diets lacking in needed vitamins and minerals. Despite these obstacles, a woman was more likely to survive her first pregnancy than subsequent ones. To understand this, it helps to consider the age at which women married. Janet Allured, studying five hundred women in Boone County (1870 and 1910), estimated that the average age at first marriage was nineteen or twenty, slightly lower than the national average of 21.6 in 1910. "The figure, nonetheless, does not fit the stereotype of the backwoods girl barefoot and pregnant at age thirteen or fourteen," she wrote.[18] (A separate examination of over eight thousand marriage records by this book's author yielded an average age, at marriage, of exactly 21.6 years.)[19] In an era when large families were common, women who married in their twenties rather than as teenagers were thus continuing to bear children at advanced ages. The four mortality schedules, while containing an admittedly small sampling of maternal deaths, still show very few teenagers dying in childbirth; what is surprising is how many women died in their late thirties or early forties, something the tombstone record concurs with.

The gradual decline in the maternal and infant death rate was something the state board of health attributed to educating and regulating midwives, including stopping their dangerous practices and superstitions. However, simultaneously other factors were playing a part in the overall improvement in public health. These factors included rural electrification (bringing with it refrigeration), improved sanitation, government-sponsored canning kitchens, screens on homes, mosquito eradication programs, the advent of county health units with visiting nurses, and public health campaigns that eradicated debilitating internal parasites and venereal diseases.

Naming—or Not Naming—Children

One obstacle to getting birth certificates filled out had to do with parents' leisurely approach to naming their offspring. The health department's solution was to urge parents to choose names prior to the birth, but it was hardly a new problem, as evidenced by toddlers' tombstones from the late 1800s labeled only "Named in Heaven."

Perhaps the parents of Henry Ward Beecher Emmet Moss (Newton County, born 1879) were exhausted after choosing multiple names for him and five of his siblings, because their seventh child (born 1888) was *not* named. "I think it was a scandalous shame that our parents were so little interested that they never gave her a name," Moss wrote. "In fact, she never had a name until she was old enough to name herself," and even then the family refused to call her by it.[20]

Other explanations for the delay include waiting to be sure the child would live before bestowing a cherished family name, waiting until a circuit-rider minister returned to hold a christening and naming, or even the perhaps apocryphal notion that the census taker would be asked to assign names. It was important to make the right choice, as it was bad luck to change a child's name later. According to Madison County genealogist Joy Russell, "Some families wanted to name the child after an elected official, so they held off naming until the next election, which might be several years off." (Supposedly, in a county where the Democratic Party predominated, one family was so determined to honor a Republican candidate when he secured a particular office that eventually their boy became "X" by default.)

Stillborn babies or ones who died shortly after birth were rarely named. "Because he never breathed, they wouldn't let me give him a name," Mary Irene Collard explained to her granddaughter, showing her a tombstone inscribed "Infant Collard" (Cleburne County, died 1899).[21] In this way, as well as by refusing to allow women to even see their stillborn infants, women were forbidden to mourn their losses.

Some families followed the custom that a child's initials should spell a word, for good luck; another practice was naming a baby for everyone present at its birth. Bud Phillips (Newton County, dates unknown) knew of two women saddled in this fashion: Mandy Mayo Pitts Violet Mac Roberts and Sarah Daisy Rosey Adeline Mary Liza Annie Jane. ("They called her Annie.")[22] Even boy babies might be named for the only male likely to be in attendance, which explains why John and Ann Campbell named their baby Doctor McFaddin Campbell, after a Dover physician by that name (Pope County, 1870); nor was he the only Ozarks baby having "Doctor" as a first name. To the delight of future genealogists, some families called their children after various states. The Fugatt family (Independence County, children born 1856 to 1892) named daughters Missouri, Texas, Virginia, Tennessee, Louisiana, Alabama, Florida, Illinois, and possibly Indiana; sons were named Maryland (called "Merlin") and Georgia ("George"). The names may have had meaning for the parents, but not one refers to the state in which the child was born.[23]

Loving Too Much

Deferred naming might seem to bolster the theory that during times of high infant mortality parents tried not to bond with their children, to lessen the pain of losing them. If this lack of attachment occurred elsewhere, it seems not to have been true in Arkansas, where memoirs are filled with descriptions of parents grieving their children's deaths. According to Allured, "Interviews with Boone County women illustrate that children were highly valued in the latter half of the nineteenth century in the Ozarks."[24] Nor did a series of losses make subsequent infant deaths any easier to bear. Napoleon Bonaparte Cowan and his wife, Rosa, had lost twins, a young son, and possibly a fourth child (Newton County, 1883 and 1885) by the time daughter Teney was born (1897). Six months later they had this original expression of their grief carved on her tombstone:

> All I love a baby's grave
> all I praye a tiney girl
> she has gone to him who gave her
> god take me too.

By the 1910 census the Cowans had lost seven of their twelve children. Another original expression of loss, found on an infant's tombstone (Sharp County, 1916): "He taught us much we did not know."[25]

Parents bonded with their offspring to such an extent that when they died, some blamed themselves for having loved their children *too much*. "I am all alone in the world now that my precious Charlie Will was the last tie that bound me to earth," widow Clementine Watson Boles wrote to her aunt, following the death of her third and last child (Washington County, 1889). Describing herself as lonely, desolate, and punished by God, Boles speculated, "Perhaps I loved my husband and children too much was why they were all taken from me."[26] Such a notion is found in a popular epitaph:

> We had a little treasure once
> She was our joy and pride
> We loved her, oh, perhaps too well
> For soon she slept and died.

Memorial poetry, epitaphs, and obituaries advised parents on coping with these losses. Children's deaths were justified on the grounds that they kept the child from sinning or saved it from experiencing pain, sorrow, or sickness ("Sleep on darling, you have missed a world of trouble").[27] Another justification was that a fragile child could not have withstood the trials of an adult life, or that the child was simply in a better place ("A mother's tears may fall, but not for worlds would she her child recall").[28] Sometimes the child was said to have died "to call our hearts to heaven," that is, to ensure that the parents led good lives in order to be reunited later. More fancifully and rather cloyingly, some parents were consoled by the notion that God needed another star, flower, musician, or singer in his "angel band" in heaven, roles that only their child could fill.

There was also the belief that some children were simply too good, pure, or intelligent to live, and for this reason it was taboo to call a living child an angel, lest he die.[29] Of her brother's death at eighteen months (Washington County, 1859), Marian Tebbetts Banes wrote, "Persons talked of his extreme beauty and many said he was too angelic for this world. His great starry black eyes, his golden hair with a glint of red in it curling around his almost perfect face, his fine disposition and angelic smile, made him a joy to remember."[30]

Infant Diseases

It's no wonder parents tried to find meaning in their children's deaths, as often no one knew what had caused them to die. (In 1860 Crawford County's census taker simply listed "infancy" as the cause of death for five children who died at one month of age.) Based on the mortality schedules, hives and croup were the most common causes of death in young children. In the mid-1800s hives, a skin eruption or type of rash, is frequently listed as the cause of death in children under age three, but true hives are not fatal. Instead, it is thought that these deaths were actually caused by croup, a throat obstruction characterized by a distinctive cough and difficulty breathing.[31]

Hives were also called "bold hives," a term once common across the South and used by both blacks and whites to describe something that, again, was not true hives. Andrew P. Cavender, in *Folk Medicine in Southern Appalachia*, defines the condition as

> an infant-specific folk illness distinctly different from the type of hives (urticaria) recognized by official medicine. From the folk medical perspective, newborns entered the world with hives—a mysterious, undefinable entity—inside their bodies. Like measles and chicken pox, hives had to be forced out before it "turned inward," thus transforming into *bold* hives. If the hives turned inward, normal body functions were adversely affected. Many people thought that bold

hives "wrapped around" or "attacked" the heart and lungs, and if not properly treated, death was inevitable.[32]

Cavender speculates that the terms "bull" or "bold" hives were a corruption of "bowel hives," a condition first described in early Scottish medical texts.[33] Vance Randolph, reporting this as *boll* hives, wrote that Ozark doctors deemed the condition "mythical" but nonetheless were often called upon to treat it. "When I get there I generally find a case of ordinary hives," he quotes Dr. J. H. Young as saying, "and they always get well."[34] Mildred Heffley, however (Newton County, born 1930), recalled her baby brother's death from "bow hives" despite having a doctor in attendance. She described the rash as being "as big around as your little finger, and it would turn purple under the skin, and this little baby was covered with it. . . . He turned purple, and them spots were everywhere."[35]

This threat terrified new mothers, told to beware of such telltale symptoms as a baby rolling its eyes[36] or "smiling and opening their eyes when they're asleep" (Izard County, 1920s).[37] After Jo Anne Rife's first child, Shara, was born (Benton County, 1949), she received daily visits from an elderly neighbor who considered herself an expert on such things. "She'd get her spectacles out and put them on, look Shara over and then say, 'You'd better be careful, child, or you'll drive those hives in, and she'd die right away.' I'd look at Shara and say, 'Why, I don't see any hives.'" The neighbor was adamant that they existed. "'They're there, right under the skin. I can see them. I've seen many of 'em.' I asked her what would 'drive them in.' 'A little too hot or a little too cold. Sometimes just a breath of air will do it.'"[38]

An infant that had broken out ("as spotted as a speckled pup") was presumed to feel better.[39] More important, it was now out of danger. The belief that hives could be fatal explains the notion that babies had to be *made* to break out. "I killed three of my mother's babies," confessed a woman whose mother, bedridden for the requisite ten days to two weeks following giving birth, told her young daughter how to prepare teas to give the newborn (Missouri Ozarks, early 1900s). Only as an adult did she realize that the teas—not hives—had killed them.[40] Some of the substances used for this included whiskey, juice from a roasted onion, mullein and catnip tea, "skillet-bark tea" made from the sooty scrapings off the underside of an iron pan, mashed sow bugs mixed with breast milk, and tea made from the hive vine or deerberry (*Vaccinium stamineum*). It's no wonder that by the 1930s licensed midwives had to sign a pledge promising "not to give any medicine or tea to mothers or their children unless ordered by a doctor."[41]

These herbal concoctions sound positively benign compared to the turpentine, kerosene, and coal oil, mixed with sugar, which was fed to children in small doses, to cure various complaints including croup. These substances were used medicinally up until recent times, though the origins of the custom have been lost.[42] Randolph, writing about the medicinal use of turpentine, stated that lots of Ozarks children died from nephritis, a kidney disease doctors attributed to their being dosed with turpentine.[43]

Sheep manure has to be the most repulsive tea ingredient of all. It has been called "sheep ball tea," "nanny tea," or the more genteel-sounding "sheep saffron tea." (Lacking a flock, dried cow manure could be used instead.)[44] This was the remedy of choice for forcing hives or measles to break out whenever they were slow to do so. Tate "Piney" Page (Pope County, early 1900s) made the distinction between old, dried droppings (used to break out hives in infants) and "hot" or fresh manure, used to make measles erupt.[45] June Eaton Geiger (Madison County, born 1927) described how the therapy was used on her sister, Doll, who got the measles but did not exhibit the telltale rash.

> Dad got Dr. [Beeby] to come to the house. He told Dad he could do nothing, but if she didn't break out by morning she would be gone by nightfall. Dad got a paper bag and told me to come along. We walked to where there was a stock pen . . . There were sheep in the pen and Dad told me to chase the sheep until they defecated. He gathered the "sheep pills" in his paper bag, took them home, placed them in a clean cloth bag and boiled them. Then he poured the liquid through another clean cloth and when it cooled he gave it to Doll to drink. He sat at her bedside throughout the night and by morning you couldn't put the head of a pin between the bumps.

In response to the surprised doctor's query, Geiger's father only said, "I made her some tea."[46]

Diarrhea, another common cause of death in young children, was also called cholera infantum, flux, dysentery, deranged digestion, choleric fever of children, cholera morbus, summer diarrhea, or summer complaint. "Back then when a little kid took that they nearly always died," recalled Trude Foster (Izard County, born 1923),[47] death occurring quickly once the child became dehydrated. This condition was treated with herbal teas, calamus root, and the blackberry plant, its roots and leaves in tea, and its fruit in cordials.

One final medicinal plant that had wide usage was asafetida (also asafoetida), colloquially pronounced "ass-a-fiddity." Latex sap from the root of this plant, *Ferula assa-foetida*, related to carrots, parsley, and fennel, was dried and placed in little cloth bags and was believed to ward off disease. Children—both white and black—wore these bags around their necks all winter, and were allowed to remove them by spring, or "when the first whippoorwill sang.[48] The substance was so foul smelling that it may have done its job simply by keeping other people and their germs at bay but, because it was believed to work better when wet, children were encouraged to chew on their asafetida bags. Asafetida has been found on the inventories of general stores as far back as 1840[49] and was worn as recently as the 1950s, according to many of the people interviewed for this book.

Unconventional Therapies

One ancient treatment used on sick children was known as scarifying. "I saw my mother lay a baby brother across her lap, prick his shoulder with a needle, draw out a drop of blood through an open end thimble, pour it in a spoonful of her own milk and feed it to him," wrote Estella Wright Szegedin (Crawford County, born 1897). She questioned a one-hundred-year-old friend about the practice. "I have seen doctors do this, but I never knew mothers who did it," the woman told her. "And I don't know why it was done."[50] Martha Poyner, a doctor's daughter (Carroll County, born 1908), described an early, related croup therapy this way: "small gashes were cut on the chest, pieces of paper were placed over the cut places and a cup of hot water [was poured] over the paper," a practice she attributed to "religious cults."[51]

Scarifying was also believed to cure thrush (or "thrash"), a contagious fungal disease characterized by a whitish substance that coats the mouths, throats, and tongues of infants and that could be fatal.[52] However, the standard cure for thrush was to get a "posthumous child," someone born after his or her father's death, to blow into the infant's mouth. Randolph wrote that "There is no excuse for a properly reared mountain baby ever having thrash anyhow, since it can be prevented by carrying the newborn babe to a small hole in the wall or chinking and allowing the sunlight which streams through to enter the child's mouth."[53] An even simpler cure: "water poured from a crack in a shoe."[54] This footgear could not belong to a relative, which explains why people came from miles around to use Swedish-born Adolf Lager's shoes for this purpose (Newton County, 1920s), knowing he could not possibly be kin to them.[55]

Children suffering from asthma usually had to outgrow the condition, but parents could resort to "plugging" in an attempt to help. "I remember my mother told me how, when she was a young girl, they bored a hole in a tree

Figure 10.2 Infant's funeral, Dutton Cemetery (Madison County), about 1920. *Courtesy Shiloh Museum of Ozark History/Wayne Martin Collection (S-98-2-105), and Dan Martin.*

and put the child's hair in the hole," said Truman Gurley of his mother when she was about ten years old (Madison County, 1900). "They backed her up to that tree, stuck her hair in, and put the plug back [to hold it] and cut it off with scissors." The procedure either hurt or scared the girl, as Gurley added, "She was really squalling!"

Randolph collected another version of this custom. "If a child does not grow fast enough, back him up against a tree and cut a notch in the bark, on a level with the top of his head. Put some of the child's hair in the notch," a practice he claimed to have seen work.[56] He also recorded that the technique was used to cure asthma in adults when hair, inserted into a black oak tree hole, was cut off flush with the sufferer's scalp. "When the bark grows back over the hole so that the peg is no longer visible, and the patient's hair grows out to replace the missing lock, the asthma will be gone forever."[57] According to different sources, cure occurs when the patient grows taller than the hole (bored in a persimmon tree), or when bark grows over the hole.

Fayrene Stafford Farmer described something similar, used by a "faith doctor" on her mother as a child (Newton County, 1890s). The cure involved nailing a lock of her hair to a big tree. "He asked her to repeat a certain phrase," Farmer wrote. "He cautioned the child to never repeat the words he told her. The lock of Mama's hair was cut and left hanging to the tree." The doctor said the girl would have three more asthma attacks, one severe, but there would be no recurrences after that. "And so it happened," Farmer wrote.[58]

There is hardly room to give a complete catalog of the remedies and therapies administered to children, but one more should be mentioned: passing a child through a hole in a tree or object to alleviate various symptoms. Mary Parler's students were told that passing a stunted child through a loop of string held by three elderly women encouraged growth,[59] or through the trunk of a hollow tree.[60] According to Bruce Vaughan, quoting old-timers, "To 'koure th' colic' in a baby, you took a well-worn horse collar and passed the child through the horse collar fourteen times."[61] Another colic cure was taking a child to the river and getting someone who was "no blood kin" to carry the child back and forth across the river three times. "After the third time he took off his shoe, dipped up some river water, and gave the baby a drink from the shoe," a sure cure according to Vaughan's source.[62]

Teething

Teething as a cause of death sounds odd but self-explanatory. However, a study of illness and death in New England (1840–1916) attributes teething deaths to cholera infantum, a form of gastroenteritis, and not true cholera. "Teething infants who were being weaned from their mothers were known to succumb to the disease quickly, causing people to believe that teething itself was the cause of the illness."[63]

Cholera infantum was noncontagious, often fatal, and usually caused by a child eating food or milk that had spoiled in hot weather. This accounts for the alternate name for the disease—summer complaint—as it most often strikes in summer or early fall. Children who were just starting to eat solid foods were most at risk of becoming sick. A cursory and hardly comprehensive perusal of the mortality schedules for the Arkansas Ozarks (1850 through 1880), combined with death records compiled in Fort Smith, yields seventy-two examples of deaths attributed to teething, equally divided between the hot and cold months of the year.

Patent medicines claimed to cure the condition, such as Mrs. Winslow's Soothing Syrup for Children Teething (late 1800s).[64] This may have merely drugged fretful children, because McGee's Baby Elixir (1908), another teething nostrum, accused its competitors of creating "baby morphine fiends" by adding narcotics to their formulas.[65] In an era before teething rings that could be sterilized, children gnawed on strings of roots, shoots and seeds, or even chicken bones, snake rattles, and vertebrae,[66] which could have led to infections. (Hence the death of a one-year-old male from "rotten gum" in 1850.)[67] Other sources of infection may be traced directly to the folk remedies used to ease teething, such as killing a rabbit and rubbing the brains on the child's gums.[68] One primitive method of tanning leather uses an animal's own brain to dress and toughen the scraped hide, possibly the origin of this teething remedy.

"Another way to make teeth come easier is to give the child a mole's foot to play with," Randolph wrote. "The old tradition is that it should be the left hind foot, but the big fleshy front paws are the only ones I have actually seen given to babies."[69] Szegedin's father used several methods on his daughter (Crawford County, born 1897) when she was cutting teeth, including tying a mole's front feet around her neck.[70] In addition to these substances, Parler's students were told about rubbing a child's gums with bacon rind, chicken brains, rabbit lungs, and either live or dead minnows.[71] Though not a teething remedy, it was recommended that urine (called "chamber lye") be rubbed in a child's mouth to cure thrush or that a child chew on a urine-soaked diaper to cure colic—either one of which could have contributed to fatal gum infections.[72]

Worms

Judging from the frequency with which worms and worm fever are listed as a cause of death on the mortality schedules, and the vast numbers of herbs, teas, and patent medicines used to expel these parasites, this was a very real concern prior to the advent of public health campaigns to eradicate intestinal worms. As a child, Opal Arnold Taylor witnessed the death of Johnnie Luther, her baby brother, attributed to an overdose of worm medicine (Searcy County, 1917). "The old-time doctor, he used vermifuge, and he [the baby] was overdosed. The worms came up through his mouth, and passed out in handfuls through his diaper. I remember seein' my daddy standing at the split fence palings, I can see him emptying that diaper over that fence, with them worms in it. And that's what killed him," she said.[73]

Taylor believed her two-year-old brother had worms because he ate dirt, which many children did. Known as geophagy, this practice has been associated with the South and was observed among blacks during slavery, although it dates as far back as colonial times and does not, in fact, cause hookworm.[74] (The cause of death listed for Mary Towson, a seven-year-old African American girl in Drew County, 1880, was "eating dirt.")[75]

It is most commonly found among both black and white women and children, though usually it is clay, not dirt, which is eaten.[76] There are people alive today who ate "clay dirt" as children and who continue to crave it.

Emma Mankin Byler well remembered her parents' remedy for treating pinworms (Izard County, born 1916). "Put two or three drops of turpentine on a spoonful of sugar and eat a little at a time or lick it till it's gone. Then rub some turpentine around the navel and hollow of the throat."[77] Newspapers were filled with ads for over-the-counter products, while home remedies included teas made from pumpkin seeds, wild sage, peach leaves, senna, and pokeroot, as well as ipecac (a purgative) and homegrown tobacco leaves. The most oft-cited remedy, however, was Jerusalem Oak seed (*Chenopodium botrys*), also called Goosefoot, Wormseed, or American Wormseed, usually administered in tea or molasses candy. It is this plant that is meant any time "vermifuge seeds" are referred to.

Parents couldn't always be positive that their children had worms, given the condition's many supposed symptoms, and some took the precaution of giving their children a yearly dose of vermifuge. Symptoms in an early medical text used by one Arkansas doctor included "grinding the teeth in the sleep," something a folklore student collected ninety years later.[78] Kickapoo Worm Killer ("a pleasant candy lozenge") ran an ad spelling out how parents could make a correct diagnosis (1913). "Peevish, ill-tempered, fretful children, who toss and grind their teeth, with bad breath and colicky pains, have all the symptoms of having worms."[79] Ads for the widely popular White's Cream Vermifuge (1908) listed a "yellow and pasty" complexion, listlessness, and flatulence as being possible symptoms.[80]

Hookworm was not suspected, though by one estimate one-fourth of all school-age children had it.[81] "The disease was not generally known or recognized, even by the medical profession, and thousands of persons had been treated for tuberculosis, chronic malaria, and other chronic diseases" but, instead, had hookworm.[82] Symptoms included weight loss, anemia, swelling of the feet and stomach, and a desire to eat dirt or chalk. This disease was eradicated after the Rockefeller Sanitary Commission undertook a public health campaign (1910–1914) that included medical tests, public education, and free clinics.[83] Treatment was also given for any pinworms, tapeworms, and roundworms found in patients' stool samples.[84]

Since most children went barefoot, except during the coldest weather, they easily contracted worms. Combine this with the fact that in many rural areas people defecated in the woods, not in outhouses, and that hogs, cattle, and chickens roamed unpenned. It's no wonder the Rockefeller Commission's emphasis on building "hygienic privies" and getting children to wear shoes to school contributed to eradicating this disease.

One of the projects undertaken by the federal government's Works Progress Administration was constructing free "pit toilets" for individual families. Though the WPA had six hundred such outhouses constructed (Montgomery County outside the Ozarks, early 1940s), Creo Jones, who worked for this program, explained, "With the toilets installed, it was difficult to get the masculine members of the household to use them. Toilets were for the women and were seldom used by the men unless they were sick and couldn't make it to the barn, cow shed, or woodland."[85] The area behind the smoke house, ash hopper, a rail fence, or (urination only) in the chimney corner outdoors were the preferred places for relieving oneself.

Even as late as the 1950s many people still didn't have an outhouse. Paul Faris, puzzled by the lack of such buildings behind the log cabins he photographed (northwest Arkansas, 1949–1952), asked where they were. "One native Ozarkian has since told me that many older families considered it 'more sanitary to go to the woods.'"[86] Nor did Faris find any evidence of outhouses behind one abandoned school, though there was a "well-beaten path" behind the building that forked into two paths and disappeared into the woods. "Bathrooms?" wrote one woman of the rural school she attended as a child (Van Buren County, 1931). "We had a 'boys woods' on the north side and a 'girls woods' on the south side" behind the school.[87]

Loving Too Little

Not all parents were loving and attentive; undertakers' records and the mortality schedules list children's deaths from starvation, exposure, and neglect. Abortion, done in secret, came to light only after a mother died or a fetus was found. Though Dr. W. E. Acree was exonerated of the charge of "aiding one Miss Haley Hensley to produce an abortion" (Madison County, 1912) and Hensley denied the charge, she pleaded guilty to "concealing the death of her child."[88] This was not the first time Hensley had disposed of unwanted offspring. Two years earlier when she, her mother, and an infant traveled through Fayetteville (Washington County, 1910), guests in the hotel where they were staying told how "the baby cried continually from the time they went to their room until its cries were hushed by death" at 4:30 in the morning. Apparently no action was taken, and the baby was buried by the county, as the women had just $1.90 between them.[89]

Sometimes doctors weren't permitted to save a child's life when the parents believed that medical intervention opposed God's will. Though Dr. T. J. Pollard was renowned for his surgical skills (Washington County, late 1830s and later) he was not allowed to insert a tube into the neck of a child who was choking to death with croup. Instead, the parents sat by and watched their child die. "What a pity! Such a little way to life," the doctor remarked sadly.[90] Another harrowing story involves a pregnant woman who died at full term (Newton County, 1958), the fetus suffocating inside her after her family refused permission for a caesarean section.[91]

Evidence of infanticide turned up from time to time, almost always without the perpetrator being discovered. Several such cases were discovered near Cove Creek (Searcy County), but whether this community had a higher incidence of the crime or merely reported it more often is hard to say. People out fishing found a baby's body in a shoebox (1909), and four years later first one baby's body was found in a creek then shortly afterward a second infant, burned, in a furnace (1913).[92] Elsewhere, newspaper accounts tell of babies' bodies discovered in ash pits (presumably having been burned, to dispose of them), in streams and rivers, in shallow graves, beside railroad tracks, and hidden under trash piled in a vacant lot. One infant was found hidden inside a threshing machine and narrowly escaped being killed (Carroll County, 1892).[93]

It's impossible to know why some parents deliberately murdered their infants, but newspaper accounts suggested incest. The Knowles family (Benton County, 1914) gave their neighbors plenty to talk about after their seventeen-year-old daughter became pregnant. Mrs. Knowles had taken the youngest children with her to Eureka Springs where she found work, leaving the oldest daughter behind with her father. After the birth, father and daughter joined Mrs. Knowles in Eureka Springs—minus a new baby—and denied all knowledge that there had ever been one. After Mr. Knowles was jailed, the daughter confessed and told officers where the infant's body could be found; nothing more is known about the participants.[94]

The trial of Ed Cox (Sharp County, 1917) was even more sensational. Daughters Lucy, age nineteen, and Eva, age sixteen, accused their father of "numberless occasions" of incest, both claiming they had borne children by him. Lucy testified that she had given birth to a baby the previous year, delivered by her father, and never saw the child again. Eva claimed to have had three babies by her father, "and what became of the children she did not know." The newspaper account concluded, "Cox is a poor man and leaves here a family of eight children, the youngest of which is nine years of age, without any visible means of support. A purse of several dollars was made up here among the citizens to help them."[95] Cox was sentenced to a life term in the penitentiary.[96]

Mothers convicted of committing infanticide were sentenced to surprisingly little jail time, as in the case of Miss Hensley, above, who was given a single day in the penitentiary, which she did not have to serve. Not all mothers were found guilty at trial, even after a chorus of witnesses testified against them. Caroline Linzy, a young African American woman, was accused of killing her first child, whose body was found partially eaten by hogs (Pope County, 1884). Despite a great deal of suspicion cast upon her, including a doctor testifying that the child had been born alive, she was acquitted of murder.[97]

Both obituaries and memoirs attest to the casual attitude people sometimes took toward finding homes for orphaned children. Large sibling groups were usually split up, the brothers and sisters sometimes not seeing one another again for years. Even so, it's hard to know what to make of the headline in a Fayetteville newspaper, "A Live Baby to be Given Away" (Washington County, 1907). Captain Ament's traveling show, which included comedy and a trained dog act, announced that it was going to give an orphaned baby ("from a respectable family") to a married couple on the night of the show. While this may have increased attendance, there was no mention of the give-away in subsequent newspapers, other than for an unexplained and likely unrelated item that a baby, "recently left at the home of Dr. H. D. Wood" had been sent to an orphanage in Fort Smith.[98]

Preserving Memories

As discussed in chapter 4, following a death families wanted to save mementos of their loved one. Often when a young child died, the family had no photograph of it. This may have been due to the superstition that it was bad luck to take a child's picture before it was six months old,[99] but not all families had money or access to a photographer. In such cases parents went to great lengths to have a postmortem photograph taken. Roberta Watts Ferguson was told the story of how her father had his firstborn child, a stillbirth, photographed en route to the burial (Searcy County, 1934). "After being dressed the baby's body was wrapped in a quilt and my dad took the baby in his car stopping at his parents' home ... where his mother covered herself in a quilt and held the baby for a picture to be taken."

Sometimes a photo was taken when a child was dying, just in case. Moss's father had a tintype made of his son (Missouri, 1884) after the five-year-old was accidentally shot and a doctor pronounced him certain to die. The family was en route from Arkansas to Nebraska at the time and stopped in the first town with a photographer's studio where he, but not his older siblings, had his photograph taken.[100]

The saddest stories concern parents who had practically nothing to save. An older Searcy County resident recalled how, as a child, she'd seen adults "drawing the hands and feet" of her baby sister after death—that is, tracing around them on sheets of paper, in order to have something to remember the

Figure 10.3 Photoceramic portrait on the tombstone of Murle May (1910–1915), Ben's Branch Cemetery (Newton County). The shoes May wears were recently found, hidden above a door lintel in the family home. *Photo by Abby Burnett.*

child by. Another source recalled how her parents found their son's tiny, bare footprint in the garden after he died, and how they kept a box over the print in an attempt to preserve it. The mother of Otto Davis even saved the piece of candy her son had been eating the day he died (Madison County, 1900).[101] It was important to save something—even information. In his funeral museum Tom Olmstead displayed the Hanson baby scales that his father, undertaker Ralph Olmstead, took with him to a family's home when picking up an infant's body for burial (Cleburne County, early 1900s). "The mother never knew the weight of the child and kind of wanted to know," Olmstead said of these home births.

It's not obvious why some mementoes were saved. Wendel and Liz Norton, restoring an ancestral log cabin (Newton County, built 1839), found a child's well-worn pair of shoes hidden above a door. These shoes match ones in the photoceramic on five-year-old Murle May's tombstone (Newton County, 1915).[102] Though one item of folklore, African American in origin, states that if a child's shoes are placed on a table or dresser "the baby will never grow any higher than that,"[103] according to Randolph children's shoes were of great importance. "For a baby to lose a shoe is regarded as a very serious matter, and all the people in the house drop their other affairs to hunt for it. Sometimes men are even called in from the fields to help. If the shoe is not found, it is a sure sign that somebody in the family will die."[104]

Participation by Children

Children were spared *nothing* when it came to witnessing death and participating in burials. Exposing them to harsh reality ensured that they understood how brief and uncertain life was, but in case they missed this point preachers were ready to remind them of it. "Ye young 'uns, don't think yer goin' to live forever," James C. Hefley quoted a minister addressing children at a revival (Newton County, 1930s). "Jist look in any graveyard, and ya'll find people yer size thar."[105] (The distance between headstone and footstone shows the length of the grave's occupant.) They didn't have far to look, either, because schoolhouses were often built in proximity to the community cemetery.

Children were expected to perform every role adults did. George Bond was sixteen (Washington County, 1908) when he decided to attend an inquest over the body of a man whose murderer was very likely the victim's own father-in-law. Bond was the only spectator, and when the coroner's jury left to view the murder scene he was asked to stay behind. The boy was told, "The body's in that room, you've seen it, you know where it is. . . . If some disturbance comes along, you can go in and see what the trouble is." After the men left, Bond *did* hear something, which worried him because the murderer was still at large. Arming himself with a fireplace poker, Bond entered the room to investigate, "only to find a big grey tom cat prowling around in the room," to his great relief.[106]

There are many stories of children having to deal with the dead. As a teenager, Viola Williams (Carroll County, 1945) had to "baby sit" a dead infant while her mother sat with the baby's mother and her father dug its grave. "I didn't think about it at the time," she said, but later it bothered her. Emma Mason Bradley, who made burial clothing and sewed linings for the caskets made by her father, expected her children to help when they were five or six years old (Conway County, outside the Ozarks, 1920s). "One time a wagon train of people came through and a woman in the group became quite ill and died. Eva Lee and Thelma were very small. They sat and swished flies and kept the cats and etc. away from the corpse while the men made the casket and I made the lining to bury that strange woman in."[107] Children also sat up with the sick, though usually without doing actual nursing.

Nor was the job of laying out the dead reserved for adults. Milbra Eaton Parker was a teenager when she had to lay out an infant (Madison County, 1940). Parker's father had sat up all night with a neighbor's sick baby, and when it died Parker was told to take over. "I had to close its eyes and put its little hands together and then dress it," she recalled. "I was just a kid then. That was hard on kids, to do things like that."[108] Another account concerns life on the poor farm (Izard County, 1930s). James Rush had bid on the job of caring for paupers, and son Jack was expected to help. Lydia Moser Rider, whose sister later married Jack, recalled that after an elderly pauper died Jack's father told him, "You go up there and wash him, and get his clothes on, and get him ready for burying." It's unknown how old Jack was at the time, but another boy helped him dress the body. Suddenly the corpse emitted a loud noise, frightening the two so badly they "nearly knocked the walls down getting out of there!" Jack reported to his father that the man wasn't dead, only to be told, "That's just air coming out," and the two were sent back to finish the job.[109]

Children also performed adult roles at the funerals of other children, walking in procession behind the coffin or serving as pallbearers. Eight-year-old Katie Pressley's obituary, written by her classmates, was as florid as anything penned by an adult writer (Benton County, 1903). "We who followed to her last resting place saw the coffin lowered into the grave, listened to the hollow sound of clods as they fell on the lid, [and] will never forget our little friend," they wrote.[110]

When the time came, children were also expected to take a farewell look into the coffin. When young Jewell Farrar died in Springdale (Washington County, 1906), "the casket was opened in the yard to give the children and playmates of Jewel an opportunity to view the remains," as was done for adults.[111] One of June Martin's earliest memories was of being taken to a funeral (Madison County, 1938) and lifted up by her father so she could look into a wicker bassinette. "He asked if I wanted to see the baby," she recalled. "I was three years old."

Children were also not spared the sight of their friends' suffering and deaths. The Sunday School classmates of four-year-old Mary Jo Buttram bore an added burden (Benton County, 1925). These children had stopped at Buttram's house with valentines and the child ran excitedly to the kitchen to show them to her parents. She tripped over a tub of scalding laundry water, burning her so badly that she died two weeks later. "I can remember Mother taking me to see my playmate and pal," an unnamed source recalled. "She was wrapped in cheesecloth and swabbed in a yellow salve." The same children attended

Buttram's funeral.[112] Another child, six-year-old Ruthie O'Neal (Izard County, 1929), was severely burned when her clothing caught fire. A mixture of sulphur and molasses was applied to her burns, and she died two days later. According to Madge Tate Stephens, five years old at the time, "They put it on her and it was horrible. . . . But they let all the children come and see her after she died. I don't know if that was bad, or good, but we did. . . . It was very traumatic."[113]

Though children in the Ozarks were exposed to both the facts of life and the reality of death, they were affected by what they witnessed. Nora Davis Standlee (Carroll County, born about 1895) was taken to her cousin Maude's funeral, held long after the actual burial. "I could see signs of hysteria especially from Maude's mother who was a highly emotional lady so I crept to the shelter of my parents' spring wagon and covered my head with a blanket in order to muffle [the] sounds of loud weeping. When my father found me I was a sorry sight," she wrote, and her parents vowed never to subject their children to such events again.[114] Thada Miller Cockrill was carried into the bedroom to view her father's body, when she was four years old (Izard County, 1912). She wrote that adults didn't explain death to their children. "You didn't tell kids that they went to heaven, they just died," she recalled.[115]

CHAPTER ELEVEN

Disenfranchised Death

Grieve not for him who dieth
    for his struggling soul is free
& the world from which it flieth
    is a world of misery.

He died to live, he sank to rise
    He left this wretched mortal shore
But brighter suns & bluer skyes
    shall shine on him forevermore.

—William Rosson, 1832–1894
Rankin Cemetery (Franklin County)

In 1867 the Arkansas State Penitentiary, adopting a practice common across the South, began leasing convicts to various industries. The owners of plantations, railroads, and coalmines housed the men and paid the state generously for their labor. There was little oversight, and not until the "Coal Hill Horrors" came to light (Johnson County, 1888) did it become known that many of these prisoners had been worked, beaten, and starved to death.[1] By the time the penitentiary's commissioners investigated the camp, sixty to seventy convicts had died, their bodies "taken about a half-mile from the stockade and buried in a marshy place in graves sixteen inches deep, in pine boxes, with a piece of blanket for a shroud and without any ceremony whatever." The *Arkansas Gazette* likened this graveyard to "a rooting place for hogs."[2] It is unlikely that the men's relatives ever learned what became of them.

This is an example of disenfranchised death, a term usually applied to ones society does not formally acknowledge, such as miscarriages and stillbirths. In this chapter, however, it is used to define deaths that, for a variety of reasons, were not mourned in the conventional manner, if mourned at all. It does not, however, refer to suicides. Unless a body was found in a deteriorated condition, or when a suicide note made a specific request ("Bury me as I am"), even these deaths were accorded the full funeral ritual.

Poor Farm and Pest House Deaths

The cliché "Death loves a shining mark" appears often in obituaries but of course death isn't choosy. It comes for the minister, the mayor, and the senator as well as criminals, the elderly poor, infants, and the insane. Long before there were welfare programs, those living on the fringes of society relied on local charity, and when they died they were buried at town expense. In Eureka Springs (Carroll County, 1886–1896) it fell to the ladies to provide aid to indigent health seekers who flocked there and, it was suspected, to others sent there by surrounding communities wishing to unburden themselves. The Ladies United Relief Association was formed to provide assistance, including burials. After ten years of doing what the county could or would not do, the ladies attempted to get the Carroll County poor farm to "do its duty toward the indigent."[3] After all, this was what a poor farm was designed to do: house the poor, elderly, sick, lame, blind, insane, and orphaned, and anyone else without means.

Arkansas's poor farms (also called poorhouses or county farms) were modeled on those created during England's Industrial Revolution in the late 1700s. An act passed by the Arkansas legislature in 1851 authorized each county to buy land, erect buildings, and accept the lowest bid submitted for the feeding, clothing, and medical care of any paupers.[4] The law was modified over the years; in 1875 an act allowed these indigents to work for the county, with any "protesting pauper" to be examined by a doctor to ensure that he was physically capable of working.[5] In 1889 an act decreed that paupers "able to perform manual labor shall be worked on said [poor] farms," the county selling any surplus crops that were produced there.[6]

Prior to the establishment of poor farms, paupers were housed with whomever charged the least amount for their care. In addition to being paid, this low bidder could use the pauper's labor for one year.[7] This is seen in one county's general fund accounting: payment to G. M. Drain for $3.15 for housing a pauper and, not coincidentally, $7.50 to Drain for hauling rocks (Madison County, 1911).[8] Eventually most counties created a poorhouse or farm, but a few continued to place paupers with individual families well into the 1900s,[9] usually when the farm was overcrowded. Some, like Cleburne County (until

1903), used both systems simultaneously.[10] With the establishment of the Social Security Act of 1935, inmate populations began to dwindle; eventually the farms were closed, though in the early 1950s some counties returned to the bidding system of pauper care. The Poor House Act of 1851 was repealed in 1977.

Living conditions were often bad because, despite the construction of the Arkansas State Lunatic Asylum in Little Rock (Pulaski County, 1882), the insane were incarcerated on these farms whenever the asylum was over-crowded, which was often.[11] In 1907 all eleven of the residents of Carroll County's farm were insane, which a reporter thought helped explain why the place was so unclean,[12] but in fairness, county judges sometimes solved their own overcrowding problems by declaring elderly paupers "insane" and bundling them off to the state asylum.[13] For this reason some poor farms had actual jail cells, complete with shackles used to restrain the insane, as well as the occa-sional violent criminal housed there. Mildred Stansell Jenkins, whose parents bought an abandoned county poor farm (Madison County, 1946), witnessed her father's attempts to dismantle a small outbuilding that sat by itself in a pas-ture. After his team of horses could not dislodge the six-by-eight-foot struc-ture, Stansell's father discovered that it was anchored deep in the ground with iron straps, evidence that it was intended to be escape proof.[14]

These farms were the dumping grounds for counties' other problems as well. Mount Comfort's farm (Washington County, late 1800s to early 1900) housed both prostitutes and children with epilepsy;[15] fifteen-year-old John Richmond, an African American orphan, died in the poorhouse after acci-dentally shooting himself (Crawford County, 1872).[16] A Mrs. R. P. Hall died after giving birth to an illegitimate baby (Washington County, 1905), and the doctor who delivered the child threatened to send it to the poorhouse unless someone—anyone—took it, which a local family finally did.[17] Orphans were routinely housed at these farms. One payment found in court records (Pope County, 1927) speaks volumes: "Dr. W. L. Mason, $25, syphilis serum and treat-ment for Whitehead children (orphans)."[18] Sometimes families used the farm as a dumping ground. Jeff Watts, a child when his father served as overseer on a farm (Lawrence County, 1933–1940), noted that during the Depression, "People who could no longer support their mothers or fathers would bring them here and drop them off. We had as many as 40 people."[19]

Paupers made desperate efforts to keep from being sent to the poor farm, or to escape once there. One elderly man, jailed for vagrancy (Benton County, 1899), refused to divulge his name or place of origin for fear of being returned to a poor farm in Kansas,[20] while William Britton, aged sixty-eight, hanged himself when illness rendered him unable to work and he feared he would be sent to the same farm whose insane inmates had rendered it so unsanitary (Carroll County, 1903).[21] Any death was preferable to dying on these farms. Counties appropriated money for burials, which were substandard. In Washington County the inmates assembled plain wooden burial boxes without lids (date unknown),[22] while in another account these inmates' bodies were merely wrapped in blankets and buried without a funeral.[23] The poor farm cemetery was society's final dumping ground, also used to dispose of unidentified bodies and county prisoners. Inmates were buried without tombstones other than field rocks and the locations of many of these cemeteries are now lost.

A similar fate awaited anyone stricken during smallpox epidemics. It would be hard to overstate the fear people had of this infectious disease that could disfigure, blind, or kill its victims. Vaccination, and prudently avoiding those who had the disease, provided the greatest protection. To facilitate the latter, hospitals posted the word "smallpox" on their buildings and wagons, and the state board of health, in 1899, threatened to prosecute anyone who did not post a yellow flag on his dwelling when there was a smallpox patient within.[24] Some towns quarantined themselves by forbidding trains to stop there.

Diarist Mary Adelia Byers (Independence County, 1864) wrote that friends "shun the house like a smallpox hospital" when a disagreeable relative visited,[25] but such a fear worked to one woman's advantage during the Civil War (Washington County). Union scavengers, stealing meat, saw her and her smallpox scabs through a window and threatened to shoot her. But, "I saw how afraid they were of me and I could not resist the temptation to open the door. The squad of Feds ran and I had saved a few hams left in our smokehouse."[26]

Once the disease was manifest, people went to extraordinary lengths to eradicate contagion. As a young child, Mary Price and her entire family had smallpox, and everyone but Mary died inside the home (Searcy County, 1840s). When neighbors realized the girl was still alive, they left food for her on the windowsill but came no closer. Eventually, "when she was able to walk outside, the neighbors built a fire under the wash pot in the yard, filled it with water and soap and called to Mary to strip off her clothes, leave them in the house and come bathe in the pot and put on clean clothing that they had left lying nearby." Even then they made her live alone in another small house until she was fully recovered, during which time they burned down the Price home.[27] Decades later houses were still being torched if a smallpox victim had died within. During Fort Smith's cholera epidemic (Sebastian County, 1866), authorities wanted to burn down the home of two former slaves, whose bodies had been inside for two days. Physicians refused to allow it, saying, "it would not do."[28]

In its early stages, smallpox, which killed 35 percent of its victims,[29] was hard to diagnose and doctors sometimes mistook it for chicken pox or measles. Fluid-filled blisters appear about twelve days after exposure to infection, so anyone who visited or nursed the sick person during that period had to be quarantined as well. These blisters, later drying into scabs, could cause deep scarring. One man, after visiting a recovering friend (Pope County, 1899), issued the reassuring news that "he has peeled off as slick as an onion and [is] almost free from blemishes."[30]

Though the wealthy were allowed to convalesce in their own homes, those without means were isolated in a pest house, located well outside of town. This term, used in England in the 1600s, originally referred to a place housing victims of the plague. In the Ozarks, however, the pest house was where smallpox victims were kept under quarantine—sometimes under guard. Though these places housed both whites and blacks, African Americans were more likely to be mentioned in connection with them.

Two crews, one black and one white, worked at opposite ends of the Frisco Railroad line and tunnel construction project near Winslow (Washington County, 1882). A doctor was sent to vaccinate the laborers in January, and it seems all too likely that he vaccinated only the white crew against smallpox,[31] as by March the disease was "raging."[32] W. A. Burgess, whose father was an employee of the project's construction company, described seeing "a great number of small cubicle-style rough-lumber shacks" up on the hillside and was told that each one housed a smallpox sufferer.[33] So many deaths resulted that four separate burial locations were needed to hold the bodies. One witness recalled seeing as many as fifteen bodies, wrapped in the blankets in which they had died, thrown into trenches and covered with dirt,[34] while another estimate put the death toll at around one hundred, only five of them white.[35]

Though vaccination provided protection, it could be risky. The sexton of Van Buren's Fairview Cemetery (Crawford County, 1850) recorded the cause of death for J. M. Ward, age twenty-two, as "spurious vaccination," adding the note that Ward's "arm swelled enormously and mortified."[36] At the very least these inoculations caused "fearful sore arms"[37] and even sickness, and inoculations that didn't "take" had to be redone. Still, during one epidemic (Boone and Marion counties, 1882), the five patients who had been vaccinated recovered, while sixteen of the thirty unvaccinated patients died from smallpox.[38] Doctors were slow to take their own medicine, and three of four doctors who treated these patients died, the sole surviving doctor having been vaccinated.[39]

Early doctors took scabs from smallpox patients and scratched or jabbed matter from a scab into the arm of a healthy person to cause immunity to develop. Even after vaccines became available, some doctors kept scabs on hand. As recently as 2000 an exhibit in a county museum contained a jar of these scabs, each attached to a small square of wood, donated to the museum along with a local doctor's medical equipment. Arkansas became the first state in the nation, in 1916, to make smallpox vaccinations mandatory for all schoolchildren and enforced the law. Still, there were outbreaks as late as 1922, and the disease was not declared eradicated worldwide until 1978.[40]

Hangings

Men about to be executed by the state were accorded almost all burial traditions: new clothing, proper coffins, the witnessing of last words and requests, a funeral oration. The difference was that the condemned received these things *before* dying, not after. All of the conventional elements were there, but occurred out of sequence.

This is illustrated by the events of one hot June morning, as an immense crowd converged on Clarksville (Johnson County, 1883). Some arrived on a special railroad coach that brought dignitaries to town, but most were on foot, on horseback, or traveling by wagon. All were in a hurry, hoping to get close to the platform where they could best witness the spectacle to come. In a nearby room, as the noon hour approached, four men ate a hearty dinner, bathed, shaved, donned new, lightweight summer suits, and pinned boutonnieres of white roses and geranium leaves to their lapels. Finally these men, whom an estimated five thousand people had come to see hang, made their appearance. These were the infamous "Mulberry train robbers." The youngest of the four, seventeen-year-old Jim Johnson, had most likely done the shooting that killed a railroad conductor, but all four were condemned to hang for the crime.[41]

Men who were about to be hanged (only one Arkansas woman was executed between 1820 and 2000, Lavinia Burnett in 1845) were always given new clothing to wear—in a way, it could be said they laid themselves out, as their bodies would be placed directly into coffins after they died. Clothing was paid for out of the sheriff's budget and not, as is popularly believed, by the hangman. Unlike those who died of natural causes, these men would see their coffins ahead of time and many would ride to the execution seated upon them. Lastly, these living men actively participated in the religious ceremonies marking their approaching deaths. These occasions also paralleled conventional death in that the condemned met with their ministers, said farewells to family and friends, and died surrounded by throngs of people.

An execution was an occasion for pageantry, both religious and otherwise. With the exception of the Fort Smith federal court's permanent gallows, on which multiple prisoners could be hanged simultaneously (Sebastian County, 1875–1896), scaffolds were erected for the occasion and dismantled afterward. Crowds assessed the condemned's demeanor, interested in whether he appeared frightened or confident, and called out to him as he arrived. Cornelius Hammon (Benton County, 1876) good-naturedly reminded the crowd, "There's no use to be in a hurry, for nothing's going to happen until I get there."[42]

Ministers held full church services once all participants had assembled. At Jerdon Grinder's execution (Crawford County, 1871) his spiritual advisor "had a season of prayer and exhortation at the jail yard" lasting about an hour, then, at the gallows, read from Psalms 139 ("O Lord, thou hast searched me, and known me. Thou knowest my down-sitting and mine uprising, thou understandest my thought afar off"), prayed, and led the singing of two hymns. The choice of one of these seems harsh, given Grinder's belief that he had sinned too deeply for God's forgiveness:

> That awful day will surely come,
> Th'appointed hour makes haste,
> When I must stand before my Judge,
> And pass the solemn test.[43]

At some point in the proceedings the condemned man was allowed to make a last statement to the crowd, and most seized the opportunity—one man talked for an hour and a half. The condemned almost always used their time in precisely the same way dying people used their last breaths: to beg loved ones to meet them in heaven. A few protested their innocence, sang a hymn, or corrected a newspaper account of their crime; others offered their lives as cautionary examples to the young men in the audience. Lee Mills (Van Buren County, 1898) delivered both a lengthy mea culpa and sang a song he'd written for the occasion, in which he urged the "rowdy boys" in the audience to mend their ways.[44]

Finally, the condemned's hands and feet would be tied and a black hood placed over his head to hide his features. Deputies—or a wooden plank—supported any prisoner who fainted or could not stand. After reading aloud the charges and the sentence, which often concluded with the theatrical pronouncement that the prisoner was to be "hanged by the neck until dead, dead, dead!" the sheriff placed the noose around the prisoner's neck, cried, "May God have mercy on your soul," and released the trapdoor beneath the man's feet.

Newspaper writers liked to say that the condemned was launched into eternity, which sounds like a speedy if acrobatic death. When done properly the person's neck was cleanly broken by the fall, with a total elapsed time upward of five minutes before death was declared. Still, the body was usually left to hang for fifteen to twenty minutes, with doctors and even reporters checking at intervals for a pulse. Done incorrectly, the condemned man would slowly, noisily, and sometimes bloodily strangle to death at the end of the rope or, worse, be decapitated by the process. Three of the four Mulberry train robbers took several minutes to die, but James "Gove" Johnson suffered the longest. Just before the trap was sprung, "his muffled voice was heard calling out, 'That rope is caught on my chin; pull it down.'" This misplacement of the noose's functional slipknot caused him to strangle at the end of the rope, "dying very hard,"[45] a process that reportedly took nearly half an hour.[46]

Despite the solemnity of the occasion, hawkers moved through the crowd selling lemonade and photos of the murderers and their victims; in the case of the four men above, pamphlets were sold titled "History of the Train Robbers," containing biographies of the participants.[47] In later years spectators took Kodak photos at hangings. Another souvenir was the rope itself, though tossing pieces to the crowd has been found in only one account (Boone County, 1913). More often the rope, cap, and straps used in hangings were borrowed from the state and had to be returned afterward to Little Rock. George Maladon, one of several men who hanged prisoners sentenced by Fort Smith's Judge Isaac Parker (serving Parker in this capacity from about 1878 to 1891),[48] reused his ropes and made money exhibiting them. He might have made even more money by selling them. English folklore credits a hanging rope with the power to cure headaches, malarial chills, and fits,[49] while blacks living in Little Rock sought such rope as a cure for epilepsy.[50]

Finally, all that remained was disposing of the body. Though parents visited their condemned sons in prison, few stayed to witness the executions, instead asking adult children or friends to bring the body home for burial. Some did more than that; the sister of murderer Owen D. Hill stayed on the platform while her brother was hanged (Fort Smith, 1888), then "arranged his hands and closed his eyes after the body was placed in the coffin."[51]

The Business of Executions

Some witnesses claimed they were sickened by the event, but executions were a popular entertainment, one that even small children attended. Newspaper accounts usually estimated the crowd as numbering in the thousands, despite the fact that in 1887 the Arkansas General Assembly had passed an act limiting the number of witnesses to twenty-five. (The U.S. marshals who carried

Figure 11.1 Odus Davidson addresses those who had come to witness his hanging for murder in Harrison (Boone County), 1913. Davidson proclaimed his innocence to a crowd that contained men, women, children, and even babies. *Courtesy Boone County Library.*

out Judge Parker's death sentences started using a board fence and restricting audience numbers in 1878.) In the event that no jail yard or private location was available, the sheriff was instructed to have an enclosure built for the occasion.[52] These twenty-five witnesses were in addition to law enforcement, doctors, clergy, and members of the press, and entrance tickets were avidly sought after. In 1901 the law was amended to allow executions for the crime of rape to be carried out without a fence hiding the proceedings.[53] According to an online index that lists 478 executions between 1820 and 1964 (an incomplete record), prior to 1950 Charles Hammons (Conway County, 1910) was the only white man hanged for rape.

According to this index, of the 464 executions for which the date is known, 370 (nearly 80 percent) took place on a Friday. Though Saturday was the day when people normally came to town, according to superstition Friday was a day of bad luck, as well as having been the day of Jesus's crucifixion. In Ozarks folklore it is an inauspicious day to start any new projects or to begin a journey. Traditionally, Friday the 13th is especially unlucky, though four hangings and six electrocutions took place on that day.

In all respects the hanging of African Americans followed the same rituals, with blacks being just as anxious as whites to view the proceedings. Still, accounts of these executions are all found outside the Ozarks, such as that of Charles Anderson (Pulaski County, 1901), which was witnessed by an estimated ten thousand people—over half of them black.[54]

Prior to 1913 all of the state's legal executions were by hanging, with the exception of four guerillas executed before a firing squad during the Civil War.[55] In 1913 the state legislature established a death chamber at the state penitentiary at Little Rock and appropriated $1,500 to build an electric chair. They also forbade newspapers from describing these events or writing anything beyond the fact that they had taken place, though few complied.[56]

The state's electric chair was built in Fayetteville by W. N. Gladson, dean of the College of Engineering at the University of Arkansas, at a cost of $750, which included travel expenses to visit states that had such chairs[57] and (perhaps apocryphally) for the cow on which the device was first tested.[58] Housed at the penitentiary in Little Rock, the chair's inaugural use was the execution of Lee Simms, a black man convicted of rape in 1913. Following this there were three more hangings around the state, alternating with electrocutions, before the full transition to the electric chair was complete in 1914. Capital punishment was ruled unconstitutional by the U.S. Supreme Court in 1972 but was eventually reinstated, and since 1983 Arkansas has given lethal injections to those sentenced to death.[59]

Lynching

Both officially sanctioned executions and lynchings were public spectacles, but beyond that the two have little in common. Lynching is usually described as a mob of whites hanging a black man accused of raping a white woman. While it is true that 231 of the 318 documented lynchings in Arkansas were those of blacks (1860s–1930s), only 51 of these cases were for an alleged rape.[60] The word actually derives from "Lynch's law" (1818) and originally referred to an unauthorized whipping, administered upon suspicion of guilt[61] and not resulting in death. It has also been used to define any assault against any marginalized group, such as Jews, Catholics, homosexuals, and criminals. In more recent times, however, newspapers referred to "Judge Lynch," and the word has come to be associated with the murder of African Americans, often at the hands of the Ku Klux Klan.

In legal hangings the condemned fell through an opening in the gallows floor, the five-foot drop designed to break the person's neck in a swift and supposedly humane way. In a lynching, however, a noose was used to haul a man upward so that the weight of his body caused him to slowly strangle. Mobs also shot and burned these bodies as they hung.

Lynching took many forms, with blacks, whites, and women killed in this way. One such event involved Cal Emory, an African American sentenced to hang for murder, and for whom a scaffold had been built when the governor commuted his sentence to twenty-one years in prison (Pope County, 1881). "They tried to get the man out and they couldn't, so they killed him in jail and drug him to the gallows and hanged him on the one that was made for him," said J. T. Odom, possibly an eyewitness to the event. Following this, Emory's body was left hanging from the gallows all night.[62]

There had been several acts of mob violence, including at least one lynching, in Pope County by the time G. L. Parker, editor of the *Chronicle* (about 1896), wrote a parody that almost surely paralleled human events. According to Parker, "a band of lawless men hurled two beings into eternity, totally unprepared for their awful fate." The piece contains all of the elements of an actual account of lynching, as "Jake and Tom," accused of being thieves, were strung up by a "howling, shrieking, gore-hungry mob" as their sobbing mother looked on. "After accomplishing the terrible deed, the mob silently dispersed . . . the victims presented a gruesome sight in the light of the early Sabbath morn and kind hands cut them down and prepared them for burial." This parody concluded: "The deceased were two young billy goats," adding the phrase often found at the end of actual news stories: "Northern papers please copy."[63]

It is difficult to document what became of victims' bodies following such killings. Given the violence involved, it's unlikely family members could have safely come forward to claim a body, nor was there always much left to retrieve. Certainly there was no squeamishness on the part of onlookers as, following the lynching and burning of Will Norman's body in Hot Springs (Garland County, 1913), the newspaper coyly hinted, "Souvenir hunters ripped the remains of the situation to riddles"[64] and, the following day, reported that the coroner would not hold an inquest, as "there was nothing to hold an inquest over."[65]

Wartime Deaths

Rest soldiers rest, thy warfare o'er,
Sleep the sleep that knows no breaking,
Dream of battle fields no more,
Days of danger, nights of waking.

—**Thomas Loftin,** 1822–Sept. 16, 1863
Alfred Loftin, 1814–Sept. 16, 1863
Auman Cemetery (Boone County)

Before discussing Civil War deaths, the subject of burial customs of blacks under slavery ought to be addressed, but this is problematic. Of the seventeen counties making up the Arkansas Ozarks in 1850, half of the region's 6,402 slaves, or 8.5 percent of the region's total population, resided in just four counties: Washington, Independence, Johnson, and Crawford. Contrast this with the rest of the state: 40,698 slaves owned outside the Ozarks, or 30.2 percent of the total population.[66] By the 1860 census, although the total population had increased, there was no significant change in these percentages. As before, four counties (now Washington, Independence, Johnson, and Pope) owned roughly half the slaves in the Arkansas Ozarks, and these slaves made up just 7 percent of the total population, while slaves in counties outside the Ozarks accounted for 33.6 percent of that total population.

The suggestion that "slaves who lived on the small farms of Arkansas may well have functioned much like hired hands"[67] likely applies to the Ozarks. The only first-person accounts of life under slavery are found in interviews conducted by the WPA's Federal Writers' Project (1936–1939). Subjects were not asked about death customs, and almost all of those who volunteered such information came from the Little Rock area (Pulaski County). As far as can be determined, none was describing life in the Ozarks, nor were accounts consistent, as practices on the various plantations were dictated by the slave owners.

Some subjects asserted that slaves' bodies were simply put into the ground without any funeral service, while others described simple funerals and wooden coffins. Slaves conducted their own services. Though slaves could join a church, and "Many masters encouraged religion among their slaves, sometimes for benevolent reasons but at times because they believed it would make their property more docile,"[68] by one estimate less than 20 percent of all slaves had any religious affiliation.[69] Several of those interviewed said slaves did not attend church, nor were preachers on hand very often for the community at

large. If whites had to delay funerals until a minister could be present, it is little
wonder blacks had no church-sanctioned ceremonies at all.

On rare occasions whites handed down stories of their ancestors' burial
of slaves. One such account, recorded by Silas Turnbo, tells how the John
Jones family (Marion County, 1864 or 1865) buried the body of a "small negro
boy" wrapped in a quilt.[70] Turnbo recorded other Civil War–era stories of
whites being buried in the same manner, so this may have been done out
of necessity. An account from the Morgan Magness family (Independence
County) states that each slave was given a "proper burial" during the war and
that many years later son William D. Magness "himself oversaw the burial of
the last one of the Col's slaves."[71]

Civilian Civil War Burials (1861–1865)

With the Civil War fully under way, whites living in the Ozark Mountains
were often forced to bury their dead in a hurried, haphazard manner, work
done by women, children, and the elderly because men were away at war
or in hiding. Burying bodies killed by troops, marauding bands of raiders
known as bushwhackers (Confederate guerillas), or Jayhawkers (Union guerillas) was a difficult, dangerous job for civilians. Those responsible for the
killing were likely to still be in the vicinity, while in some instances witnesses
were ordered to leave bodies unburied, to dishonor the dead and intimidate
the populace.

Civilians sometimes had to redo military burials. E. M. Bailey (Randolph
County, born 1851) recalled how a passing company of Union soldiers buried
the body of one of their men in loose creek gravel. "Some women passed and
saw his toes sticking out of the grave," he told a WPA interviewer in 1941. "Old
man John Barrett and some women and several boys took him up, put him in
a box, and buried him on the hill near where the church now stands."[72] Such
labor required physical strength that undernourished women scarcely had.
In some accounts elderly men did the digging, but were afraid to help further. Lavinia Holmes had no help when two neighbors were killed by robbers
(Boone County, then part of Carroll, some time during the Civil War). She
borrowed a yoke of oxen, hauled the bodies to Holmes Cemetery, and buried
the men. "This task was all hers and at the same time all her quilts, feather
beds and pillows went with the raiders."[73]

It was often impossible to observe traditions of respect. When six-month-
old Jasper Faught died (Newton County, 1864), Mr. Davis, a neighbor, volunteered to take the infant's coffined body to the nearest cemetery. "Mrs. Faught,

though a deeply grieving mother, allowed sensibility to reign over emotion. She told Mr. Davis that if he perchance might encounter and be pursued by the dreaded bushwhackers, to drop the coffin ('the child is dead and you can't hurt it,' she said) and to save himself."[74] Davis succeeded in his mission and buried the baby; according to one version of events, he disguised himself in a woman's dress and bonnet while making the trip.

In the first years of the Civil War, especially in more affluent communities, bodies were buried in conventional coffins. As the war progressed, however, materials became increasingly scarce. Families were forced to make do by wrapping bodies in fabric or, lacking even that, by placing a piece of fabric over the corpse's face to protect it from dirt. When containers are mentioned, they often involve unconventional elements, such as planks from a wagon bed (Newton County, 1866)[75] or a split, hollow log.

Families went to extraordinary lengths to retrieve bodies killed in battle, but Mollie Williams's efforts were heroic. Her husband, Henry, was murdered as he waited to take an oath of allegiance releasing him from the Confederate army, and his body was thrown into the Arkansas River and presumed lost. Mollie made the eighty-mile trip from her home in the Boston Mountains (Searcy County, 1865) to the site of the killing (Dardanelle, Yell County) to find out what she could about his murder, returned home to relieve her anxious mother-in-law, then returned to the Arkansas River to search for his body. This time Williams had the good fortune to meet a man who had been present when a body was buried in the sandbar where it had been found, and he told her that one of the grave diggers had removed a silver ring from the corpse. A description of the ring convinced Williams that it had, indeed, been taken from her husband's hand.

"I at once started home to make the needed preparations to bring him home and have him buried in the country graveyard near where he had been born and raised," she wrote many years later. Williams borrowed a wagon and a pair of oxen, had a rough coffin built and waterproofed inside with tar, and returned to the river. There, Williams was informed that her earlier inquiries had convinced "certain parties" that the corpse had money on it. While she was gone they had dug up the body, searched it, and thrown it back into the river. She put the coffin in the attic of an abandoned house, and again made the long trip home—her sixth over the Boston Mountains—having spent a total of forty-two days in her search.

Our sad and wearisome task was done. My husband's body rested somewhere enshrouded in the ever shifting sands of the Arkansas River, and his soul drifted out into the great unknown to meet such destiny as inexorable Fate might dictate, and I was left alone to renew the fearful struggle of life under the most discouraging difficulties.[76]

Military Civil War Burials: "That terrible carnival of death"[77]

Soldiers died far from their families, and this weighed on the mind of Rev. William Baxter as he witnessed wounded Union soldiers being brought to a makeshift hospital in Fayetteville, following the Battle of Prairie Grove (Washington County, 1862). Watching as the injured "in every form of mutilation and disfigurement" were carried in, the minister expressed special pity for the injured who were "hundreds of miles from home, among strangers and even enemies, no kind voice to console, no soft hand to soothe; the lip parched, the wound burning; or the life-blood, from wounds that skill cannot stanch, ebbing slowly away."[78]

At least these Union dead received decent burials, complete with funeral services; Confederate bodies were buried by their enemies. Retreating Confederate soldiers had stripped the dead of valuables, clothing, and shoes, and robbed the wounded lying exposed in the extreme cold. This angered Union soldiers responsible for burying the huge piles of bodies left behind, and they retaliated by throwing Confederate corpses into trenches, "with but little ceremony."[79] Another member of this burial party added a chilling detail: "I noticed in one slaughter pen [burial trench] 38 rebels, one of whom was still alive. He would follow us with his eyes."[80]

Families had to move quickly if they wanted to retrieve their relatives' bodies. Children in Fayetteville saw "a grim, white haired man on horseback, holding a gray blanketed figure in the saddle in front of him, its two stark legs protruding on either side." A parent explained, "Someone was taking a loved one home."[81] At least this man had been able to find his son. The military did not issue identification tags, though men could purchase an engraved "Soldier's pin" via mail order, or from peddlers who sold goods to the troops.[82] Some soldiers, hoping to make subsequent identification easier, made their own badges or wrote their names and military units on pieces of paper, attaching them to their clothing. They did this, that is, if they had access to paper and ink, but not all did. Mollie Williams, mentioned above, received a letter from her soldier lover written in his own blood, "a habit many of the confederate soldiers had to resort to in the early history of the war."[83]

Members of the Ladies Southern Memorial Association (Washington County, 1872) oversaw the exhumation of bodies of men killed in battles around northwest Arkansas, and had them reburied in the Confederate

Figure 11.2 The Confederate Cemetery, Fayetteville (Washington County), founded by the Southern Memorial Association in 1872, and containing the dead from numerous Civil War battles in northwest Arkansas. The war memorial in the center was dedicated in 1897. *Photo by Abby Burnett.*

Cemetery they established in Fayetteville. Though it had been nearly a decade since these bodies were first interred, the women searched the corpses' clothing, looking for names. Instead, "We found in their decayed and mouldering pockets acorns, and the dust of parched corn," Lizzie Pollard said in a speech given a quarter-century later. She admonished the young people in the audience, "You . . . cannot comprehend the hunger and heroism that represents."[84]

World War I (1914–1918)

Though a heartbreaking and gruesome task, it was at least possible for some families to retrieve bodies following Civil War battles. This could not be said of the two World Wars, fought on foreign soil. Still, bodies of all soldiers killed in the Spanish-American War (1898), the Philippine-American War (1899–1902), and the Boxer Rebellion in China (1899–1901) had been returned to this country as a matter of policy, and the government expected to do so again at the close of World War I.[85]

In 1918 the plane piloted by Lt. Quentin Roosevelt, the son of Theodore Roosevelt, was shot down over France. On behalf of all bereaved parents

Roosevelt protested the military's plan to return his son's body to this country. "Where the tree falls, let it lie," Roosevelt wrote,[86] a sentiment later endorsed by other American parents. Quentin's body was later moved to Normandy American Cemetery, established after World War II at Colville-sur-Mer, France, and buried next to his brother, Brig. Gen. Theodore Roosevelt Jr., who died 1944.

During wartime, families were in limbo once they received the military's telegram, announcing their son's death overseas. Having neither a body to bury nor the emotional closure of a funeral, some families held memorial services. As was the norm during conventional funerals, local businesses closed out of respect. (Bodies of soldiers who died while still in training, during the influenza epidemic, were returned to their families immediately.) Once again there was the added sadness of the deaths having taken place away from loved ones. As expressed by a Masonic resolution of respect for three of its members (Searcy County, 1919): "To die in one's own homeland . . . adds a solemn sweetness to the last sad rites of memory and honor; but to die on foreign soil, mangled and torn, buried in a grave disturbed by the flash and roar of the war cannon, wrings the heart with unspeakable sorrow."[87]

The military telegram that announced a death contained little information, and some families needed to know more. To this end, the parents of Martin Lynn Shelton (Washington County, 1918) contacted four men known to have been present on the battlefield when their son died. "He was instantly killed by a piece of shell penetrating the skull and brain," William Petrie wrote them (Ohio, 1919). "His body was not in the least mangled, nor did it lie around any length of time." Paul Lutz, writing from a convalescent hospital (Arizona, 1919), also did his best to reassure the Sheltons. "Comparatively speaking, Martin is a whole lot better off resting in a quiet grave in the blood-drenched soil of France, than many of us who are struggling hard to try to regain what little health we may, having gone through the living hell of gas, shell, shrapnel and all of those other modern modes of wholesale destruction."[88]

According to a report by the Army Quartermaster Corps, "a growing sentiment among relatives in the United States to let the dead remain where they fell in battle"[89] prompted the War Department to let each soldier's next of kin decide the disposition of the body. Of the 116,516 members of the army, navy, and marines who died in this war (53,402 of them in battle),[90] about 77,000 were buried in 2,400 battlefield graves scattered across England, France, Belgium, Italy, Russia, and Germany. (A great many were missing in action, their bodies never recovered.) Of the 63,708 families who responded to the government's notification, 43,909 requested the return of the bodies to this country.[91]

Figure 11.3 John Flake Matheny died of pneumonia in France, 1919, and was brought back to Leslie (Searcy County) in about 1920. His was the county's first military funeral following World War I. *Courtesy of George and Sally Matheny Family.*

Families requesting this repatriation were finally able to hold full-fledged funerals, complete with casket. One of these was Pvt. Charles Magness Mc-Kinney, who died of a ruptured appendix in France in 1918. In 1920 McKinney's body was disinterred and returned to Newark, Arkansas, with a military escort.[92] Once home it was discovered that the casket, in a shipping container, was too large to fit through the front door, and it remained on the front porch until the funeral the following day.[93]

Bodies tended to be sent back in the order in which the soldiers died, the first returns receiving the most elaborate funerals and drawing the largest crowds. Bodies continued to arrive back in this country over the next several years. Despite so much time having elapsed, some families insisted on opening the sealed burial containers, intent on seeing their sons again or to ensure they were burying the right person.

These men's tombstones occasionally mention reburial or justified repatriation. The parents of Charles Meeks (Lawrence County, 1919) chose a verse from a Civil War–era poem: "Your own proud land's heroic soil / Shall be your fitter grave,"[94] an argument also made in the poem, "Take Me Home," that Shelton's mother saved in her scrapbook.

> And they tell me t'would be grand
>> Just to leave him in that land
>>> This I know.
>
> But I fain would have him lifted
>> From that loam,
> If my brave lad could speak
>> He would say in accents meek:
> "Take me home."[95]

Gold Star Mothers and Widows

Ultimately, nearly 31,000 burials (including remains that could not be identified) remained in Europe. These were consolidated into eight permanent American military cemeteries, six in France, one in England, and one in Belgium, established and maintained with money appropriated by Congress in 1919.[96] In 1929 Congress passed Public Law 592 recognizing families' sacrifices, as well as the expense and energy saved by *not* returning their dead. This bill appropriated over $5 million to send widows (provided they had not remarried) and mothers overseas to view their husbands' and sons' graves, and tour the battlefields where they died. Of the nearly 16,500 women eligible to go on this Gold Star Pilgrimage, 6,674 women undertook the trip between 1930 and 1933.[97] (According to an account written at the time, nearly 9,000 women initially accepted the offer to go and over 5,000 of them made the trip during the first year of the program.)[98] These trips were controversial, and some felt the $650 expenditure per woman would have been better spent on veterans.

A "Gold Star Mother" was one whose child had died in battle, and the term "Gold Star Widow" was also used. The name derives from the service flags churches created to honor local men serving in the military. Blue stars were used to represent those who had just joined up; these were ceremoniously changed to red ones when the men were sent overseas, to gray if they were wounded, and to gold if they were killed. In a related practice, families displayed a blue star in a window for each member serving in the military, replacing one with a gold star if the person was killed. John Branscum's epitaph (Searcy County, 1919) notes the distinction: "The service star of one we love / Has changed its blue to gold."[99]

Of the women who went on the pilgrimage, 95 percent were Gold Star Mothers, not widows;[100] the few husbands who accompanied their wives ("Gold Star Fathers") had to pay their own way. Eliza Baker Smith (Pope County, 1930), whose youngest son, Pvt. Joe F. Smith, died of pneumonia after being gassed on the front lines in 1918, received coverage in her local newspaper, which noted that she'd never been outside her county before this. "The beauties of the sea, the wonders of the foreign country will no doubt slip her vision, for 'to visit' her boy's grave is more to her than the 'dreaded trip.' Perhaps she'll have a story when she returns, but it's doubtful."[101] This was a self-fulfilling prophecy, as no follow-up article was written.

The S.S. *America* brought the first 231 Gold Star Mothers to France on 16 May 1930, with other ships arriving quickly so a large contingent of women could attend Memorial Day services in the five military cemeteries outside Paris. The women must have been overwhelmed by the reception they received, which included military planes escorting their ship and a "tumultuous welcome" by thousands of people who greeted them at the dock.[102]

When interviewed, these women remarked, repeatedly, on how impressed they were by the military cemeteries' beauty and upkeep. "Back home in America, cemeteries were a visual hodgepodge of gravestone designs and types of stone, and while marble stones were common, they were seldom carved in the form of crosses. Nor were lush green lawns and carefully planned landscaping and fountains always found in American small town cemeteries," something especially true of the Ozarks' rural burial grounds.[103]

Immediately after the war the Red Cross had sent families photos of their sons' graves, but now they looked different, the wooden crosses having been replaced by marble markers. Seeing the actual grave was a revelation. "Some mothers had never fully grasped the idea that their boys were dead," wrote Grace Robinson, a reporter who traveled with the women, also aboard the S.S. *America*, and observed them as they came to terms with the reality of their losses. Robinson explained, "It is hard to nurse your dear ones through an illness, to watch life ebb from the loved body. There is at least the relief of expression in the poor show of the funeral and consolation of friends. But it is harder and more cruel to receive a telegram from the War Department and a studied, kindly letter from your boy's commanding officer—and then to hear and see no more."

Robinson, who accompanied some of these women to a cemetery, likened their first view of the headstone to that of a condemned man seeing the electric chair for the first time. Nor did she spare readers these women's anguished reactions, describing them prostrating themselves on the graves, and crying out "My baby!" "Oh Johnny, my boy!" and, "My son, can you hear me!" Some of the women, caught up in their grief, were unable to operate the small cameras they'd brought with them from home. Then newspaper photographers, there to record the event but staying back so as not to intrude, came forward and used the women's cameras to record photographs of the graves. Despite the terrible expressions of sorrow, Robinson wrote that the visits ultimately made the women feel better. At least, as one mother told her, her son had died for a noble and valid cause, fighting in a war "to end all wars."[104]

Susie W. Shelton, the mother mentioned above, despite saving the poem "Take Me Home" was among the arrivals aboard the S.S. *America* and one of four Gold Star Mothers from Arkansas in the first wave to reach France.[105] John J. Noll, another reporter covering the story, accompanied Shelton's contingent to Somme American Cemetery and described the women's arrival there as being one without further ceremony or speech making.

"Quietly each mother or widow was shown the grave she sought. . . . Here rested her dead. Carefully and reverently the wreaths and flowers were placed before the cross—with them, an American flag brought from home," he wrote. "After communing with their dead, many gave thought to the sons of other mothers who had either gone to their rest or who were unable to make the long journey,"[106] and they did their best to decorate these graves, as well. Shelton had brought two potted hydrangeas with her to plant on her son's grave, and was assisted with this work by a cemetery laborer.[107] Military cemeteries do not allow the planting of flowers and shrubs, so such things would have been removed after the women returned home.

"I wish that every mother who has a son buried in France would make the trip," Shelton told a local reporter on her return. "I am sure they would come home with a heart full of gratitude for the care that is given not only by the United States government but also by the people of France."[108]

World War II (1939–1945)

When the Second World War ended there was, again, debate over the repatriation of bodies. Kenneth C. Royall, undersecretary of war (1945–1947), said the troops he'd spoken with had all preferred burial "in the lands they fought to liberate,"[109] and Brig. Gen. T. Bentley Mott, director in Europe of the American Battle Monuments Commission, protested a bill before Congress authorizing families to again decide on the return of their dead. "Remembering what took place after the last war, I should think that an effort could be made to do some educational work before the undertaker's union or some other organization had already started a crusade to have the bodies returned," he wrote in a letter to Washington, D.C. (1945).[110] If the country's National Funeral Directors Association had spearheaded any such "crusade" they made no mention of it in the history of their industry they commissioned ten years later. They did, however, praise local undertakers' efforts in assisting families with taking delivery of returned remains, holding funerals and burials, and helping make sense of the military's repatriation program, which the previous war had given them experience in dealing with. In all subsequent conflicts the military has brought all bodies back to the United States for burial.

Once again, the term "Gold Star Mother" was used to denote someone whose child had died in the military—a term still used today. This time, however, there would be no Gold Star Pilgrimage. As before, bad news came via military telegrams, ones stamped with a single star to denote a soldier missing in action and two stars when one was killed. Bruce Vaughan delivered wartime telegrams for the Western Union Telegraph Company (Washington County), some of them stamped with two black stars on both the telegram and its envelope. "Death messages were something I dreaded. Some women would literally fall in your arms, overcome with grief." Recipients who lived outside city limits were notified by telephone whenever possible, but Vaughan had to take telegrams to homes that had no phones. Delivery in town cost ten cents, but Vaughan said he was rarely able to collect the twenty-five-cent fee for out-of-town deliveries, nor did he ever receive a tip.[111]

The Army Quartermaster Corps supplied all materials needed by the troops; when soldiers were killed, the Graves Registration Service, under the auspices of the Quartermaster, provided caskets, oversaw burials, and was responsible for all "cemeterial activities."[112] After the war ended, this service was also responsible for disinterring remains. John D. Little (Madison County, born 1924) was assigned to the Graves Registration Service, now called Mortuary Affairs, and received specialized training. "I'd seen a lot of dead bodies before I was nineteen years old," he said, referring to the open-casket funerals he attended as a child. It was for this reason, he believed, that the military specifically chose country boys for the job.

"They had to toughen us up for the situation," he said. "Well, we went to the Denver City Morgue and watched them cut up dead bodies. We had to eat our dinners right in the place [in amphitheater seating surrounding a dissected cadaver] then the doctor would take a volunteer out of the audience to sew the body back up, and to put the parts back in the body." Little had to do this on occasion but, he said, "I was nineteen and nothing bothered me."

Little was sent to England in 1944, landing on Omaha Beach shortly after the D-Day invasion of Normandy, France, in order to begin the process of collecting and processing bodies, or pieces of bodies, for burial. This job involved such things as recording dental records ("tooth charting"), removing live ammunition found on the bodies and burying it, collecting soldiers' personal effects to be sent back to their families, marking the graves, and overseeing grave digging. Despite the immense carnage, "We had a pretty good record," Little recalled. "We buried [only] one percent of our troops unidentified." In some instances, information they gathered was sent on to Kansas City where a final identification might be made.

According to a report by the Graves Registration (1946), "The painstaking efforts made by search teams to identify bodies rival the methods of detectives in fiction." If unable to use fingerprints, dental work, or dog tags, practically any clue was used to trace a soldier's identity: a high school class ring, laundry marks in clothing, handwriting on scraps of paper, or the serial numbers found inside wristwatches.[113] Little said they also recorded anything unusual on the body, such as tattoos, that might aid with later identification.

Graves Registration also buried Red Cross and medical personnel, as well as civilians—the latter made easier because everyone carried identification papers, although military regulations forbade burying American and enemy soldiers together. American soldiers were usually identified using the paired metal "dog tags" worn around the neck, the earliest versions of which were stamped with the soldier's name, serial number, next of kin's name and address, date of tetanus inoculation, blood type, and religious affiliation (Protestant, Catholic, or Hebrew). Starting in 1943 these tags no longer carried the next of kin but were otherwise the same. At burial the two tags would be separated; one remained with the body and the other was attached to the wooden grave marker.

The army started issuing aluminum identification disks in 1913, and by 1917 all soldiers wore pairs of these disks around their necks. During World War II, however, the design was changed to a metal rectangle, notched at one end. "Battlefield rumor held that the notched end was placed between the front teeth of battlefield casualties to hold the jaws in place," according to the U.S. Army Quartermaster Foundation. However, "the only purpose of 'the notch' was to hold the blank tag in place on the embossing machine," something no longer needed by today's technology.[114] (Another myth was that one of the two tags was placed in the corpse's mouth before burial.) According to Little, even a body wearing dog tags had to be initially buried as "unidentified" if it was found to have someone else's tags in a pocket, though these additional tags would be listed in the paperwork so that a determination could be made later.

Families could begin the application process for the return of bodies within six months of the end of the war. According to one report, the work of processing the remains began after C-Day ("Casket Availability Day") and E-Day ("Exhumation Day"), when enough caskets had been shipped to Europe for digging to begin.[115] Cemetery by cemetery, "letters of inquiry" were sent to the next of kin, and disinterred remains in caskets were stacked above ground until all responses had been received. According to Little this meant that some caskets were above ground for as long as two years awaiting families' replies.

The government had anticipated that 80 percent of bodies would be returned to this country at the families' request, in part because all of the cemeteries established by the United States military after World War I (with the exception of Brookwood American Cemetery in England) had been over-run by the German army during World War II. The actual return rate was 71.4 percent, practically identical to the 68.9 percent of return following the previous World War.[116] After all requests had been processed, the remaining caskets were reburied in fourteen permanent military cemeteries in eight countries: the Philippines, Tunisia in North Africa, England, Italy, France, Belgium, Luxembourg, and the Netherlands.

"This is one thing civilians didn't realize after World War II, when they requested that their boys' bodies be brought home," Little said. "We had buried them in mattress covers, nearest I can explain it, like a cotton sack. It was made out of canvas and slipped over a one-man bunk. That's what we buried them in," and these sacks had deteriorated from being in the ground. "You dig them up, and you dig the dirt up around them, that's why the caskets are so heavy, there's a lot of dirt." He added, "I believe that if the people in America understood the moving of graves when they request a body back, they wouldn't do it."

CHAPTER TWELVE

Early Undertaking

There are thoughts that never perish
Bright unfading through the years,
So thy memory we cherish
Shrined in hope, embalmed in tears.

—**J. H. Martin,** 1854–1899
Powhatan Cemetery (Lawrence County)

Thirty restless undertakers sat in a Searcy lecture hall (White County, 1891), waiting to hear Professor Lutz, a New York City embalmer, present an illustrated lecture on "the art restorative." The problem was that no corpse was available on which Lutz could demonstrate his techniques. Undertaker John H. Neal, an event organizer, had the task of procuring a body and knew of a female prisoner who lay dying in the city jail. He feared that she might rally.

Finally, however, Neal entered the lecture hall to make the happy announcement, "She is dead!" Soon the professor was able to proceed with his demonstration of embalming (the chemical treatment of a dead body to delay decomposition), a lucrative skill that his audience, which had traveled there from all parts of Arkansas, was anxious to learn. Then, if this second annual convention of the Arkansas Undertakers' Association was anything like the first, members adjourned to eat a hearty dinner and take in some light opera. Afterward they departed, leaving Neal to dispose of the embalmed body.[1]

The association had paid for the woman's burial but her indigent status meant there would be neither a funeral nor a public viewing. Rather than lose a valuable opportunity, Neal used it to educate the public. For the next month the body was displayed in the front window of first one mercantile store, then a second. Far from impressing the populace with its state of preservation,

Figure 12.1 Blocksom, Weaver & Co. Undertaking Rooms, Eureka Springs (Carroll County), circa 1902. Blocksom, as was common with many businesses at this time, combined undertaking with other lines of work. *Bank of Eureka Springs Historic Museum Photo Collection.*

however, the corpse did little more than scare local children, who had to pass it on their way to school.[2]

This illustrates an early attempt by the funeral industry to publicize its services, necessary in order to convince the public of the value of a burial overseen (or "undertaken") by professionals. The changeover from home burials to professionally managed ones occurred gradually, as undertakers assumed an increasing number of the jobs once performed by members of the community. By the end of World War II the transition was complete.

From Furniture to Funerals

In the beginning undertakers—or funeral directors, as they are now called— did not ply their trade full time. In the same way that doctors also owned pharmacies, blacksmiths built coffins, and tombstone carvers made marble tabletops, basic undertaking was once a sideline for those in the business of making and selling furniture. This combination prompted one business (Ouachita Mountains, Clark County, 1927) to adopt the very literal slogan, "From the cradle to the grave."[3] Stores that sold coffins often carried undertaking supplies and burial clothing as well.

In the late 1800s anyone could do a little undertaking on the side. The words "Undertaker's Goods" or "Undertaking a specialty" have been found tucked into advertisements for businesses selling mattresses, picture frames, lace curtains, curtain rods, window shades and screens, oilcloth, carpets, doors, sashes, molding, brackets, and wallpaper. Some businesses also did upholstery (relevant because some coffin lids were upholstered), furniture repair, carpentry, and house building—all trades that worked with wood. One rather startling combination, while not located in the Ozarks, was the one offered by C. F. Kroeger, of Arkansas City (Desha County, 1892). His business directory ad touted his fancy groceries, bread, cakes, undertaking, and coffins.[4]

By the 1900s such businesses, rather than becoming more specialized, now combined undertaking with an even wider array of goods and services. These included the sale of sewing machines, dry goods and clothing, glassware and Queensware (white ceramic dishes), and groceries. The Mammoth Spring Hard-Ware Co. (Fulton County, 1906) offered undertaking along with hardware, wagons, furniture, fence wire and nails, and Oliver Chilled Plows, while the Nix-Callison Undertaking Company (Washington County, 1924) promoted its Art Congoleum rugs, stains, wood varnishes, floor wax, O'Cedar floor mops, wallpaper, and house paint, and "our gift shop line of novelties."[5] By one estimate the affiliation between furniture and hardware stores and undertaking existed in the smaller, rural towns as late as the mid-1900s.[6]

J. Frank Moore, who got his start as a grave digger, was unusually diversified, having business listings under the following headings in the Fayetteville phone book (Washington County, 1927–1928): Ambulance Service, Art Novelties, Books, Funeral Directors, Gift Shops, and Picture Framing; by 1932 he'd added Leather Goods to these offerings, all listed at the same address.[7] Clarksville's Griffin Funeral Home (Johnson County, 1935) tailored its offerings to its audience by selling peach baskets.[8]

Only one man in the state, on the 1870 census, listed undertaking as a full-time profession, Little Rock's James Cook, a junior partner in Fred J. Ditter's furniture business. Following Ditter's death that same year, Cook purchased the firm, closed down its woodworking shop, and renamed the business "James Cook, Undertaker."[9] In 1880 there was one seller of "coffins, burial cases and undertakers' goods" in Arkansas (this manufacturing census did not have a heading for undertakers), probably James Cook. There is a twenty-year gap in the census but, by 1900, 77 undertakers were listed statewide, and in 1910 there were 135.

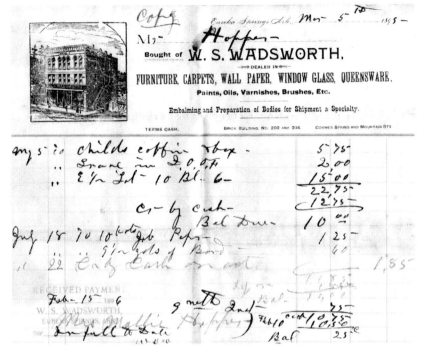

Figure 12.2 Receipt for a child's coffin, box vault, and gravesite, paid to undertaker W. S. Wadsworth, Eureka Springs (Carroll County). This was for the burial of six-month-old Irene Hopper; the Hoppers would lose another infant the following year. *Bank of Eureka Springs Historic Museum Photo Collection.*

Proving Their Worth

Under normal circumstances rural residents had the time, materials, and know-how needed to bury their own dead. An outsider's help was sought only when dealing with bodies in a deteriorated condition or when transporting one over long distances. Railroads required that bodies be embalmed for shipping, and for this reason some of the Ozarks' earliest embalmers are found in the towns whose healing waters attracted visiting invalids.

Within two years of its founding, Eureka Springs had two furniture dealers selling coffins and metallic burial cases (Carroll County, 1881). One of these was J. W. Willett and Co., whose advertising offered funeral paraphernalia, Fisk's Patent Metallic Cases and Caskets, burial robes, shrouds, and "everything kept by the finest undertaking establishments of the largest cities." Willett also laid out bodies and touted "Embalming for shipment a specialty."[10]

Eight years later W. S. Wadsworth would advertise that he was "the oldest established Undertaker and Embalmer in the city,"[11] unfair considering that Willett was still in business. Other firms also came and went over the years, with as many as eight undertakers in business in Eureka Springs at one time.[12]

Other spa towns also used embalmers from an early date. Sulphur Springs's resident undertaking family, headed by W. W. Dunn, was in business at least as early as 1888 (Benton County), shipping bodies as far away as Illinois, Ohio, Kansas, and Missouri, but the firm did not record an embalming charge until July 1903. The railroad had begun bringing invalids to Sulphur Springs in 1889, but the town's real prosperity didn't arrive until 1909, when the multistoried Kilhberg Hotel opened. The resulting increase in visitors is reflected in Dunn's records, as his embalming business became steady starting that same year.

Handling the Worst Cases

Undertakers were hired when bodies were too unpleasant for the public to deal with. They buried indigents, those who died from contagious diseases or massive injuries, or ones found in a state of advanced decomposition. Coroners did not handle such bodies. Their role was merely to determine a cause of death, aided by a twelve-man "coroner's jury" convened solely for this purpose. Even in the late 1930s the coroner's job was to summon this jury to view the body where it was found, then to "inquire into the cause, manner and circumstances of the death," including questioning witnesses and suspects— even exhuming any body buried in advance of such formalities.[13] If the coroner lived more than twenty miles from where a body was found, the nearest justice of the peace could do the job.

Undertakers needed strong stomachs for their work. In Benton County alone, these professionals were called in to deal with the "ghastly remains" of E. S. Newsom, found eleven days after he drowned in the Illinois River (1898)[14]; Ed Preston, an African American man "mashed horribly" by a freight train (1902)[15]; elderly Alex Crane, whose death wasn't discovered until rats and mice had partially eaten his face (1906)[16]; and Joe Ellis, decapitated by a train (1910).[17] Professionals were also called to dispose of a Mr. Dawdy, left hanging in his barn for four days until a jury could convene (1911),[18] as well as to remove the oversized remains of another suicide not found for quite some time (1913).[19]

These professionals worked at a time before the invention of disposable gloves and other protective gear. They could, however, paint their hands with "Biosote liquid court plaster," a product sold by the Embalmers' Supply Company, of Westport, Connecticut. According to ads, Biosote was superior to other products used to protect the hands such as "collodion preparations" and adhesive bandages. The product claimed to disinfect the hands and heal wounds without, most importantly, impairing the sense of touch.[20]

Embalming

In 1865 the embalmed body of Abraham Lincoln began an eighteen-day, 1,654-mile journey from Washington, D.C., where the president had been assassinated, to Springfield, Illinois, where he was to be buried. By one estimate as many as a million people along the route viewed his body, seeing a corpse in an impressive state of preservation despite the nature of its injuries. His appearance was the work of a professional embalming company, with additional touch-ups made along the route, needed to keep Lincoln in a "presentable viewing condition." By the end of the journey, however, it was necessary to apply a thick coating of makeup to hide evidence of decomposition.[21] Though not the first public figure to be preserved in this way, Lincoln was the most famous. His embalming has been cited as the beginning of public acceptance of a practice that had been used in this country as early as the 1840s.[22]

That the president's body was treated in this manner was due, in part, to the death of twelve-year-old son Willie Lincoln, who died in 1862 and was embalmed by the firm of Brown and Alexander.[23] Pending the expiration of Lincoln's second term in office and his return to Springfield, Willie's body was placed in a borrowed cemetery crypt. Supposedly, on at least two occasions the president had the coffin opened so he could look at his son again, an act that comforted the grieving father.[24] Three years later Mary Lincoln authorized this same firm to embalm her assassinated husband.

During the Civil War families of both the Union and Confederate dead could pay to have their relatives' bodies embalmed by independent, civilian operators,[25] though officers' bodies were more likely to receive this treatment than those of enlisted men. Some accounts have incorrectly stated that military employees did this work, but the embalmers were civilians, similar to the sutlers, or peddlers, who sold a variety of goods and services to the troops. Though the army quartermaster would, in future wars, process the dead, during the Civil War the federal quartermaster was responsible only for keeping death records and providing material for grave markers.[26]

Embalming in the Home

Arkansas's first attempt at forming an undertakers' association did not survive, but its second, in 1900, resulted in the present Arkansas Funeral Directors Association.[27] The state legislature created a state board of embalmers in 1909 to license those doing this work, ostensibly to control the spread of disease.[28] In 1953 the state passed laws requiring the licensing of funeral directors and their assistants.[29]

Up through the 1940s it was common for undertakers to bring their trade to rural families, embalming in the family home—or, more precisely, on its porch or in its kitchen. As a child Tom Olmstead accompanied his father, Ralph, on trips into the country to do this work. Tom's job was disposing of bodily wastes and fluids, even in cases where the person had died from a contagious illness. Olmstead gave his biographer an account of one such event, which occurred when he was nine (Cleburne County, 1939):

> It was dark and cold, and they performed the embalming by lanterns and candlelight with no heat. Tom carried a bundle of newspapers into the kitchen [used to collect bodily waste as the bowels relaxed], where most home embalmings occurred because kitchens usually had floors that could be mopped. Ralph set up the cooling board, a portable embalming table with a washable rubber sheet. They rolled the body on a wheeled cot into the kitchen, lifted it onto the cooling board and bathed it. Afterwards Tom gathered the newspapers in a bucket, carried them outside, dug a hole with a shovel and buried them. Then he returned and spread more newspapers.

The next step was inserting a rubber tube into an artery where embalming fluid would be pumped in, and a second tube (in either groin or armpit) where blood would be forced out, using a hand pump that was operated in turns by Ralph and Tom. Though Ralph owned a machine that did the same thing, few rural homes had electricity.

> Meanwhile, a crowd of about 30 gathered on the front porch. It was freezing cold and the wind was blowing, and with no other means of entertainment everyone wanted to see the procedure. Ralph allowed one at a time inside as long as they stayed out of the way.... Finally, the group's "spokesman" entered the room and said, "Doctor, we've taken a poll of the crowd outside, and rather than having all of this coming in and out one at a time, we've elected that you just move everything out on the front porch and continue this operation out there where we can all see at one time and then we'll know a little bit more

about what's going on." Ralph responded clinically, "Sir, I'm just real sorry. I'm at a position at this time where we cannot quit this operation and start over again. We must continue where we are." That was true, but it also kept him and Tom off that cold porch.[30]

Some embalmers' wives helped out, but not everyone traveled with an assistant. In one account, William Dunn became the first person in the Dolph community to be embalmed (Izard County, 1934), but only after a local man helped the undertaker hand-pump his embalming machine, as there was no electricity. (At least undertaker Couch did his own cleaning up, personally burying the blood that had been extracted.)[31] Home embalming continued well into the 1940s but even when they didn't embalm, undertakers would still bring coffins to the home and lay out bodies there. In some instances they would take the body to their place of business to embalm it, returning the casketed remains to the home so neighbors could sit up.

Though the undertaker certainly saw bodily fluids entering and exiting during the procedure, it's difficult to know what to make of nineteen-year-old Braden Shipley's death from influenza (Madison County, 1919). "His under-taker remarked to his mother that she should be proud of him for there was not a drop of impure blood in his veins."[32]

Women in the Profession and Other Business Promotions

Long before homes had radios or televisions, newspapers were the primary way undertakers reached a wide audience. Though the Arkansas State Board of Embalmers' 1916 code of ethics cautioned that, "It is derogatory to the dig-nity of the profession to resort to public advertisements,"[33] no one paid any heed—just the opposite. According to *Ethical Advertising for Funeral Directors* (published in 1924, owned by a Carroll County undertaker), advertising was the perfect way for a funeral director to "say what he wishes without offend-ing." It all depended on the wording. Those in the business were advised to stress their state-of-the-art equipment but never to brag about "demisurgical work" or the "lifelike appearance" of the bodies they embalmed.[34]

Putting one's business name on items to give to the public was another popular way to advertise. The best-known example is the funeral home fan, a piece of stiff cardboard attached to a wooden handle. These items, greatly appreciated by congregations sweltering through long, hot church and revival services, are still in use today. Some firms gave away pens and pencils, let-ter openers, calendars—even kitchen gadgets. Huntsville undertaker Bruce

Brashears (Madison County, after 1936) gave away pink and blue baby rattles with his business name printed on them, and both Bruce and his son Felix handed out fans, fly swatters, yardsticks, and outdoor thermometers.

Ethical Advertising was against such gimmicks on the grounds that people who wanted these giveaways were "of the very poorest class, and hence were not, normally, profitable prospects for future business." Besides, the writer snobbishly insisted, "People of the better class, those who can afford to pay for a funeral from which you realize a sizeable profit, are not going to have their home or their desk littered up with any sort of material bearing a funeral director's name and address."[35] During the Depression, however, such trinkets were appreciated by young and old. When Tom Olmstead gave away almost all of his father's stock of three hundred imprinted toy balsa airplanes without permission (Cleburne County, 1939), he confessed to what he'd done, "I thought it was good advertising." His father's only comment was, "Okay, son, that's good."[36]

One of the most important things a funeral home could promote was the presence of a female employee. "Instinctively one hates to think of some feminine loved one going into the hands of a male funeral director. No matter how much trust may be imposed in the funeral director, there is a certain sex-consciousness that makes a man shrink from turning over the body of his mother, wife, sister or daughter to a male operator," *Ethical Advertising* cautioned. The solution was to have a woman on staff, either as an assistant or, better yet, a licensed embalmer. This allowed for the all-important words, "Lady Attendant" or "Lady Assistant" in the company's advertising, though the word "embalming" was to be avoided at all costs.[37]

Lina Odou has the distinction of being the United States' first female embalmer, an art she learned in Switzerland in 1896. In 1899, not long after coming to this country Odou, a former nurse and friend of Florence Nightingale, taught embalming to women in New York City, then established her own school. She also wrote editorials for industry trade journals, successfully convincing colleagues of the need for more women in the profession.[38]

The 1900 U.S. Census, tabulating numbers of men and women working in various professions, recorded one female and seventy-six male undertakers in Arkansas.[39] In 1893, however, a credit ratings book for Arkansas listed two women undertakers, a Mrs. John A. ("Bell") Erwin in Russellville (Pope County) and, just outside the Ozarks, a Mrs. J. B. Robertson (Fort Smith, Sebastian County).[40] Other early female undertakers include Mrs. J. D. Caudle of Pea Ridge and Mrs. W. E. Fowler of Rogers (both Benton County, 1902).[41] Another, Mrs. W. W. Ocker, who had worked alongside her husband in the business, made news when she received her state embalmer's license a year

Figure 12.3 Glass vessel, part of an early, gravity-fed embalming apparatus. *In the collection of the Heritage Center Museum, Berryville, Carroll County Historical Society; photo by Vineta Wingate.*

after her husband's death during the influenza epidemic (Crawford County, 1919).[42] By the 1940s women were appearing in advertisements, either as the ambiguous "Lady Attendant" or as licensed embalmers. Genevive Holt Ragan, one of only two women in her graduating class from Kansas City's Williams Institute of Mortuary Science, pursued her profession after her brother, an undertaker in their father's funeral business (Harrison, Boone County, 1941), joined the navy.

The practice of home embalming had given the public a pretty good idea of what was involved. Ragan certainly found plenty of work, taking gravity-fed equipment with her to rural homes that lacked electricity. This apparatus had a bottle of embalming fluid that hung from a tall pole whose height could be adjusted, thus regulating the flow of fluid into the body. Though health problems finally forced Ragan into semi-retirement, she continued to attend viewings held in her funeral home. According to daughter-in-law Glenna Ragan, "People had gotten used to seeing a woman in the business. They expected it."

Other Goods and Services

Laying out and preserving bodies were just two services offered by undertakers, jobs they performed using equipment and chemicals not available to the public. Professionals had cooling boards (small, portable tables on which to lay out a body), devices to position the hands, and machinery, such as casket-lowering devices, used at the cemetery. "We also have all the latest appliances for handling the dead," the Bentonville Furniture Company (Benton County, 1902) assured the public.[43]

No matter who did the work, it was always imperative to act quickly once death occurred. For this reason professionals advertised daytime and nighttime phone numbers and addresses, making themselves available to the public around the clock. "We never sleep" was the somewhat unsettling motto of Mr. and Mrs. Robert Owens of North Little Rock (Pulaski County, about 1916).[44] This availability has continued up to the present day; as Lucina Brashears, third-generation funeral director, expressed it, "We've been open for getting on eighty years, and somebody has answered the phone round the clock for that entire time." Once notified, the undertaker often had a long journey ahead of him. According to Norman Powell, an assistant to John Thomas Greer of Ozark (Franklin County, early 1900s), Greer saved time by suspending his horse's harness from a spring in the barn. This allowed him to walk his horse under the apparatus, lower the harness, and hitch up his buggy in record time.

By the 1920s professionals were offering a long and varied list of goods and services. These included selling flowers ("sprays"), hauling chairs to the home or cemetery, providing certified death certificates, and putting funeral notices in newspapers. Personal services for the deceased included washing and dressing the body, shaving men, and doing women's hair. There were separate charges for burial suits, dresses, slippers, men's hose, and women's stockings. Most funeral homes required that bodies be dressed in "unions" (one-piece underwear, worn under the shroud); others billed families for such miscellaneous items as gloves, cuff buttons or cufflinks, garters, collars, and men's ties. There were also charges for ironing or cleaning the deceased's burial garments when provided by the family, or for lengths of fabric, sold to neighbors who were making the burial garment. A business could cut corners when dressing parts of the body that weren't on view. A bill from the Hatchett Brothers undertaking firm (Van Buren County, 1921) includes a $19 charge for "suit less pants," presumably because the casket's divided lid hid the body from the waist down.[45]

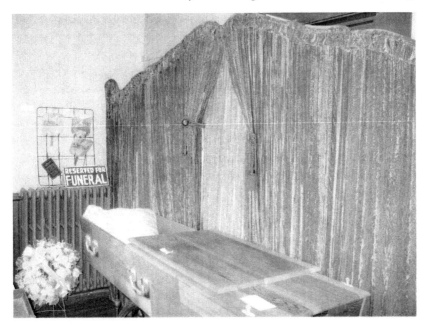

Figure 12.4 Swagged fabric backdrop, called a jack-in-the-box, set up behind a coffin at home funerals, and loaned out by funeral homes. *In the collection of the Heritage Center Museum, Berryville, Carroll County Historical Society; photo by Vineta Wingate.*

In the 1920s and 1930s some undertakers began billing for the rental of plants and tents, for use of a mechanized device that lowered the casket into the grave, and for singers' and ministers' fees. Some undertakers also sold cemetery plots and vaults, hired grave diggers, and provided temporary grave markers and such niceties as special ribbons, swathes of crepe with which to decorate the home, and candles. Others included an engraving fee when a casket escutcheon plate was ordered. During the Depression, funeral homes also billed clients for long-distance phone calls to notify family of a death, often the only telephone available in a community. As early as 1909 undertaker J. W. Sloan (Searcy County) advertised a "Farmers 'Phone at Store and Residence."[46]

One source of information comes from the billing ledgers used by the funeral industry nationwide. These contained blank forms listing a variety of charges, one being "Lining Grave with Evergreen or Muslin." An introductory section at the front of one ledger offered the advice that "Lining with evergreen helps very materially to make a grave seem less distressing during interment." Over the years, records kept by the Bryant Hardware Company

(Benton County, 1899–1936) show charges for a variety of grave linings including eleven yards of fabric, usually muslin, for an adult grave, as well as a special fee paid to the man who did this work.[47]

Undertakers also sought to bring refinement to the home funeral, by renting out folding chairs (also delivered to the cemetery), candelabrums, and torchere-style lamps, brought even into homes lacking electricity. Another elegant item, informally called a jack-in-the-box, was a large, swagged drapery (often crushed velvet) that hung from a folding metal frame, placed behind the coffin as a backdrop. The device folded up into a compact carrying case for easy transport. However, most rural homes were too small to accommodate this device.

Hearses and Ambulances

A variety of vehicles were needed to convey a coffin, mourners, pallbearers, flowers, and graveside equipment to the cemetery. Early billing records show rental charges for carriages, wagons, wagonettes, "buggy phaetons," surreys, hacks, drays (for hauling crated coffins to the railway station) and, of course, hearses. Teams of horses were used to pull all of these vehicles, giving anyone with a livery stable a connection to the funeral industry.

Horse-drawn hearses, which had glass sides showing off the casket within, were highly ornamented and had only one use. Any business that owned one was making a statement about how successful and up-to-date it was. "We are pleased to know that Messrs. Lytle & Carson and Mr. Henry Glass, having long felt the need of a new hearse in Van Buren, have just completed a superb one," the newspaper enthused. "The sides and back are set with large plate glass, elegantly trimmed with fringe and mounted with handsome plumes, which makes it as handsome a hearse as will . . . be found in the larger cities" (Crawford County, 1873).[48] Such things were not cheap. J. S. Owen's purchase, called "one of the finest and best equipped hearses in the state" though not the only one in Harrison (Boone County, 1905), set him back over $1,000, or about $25,000 in today's money.[49] Matched teams of black horses, decked out in plumes and other trappings, were often used to pull these hearses.

Some undertakers purchased new, motorized vehicles as soon as they came onto the market, reserving their older, horse or mule-drawn models for rural burials. In the 1920s quite a few undertakers simply converted their horse-drawn hearses to motorized ones by putting the original glass-sided body onto an automobile chassis. W. W. Ocker was credited with a number of innovations at his Van Buren business (Crawford County, before 1918), one

Figure 12.5 A. D. Callison Undertaking Company motorized hearse (Benton County), about 1917. Callison bought a hardware and funeral goods store in 1912, and began specializing in undertaking. *Courtesy Shiloh Museum of Ozark History/Herbert Locke Collection (S-90-196-15).*

being that he had his town's first motorized hearse. He accomplished this by ordering a standard horse-drawn hearse from Bentonville, then hiring the Armbruster Stageway Company to "mechanize" it.[50] The G. A. Mayhan and W. M. Boultinghouse Company of Newark (Independence County, 1920s) also recycled vehicle parts. "After a motorized hearse replaced the horse drawn one, its wheels were removed and sold. The body of the old hearse was then abandoned in a pasture where the local children used it as a stagecoach while playing cowboys and Indians."[51]

Nationally, starting around 1910, the funeral industry also provided ambulance service. This makes sense, as the hearse was the only vehicle in town long enough to accommodate a person lying down, whether in a coffin or on a stretcher. The appearance of most motorized hearse-ambulance combinations could be altered depending on its function. The driver attached a domed red light to the roof of the cab when on an ambulance call, removing it for funerals. Some models even came with panels that could be snapped over the ambulance's rear windows, converting it to a landau-style hearse. This dual-purpose vehicle, called a "combination coach," predates the era of emergency medical services. To modern sensibilities, however, an undertaker driving an ambulance suggests a possible conflict of interest.

"Not much first aid was given at first; the main service was a quick trip to the hospital," wrote Jim Moshinskie, funeral director and historian. Newspaper ads for Yellville's Holt Furniture & Undertaking Co. (Marion County, 1928) included the drive time to the surrounding towns of Flippin, Cotter, Gassville, and Mountain Home, perhaps to reassure ambulance clients that they would arrive quickly.[52] According to Moshinskie, in 1953 the state outlawed burial insurance policies that provided free ambulance service, and all such services ended by the 1970s when the state-funded Emergency Medical Service became available.[53]

Olmstead recalled that providing ambulance service was an added headache for undertakers. The system was easily abused, especially during World War II when gas and automobile tires were rationed for civilians. Paying just fifty cents for a three-month membership guaranteed transportation for an entire family. "Before long ... someone who easily could walk out of the hospital instead called the service because his family had four bald tires and no gas stamps," said Olmstead, who received a driver's license at age twelve so he could help out. "On the way home, he'd want to stop by the grocery store or the drugstore or even visit a relative, and it was hard not to oblige."[54] The other downside was that patients sometimes waited on transport when a funeral was in progress.

Undertakers covered a lot of miles on behalf of the dead, including traveling by train from one city to another to pick up or embalm a body. Olmstead said that on rare occasions he traveled on behalf of a family to bring a body home for burial or to help with a funeral in a distant city, where the family would meet him. "I didn't act as a funeral director as much as a friend of the family ... and to make sure everything was done," he said.[55] This was in keeping with the State Board of Embalmers' 1916 Code of Ethics: "When a funeral director accompanies a funeral party to a distant place where burial is to take place, and a funeral director is at its destination to take charge, the attitude of the accompanying funeral director should be that of a friend of the family, and assistant to the funeral director in charge of the interment."[56]

Cremation

Language used in obituaries and on tombstones should not always be taken literally. The expressions "Here rests the ashes of" or "Peace be to his ashes in the grave / Perfect be his soul in heaven" do not refer to cremation but are, instead, reminiscent of the burial refrain "ashes to ashes, dust to dust." Cremation was all but unknown in Arkansas until fairly recent times. According to Olmstead, prior to the construction of gas-fired crematories in Mountain

Home (Baxter County) and Little Rock (Pulaski County) in the early 1960s, the nearest such facility was a coal-fired crematory in Memphis, Tennessee.[57]

Though bodies have been disposed of by burning as far back as the early Stone Age, or 3000 B.C., the methods used today are the invention of Italy's Dr. Brunetti, who exhibited a "cremation apparatus" at the Vienna Exposition of 1873.[58] Sir Henry Thompson, surgeon to Queen Victoria, established the Cremation Society of England in 1874 and England's first crematorium was built in 1879. However, human remains were not cremated there until a court ruling cleared the way five years later, but the procedure remained so unpopular police sometimes had to guard the premises.[59]

Col. Henry Laurens has the distinction of being the first U.S. citizen to be cremated, a job performed by relatives at his request (South Carolina, 1792), but not until 1876 did this country have an official crematorium. It was built by Pennsylvania physician F. Julius Le Moyne and used for the first time that December. This facility closed in 1900, having been used just forty-two times in all (including to incinerate Le Moyne's remains), but by then there were twenty working crematories in this country.[60] The practice continued to grow, and by 1913 the Cremation Association of America was founded.[61]

It was rare for an Arkansan to request cremation, because this destroyed the physical body that Christians believe will rise during the Resurrection. Still, on rare occasions someone wanted cremation, such as John Withrow, a former Benton County resident (1896). Withrow was so determined that his body be cremated after he committed suicide that he traveled to Davenport, Iowa, in order to be close to the Northwestern Cremation Society when he did the deed. He had previously corresponded with this society "as to their methods and terms for incinerating bodies," and presumably got his wish.[62]

It was more common—if this word can be used for so a rare an event— to take bodies to St. Louis for cremation. One early example comes from the Birnie Brothers' records, as they made the arrangements to have Henry Bowring's body transported from Fort Smith to St. Louis following his death from a surgical procedure (Sebastian County, 1891).[63] The New England–born Dunbar family was especially keen on the process, as both father Henry Dunbar and son George W. Dunbar (Benton County, dying 1907 and 1912, respectively) expressed the wish to be cremated. In each instance, a local undertaker personally transported the bodies to St. Louis.[64]

Burial Insurance

"Knowing of the inborn horror with which mankind, particularly the very poor, regards the Potters' Field, certain ingenious gentlemen have, from time to time, endeavored to coin this aversion into dollars by the organization of burial associations, funeral benefit societies, and similar schemes." According to this source (written in 1933, and owned by a Carroll County undertaker) the sole purpose of burial insurance was to enrich those who sold it.[65] Few people in the Ozarks would have concurred, certainly not during the Depression.

Burial societies in this country were modeled on ones in England that dated back to the early 1800s, but they didn't reach the Ozarks until the early 1900s. These societies worked in one of two ways. An individual or family could pay a regular insurance premium, its amount determined by the age of the person and the type of funeral he or she desired (usually $100 to $300 paid out for an adult's funeral). The second type, known as a pool, asked for only a small membership fee upon joining. No additional money was requested until another member of the pool died, at which point the remaining members would all be assessed a small amount. One Eureka Springs firm (Carroll County, 1904) offered a $100 funeral benefit for the initial buy-in of twenty cents, then assessed its members ten cents apiece each time someone in this burial society died.[66] The downside to this was that members never knew how much, or how often, they would be billed.

Sumner and Lucina Brashears, recalling the burial insurance policies sold by their grandfather, agreed that during the Depression this was practically the only way he got paid for funerals. (The two exceptions were affluent clients and those on welfare.) "In the old days, when you got married you came to the funeral home and got the wife off of her folks' policy and started a family policy," Sumner Brashears explained. Furthermore, once that couple started having children they were expected to insure them, too, when each child reached three months of age, increasing coverage as the child grew up.

Insurance companies used salesmen to canvas neighborhoods. Some put "salesman wanted" in their advertising as a not-so-subtle way of publicizing their plans' popularity. Still, anyone attending funerals in the 1930s would have seen the value of such insurance. Ocker Funeral Home (Crawford County, 1938) offered a variety of casket styles and burial garments to those holding a policy for a $100 funeral, with the family owing only one dollar or so in taxes when the time came. A family that paid out of pocket for even a modestly priced funeral often needed years to pay it off.

Funeral Chapels

The terms *undertaking parlor* and, later, *funeral parlor* were calculated to draw parallels between a business's facilities and the best room in the family home.

This was, after all, the room where anyone affluent enough to have a parlor would sit up with a body overnight, as well as being the room where company was received. The term *funeral parlor* was gradually replaced by *funeral home*, as the services provided by the undertaking industry grew to encompass many rooms and the need for larger buildings. This shift in language was again intended to evoke a particular emotion. Lest anyone miss the point, Batesville's Crouch Funeral Home (Independence County, 1940) advertised its services under the headline, "A Genuine Home," followed by a description of its facility: "Beautifully and comfortably furnished, it has an air of restfulness which is truly soothing to the family at time of bereavement. This home is at the complete disposal of our clients at no added cost."[67]

When Prairie Grove's Southern Funeral Home (Washington County, 1938) changed locations, newspaper readers got a preview of the new, remodeled and redecorated building that included a funeral chapel and living quarters for the owner and his family.

> The lower floors are covered by a velvety burgundy colored carpet and the draperies are of a slightly lighter color. The chapel, which has a seating capacity of about fifty people, is dignified and tastefully furnished. The walls and ceiling are light colored. An overstuffed suite, which blends in color with the rugs and draperies, furnishes seating for the choir. The audience is seated in metal folding chairs with padded seats and backs.[68]

African American Funeral Homes

The luxury and comfort advertised by funeral homes meant little to African Americans as, in most cases, they weren't allowed to use these facilities. According to Jesse Bryant, only one undertaker in Fayetteville would come to African American homes and pick up bodies for embalming, but would not allow them to remain at the business overnight (Washington County, 1930s). Little Rock (Pulaski County), with large numbers of blacks, had facilities for them at least as early as 1918. In that year the United Friends, a "self-help organization," was founded to meet the needs of blacks. To this end they sold insurance, established the United Friends Hospital, and set up the United Friends Undertakers. (Motto: "We Serve in Life, We Serve in Death.")[69]

Cities with substantial African American populations had black embalmers, or whites who would bury them. Birnie Brothers (Sebastian County, 1882–1904) dealt with all members of Fort Smith's varied population, including blacks, Native Americans, Jews, Catholics, prisoners, paupers, indigents, criminals executed on Judge Isaac Parker's gallows, and those who died of contagious diseases. The Birnies' records show who paid for burials, and the Baptist church and fraternal lodges were responsible for many black burials. A "Colored Society" paid for one adult male's burial in February 1882; the next month the Order of Wise Men paid sixteen dollars for a glass-topped coffin for "Hawkins Col'd [colored] Teacher." Still, these burials are few and far between in the Birnies' records. Godbey Funeral Home in Atkins (Pope County, 1927–1935) also recorded the occasional black burial, the most unusual being Helen Wilson, a thirteen-year-old whose cause of death was listed as "menaupause."[70] Most undertakers didn't bother recording the race of those they buried, presumably because all were white.

African Americans were licensed embalmers, though the state's earliest indexes for this profession do not list race. By cross-referencing these names against its 1916 index, which does include race, it is known that F. J. Goodrich and B. W. Jackson (of "Jackson Bros."), both of Little Rock, were licensed embalmers in 1906 through at least 1916. In 1913 Willis S. Conner of Helena (Phillips County), Walter S. Hubbel of Newport (Jackson County), R. C. Mitchell and A. W. Weatherford, both of Texarkana (Miller County), and I. N. Nelson, Forrest City (St. Francis County), were all licensed embalmers. By the 1916 directory there were a total of eighteen African Americans doing such work across the state, though none in the Ozarks.[71] Other towns with sizable African American populations certainly had undertakers who never made it into the directories, such as Graham and Warren, who did "good business" during a smallpox outbreak in Hot Springs (Garland County, 1895).[72]

Some of the bodies of Fayetteville's blacks were taken to Fort Smith, perhaps because it was home to the nearest African American funeral home. Rev. A. J. Parish, funeral director and owner of the Rowell-Parish Funeral Home, says that Our Funeral Home, owned by a brother and sister, was in business when he moved there in 1966. Reverend Parish, who is black, learned the basics of the trade at age eight, in Little Rock, when spending time with his uncle, who was in the funeral business. This led to Parish attending mortuary school and, in 1985, purchasing his present business.

Parish grew up helping his uncle embalm bodies in homes in the Pine Bluff area (Jefferson County), both in rural communities and downtown. He estimates that home embalming finally ceased in the late 1940s, after undertakers managed to convince families that a better job could be done at the funeral home. Embalming was standard procedure when he was growing up, something absolutely necessary given the traditional long waiting period between death and burial. There was one exception to this, however. "In the days before embalming, if the preacher didn't live right in that community, and the pastoral Sunday was the second and fourth Sunday of each month, then the body would be buried," Parish said. "They'd have a service that Sunday afternoon, a morning service and come back for a funeral service."

Getting Paid

During the Depression, funerals were often paid for in installments. Unlike doctors, however, it is rare to find an undertaker writing off a bill as a complete loss. H. F. Morton of Eureka Springs (Carroll County, 1925–1938) had many ways of getting paid. He accepted two diamond rings as security on one funeral bill, and a life insurance policy on another. Tucked between the pages of his account ledger are two different household inventories, a deed for real estate, and responses to dunning letters he sent, all attempts to collect money he was owed. In addition to the standard services he rendered as an embalmer and undertaker, Morton also received payments for acting as administrator to one estate and for disinfecting a house, perhaps after a death from a contagious disease.[73]

Morton used the code word "clean shirt," jotted in an inconspicuous corner of his ledger, to keep track of how much he marked up his merchandise. Each letter in the word corresponded to a number:

C	L	E	A	N	S	H	I	R	T
1	2	3	4	5	6	7	8	9	0

Thus "coffin L.L." cost Morton $22; he sold it for $50. "Coffin E.A.—H.N." wholesaled for $34.75 and was marked up to $135. It would be nice to believe that Morton did, indeed, sell Cornelia Clark's coffin at cost, but his code reveals that he charged her African American family L.I.S.T. price, or a whopping $90 for her $28.60 coffin (a markup of over 214 percent), which they worked off by doing plumbing for Morton. Nor was this his largest profit. "Casket H.A.N.T.," cost him $74.50, but retailed for $275 in 1924—a 269 percent markup.

Transition

Little by little, the funeral industry took over all jobs associated with burial. As a book on funeral psychology (published in 1945 and owned by a Carroll County undertaker) expressed it, "with the dead body today removed to a modern mortuary as soon as death occurs, giving the family opportunity to regain their composure ... with the mortician relieving the family of burdensome responsibilities and details as much as possible, the period of grief, while not felt any the less severely, is made easier."[74]

A few people have written that laying out a body was a privilege, the last thing they could do for the deceased. More often, however, people were relieved to no longer have to do such jobs. Jeanetta Richardson Grigg recalled how one month before her grandfather died he bought a burial policy from the Adams Funeral Home at Cotter (Baxter County, 1937), and which meant that he was embalmed in the home. "Always before, people had to be buried soon after death if the weather was warm," Grigg wrote. "I've been at the cemetery when the body smelled very bad and the flies were many. This was a blessing to have Grandpa's body taken care of."[75]

Of all the jobs associated with death, one of the last to go was sitting up with the body. Some undertakers permitted friends to sit up all night in their funeral homes while the body was in residence, while the Bryant Hardware Company (Benton County, between 1912 and 1936) billed families from $1.50 to $5 for an employee to do "night watch."[76] Once undertakers and their families began living on their business's premises there was no longer any need for sitting up, as the body was not, technically, left alone. According to Robert Newton, an employee of Harrison's Holt Memorial Chapel (Boone County, starting 1960s), it was once common for families to spend the extended viewing period at the funeral home. "The family would stay all night," he recalled. "They brought food, and the next day there would be baloney skins and empty Pepsi bottles everywhere. The insurance companies finally stopped this, due to the liability," and by his estimate 1964 was probably the last year in which this was done.

By the end of World War II almost all Ozark burial customs had been abandoned. The reasons for the oldest traditions and superstitions had long been forgotten, and there was no longer the labor force needed to perform the complicated, time-consuming jobs. As the overall way of life changed, so, too, did people's willingness to turn all aspects of burial over to funeral industry professionals.

CONCLUSION
Walking the Buckeye Log

Amid the plans and toil
    of busy years,
The millwheels silent grow
    And death appears.
What matters all our care,
    And hurried pace,
At last to some one else
    We yield our place,
And go to meet our maker
    Face to face.

—**A. L. Budd,** 1886–1942
Brentwood Cemetery (Washington County)

No matter how many customs, superstitions, medicines, remedies, and therapies were employed in an attempt to keep death at bay, eventually the inevitable had to occur. Members of the community managed the burial process, but
once the funeral rites had been observed the deceased's dependents were left
to carry on. Lacking social welfare programs, charities, and insurance, only the
poor farm provided a safety net, a dreaded one at that. This gave men a real
incentive to join fraternal lodges, such as the Masons, Odd Fellows, Ancient
Order of United Workmen (A.O.U.W.), Knights of Pythias, Woodmen of the
World, Red Men, or any of the other societies that flourished between the end
of the Civil War and the Depression. These organizations, also called fraternal
lodges, mutual aid societies, benefit societies, and friendly societies, provided
members with life insurance; some established orphanages and hospitals or
sent members out of state for medical treatment.

"In times of epidemics, in the hour of distress and need, is when these secret societies shine forth in all their beauty," one newspaper enthused, citing the Odd Fellows' and Knights of Honor's fund that paid for medical care during a smallpox epidemic (Washington County, 1882).¹ Such help was given *only* to members, however, which the public understood because newspapers weren't reticent about naming a cash payout to a widow or describing a family's impoverishment caused by a husband's failure to join a lodge.

It wasn't difficult to find one to join—newspapers regularly published listings headed "Secret Society Directory" that gave the groups' meeting times and locations. Nor was there any limit to how many societies a man could join or how many insurance benefits he could rack up, provided he paid his dues and policy premiums; men could also insure their wives. Benefits were paid even in the event of suicide.

Membership conferred all kinds of protection, as illustrated by the story of the Largent family, en route from South Dakota when their child died in Bentonville's city park (Benton County, 1895). It happened that several fraternal lodges were holding an Independence Day celebration and, as they paraded past, Mr. Largent caught the eye of an A.O.U.W. member and "gave the distress sign and soon from lip to lip among the members of that lodge passed the word that 'a brother was in distress.'" The lodge took charge of the child's burial, housed the Largents with a fellow member, and then, just three months later, oversaw Mr. Largent's funeral and burial.²

Another type of protection came in the form of widows' homes and orphanages for lodge members' dependents. Both the Masons and the Odd Fellows had such establishments in Batesville (Independence County), but the two weren't equally successful. The Odd Fellows' home for widows and orphans (founded 1898)³ had the lofty goal of training children to be "self-reliant, generous, tolerant, patient, kind, obedient and industrious,"⁴ but by the early 1900s there were reports of mismanagement and child abuse, and the facility was finally closed in 1931.⁵ Batesville's Masonic orphanage (1907–1947) lasted longer and left its residents with happier memories of their care there. Dale Smith recalled his father's faithful attendance at lodge meetings and how he likened this to "a payment on an insurance policy." Because he did this, the six Smith orphans were raised at the home after their father's death. Smith, in an address at the home's reunion in 1985, said that his father's "insurance" was actually, "an annuity that has paid dividends for as long as I live, and will, I hope, as it did with my father—pay dividends beyond the grave."⁶

African Americans also established fraternal lodges. John E. Bush, one of the fourteen founders of the Grand Mosaic Templars of America in Little Rock (Pulaski County, incorporated 1883), explained that he did so primarily to help fellow blacks when there was a death. "I have so often been embarrassed while talking to some prominent white person when some old colored woman would come up and ask for a donation to bury some colored man who had been a citizen of the community all his life and held good positions. The white man would often give her the donation and then turn to me with an oath and ask, 'Why Negroes did not save some money in order that they could be buried decently when they died?'"[7] Insurance companies' higher rates for African Americans, or refusal to insure them at all due to their higher mortality rates, have also been credited as the impetus for this organization's founding.

Decent burial was just one of the benefits blacks received when joining the Mosaic Templars, which provided members with both a death policy and a marble headstone bearing its distinctive "3 V's" ("Veni, Vedi, Vici") logo. Though the Depression brought about the end of this organization, during the 1920s the Templars had over 100,000 members in chapters spread across twenty-six states, and established a building and loan association, hospital and nursing school, and a newspaper with national distribution.[8]

This was just one of many such organizations founded by and for African Americans, who despite their smaller numbers in the Ozarks had their share of fraternities there. These included the United Brothers of Friendship and its women's branch, the Sisters of the Mysterious Tens (established in Louisville, Kentucky, 1861), the Supreme Royal Circle of Friends and the Knights and Daughters of Tabor. Fayetteville, a county seat having just 404 black residents (Washington County, 1893), still managed to support numerous black lodges, including the Odd Fellows, Knights of Tabor, the Mosaic Templars, and "the Daughters" (likely the Daughters of Tabor). "All of these institutions are doing well," reported a black newspaper. "Thank God for this."[10]

From the Past to the Present

Joining a fraternal lodge or helping one's neighbor in times of sickness and death, in the expectation that aid would be reciprocated, were both safeguards against an uncertain future. Such considerations are unimaginable today, and largely forgotten by those who talk longingly of simpler times and "the good old days." This is just one difference between the fairly recent past and our present. Another forgotten difference is how little privacy there once was, most especially when it came to dying. Rural columnists who sent news items to their local newspapers routinely named the doctors making house calls and the patient's name and illness. Everyone knew who was in labor, who was ill, and who was dying—it was their business to know. Those who sat up with the sick and laid out the dead were privy to the patient's physical condition, and afterward obituaries gave very frank descriptions of sickness and suffering.

Forgotten, too, by those yearning after a nostalgic past is how large a role death played in everyone's lives. It was once the norm for people to signal a loss by wearing mourning garments, black armbands, or ribbons, for schools and businesses to close during funerals, to hear bells tolling to announce a death, or to see glass-sided hearses roll past with the coffins visible within. Today, however, we can avoid the subject entirely.

Of all the burial customs, only the southern tradition of Decoration Day has continued unabated, albeit significantly altered. Families no longer spend a day cleaning and mowing the cemeteries, share a picnic lunch, or sit through a religious program. Instead, the grounds are mowed and graves maintained throughout the year, and at most all families do is place arrangements of store-bought, silk flowers on the graves and take their leave. Yet the tradition of respect continues. Ozark families still take their children to cemeteries so they can help decorate graves, and they use the occasion to tell stories of the relatives who preceded them on earth. They will note a tombstone that needs leveling or repair, make a donation toward the cemetery's upkeep, and leave expecting to return the following year.

Now and then in the Ozarks other traditions are briefly revived. In one village an elderly farmer's dying request is honored, and his casket is conveyed to its grave in a wagon pulled by his team of mules. In another town the death of the bank's oldest shareholder is cause to decorate the business's front door with a black wreath, as would have marked the occasion a century ago. And very, very rarely a body will be brought back to the home, to rest in the front room overnight. This does not mark a return to an earlier time, nor would anyone who has laid out a body wish it to be otherwise. But these customs are deeply rooted and have been practiced for so long that perhaps the Ozark Mountains hold a vestigial memory of how things used to be done. There, on rare occasions, someone remembers and asks that a particular, vanished tradition be observed when the time comes.

NOTES

Preface

1. Walz, "Migration into Arkansas," 118.
2. Blevins, *Hill Folks*, 18–19.
3. Walz, "Migration into Arkansas," 58.
4. Jordan-Bychkov, *The Upland South*, 8.
5. Frank C. Brown, *North Carolina Folklore*, 3–98.

Chapter One

1. *Rogers Democrat*, 29 March 1900.
2. *Springdale News*, 22 June 22 1900.
3. *Madison County Record*, 4 July 1940.
4. *Fayetteville Democrat*, 15 April 1876.
5. Arkansas State Board of Health, *Biennial Report*, 19.
6. *Gravett[e] News*, 8 June 1885, reporting on Jefferson City, Missouri; *Rogers Democrat*, 1 August 1901, reporting on Muskogee, Oklahoma; *Benton County Democrat*, 31 December 1908, reporting on Marked Tree, Arkansas.
7. *Springdale News*, 10 August 1894.
8. "Arkansas in Vital Statistics Area," *Journal of the Arkansas Medical Society* (October 1927): 167.
9. "Better Birth Registration," 2.
10. James Byars Carter, "Disease and Death in the Nineteenth Century," 293; Saxbe, "Nineteenth-Century Death Records," 43–54.
11. U.S. Bureau of the Census, 10th U.S. Census, 1880, Conway County, Gregory and Griffin townships, enumerator Will W. Stout.
12. WPA, Historical Records Survey (Lawrence County).
13. Webster, *Under a Buttermilk Moon*, 144.
14. Ash Flat Historical Society, *Ash Flat History*, 214.
15. Mecklin, *The Mecklin Letters*, 14, 18, 27.
16. Moyers, "From Quackery to Qualification," 12.
17. *Encyclopedia of Arkansas History and Culture*, Dougan, "Health and Medicine."
18. Ibid., Harris, "Arkansas Medical, Dental."

19. Kirby, 1878–1879 billing ledger.

20. *Acts of Arkansas*, Act 178, 1903, 342–45.

21. Gunn, *Gunn's Domestic Medicine*; Pierce, *The People's Common Sense Medical Advisor.*

22. Banes, *Journal*, 52.

23. Wolf, *Life in the Leatherwoods*, 103.

24. Coger, "Memories of Kingston," 64.

25. "History of Patent Medicine," online.

26. Warren, *Truth Twisters*, 75.

27. Package in the collection of the Johnson County Heritage Center, Clarksville.

28. *Huntsville Republican*, 10 April 1890.

29. *Decatur Advance*, 9 August 1895.

30. *The People's Home Library*, 286–302.

31. Moyers, "From Quackery to Qualification," 18–19.

32. Ibid., 23.

33. Ibid., 23–24.

34. Lemke, "The Account Books of W.H. Rhea," 19.

35. Wayne Clark, *Letters & Diaries of Isaac A. Clarke*, 381–94.

36. Ewing, "Chronicle of John Guin Bledsoe (Part 1)," 101, 114.

37. *Fayetteville Democrat* throughout 1899; *St. Paul (Madison County) Republican*, throughout 1887; *Fayetteville Democrat*, 31 May 1887.

38. *Fort Smith Journal*, 5 September 1889.

39. *[Little Rock] True Democrat*, 4 October 1854.

40. Claude E. Johnson, *The Humorous History of White County*, 30.

41. Mooney Barker store charge slips, Shiloh Museum of Ozark History, Springdale, compiled by Susan Young.

42. Turnbo, "Died at an Extreme Old Age," vol. 18.

43. WPA, Early Settlers' Personal History Questionnaire, all Van Buren County: Garner Fraser (born 1874), J. W. Hatchett (born 1873), Charles W. Hershey (born 1853).

44. Sebastian County Medical Society, *Physicians and Medicine*, 124, 211–12.

45. Campbell, "Growing Up In Zinc," 15.

46. Vaughan, *Growing Up Rich, Though Dirt Poor*, 81–84.

47. Hefley, *Way Back When*, 201–2.

48. Rothman, *Living in the Shadow of Death*, 2.

49. *Benton County Democrat*, 28 June 1900.

50. Wolf, *Life in the Leatherwoods*, 105.

51. J. H. Schenck, M.D., "The Cause and Cure of Consumption," *Arkansas Gazette*, 17 November 1871.

52. "Atmospheric Diseases," *Fayetteville Democrat*, 4 May 1872.

53. *Daily Arkansas Gazette*, 8 August 1880.

54. *[Marshall] Mountain Wave*, September and December 1909.

55. Ibid.

56. Montague, "Growing Up With the Century," 25–26.

57. Stephan, "Changes in the Status of Negroes," 48.

58. Holmes, "Home Care for Patients," 501–4.

59. WPA, Historical Records Survey, Crawford County Health Unit documents pertaining to Burr Cottages, 1937.

60. Eureka Springs Centennial Commission, *A Post Card History.*

61. Polk, *State Gazetteer, 1884–1885,* 15.

62. Rafferty, *The Ozarks,* 200.

63. Blevins, "'In the Land of a Million Smiles,'" 6.

64. Wayne Clark, *Letters & Diaries of Isaac A. Clarke,* 437.

65. Bair, "Report on an Investigation."

66. *[Boone County] Elixir Bugle,* 20 October 1883.

67. "Sulphur Rock Described as Health Resort," 32–34.

68. "Local and Personal," *[Harrison] Times,* 9 December 1882.

69. Edith Gregson, "Fountain-Of-Youth Fluid Sold Cheap Thirty Years Ago," *Fayetteville Democrat,* 3 July 1928, Independence and Centennial issue.

70. Berry, *Sugar Loaf Springs,* 19.

71. Elizabeth Tindle, age three (Randolph County), 1860 mortality schedule. William McElhaney, age seven (Madison County), 1870 mortality schedule.

72. Bud Phillips, *New Ozark Cousins,* 293.

73. Randolph, *Ozark Magic,* 123.

74. Rayburn, *Ozark Country,* 254–55.

75. Randolph, *Ozark Magic,* 123–24

76. Page, *Voices of Moccasin Creek,* 325.

77. Parler, *Folk Beliefs from Arkansas,* vol. 1, #841–42, 286.

78. Mullen, *An Arkansas Childhood,* 155; Mumey, *University of Arkansas School of Medicine,* 162.

79. *Fayetteville Democrat,* 6 June 1890.

80. Bowling, "William Sherman Rogers M.D.," 10.

81. Hansen, "America's First Medical Breakthrough," 407; Pasteur Foundation website.

82. *Journal of the American Medical Association* (July 1907), 430.

83. Rayburn, *Ozark Folk Encyclopedia,* Masnor, "Keeps Madstone In Bank Vault."

84. *Arkansas Gazette,* 12 June 1872.

85. Watson Smith, "Madstone—Medicine or Myth?" 20–21.

86. *Sharp County Record,* 18 June 1891.

87. Henning, "My Grandfather, Willis Taylor Inman," 6–7.

88. Duvall, *Hoopsnakes and Horseshoes,* 78.

89. *Arkansas Gazette,* 16 April 1893.

90. Forbes, "The Madstone," 11–19.

91. "Mad Stones Condemned," *North Arkansas Star,* 10 May 1906.

92. "Bitten By a Mad Dog," *Arkansas Gazette,* 28 March 1890; "Bitten by Rabid Dogs; A Suggestion to the State Medical Association," *Arkansas Gazette,* 29 March 1890.

93. *Journal of the Arkansas Medical Society,* "Personals" (August 1912), 3.

94. Ibid., "Personals" (December 1912), 173.

95. Ibid., "Personals" (September 1914), 106.

96. "How Pasteur Antirabic Vaccine is Supplied," 67.

97. *Arkansas Gazette*, 22 December 1891; Hinkle is found on all U.S. Federal Censuses, 1900–1940.

98. *Benton County Democrat*, 18 July 1907; *Washington County Review*, 20 June 1907.

99. *North Arkansas Star*, 18 July 1924.

100. Rayburn, *Rayburn's Ozark Guide*, "Folklore by Mail," 18.

101. Rayburn, *Ozark Country*, 160; Randolph, *Ozark Magic*, 142.

102. *Sharp County Record*, 22 February 1901.

103. "Muzzle Your Dog Or Keep At Home," *Fayetteville Democrat*, 25 August 1928.

Chapter Two

1. Halbrook, *A School Man of the Ozarks*, 21–22.

2. Hogue, "The Cat and the Corpse," 7.

3. "Extracts From the Marble City Highlander," 37.

4. McCollum and Chrisco, "Evadean Phillips Sloan," *Down Memory Lane*, vol. 3, 72.

5. McChristian, *Bits and Pieces for Joan*.

6. Whittemore, "Kendall and Grace Bohlen," *Fading Memories*, vol. 2, 134–38.

7. Vaughan, *Growing Up Rich, Though Dirt Poor*, 111.

8. McCollum and Chrisco, "Herron Thompson Whitfield," *Down Memory Lane*, vol. 4, 173.

9. Burleson, *History of Cedar Grove*, 14.

10. *Fayetteville Democrat*, 19 January 1882.

11. Walden, *Journals*, part 2, 84.

12. Turnbo, "The Prayers of a Devoted Wife," vol. 26.

13. *Rogers Democrat*, 3 April 1902.

14. McCollum and Chrisco, "James Winford Franks," *Down Memory Lane*, vol. 7, 281.

15. *Springdale News*, 15 November 1901.

16. Britton and Griffith, "The Elvena Maxfield Journals, 1861–1866, Vol. 1," 12.

17. Ibid., 18.

18. Wilhoit, "A Doctor's Saddle-Bags of Cures," 2–6.

19. McColloch, "The Doctors of Old Cane Hill," 1.

20. McLane et al., *Observations of Arkansas*, 63–64.

21. Adams, *Doctors in Blue*, 39.

22. Ibid., 38–41.

23. Hodges, *Johnson County, Arkansas Funeral Book*.

24. Vest, *Remembering the Small Communities*, 91.

25. "Dr. I. Harmon Pavatt," 7.

26. Dawson, M.D., *Daybook*.

27. Lesh, M.D., "A Century of Medicine in Northwest Arkansas"; Turpentine, "Reminiscences," 26.

28. Britton and Griffith, "Elvena Maxfield Journals, Vol. 2," 21.

29. 1880 Census of the blind, deaf, and senile (Washington County).

30. Murphy, *Naked Ears*.

31. *Benton County Democrat*, 16 March 1893.

32. *Randolph [County] Herald*, 2 March 1885.

33. *Marshall Republican*, 21 July 1893.

34. "Fayetteville Female Seminary Was City's Top Girls' School," *Northwest Arkansas Times*, 14 June 1960, Centennial Edition.

35. Whittemore, "LaVera Beeby," *Fading Memories*, vol. 1, 73–75.

36. Szedegin, *As I Remember Piney*, 32.

37. Opie and Tatem, *Dictionary of Superstitions*, 15–16.

38. Edward Martin, *Psychology of the Funeral Service*, 12.

39. Whittemore, "Chloe Phillips Strode Baker," *Fading Memories*, vol. 3, 128.

40. Wolf, *Life in the Leatherwoods*, 129.

41. *Rogers Democrat*, 17 February 1898.

42. *Benton County Democrat*, 30 July 1891.

43. John Acheson, 1807–1833, Masonic Cemetery, Pocahontas (Randolph County).

44. *Benton County Democrat*, 21 November 1901.

45. *Russellville Democrat*, 22 November 1888.

46. *Benton County Democrat*, 4 August 1898.

47. *Benton County Democrat*, 12 August 1909.

48. Sarah "Belle" Nash, 1850–1911, Buckeye Cemetery (Madison County).

49. Vaughan, *Growing Up Rich, Though Dirt Poor*, 100.

50. Szegedin, *I'm Thinking About That Tree Yet*, 23–24.

51. *Fayetteville Democrat*, 19 February 1885.

52. Charles William Boles, 1883–1886, Evergreen Cemetery, Fayetteville (Washington County).

53. J. H. Williams, 1894–1899, Etna Church Cemetery (Franklin County).

54. Ronald Crockett, 1889–1904, Carrollton Cemetery (Carroll County).

55. Sarah Kelly, 1855–1890, Austin Cemetery (Benton County).

56. Rayburn, *Ozark Country*, 273.

57. *St. Paul Republican*, 30 March 1888.

58. *Benton County Democrat*, 18 January 1906.

59. "Mr. Axton," *Gravett[e] News*, 11 January 1896.

60. Mary Borland, 1837–1910, Highland Cemetery (Franklin County).

61. Swinburn and Stevenson, *History in Headstones*, 125; tombstone now missing.

62. Turnbo, "A Dying Man Tells How He Is Haunted," vol. 24.

63. Frank James, alias Joe Vaughn, 1844–1925, Snow Cemetery Ozark (Newton County).

64. Ray Robinson, "The Legend of Frank James," *Ozark Trails*, 21.

65. Whittemore, "Iva Haskins Williams," *Fading Memories*, vol. 2, 6.

66. "Death of Johnnie Chism," *[Marshall] Mountain Wave*, 4 November 1898.

67. Opie and Tatem, *Dictionary of Superstitions*, 25–26.

68. Turnbo, "In the Midst of Death," vol. 26.

69. "The History of Melvin Elmo Curry," transcribed by Wilson family descendants.

70. Parler, *Folk Beliefs from Arkansas*, vol. 8, # 7941–48, 2673–77.

71. "Miscellany," 38; McGrew, "Memories of Grandfather and Grandmother King," 193.

72. Ewing, "Chronicle of John Guin Bledsoe (Part 1)," 108.

Chapter Three

1. Epitaph contains additional verses describing laying-out and burial.

2. Tom Olmstead interview.

3. Randolph, *Ozark Magic*, 312–13.

4. Harral, "Pioneer Funerals."

5. Connell J. Brown, *Hard Times*, 94–97.

6. Pipes, *Strange Customs of the Ozark Hillbilly*, 12–13.

7. "White Ladies Prepare 'Old Mammy' in Grave," *Baxter Bulletin*, 17 July 1908; *Cotter Courier*, 17 July 1908.

8. Edge, *Was It Murder?* 207.

9. McCollum and Chrisco, "Louis, Abbie & Addie Adkisson," *Down Memory Lane*, vol. 5, 7.

10. Whittemore, "Iva Gross," *Fading Memories*, vol. 1, 111.

11. Page, *Voices of Moccasin Creek*, 46.

12. Rayburn, "Ozark Cyclopedia," 50.

13. Lemke, *Early Colleges and Academies*, 40.

14. "Poem Written 80 Years Ago," 7.

15. Mayer, *Embalming*, 117–18.

16. Randolph, *Ozark Magic*, 313.

17. Ibid., 315.

18. Allsopp, *Folklore of Romantic Arkansas*, 128, coins worn to cure consumption and halt bleeding.

19. Rose, *Gone to a Better Land*, 61.

20. Roberta Hughes Wright et al., *The Death Care Industry*, 11.

21. McCollum and Chrisco, "Lydia Moser Rider," *Down Memory Lane*, vol. 3, 128.

22. Mira Leister was told this story, 1960s; Brelowski, "Gone But Not Forgotten," 34.

23. Goss and Steward, "Rockabye Baby; Raising Babies in the Early 1900s," 36.

24. Winslow Centennial Book Committee, *Winslow, Arkansas*, 83.

25. Randolph, *Ozark Magic*, 302.

26. Laderman, *The Sacred Remains*, 29.

27. *Fayetteville Republican*, 15 March 1889.

28. *Rogers Democrat*, 29 April 1915.

29. McCollum and Chrisco, "Vera Ann Cypert Jacobs," *Down Memory Lane*, vol. 2, 179.

30. Edward Martin, *Psychology of the Funeral Service*, 56–57.

31. Geraldine Hatfield, "Old Time Burials," 75.

32. Crabtree et al., *Pea Ridge 1850–2000*, 12.

33. Skelton, "The William and John Thaddeus Skelton Families," 12.

34. Parler, *Folk Beliefs from Arkansas*, vol. 8, #8287, 2878; #8289–91, 2879.

35. Dunn Funeral Home Records.

36. Slocum, "Customs and Beliefs," 14.

37. Opal Arnold Taylor interview, Searcy County oral history project.

38. Ruth Wise, "Burials, Back When," 132.

39. F. M. McConnell, "History of the Middle Fork," 15.

40. Dunn Funeral Home records.

41. Hugh L. Routh, 1844–1919, Rose Hill Cemetery, Harrison (Boone County).

42. *Bentonville Sun*, 23 March 1895.

43. Puckett, *Folk Beliefs of the Southern Negro*, 84.

44. Rose, *Gone to a Better Land*, 133.

45. Parler, *Folk Beliefs from Arkansas*, vol. 8, #8245, 2855.

46. Mainfort and Davidson, *Two Historic Cemeteries*, 183, 221.

47. Carreiro, "Burge Family Reminiscences," 259–60.

48. *[Fayetteville] Free Press*, 28 May 1896.

49. Morton Mortuary Funeral Home records, pricing decoded by David Zimmerman.

50. Rahm, "The Crumrine Family of Mountain Home," 32.

51. Wise, "Burials, Back When," 132.

52. Fischer, *Albion's Seed*, 700.

53. Parler, *Folk Beliefs from Arkansas*, vol. 8, #8242, 2854; #8244, 2855.

54. Jamieson, "Material Culture and Social Death," 53.

55. Randolph, *Ozark Magic*, 313 and 282.

56. Rose, *Gone to a Better Land*, 96, burial believed to be that of a female, fifty-plus years old.

57. Flossie Cook Smith interview, Shiloh Oral History Collection.

58. Lankford, *Bearing Witness*, 134.

59. Key, "History of the Blackburn Family," 3.

60. Abbott, "The Way That Was . . . War Eagle Revisited," 88.

61. Counts, "Gladys Counts' Life Story," 115.

Chapter Four

1. Bruce Vaughan interview.

2. Vaughan, *Growing Up Rich, Though Dirt Poor*, 112.

3. Turnbo, "Several Old Time Items Worthy of Interest," vol. 19.

4. "Cleansing Garments by Heat," *Van Buren Press*, 6 January 1874.

5. Coffin, "Pioneer Days," 10.

6. Russell and Russell, *History of Hindsville*, reprinting Billie Jines, "Lots of Hindsville Doctors," *Madison County Record*, 28 March 1957.

7. Randolph, *Ozark Magic*, 212.

8. Rayburn, *Ozark Folklore Encyclopedia*, May Kennedy McCord, "Hillbilly Heartbeats," quoting Sylvia Hill, of Thayer, Missouri.

9. McCollum and Chrisco, "Ernest Don Tomlinson," *Down Memory Lane*, vol. 3, 225.

10. Pauline Davis Steele, "Angel Wreaths," *Hill Country Sayin's*.

11. Parler, *Folk Beliefs from Arkansas*, vol. 8, #s 7897–7911, 2645–52.

12. Rayburn, *Ozark Folk Encyclopedia*, (May Kennedy McCord?), "'Feather Crown' Omen of Death?"

13. Randolph, *Ozark Magic*, 322.

14. McCord, "Hillbilly Heartbeats," quoting Sylvia Hill.

15. *Springdale News*, 14 September 1906.

16. Randolph, *Ozark Magic*, 323–26.

17. Rayburn, *Ozark Folk Encyclopedia*, "'Feather Crown' Omen of Death?"

18. Garland County Historical Society collection, Hot Springs.

19. Mainfort and Davidson, *Two Historic Cemeteries*, 56–58.

20. Unsigned, "Letter of General Moore," 18.

21. *Encyclopedia of Arkansas History and Culture*, Dougan, "Archibald Yell."

22. Varno and Tyree, "One Dead as Result of Stabbing Affray," 17.

23. Lemke, "An Unusual Execution in Fayetteville," from the *Fayetteville Democrat*, 26 April 1894.

24. C. L. Miller, *Postmortem Collectibles*, 47; Wendell catalog (1904?) from the private collection of Bob and Patty Besom.

25. McLane et al. *Observations of Arkansas*, 57.

26. May, *The Victorian Undertaker*, 20.

27. Lemke, "Judge Sebron Graham Sneed," 9–10.

28. *Springdale News*, 1 September 1911.

29. Hasson, *Widows, Weepers and Wakes*, 2.

30. McCollum and Chrisco, "Floyd Foster Copeland," *Down Memory Lane*, vol. 6, 149.

31. Carolyn Banks, Cooper's granddaughter, e-mail 2006.

32. Phillip W. Steele, *Two Longs and a Short*, 88.

33. Ash Flat Historical Society, *Ash Flat History*, 216, citing an undated video interview made by Chris Beller.

34. Hetrick, *Plumerville Foundations*, 134.

35. McCollum and Chrisco, "Louis, Abbie & Addie Adkisson," *Down Memory Lane*, vol. 5, 13.

36. Marion Stark Craig, "Death of Dr. Daniel J. Chapman: 1857," 17.

37. Rayburn, *Ozark Folk Encyclopedia*, Karr Shannon, "Run of the News."

38. Mildred Smith e-mail, 2006.

39. Rayburn, *Rayburn's Ozark Guide*, "Ozark Fact and Folklore," 51–52.

40. Wassell, "Negro Folklore," 174.

41. Opie and Tatem, *Dictionary of Superstitions*, 63–64.

42. Randolph, *Ozark Magic*, 313.

43. Parler, *Folk Beliefs from Arkansas*, vol. 8, #8232, 2849.

44. Ibid., #8233, 2849.

45. Wayne Martin interview.

46. Rayburn, "Ozark Folk-Ways," *Will-O'-The-Wisp*.

47. Randolph, *Ozark Magic*, 313, quoting May Kennedy McCord on Springfield, Missouri, practices.

48. Edith Simmons Martin, "A History of the Rushing Community," referring to David E. Rushing (born 1889), Pope County.

49. "Funeral Ethics," undertaker's record-keeping book published by F. J. Feineman, St. Louis, Missouri, in a private collection.

50. Whittemore, "LaVera Beeby," *Fading Memories*, vol. 1, 73–75.

51. Tom Dillard, "Ice, ice, baby," *Arkansas Democrat-Gazette*, 15 August 2010.

52. Ibid.

53. Phillip W. Steele, *Two Longs and a Short*, 30.

54. McCollum and Chrisco, "Goldie Marie Sears Estes," *Down Memory Lane*, vol. 7, 158.

55. United States Patent Office, patent nos. 214,998 and 215,055, both issued on 6 May 1879

56. Dunn Funeral Home records.

57. Notebook of collected funeral notices, Crawford County Genealogical Library, Alma, Arkansas.

58. Knotts, *Death Notices in Pocahontas, Randolph County*.

59. Morton Mortuary records, in the private collection of David Zimmerman.

60. Dunn Funeral Home records.

61. *Springdale News*, 10 August 1906.

62. *Washington County Review*, 11 October 1906.

63. Rayburn, "Folklore By Mail," *Rayburn's Ozark Guide*, 17.

64. McCollum and Chrisco, "Erma Rhea 'Reedie' Williams Moore," *Down Memory Lane*, vol. 2, 73–74.

65. Bondeson, *Buried Alive*, 14.

66. "Blister sign of death," 372.

67. *Springdale News*, 23 August 1901.

68. "Slaughter Alive," *Arkansas Gazette*, 8 May 1892.

69. *Fayetteville Democrat*, 2 February 1923.

70. Turnbo, "A Part of an Account of the Coker Family," vol. 18, concerning Redissa ("Dicy") Trimble, born 1814.

71. *Pocahontas Star Herald*, 30 October 1914.

72. McCollum and Chrisco, "Louis, Abbie & Addie Adkisson," *Down Memory Lane*, vol. 5, 14.

73. Bondeson, *Buried Alive*, 241–42.

74. Lang, "Coffins and Caskets," 40–42.

75. Information provided by William Flanagan, former groundskeeper of Evergreen Cemetery, Fayetteville (Washington County), date unknown.

76. Turnbo, "The Old Pioneer Joe Magness," vol. 17.

77. Lankford, *Bearing Witness*, 277–78; both the date and location (presumably Little Rock) are uncertain.

78. Wiggins, "Remembering Annie Eliza Acord Eubanks," 41–42.

79. Witnessed by Hubert Criner, born about 1900, and told to Charles Stockton in the 1970s.

80. Wolf, *Life in the Leatherwoods*, 35–36.

Chapter Five

1. Vaughn, *Heartbeats of Home*, 53–54.

2. Dunn Funeral Home records.

3. Haberstein and Lamers, *History of American Funeral Directing*, 253, 270–71.

4. Tom Olmstead interview.

5. David Matlock interview.

6. Ash Flat Historical Society, *Ash Flat History*, 216.

7. Bud Phillips, *The New Ozark Cousins*, 212.

8. Tessie Phillips Taylor, "James Willis Phillips," 58.

9. *Southwest Independent*, 30 September 1854.

10. Witherspoon, *Pioneer Life in Rural Missouri*, 22.

11. Payne, "The Cincinnati Story," 35.

12. "Sulphur Rock Described as Health Resort," 34.

13. Jesse Moody papers, Shiloh Museum of Ozark History, Springdale, Arkansas.

14. Wayne Martin, *Pettigrew, Arkansas*, 205–6.

15. Eric Allen, "I Can Make Anything Out of Iron, Steel or Wood," *Fort Smith Times Record*, 25 August 1968.

16. Ibid.

17. Hill, *I Remember St. Paul*, 25–27.

18. Chalk, "Coy Cleveland Roten," 154–55.

19. Wayne Martin, *Pettigrew, Arkansas*, 199.

20. *Pocahontas Star Herald*, 19 June 1930; additional biographical information provided by Wilson descendants.

21. Harrell, "The Night Uncle Lum Died," *History and Folklore of Searcy County*, 420.

22. McCollum and Chrisco, "Lena Jane Cantrell Coder," *Down Memory Lane*, vol. 8, 27.

23. Vester Williams, "The Pioneer Coffin Makers," 77–78, originally published in the *Salem Headlight*, 12 January 1967.

24. Counts, "Gladys Counts' Life Story," 117.

25. McCollum and Chrisco, "Erma Rhea 'Reedie' Williams Moore," *Down Memory Lane*, vol. 2, 73.

26. Rex Harral, "Pioneer Funerals."

27. Rahm, "The Crumrine Family of Mountain Home," 32.

28. Amy Sherrill, "Ozark Man in Touch With Local History," *[Fort Smith] Southwest Times Record*, 9 August 2004.

29. Putnam Funeral Home records.

30. *Benton County Democrat*, 29 March 1906.

31. Standlee, "Life as It Was," 164.

32. Murphy, *Naked Ears*.

33. McCollum and Chrisco, "Louis, Abbie & Addie Adkisson," *Down Memory Lane*, vol. 5, 13.

34. Rayburn, *Ozark Folklore Encyclopedia*, "A Backwoods Buryin'," vol. D-2.

35. McCollum and Chrisco, "P. O. Wren," *Down Memory Lane*, vol. 2, 93.

36. McCollum and Chrisco, "Nina Zoe Davis Blair," *Down Memory Lane* [unnumbered first vol.], 169.

37. *Pocahontas Star Herald*, 29 November 1918.

38. Cave Springs Library Board, *Cave Springs Memories*, account given by Iva Heagerty-Nichols (born 1897).

39. Hope Hodgdon Creek, family reminiscence.

40. Lilian Baker Carlisle, "A History of Casket Plaques," *Antique Trader Weekly*, 8 March 1989.

41. *Edmiston Store Day Book, 1882*.

42. Estes, *Early Days and War Times*, 14.

43. Mainfort and Davidson, *Two Historic Cemeteries*, 156.

44. Ibid., 163.

45. Garner Hardware inventory ledger, Calico Rock.

46. Bryant Hardware Store records; Ocker Funeral Home records.

47. *Fayetteville Democrat*, 23 June 1905.

48. Page, *Voices of Moccasin Creek*, 304.

49. Roach, *Gulp, Adventures on the Alimentary Canal*, 157–63.

50. Acts of the General Assembly of the State of Arkansas, 1873, No. 45.

51. Akins, "Hangin' Times in Fort Smith: The Execution of Kitt Ross," 50; Akins, *Hangin' Times in Fort Smith*, 143.

52. "A Convict Cemetery," *Arkansas Gazette*, 12 December 1893; "A Convict Cemetery," *[Morrilton] Pilot*, 5 January 1894.

53. Baker, *Historical Perspectives*, 66.

54. Ibid., 66.

55. *Encyclopedia of Arkansas History and Culture*, Puryear, "University of Arkansas Medical Sciences (UAMS)."

56. "'I'll Shoot 'Em.'; A Belief Now Prevailing Among the Colored People," *Daily Arkansas Gazette*, 28 October 1879.

57. Flossie Cook Smith interview, Shiloh Oral History Collection.

58. Garner Hardware records, 1927, listing "2 sets child coffin handles" at $1.32 per set.

59. Boise, "A Pioneer Tragedy," 21–22.

60. McCollum and Chrisco, "Louis, Abbie & Addie Adkisson," *Down Memory Lane*, vol. 5, 16.

61. Turnbo, "The Old Pioneer Joe Magness," vol. 17.

62. *Pocahontas Star Herald*, 14 July 1916.

63. Boulden, David Matlock interview.

64. *Frigid Fluid Company, Embalmers, Undertakers and Cemetery Supplies*; Kregal Casket Co., *Illustrated Catalogue*.

65. "The Account Book of Orren M. Reiff," 25–27.

66. Huhn, "The B. F. Hobbs Account Book," 48; Lemley, "Business Houses of Russellville," 105.

67. Birnie Brothers records (14 January 1882–14 September 1904); no death records date to 1875, the start of Judge Parker's tenure.

68. Britton, *Independence Pioneers*, vol. 2, 35.

69. Black, *History of Benton County*, 492.

70. Bart H. Atkinson records.

71. David Matlock interview.

72. *Sharp County Record*, 10 August 1917.

73. Boyertown Burial Casket Company.

74. E. A. Medley ad, *Izard County Register*, 6 July 1905.

75. L. V. Parker ad, *Madison County Record*, 5 May 1927.

76. Coffin ledger, courtesy of Charles K. Grubbs. Thomas "Lee" Grubbs added an "s" to the family's surname.

77. Charles K. Grubbs interview.

78. McChristian, *Bits and Pieces for Joan*.

79. Grubb/Grubbs family history, courtesy Charles K. Grubbs.

80. "Fort Smith Casket Company," *Southwest American*, 25 July 1907.

81. Boulden, David Matlock interview.

82. Ibid.

83. Butler, "The Forgotten Soldiers," 60–61.

84. WPA, Early Settlers' Personal History Questionnaire, George Meriwether interview (Independence County, born 1852).

85. Tunstall family history, courtesy of descendant Jim Barnett.

86. Ober, *Mark Twain and Medicine*, 89–90.

87. U.S. Patent No. 5920, 14 November 1848.

88. Habenstein and Lamers, *History of American Funeral Directing*, 263–72.

89. Crane & Breed Mfg. Co.

90. Tharp, "Preserving Their Form and Features," 185.

91. Kalklosch, *The Healing Fountain*, unnumbered advertising pages.

92. Fisk Metallic Burial Case Co., approximately 1866 or 1867.

93. *Benton County Democrat*, 30 March 1911.

Chapter Six

1. *Washington County Review*, 11 October 1906.

2. McMurry, *Mama's Trunk of Memories*, 10.

3. Bud Phillips, *The New Ozark Cousins*, 280.

4. Mooney, *Mrs. Lola Brown Diary*.

5. Ellen Earle Richardson, *Early Settlers of Cane Hill*, 56; Conrow R. Miller, *The Cane Hill Story*, 13.

6. Young, "So Big, This Little Place," 97–98.

7. Maddox, "Calling Central," 20.

8. *Fayetteville Democrat*, 21 August 1875, 16 February 1882.

9. Brawner, *My Life in the Funeral Business*, 37.

10. *Rogers Democrat*, 18 January 1917.

11. Lyon, *Hurrah For Arkansas*, 226; William Pleas Spears, 1862–1945, Jasper City Cemetery (Newton County).

12. Mrs. T. Moore, "Diary," entry written by Moore's daughter, Mrs. W. C. Bill, 15.

13. Scroggins, *Old Obituaries*.

14. "The Tracy Family of Fulton and Baxter Counties," 8.

15. Funeral notices collected by Nellie (Tracy) Mitchell and Garvin Carroll, both of Mountain Home; notebook in the collection of the Baxter County Heritage Museum, Gassville.

16. *Benton County Democrat*, 14 September 1899, shared obituary for Bagby wife, baby, and child.

17. Starck, *Life After Death*, 1–4, 26.

18. *Benton County Democrat*, 24 March 1888.

19. *Springdale News*, 15 July 1898.

20. *Russellville Democrat*, 30 June 1886.

21. *Rogers Democrat*, 23 May 1912.

22. *Rogers Democrat*, 5 October 1904.

23. *Fayetteville Democrat*, 8 October 1886.

24. *Rogers Democrat*, 4 May 1899.

25. *Rogers Democrat*, 16 August 1900.

26. *Elixir Bugle*, 21 March 1883.

27. *Benton County Democrat*, 15 June 1911.

28. *Springdale News*, 17 February 1899.

29. *[Marshall] Mountain Wave*, 23 February 1917.

30. *Rogers Democrat*, 26 July 1917.

31. *[Marshall] Mountain Wave*, 10 December 1906.

32. Ibid., 27 June 1924.

33. *Pocahontas Star Herald*, 23 February 1917.

34. *Russellville Democrat*, 22 May 1885.

35. *Springdale News*, 25 December 1908; correct name is Randell Emert.

36. *Sharp County Record*, 26 June 1890.

37. *Courier-Democrat*, 11 March 1909.

38. *Benton County Democrat*, 11 May 1911.

39. 1850 Census, Mortality Schedules, William White, age fifty-three, Carroll County, cause of death: old age.

40. *Sharp County Record*, 12 January 1917.

41. *Benton County Democrat*, 7 February 1901.

42. *Pocahontas Star Herald*, 12 August 1912.

43. *Courier-Democrat*, 4 May 1905.

44. *Rogers Democrat*, 3 February 1904.

45. *Benton County Democrat*, 22 and 29 April 1909.

46. *Fayetteville Democrat*, 6 July 1882.

47. *Rogers Democrat*, 3 April 1902.

48. *Fayetteville Democrat*, 3 May 1883.

49. Walker, "Some Items From Mrs. Walker's Collection," 30.

50. *Fayetteville Democrat*, 19 May 1877.

51. Stanley, *Fort Smith Well Remembered*, 42; there is no mention of the monkey in undertaker J. G. Putnam's records.

52. *Madison County Record*, 31 January 1924.

53. *Sharp County Record*, 17, 24 September, 1, 15 October 1897.

54. Key, "Some Early Business Men of Rogers," 9–10.

55. Page, *Voices of Moccasin Creek*, 393.

56. Russell, *Stepping Back Into Time*, 22.

57. *[Marshall] Mountain Wave*, 28 July 1892.

58. Gibson, "Mabel Wilson," 11–17.

59. McChristian, *Bits and Pieces for Joan*.

60. A. B. Macdonald, "Shepherd of the Hills Transforms Arkansas Backwoods Into a Modern Canaan," *Kansas City Star*, 9 December 1928, quoting from a sermon delivered in 1919.

61. Bud Phillips, *The New Ozark Cousins*, 300.

62. Page, *Voices of Moccasin Creek*, 139–40.

63. Jenkins, "The Montgomery Family," 124.

64. Parler, *Folk Beliefs from Arkansas*, vol. 8, #s 8266–67, 2867–68; #8274, 2871.

65. McDonough, *Garden Sass*, 150.

66. Turnbo, "A Death Stricken Family," vol. 19.

67. Tackett, "Memories," written for family, 1998, courtesy of Judy Bancerowski, 2007.

68. Judy Bancerowski e-mail, 2006.

69. Columbus Vaughn, "Heartbeats of Home," *Newton County Times*, 12 January 1984.

70. *[Marshall] Mountain Wave*, 13 May 1899.

71. Opal Arnold Taylor interview.

72. Standlee, "Life as It Was," 164.

73. *Fayetteville Democrat*, 18 October 1889.

74. *Madison County Record*, 10 August 1922.

75. F. J. Tennison, "In Eternity; Andy Hudspeth Hanged; He Wept Piteously, When Prayed for by the Minister," *(Marshall) Mountain Wave*, 5 January 1893.

76. Turnbo, "Disinterment of a Young Lady," vol. 27.

77. Sargent, *Dealings with the Dead*, 45–46.

78. Winn, *The Story of Winslow's Maud Duncan*, 25–26.

79. Robert G. Winn, "Two Children—A bizarre tale based on local history," *Washington County Observer*, 6 April 1987.

80. Winn, *The Story of Winslow's Maud Duncan*, 26.

81. McChristian, *Bits and Pieces for Joan*.

82. Rayburn, *Ozark Folklore Encyclopedia*, "A Backwoods Buryin'," vol. D-2.

Chapter Seven

1. Page, *Voices of Moccasin Creek*, 418.

2. Standlee, "Life As It Was," 163.

3. Moshinskie, "Western Undertaker," *Early Arkansas Undertakers.*

4. McCollum and Chrisco, "Mary Pauline Lewis Killian," *Down Memory Lane*, vol. 7, 73.

5. Turnbo, "Shocking Scenes Enacted at Yellville," vol. 2.

6. Russell, *Stepping Back Into Time*, 19–20.

7. Leach, "Happenings In and Near Floyd," 31.

8. Mainfort and Davidson, *Two Historic Cemeteries*, 97, 100.

9. Turnbo, "Visiting the Grave of Her Affiance," vol. 3, "More Killing in War Days," vol. 2.

10. McCollum and Chrisco, "John Henry Owen William Harvell," *Down Memory Lane*, (unnumbered first volume), 39.

11. *Gentry Journal-Advance*, 7 January 1910.

12. *Searcy County Obituaries*, 3.

13. Russell, *Stepping Back Into Time*, 19.

14. Randolph, *Ozark Magic*, 319.

15. Parler, *Folk Beliefs from Arkansas*, vol. 8, #8300, 2884, #8301–2, 2885.

16. McCollum and Chrisco, "Lydia Moser Rider," *Down Memory Lane*, vol. 3, 107.

17. Jenkins, "The Montgomery Family," 124.

18. Parler, *Folk Beliefs from Arkansas*, vol. 8, #8303, 2886.

19. Slocum, "Customs and Beliefs," 14–15.

20. Ibid., 74–85.

21. Jeane, "The Upland South Folk Cemetery," 111.

22. *American Folklore: An Encyclopedia*, Meyer, "Cemeteries," 132–34.

23. *How To Beautify Your Cemetery Plot*, 18.

24. Turnbo, "The Old Pioneer Joe Magness," vol. 17.

25. Jordan-Bychov, *The Upland South*, 75.

26. Jabbour and Jabbour, *Decoration Day*, 58.

27. Pye, "Where Death Sows Rotting Seeds," 2, 17.

28. "McKinney Cemetery," 21.

29. McCollum and Chrisco, "Nina Zoe Davis Blair," *Down Memory Lane*, (unnumbered first volume), 169–70.

30. Samuel Vaughan, Vaughan-Whitener Cemetery, Hindsville (Madison County).

31. W. R. Jones, *Gleanings of Pioneer History*, 37.

32. Hearn, "The Ingram Cemetery," 161.

33. "The First Grave at Prairie Grove," *Fayetteville Democrat*, 29 January 1885.

34. Crabtree et al., *Pea Ridge: 1850–2000*, 83.

35. Wayland, "Batesville's Memorial Park Cemetery," 2–8.

36. Pat Donat, "Doctor's Letters Reveal the Past," *Northwest Arkansas Times*, 24 October 1961.

37. Thielemier, *The Making of Catholic Hill*, 2.

38. *[Marshall] Mountain Wave*, 23 June 1906.

39. Russell, *Pre-1920 Obituaries*, 227–28.

40. *Fayetteville Evergreen Cemetery Association Records.*

41. Tom Olmstead interview.

42. Randolph, *Ozark Folksongs*, 458–60, song written by train porter Gussie L. Davis in 1899.

43. Kammen, *Digging Up the Dead*, 22–23.

44. *Springdale News*, 30 August and 6 September 1907.

45. *Springdale News*, 11 March 1910.

46. Remsberg, "From Coffin-Making to Undertaking," 34.

47. *Encyclopedia of Southern Culture*, Jeane, "Cemeteries," 463.

48. Jewell Willey Phillips, "Liberty Hill Cemetery," 56.

49. Turnbo, "Among the Dead," vol. 20.

50. Abby Burnett, "Cemetery Myth Debunked," *Morning News of Northwest Arkansas*, 20 June 2005, interviewing June Westphal.

51. Shull, "Who Is Mandy?" 33–34.

52. *Benton County Democrat*, 24 October 1901.

53. Turnbo, "She Did Not Want to be Dead," vol. 27.

54. Rayburn, *Ozark Folklore Encyclopedia*, vol. D-2, undated letter from W. S. Cazort.

55. Tom Olmstead interview.

56. Page, *Voices of Moccasin Creek*, 418.

57. Moshinskie, "Conducting Home Funerals," *Early Arkansas Undertakers*.

58. Tom Olmstead interview.

59. Watts, "Great God! I own thy sentence just," Hymn 6, based on the passage from Job 19: 26.

60. *Springdale News*, 20 December 1909.

61. Randoph, *Ozark Magic*, 202.

62. Lemke, "Violent History or Historical Violence," 1.

63. Jines, "Bushwhackers Lose Head, Arm," 57–58.

64. Vaughan, *Growing Up Rich, Though Dirt Poor*, 47–48; first name taken from tombstone.

65. Parler, *Folk Beliefs from Arkansas*, vol. 3, #s 1385–88, 430.

Chapter Eight

1. Avon Neal, "Gravestone Carving," 4.

2. Lemke, "Come All You Sons of Ioway," 23; later changed to "placed a stone at each man's head."

3. "Captain E. G. Miller: His War," 47.

4. Crawford, *Jubilee: Mount Holly Cemetery*, 9, 67.

5. WPA, Early Settlers' Personal History Questionnaire, Mary E. Hays interview (Searcy County, born 1846).

6. Wayne Clark, *Letters and Diaries of Isaac A. Clarke*, 94–96, 98, 110, 111, 113, 117.

7. *Encyclopedia of Arkansas History and Culture*, Abby Burnett, "Nick Miller."

8. "Suicided," *North Arkansas Star*, 17 August 1898.

9. Black, *History of Benton County*, 256.

10. "Some Women Marble Cutters," *Monumental News*, December 1939, reprinting an earlier, undated article.

11. *Encyclopedia of Arkansas History and Culture*, Burnett, "Lucy Daniel."

12. Cole and Creighton, P. E. Stone interview.

13. *[St. Paul] Mountain Air*, 11 April 1908.

14. *Arkansas Gazette*, 4 March 1937.

15. Blackwell Bros., Bentonville Monument Works ad, *Benton County Democrat*, throughout 1894.

16. *Huntsville Republican*, 18 December 1913.

17. *Arkansas Gazette*, 4 March 1937.

18. *Encyclopedia of Arkansas History and Culture*, Howard, "Dimension Stone Mining," 2010.

19. Hopkins, "Marbles and Other Limestones," 101.

20. Nabors, "Elmwood."

21. Hensley, "The Arkansas Commemorative Stone," 49–51.

22. Victor A. Croley, "Marble Falls Has Had Many Names," *Arkansas Gazette*, 23 March 1969.

23. *Harrison Times*, 29 December 1883.

24. Powell, "The Kruegers of the Pfeiffer Stone Company," 13–35.

25. "Batesville, Arkansas Crystalline Oolitic Marble," inside cover.

26. Ibid., 6.

27. Powell, "The Kruegers of the Pfeiffer Stone Company," 33.

28. Longfellow, "Resignation," 51–54.

29. Wasserman, *Gravestone Designs*, 26–27.

30. Martha A. Hambrick, 1843–1880, Reiff's Chapel (Washington County).

31. Marshall City Cemetery (Searcy County).

32. Case, aka Cowan Cemetery (Newton County).

33. John C. McKinney, murdered 21 January 1869 (Washington County); Dr. Archibald McKennon, 1803–1883 (Johnson County); Marion C. Shaddox, 1854–1884, Shaddox Cemetery, Pruitt (Newton County), respectively.

34. Mary Beller Russell, 1840–1902, Bellefonte Cemetery (Boone County).

35. Auman Cemetery, outside Alpena (Boone County).

36. *Fayetteville Democrat*, 26 June 1905.

37. Fairview Cemetery, Van Buren (Crawford County).

38. "Engineer Killed," *Arkansas Gazette*, 1 December 1896, J. R. Beaty, 20 October 1860–1896.

39. Joseph Buchanan, 1827–1864, Cherry Grove Cemetery (Newton County).

40. Kimbrell Hill, 1818–1901, Yale Cemetery (Franklin County).

41. Sylvanus Hinds, 1843–1863, Farmer Cemetery, Hindsville (Madison County).

42. Information provided by Joy Russell, citing Hinds in California on the 1870 and 1880 censuses.

43. Information provided by Youngblood family researchers Vineta Wingate and Dorothy Quaife.

44. Hattie Youngblood, 1888–1906, Youngblood-Richiesin Cemetery (Boone County).

45. "A Tale of Horror," *Ft. Smith Weekly New Era*, 1 December 1871; "Horrid Crime in Franklin County—Speedy Justice Administered to the Murderer," *Van Buren Press*, 28 November 1871.

46. Obed Hill, 1888–1918, Yale Cemetery (Franklin County).

47. Hankins Monument Company ledgers (1947–1951), in the author's collection.

48. "Daguerreotypes on Tombstones," 519.

49. "Monuments[,] Tombstones and Markers," 28.

50. Horne, *Forgotten Faces*, 13.

51. *How to Beautify Your Cemetery Plot*, 18.

52. Russel M. Byrd, 1856–1885, Salem Lutheran Cemetery (Washington County).

53. Patterson, "United Above Though Parted Below," 192.

54. Ball, "Further Observations on Gravehouse Origins," 26–27.

55. John Waggoner e-mail, 2010.

56. *Baxter County*, "Grisso Cemetery," 136.

57. Whittemore, "Dexter Kilgore Shastid," *Fading Memories*, vol. 2, 1; Mahalia Jane Richardson Kilgore genealogy courtesy of Joy Russell.

58. Information posted inside Guffrey Agee's gravehouse.

59. Lankford, *Bearing Witness*, 24.

60. Smiley, "Buried Twice," 32.

61. Heritage Center Museum collection, Berryville (Carroll County), donated by Charles M. Nelson, Nelson Funeral Home.

62. *Sharp County Record*, 23 August 1901.

63. Illegible name, died 1887, Bass (Newton County); Melvnia Megehee, 1847–1882, Cherry Grove (Newton County).

64. Rotundo, "Monumental Bronze," 263–64.

65. *[Fayetteville] Arkansas Sentinel*, 1 September 1908.

66. Ibid.

67. Rotundo, "Monumental Bronze," 277.

68. Ibid., 266–67.

69. Mary Ollie Whitlow, 1889–1900, Wesley Cemetery (Madison County).

70. "Monument Sign Holder," U.S. Patent #359639 issued to James K. P. Shelton, Gaston, Alabama, 22 March 1887.

71. Sears, Roebuck and Co., catalog, 1900, 739.

72. Cohn et al., *The Good Old Days*, 233–34.

73. Sears, Roebuck, *Catalogue No. 117*, 160.

74. Monuments[,] Tombstones and Markers, unnumbered first page.

75. Stott, "The Woodmen of the World Monument Program," 1–29.

76. Woodmen of the World, *Ritual*, 75–85.

77. *[Yellville] Mountain Echo*, 22 July 1910.

78. Abby Burnett, "No Pompous Marble to Thy Name We Raise," 115–45.

Chapter Nine

1. Karns, "Uncle Fate," 87–88, regarding Alfred Lafayette Firestone.

2. O'Neal, "The Canaan Cemetery," 14.

3. Karns, "Uncle Fate," 87–88.

4. O'Neal, "The Canaan Cemetery," 14.

5. Goodspeed, *Benton County*, 120.

6. Information provided by June Westphal.

7. *Benton County Democrat*, 25 May 1905, full obituary; death notice 5 January 1905.

8. *Gravette News-Herald*, 14 May 1915.

9. *Springdale News*, 11 February 1888.

10. Bearden, "The Romance of Arkansas Methodism," 1.

11. "History of the Pottsville Circuit," 20.

12. Walden, *Journals*, part 2, 31; after 1874 Walden did not itemize his mileage.

13. Standlee, "Life as It Was in Early Carroll County," 115.

14. Kephart, *Our Southern Highlanders*, 335.

15. Randolph, *Ozark Magic*, 317.

16. Wassell, "Negro Folklore," 169.

17. Abby Burnett, "At the Gallows," *Morning News of Northwest Arkansas*, 8 August 2004.

18. "Funeral of Miss Ella Barham Held at Pleasant Ridge," *[Marshall] Mountain Wave*, 31 May 1913.

19. "State News," *Arkansas Gazette*, 5 February 1882.

20. Arkansas State Board of Health, *Rules and Regulations*, 1928, 10.

21. *Springdale News*, 14 June 1912.

22. "Sebern J. Davis' Funeral," 27.

23. Brawner, *My Life in the Funeral Business*, 66–67.

24. *[Berryville] North Arkansas Star & Carroll Progress*, 28 January 1921.

25. *Fayetteville Democrat*, 29 June 1872.

26. Bruce Vaughan e-mail, 2011.

27. Randolph, *Ozark Magic*, 320.

28. Bruce Vaughan interview.

29. Starr, *Climb the Highest Mountain*, 36.

30. Pearl Thomas Williams, *Come Go With Me*, 143–44, quoting her husband (born Cleburne County, date unknown).

31. Massey, *Bittersweet Country*, 276.

32. James P. Neal, "The Memoirs of Col. James P. Neal," 15–16; the tombstone erected in 1941 gives 1831 as the death date.

33. Albertson, *A Service Book*.

34. Sherman, "Funeral Notes."

35. Ibid., funerals of Mary Louise Gregory, 1951; Felix Anderson, 1955; Martha McFarlin Tribble, 1956.

36. Deane G. Carter, "Brother Sherman," funeral of Mary A. Schoolfield, 1931, 29.

37. Sherman, "Funeral Notes," funeral of Fannie Wooddy, 1949; unnamed cemetery.

38. Sherman, *A Brief Account of the Life*.

39. "Green Kuykendall: Gone But Not Forgotten," *Franklin County Historical Association Observer*, 16.

40. *Encyclopedia of Southern Culture*, Wilson, "Funerals," 478–79.

41. *Benton County Democrat*, 12 May 1904.

42. Opal Arnold Taylor, *Medicine Time*, 10.

43. Sanford F. Bennett, "In the Sweet By and By," 1868; Robert Lowry, "Shall We Gather at the River," 1864; James M. Black, "When the Roll is Called Up Yonder," 1893.

44. J. A. McClung, "Just a Rose Will Do," 1942.

45. Hunter, *Trees, Shrubs, and Vines*, 88.

46. *Springdale News*, 6 September 1895.

47. Elise Mellard obituary, *Daily Graphic*, 30 May 1893.

48. Conner, "Moving Forward," 21; Norma Conner interview, age seventy-three.

49. Edge, *Was It Murder?* 212.

50. *Rogers Democrat*, 7 September 1899.

51. Freemasons, *Masonic Monitor*, 128–57.

52. Habenstein and Lamers, *Funeral Customs*, 835.

53. "Sebern J. Davis' Funeral," 27.

54. McCollum and Chrisco, "Louis, Abbie & Addie Adkisson," *Down Memory Lane*, vol. 5, 16–17.

55. *[Russellville] Courier-Democrat*, 6 November 1930.

56. Mrs. T. Moore, "Diary," 17, entry written by Moore's daughter, Mrs. W. C. Bill.

57. *[Marshall] Mountain Wave*, 23 January 1925.

58. Story used on condition of anonymity.

59. *[Marshall] Mountain Wave*, 18 January 1924.

60. Jabbour and Jabbour, *Decoration Day*, 116–23.

61. Roxie Smith Cook interview, Shiloh Oral History Collection.

62. *[Russellville] Courier-Democrat*, 14 May 1903.

63. Poteet, "Our Country Cemeteries," 11.

64. Story used on condition of anonymity.

65. Rayburn, *Ozark Folk Encyclopedia*, France, "The Hills of Home," referring to Sunset Cemetery, probably World War II era.

66. Flossie Cook Smith interview, Shiloh Oral History Collection.

67. Sparks, *Walking the Wagon Road*, 115.

68. Pauline Davis Steele, *Hill Country Sayin's*.

69. McChristian, *Bits and Pieces for Joan*.

70. *How To Make Crepe Paper Flowers*.

71. Creo Jones, *"I Remember When,"* 31–40.

72. McChristian, *Bits and Pieces for Joan*.

73. Bradley House Museum, Jasper, Arkansas, photo collection.

74. Opal Arnold Taylor, Searcy County oral history project.

75. Grand and Grimes, "Graves and Graveyards."

76. Barker, *Yesterday Today*, 210, unidentified county and cemetery.

77. *Encyclopedia of Southern Culture*, Patterson, "Grave Markers," 480.

78. Jeane, "The Upland South Folk Cemetery Complex," 114.

79. Evans and Dewberry, *Evans, Oark, Patterson Springs, and Yale*, 29–30.

80. Torian, "Ante-Bellum and War Memories," 352.

81. Holloway, *Passed On*, 210–11.

82. Grand and Grimes, "Graves and Graveyards."

83. "Little Rocking Along," *Arkansas Gazette*, 18 December 1938, magazine section.

84. Kevin Hatfield, *The Huntsville Massacre*, 36.

85. Keister, *Stories in Stone*, 87.

86. Montell, *Ghosts along the Cumberland*, 84.

87. Birnie Brothers records.

88. Boles's letter to "Aunt Sarah" dated 19 September 1889, collection of Shiloh Museum of Ozark History, Springdale, Arkansas.

89. Jabbour and Jabbour, *Decoration Day*, 61.

90. Fountain, *Sisters, Seeds, and Cedars*, 203; Clara Dunlap writing to Cornelia Dickson.

91. Shults and Martin, "What is a Beegee Tree?" in *Randolph County*, 90.

92. Randolph, *Ozark Magic*, 308.

93. Poteet, "Our Country Cemeteries," 11.

94. Pile, "Decoration Day at Lowes Creek," 124.

95. "News from the Rural Districts," 35.

96. Sparks, *Walking the Wagon Road*, 115.

97. "Duncan News," *Madison County Record*, 5 June 1930.

98. "Decoration at Witt Springs," *[Marshall] Mountain Wave*, 20 May 1898.

99. *[Marshall] Mountain Wave*, 20 May 1898.

100. Johnson, "Annual Decoration of Cemeteries," 56.

101. McCollum and Chrisco, "Jackie Stanley Helm," *Down Memory Lane*, vol. 8, 222.

Chapter Ten

1. Flossie Cook Smith interview, Shiloh Oral History Collection.

2. Ibid.

3. Fannie Duck interview, "This Is Newton County."

4. Parler, *Folk Beliefs from Arkansas*, vol. 1, #157–60, 53.

5. *Encyclopedia of Southern Culture*, Dougherty, "Healers, Women," 1547.

6. Thomas, *Arkansas and Its People*, 553.

7. Bakey, "James Robert Arnold Underdown," 19.

8. Scholle, *The Pain in Prevention*, 69.

9. Arkansas State Board of Health, *Biennial Report*, 134.

10. Ibid., 553.

11. WPA Historical Records Survey, Baxter County Health Unit, 1940, and Johnson County Health Unit, 1941.

12. Arkansas, State Board of Health, *Rules and Regulations*, 1952, 197.

13. Information provided by Shirley Burnett, Doty's daughter.

14. "Midwife Practice in Arkansas—1940–1961," 149–51.

15. Tom Dearmore, "The Ozark Outlook," *Baxter County Bulletin*, 20 November 1952, quoting an untitled article by Hartzell Spence, *Saturday Evening Post*, 8 November 1952.

16. Cave Springs Library Board, *Cave Springs Memories*.

17. Allured, *Families, Food, and Folklore*, 96, 115.

18. Allured, "Ozark Women and the Companionate Family," 238–40.

19. Marriage records (1880–1904) from Washington, Carroll, and Crawford counties.

20. Moss, *Beecher Moss's . . . Coming of Age Memoir*, 14.

21. Louel Collard Smith, *Descendants of Elijah Collard*.

22. Phillips, *The New Ozark Cousins*, 299.

23. Norton and Matthews, "More Independence County Pioneers," 3–24.

24. Allured, *Families, Food, and Folklore*, 101.

25. Paul Thompson, 1912–1916, Hasty Cemetery (Sharp County).

26. Boles, Letter to "Aunt Sarah."

27. William Roscoe Jeffers, February–May 1885, Duncan Cemetery (Franklin County).

28. Infant Sooter, 1887–1888, Marshall City Cemetery (Searcy County).

29. Parler, *Folk Beliefs from Arkansas*, vol. 1, # 604, 200.

30. Banes, *Journal*, 47.

31. Carter, "Disease and Death in the Nineteenth Century," 296–97.

32. Cavender, *Folk Medicine in Southern Appalachia*, 136.

33. Ibid., 137–38.

34. Randolph, *Ozark Superstitions*, 111–12.

35. "Oral History Concerning the Hurricane Creek," 27.

36. Parler, *Folk Beliefs from Arkansas*, vol. 1, #733–34, 247.

37. McCollum and Chrisco, "Erma Rhea Williams Moore," *Down Memory Lane*, vol. 2, 70.

38. Parler, *Folk Beliefs from Arkansas*, vol. 2, #2485, 708.

39. Murphy, *Naked Ears*.

40. Goss and Stewart, "Rockabye Baby," 27.

41. WPA, "Midwife Pledge Card," 1938.

42. Peacock, "Turpentine," 117–26.

43. Randolph, *Ozark Superstitions*, 120.

44. Downs, *Stories of Survival*, 173, 177.

45. Page, *Voices of Moccasin Creek*, 327.

46. Whittemore, "June Eaton Geiger," *Fading Memories*, vol. 3, 125.

47. McCollum and Chrisco, "Trude Foster," *Down Memory Lane*, vol. 5, 129.

48. Szedegin, *As I Remember Piney*, 38.

49. Lemke, "Rare Old Collection of Correspondence," 10–11.

50. Szedegin, *As I Remember Piney*, 47.

51. Poyner, "Early Medicine," 155.

52. Parler, *Folk Beliefs from Arkansas*, vol. 1, #874, 297.

53. Randolph, *Ozark Superstitions*, 137.

54. Parler, *Folk Beliefs from Arkansas*, Vol. 1, #882, 299.

55. Information provided by Toinette Madison, concerning Adolf Lager (1867–1950).

56. Randolph, *Ozark Superstitions*, 134.

57. Ibid., 134–35.

58. Farmer, *The Home Place*, 32.

59. Parler, *Folk Beliefs from Arkansas*, vol. 1, #486, 162.

60. Ibid., #488, 163.

61. Bruce Vaughan, *Shiloh Recollections*, 121.

62. Bruce Vaughan e-mail, 2011.

63. Swedlund, *Shadows in the Valley*, 49.

64. *Russellville Democrat*, 30 June 1886; *Gravett[e] News*, 22 September 1894.

65. "Baby Morphine Fiends," *Fayetteville Democrat*, 8 August 1908.

66. Parler, *Folk Beliefs from Arkansas*, vol. 1, #809–11, 276; #813–14, 277; #815, 278.

67. U.S. Bureau of the Census, 1850 Mortality Schedule (Drew County), Lemuel Bowden.

68. Randolph, *Ozark Superstitions*, 144.

69. Ibid., 144–45.

70. Szedegin, *As I Remember Piney*, 9.

71. Parler, *Folk Beliefs from Arkansas*, vol. 1, #834–36, 284; #840, 286; #844–45, 287.

72. Ibid., #873–74, 296; #822–27, 280–82; #720a. & #721b., 242; #722, 243; #703, 234.

73. Opal Arnold Taylor, Searcy County oral history project.

74. *Encyclopedia of Southern History*, Roller and Twyman, "Clay Eaters," 238–39.

75. U.S. Bureau of the Census, 1880 Mortality Schedule (Drew County).

76. *Encyclopedia of Southern Culture*, Frate, "Dirt Eating," 1368–69.

77. McCollum and Chrisco, "Emma Mankin Byler," *Down Memory Lane*, vol. 4, 157.

78. Biggs, *Botanico Medical*, 408–9; Parler, *Folk Beliefs from Arkansas*, vol. 1, #900, 307.

79. *North Arkansas Star*, 27 June 1913.

80. "Have You a Baby?" *Fayetteville Democrat*, 8 September 1908.

81. John L. Ferguson and J. H. Atkinson, *Historic Arkansas*, 262.

82. Thomas, *Arkansas and Its People*, vol. 1, 558.

83. *Encyclopedia of Arkansas History and Culture*, Haden, "Hookworm Eradication."

84. *Clarksville Democrat*, 3 March 1914.

85. Creo Jones, *"I Remember When,"* 77.

86. Faris, *Ozark Log Cabin Folks*, 95.

87. Crowder, "Stumptoe School," 17.

88. *Madison County Democrat*, 15 March 1912.

89. *Springdale News*, 28 January 1910.

90. "County's Medical History is One of Heroism AND Tragedy . . . But There was Grim Humor as Well as Great Dedication," *Northwest Arkansas Times*, June 24, 1960, Centennial Edition.

91. Story used on condition of anonymity.

92. *[Marshall] Mountain Wave*, 10 December 1909; *[Marshall] Mountain Wave* 26 April 1913.

93. "State News," *Arkansas Gazette*, 13 September 1892.

94. *Rogers Democrat*, 22 January 1914.

95. *Sharp County Record*, 26 January 1917.

96. Ibid., 20 July 1917.

97. "Death of Newborn Leads to Murder Trial," 15–22.

98. *Fayetteville Democrat*, 6, 7, and 9 August 1907.

99. Parler, *Folk Beliefs from Arkansas*, vol. 1, #607, 201.

100. Moss, *Beecher Moss's . . . Coming of Age Memoir*, 23.

101. Whittemore, "Geneva Faulkner," *Fading Memories*, vol. 3, 88.

102. Murle May, 1910–1915, Ben's Branch Cemetery (Newton County).

103. Parler, *Folk Beliefs from Arkansas*, vol. 1, #480, 160.

104. Randolph, *Ozark Magic*, 309.

105. Hefley, *Way Back When*, 199.

106. Wilson, *Cincinnati, Arkansas*, 67.

107. Cralle, *A Part of All She Touched*, 100.

108. Milbra Eaton Parker interviewed by Bob Besom; infant was Verna Villines, June–August 1940.

109. McCollum and Chrisco, "Lydia Moser Rider," *Down Memory Lane*, vol. 3, 138–39.

110. *Rogers Democrat*, 28 October 1903.

111. *Springdale News*, 12 January 1906.

112. Crabtree et al., "James Henderson Buttram and Sadie 'Babe' Head," *Pea Ridge*, 19; Mary Josephine Buttram obituary, *Benton County Record*, 6 March 1925.

113. McCollum and Chrisco, "Madge Tate Stephens," *Down Memory Lane*, vol. 8, 297–98.

114. Standlee, "Life as It Was," 164.

115. McCollum and Chrisco, "Thada Miller Cockrill," *Down Memory Lane*, vol. 4, 6.

Chapter Eleven

1. Bayliss, "The Arkansas State Penitentiary," 207–8.

2. "A Hell in Arkansas," *Arkansas Gazette*, 24 March 1888.

3. Westphal and Osterhage, *A Fame Not Easily Forgotten*, 105–7.

4. Sandels and Hill, *A Digest*, 380–81.

5. *Acts of Arkansas*, Act 1, 1876, 1–2.

6. *Acts of Arkansas*, Act 103, 1889, 143–45.

7. *Encyclopedia of Arkansas History and Culture*, Wilcox, "Poor Houses."

8. "County Court Proceedings, Jan. 9, 1911, Accounts Allowed—County General Fund," *Huntsville Republican*, 19 January 1911.

9. *Sharp County Record*, 12 January 1917.

10. Baldridge, "Paupers and the Poorhouse," 121.

11. Henker, "The Evolution of Mental Health," 223–39.

12. *Berryville Star*, 11 October 1907; *Rogers Democrat*, 10 July 1902.

13. *Sharp County Record*, 13 October 1899.

14. Abby Burnett, "At Home a Helping Hand," *Morning News of Northwest Arkansas*, 3 October 2004.

15. Ashworth and Lankford, "Olden Days of Mount Comfort, Part 1," 2.

16. *Van Buren Press*, 26 March 1872.

17. *Springdale News*, 27 January and 3 February 1905.

18. Shull, "The Forgotten of Pope County," 22.

19. Bland, "The Poor Farm," 16–17.

20. *Benton County Democrat*, 31 August 1899.

21. *Rogers Democrat*, 23 September 1903.

22. Robert G. Winn, "The County Home," *Washington County Observer*, 26 August 1982.

23. Ashworth and Lankford, "Olden Days of Mount Comfort, Part 2," 2.

24. "Smallpox Proclamation, Important Notice," *Sharp County Record*, 7 April 1899.

25. Samuel R. Phillips, *Loyalties Divided*, 139.

26. Rothrock, "Sarah Elizabeth Banks," 16.

27. Harrell, "Price-Smith and Related Families," *History and Folklore of Searcy County*, 385.

28. Pollan, "Diary," 60.

29. *Encyclopedia of Arkansas History and Culture*, Lancaster, "Smallpox."

30. "Smallpox in Russellville," 12.

31. *Fayetteville Democrat*, 19 January 1882.

32. "State News," *Arkansas Gazette*, 19 March 1882.

33. Burgess, "Building the Frisco Roadbed," 278–79.

34. Winn, "A Smallpox Epidemic," 27–29 (article contains numerous errors).

35. Brotherton, "The Train Whistle Cries for Them," 34–36.

36. Joe E. Smith, *Sexton's Record*, 4–5.

37. *Fayetteville Democrat*, 12 January 1882.

38. A. J. Vance, M.D., "Small-Pox in Boone and Marion Counties," *Arkansas Gazette*, 5 April 1882.

39. "State News," *Arkansas Gazette*, 19 March 1882, thought to be Dr. Leonidas Kirby.

40. *Encyclopedia of Arkansas History and Culture*, Lancaster, "Smallpox."

41. Mayme Ferguson, *Hangman's Harvest*.

42. "Big Crowd Turns Out For Benton County Hanging," *Northwest Arkansas Times*, 14 June 1960, Centennial Edition.

43. *Van Buren Press*, 7 February 1871; Isaac Watts, "That Awful Day Will Surely Come," written 1707–1709.

44. "'Black Friday,' The Lee Mills Hanging," 4–5; Ruby Neal Clark et al., *Van Buren County History*, 28.

45. *Arkansas Gazette*, 23 June 1883.

46. "Hangman's Day," *New York Herald*, 23 June 1883.

47. Hogue, *Back Yonder*, 193.

48. Akins, "George Maladon," 34–38.

49. Opie and Tatem, *Dictionary of Superstitions*, 189.

50. "A Hangman's Rope," *Arkansas Gazette*, 21 February 1893.

51. Akins, "Hangin' Times in Fort Smith; Three of Seven Men Hang," 35.

52. *Acts of Arkansas*, Act 24, 1887, 29–30.

53. *Acts of Arkansas*, Act 58, 1901, 105–6.

54. *Arkansas Democrat*, 26 July 1901.

55. "Execution of Bushwhackers."

56. *Acts of Arkansas*, Act 55, 1913, 171–75.

57. "Electrocution Replaces Hanging."

58. Tom Dillard, "The Last Hanging," *Arkansas Democrat-Gazette*, 21 November 2010.

59. *Encyclopedia of Arkansas History and Culture*, Rickard, "Capital Punishment."

60. Buckelew, *Racial Violence in Arkansas*, 52–53, 55; *Encyclopedia of Arkansas History and Culture*, Riffel, "Lynching."

61. *Encyclopedia of Southern History*, Shapiro, "Lynching," 762–64.

62. WPA, Early Settlers' Personal History Questionnaire, J. T. Odom (Pope County, born 1856); Bynum, "Russellville Lynching," 5.

63. Gillespie, "The Chronicle," 45–46, excerpting early issues of the newspaper.

64. *[Hot Springs] Sentinel-Record*, 20 June 1913.

65. Ibid., 21 June 1913.

66. 1850 Census, University of Virginia Library, Historical Census Browser, accessed 2011 at http://mapserver.lib.virginia.edu/php/county.php.

67. Bolton, *Arkansas, 1800–1860*, 129.

68. *Encyclopedia of Arkansas History and Culture*, Moneyhon, "Slavery."

69. Bolton, *Arkansas, 1800–1860*, 135.

70. Turnbo, "Bewildered in the Wild Woods," vol. 23.

71. Craig, "The Magnesses: Pioneers of Big Bottom," 59–60.

72. WPA, Early Settlers' Personal History Questionnaire, E. M. Bailey (Randolph County, born 1851).

73. WPA, Early Settlers' Personal History Questionnaire, John Ed Watkins (Carroll County, born 1854).

74. Phillips, *The New Ozark Cousins*, 145; Jasper M. Faught, 1863–1865, Deer Cemetery (Newton County).

75. Phillips, *The New Ozark Cousins*, 344.

76. Mollie E. Williams, *A Thrilling Romance of the Civil War*, 39–47.

77. Atwoods Gibbs obituary, unknown newspaper, August 1913.

78. Baxter, "The Battle of Prairie Grove," 42.

79. Wilder, "Thirty-Seventh Illinois at Prairie Grove," 18.

80. Lemke, "Come All You Sons of Ioway," 38.

81. Banes, "Tebbetts Family History," 19.

82. Wooley, "A Short History of Identification Tags," 1.

83. Mollie E. Williams, *A Thrilling Romance of the Civil War*, 13–14.

84. *Fayetteville Democrat*, 17 June 1897.

85. Eudora Ramsay Richardson and Sherman Allan, *Quartermaster Supply*, 1.

86. Ibid., 87.

87. "In Memory of Our Hero Dead," *[Marshall] Mountain Wave*, 18 April 1919.

88. Shelton scrapbook, undated letter.

89. Eudora Ramsay Richardson and Sherman Allan, *Quartermaster Supply*, 1.

90. Leland and Oboroceanu, *American War and Military Operations Casualties*, 2.

91. Sledge, *Soldier Dead*, 150.

92. McKinney family papers, Old Independence Regional Museum, Batesville (Independence County).

93. Robert D. Craig, *History of Newark, Arkansas*, 74.

94. Charles C. Meeks, 1893–1919, Masonic Cemetery, Pocahontas (Lawrence); Theodora O'Hara, "The Bivouac of the Dead."

95. Shelton scrapbook, "Take Me Home," undated, unsigned.

96. Eudora Ramsay Richardson and Sherman Allan, *Quartermaster Supply*, 1.

97. Meyer, "Mourning in a Distant Land," 31–75.

98. Noll, "Crosses," 14–17, 52–54.

99. John Branscum, 1894–1919, Marshall City Cemetery (Searcy).

100. Meyer, "Mourning in a Distant Land," 34.

101. *[Russellville] Courier-Democrat*, 24 April 1930.

102. "France Welcomes War Mothers; City Turns Out En Masse As In 1918 When U.S. Soldiers Landed," *Fayetteville Democrat*, 16 May 1930.

103. Meyer, "Mourning in a Distant Land," 68.

104. Grace Robinson, "Mothers Remember," 7–11.

105. "Paris Dresses Up For War Mothers," *Fayetteville Democrat*, 17 May 1930.

106. Noll, "Crosses," 53.

107. Peel, "Gold Star Mother Returns From France."

108. Ibid.

109. "Graves Registration; Quartermaster Review," 3.

110. Eudora Ramsay Richardson and Sherman Allan, *Quartermaster Supply*, 8, 11.

111. Bruce Vaughan e-mail, 2008

112. Eudora Ramsay Richardson and Sherman Allan, *Quartermaster Supply*, 5.

113. "Graves Registration; Quartermaster Review," 2–3.

114. Wooley, "A Short History of Identification Tags," 1.

115. Eudora Ramsay Richardson and Sherman Allan, *Quartermaster Supply*, 89

116. American Battle Monuments Commission.

Chapter Twelve

1. "The Undertakers; The Arkansas Association Meets in Second Annual Session; Searcy Supplies a Cadaver for an Illustrative Lecture on Embalming, From Her Jail, by the Death of a Woman Prisoner," *Arkansas Gazette*, 13 November 1891.

2. Muncy, *Searcy, Arkansas*, 172.

3. McCollum and Chrisco, "Vera Ann Cypert Jacobs," *Down Memory Lane*, vol. 2, 179.

4. *Polk's Gazetteer*, vol. 3, 75.

5. "The Gift Book," Nix-Callison funeral home ad.

6. Moshinskie, "Easing the Burden," *Early Arkansas Undertakers*.

7. *Interstate Directory, 1927–1928*, 186–87, 189, 192; *Interstate Directory, 1932–33*, 186.

8. King, *The Dunlap Opera House*.

9. Moshinskie, "Little Rock: First Full Undertaker," *Early Arkansas Undertakers*.

10. Schaefer, *Signs of the Past*, 1881 business directory facsimile.

11. *[Eureka Springs] Times*, 28 December 1889.

12. Moshinskie, "Unique Eureka Springs," *Early Arkansas Undertakers*.

13. WPA Historical Records Survey, "Coroners," 1938.

14. *Springdale News*, 22 April 1898.

15. *Rogers Democrat*, 12 June 1902.

16. *Benton County Democrat*, 22 November 1906.

17. *Gentry Journal-Advance*, 1 April 1910.

18. *Benton County Democrat*, 18 May 1911.

19. Ibid., 24 April 1913.

20. Birnie Funeral Home records, loose ad for Biosote Liquid Court Plaster (date unknown).

21. Laderman, *The Sacred Remains*, 160–61.

22. Mayer, *Embalming*, 41.

23. Ibid., 42–43.

24. Kunhardt and Kunhardt, *Twenty Days*, 137; James M. Cornelius, Curator, Lincoln Collection, Abraham Lincoln Presidential Library, Springfield, Illinois, e-mail, 2011, stating that this story, though lacking a source, is believed to be true.

25. *Richmond Times-Dispatch*, 31 July 1863; information provided by Jon Austin, authority on Civil War embalming.

26. Edward C. Johnson, "Civil War Embalming."

27. Moshinskie, "Arkansas Funeral Directors' Association," *Early Arkansas Undertakers*.

28. Thomas, *Arkansas and Its People*, vol. 2, 555.

29. Moshinskie, "Arkansas Funeral Directors' Association," *Early Arkansas Undertakers*.

30. Brawner, *My Life in the Funeral Business*, 34–37.

31. Varno, "Trimble Campground Cemetery," 13.

32. *Madison County Democrat*, 23 January 1919.

33. Moshinskie, "State Board of Embalmers of Arkansas," *Early Arkansas Undertakers*.

34. Sewell Peaslee Wright, *Ethical Advertising*, 21.

35. Ibid., 10.

36. Brawner, *My Life in the Funeral Business*, 38.

37. Sewell Peaslee Wright, *Ethical Advertising*, 21, 24.

38. "Pioneer Woman Embalmer."

39. U.S. Bureau of the Census, 1900 Census, *Population, Part 2*, 514.

40. Bradstreet, 21, 10.

41. R. G. Dunn, *Mercantile Agency Reference Book*.

42. *Benton County Record*, 18 July 1919.

43. Black, *History of Benton County*, 492.

44. Moshinskie, "Owens & Company," *Early Arkansas Undertakers*.

45. E. E. Burnett, "John J. Hunter Dies," 16.

46. *Leslie News-Standard*, 20 May 1909.

47. Bryant Hardware Company records.

48. *Van Buren Press*, 22 July 1873.

49. "A Fruitful Past, Coupled With a Bright Future," *Harrison Times*, 7 January 1907; $25,000 determined using online inflation calculators.

50. "The Ocker/Byars Family Heritage," 16–26.

51. Robert D. Craig, *History of Newark, Arkansas*, 63.

52. *[Yellville] Mountain Echo*, 22 March 1928.

53. Moshinskie, "Aiding the Injured," *Early Arkansas Undertakers*.

54. Brawner, *My Life in the Funeral Business*, 44–45.

55. Tom Olmstead interview.

56. Moshinskie, "State Board of Embalmers of Arkansas," *Early Arkansas Undertakers*.

57. Tom Olmstead interview.

58. Kenevich, "Cremation," 22.

59. Iserson, *Death to Dust*, 242.

60. Ibid., 245.

61. Kenevich, "Cremation," 24.

62. *Rogers Democrat*, 24 December 1896.

63. Birnie Funeral Home records.

64. Henry Dunbar obituary, *Benton County Sun*, 12 September 1907; George W. Dunbar obituary, *Gravette News-Herald*, 22 March 1912.

65. Quinn, *A Syllabus*, 73.

66. *Green Forest Tribune*, 3 September 1904.

67. "Mountain View Telephone Company Directories," 12.

68. *Prairie Grove Enterprise*, 3 February 1938.

69. *Encyclopedia of Arkansas History and Culture*, McDowell, "Frank Barbour Coffin."

70. Godbey Funeral Record Book.

71. Moshinskie, "Business Directory, Undertakers and Embalmers, 1906–1907," *Early Arkansas Undertakers*.

72. Percefull, "A Public Health Response," 189.

73. Morton Mortuary Funeral Home records; Bryant Hardware records show one disinfecting charge in 1906.

74. Edward A. Martin, *Psychology of the Funeral Service*, 57.

75. Grigg, *Dear Jean*, 82.

76. Bryant Hardware Company records.

Conclusion

"Walking the Buckeye Log" attributed to St. Paul blacksmith Jesse Moody, who would say, "Mr. Johnson walked the buckeye log" to mean that the person had died.

1. *Fayetteville Democrat*, 9 February 1882.

2. *Bentonville Sun*, 6 July 1895; *Benton County Democrat*, 3 October 1895.

3. Wolfe, *Album of Odd Fellows Homes*, 73.

4. Powell, "Independence Lodge No. 4," 12.

5. *Journal of Proceedings, Grand Lodge I.O.O.F.*, 41.

6. Bowen, *Yea! I'm an Orphan*, 71–72.

7. Gordon, *Caste and Class*, 76–77.

8. *Encyclopedia of Arkansas History and Culture*, Wintory, "Mosaic Templars of America."

9. Gatewood, "Arkansas Negroes," 311, quoting the *Freeman*, 23 December 1893.

BIBLIOGRAPHY

Although numerous sources were consulted during the research of this book, this bibliography contains only those sources directly cited. This includes unpublished memoirs, listed here by author, title, and the repository or private collections where they were found. It should be noted that there is a wide divergence in the way historical societies number their journals, bulletins, and quarterlies, in some cases sequentially numbering of their issues, rather than using the conventional method of starting the numbering over each year.

"N.p." stands for "No publisher" and "N.d." stands for "No date."

Abbott, Virginia. "The Way That Was . . . War Eagle Revisited." *Benton County Pioneer* 16, no. 3 (1971).

"The Account Book of Orren M. Reiff." *Flashback* (Washington County Historical Society) [unnumbered first volume], no. 6 (1951).

Acts of Arkansas:

Acts, Resolutions and Memorials of the General Assembly of the State of Arkansas. Little Rock, AR: P. A. Ladue, Printer, 1876.

Acts and Resolutions of the General Assembly of the State of Arkansas. Little Rock, AR: [various state printers], 1887, 1889, 1901, 1903.

Public and Private Acts and Joint and Concurrent Resolutions and Memorials of the General Assembly of the State of Arkansas. Little Rock, AR: Democrat Print. & Litho. Co., Printers, 1913.

Adams, George Worthington. *Doctors in Blue: The Medical History of the Union Army in the Civil War.* Baton Rouge: Louisiana State University Press, 1952.

Akins, Jerry. "George Maladon: The Man and the Myth." *Journal* (Fort Smith Historical Society) 30, no. 2 (2006).

———. *Hangin' Times in Fort Smith: A History of Executions in Judge Parker's Court.* Little Rock, AR: Butler Center Books, 2012.

———. "Hangin' Times in Fort Smith: The Execution of Kitt Ross, 1886." *Journal* (Fort Smith Historical Society) 30, no. 1 (2006).

———. "Hangin' Times in Fort Smith: Three of Seven Men Hang." *Journal* (Fort Smith Historical Society) 31, no. 2 (2007).

Albertson, Charles Carroll. *A Service Book.* Chicago, IL: National Selected Morticians, 1925, revised edition, 1936.

Allured, Janet. "Families, Food, and Folklore: Women's Culture in the Post-bellum Ozarks." Ph.D. dissertation, University of Arkansas, 1988.

———. "Ozark Women and the Companionate Family." *Arkansas Historical Quarterly* 48, no. 3 (Autumn 1988).

American Battle Monuments Commission, online: http://abmc.gov/wardead/listings/wwii .php.

American Folklore: An Encyclopedia, ed. Jan Harold Brunvand. New York: Garland Publishing, 1996.

    Meyer, Richard E., "Cemeteries."

Arkansas State Board of Health. *Arkansas State Board of Health, Division of Communicable Diseases First Annual Report, For the Year Ending Dec. 31, 1937.* N.p.

———. *Biennial Report of the State Board of Health, State of Arkansas, July 1, 1926–June 30, 1928.* Little Rock, AR: n.p.

———. *Rules and Regulations of the State Board of Health of Arkansas.* Little Rock, AR: n.p., 1928.

———. *Rules and Regulations of the State Board of Health of Arkansas.* Little Rock, AR: n.p., 1952.

Ash Flat Historical Society. *Ash Flat History.* Mt. Vernon, IN: Windmill Publications, 1998.

Ashworth, Dottie, and Deb Lankford. "Olden Days of Mount Comfort: Homeless in 1900: The County Poor Farm, Part 1." *Mount Comfort Community Gazette* 1, no. 5 (1992).

———. "Olden Days of Mount Comfort: Homeless in 1900: The County Poor Farm, Part 2." *Mount Comfort Community Gazette* 1, no. 6 (1992).

Atkinson, Bart H. General store records, Heritage Center Museum collection, Carroll County Historical and Genealogical Society, Berryville.

Bair, M. Z. "Report on an Investigation of the Prevalence of Typhoid Fever at Eureka Springs," 20 December 1920, in "The Springs of Eureka Springs: Historic Archive." CD-Rom. Eureka Springs Historical Museum, 2008.

Baker, Max L., ed. *Historical Perspectives: The College of Medicine at the Sesquicentennial.* Little Rock: Arkansas Sesquicentennial Commission, 1986.

Bakey, Alma Marie (Arnold). "The James Robert Arnold and Florence Texas Underdown Family." *Izard County Historian* 12, no. 1 (January 1981).

Baldridge, J. M. "Paupers and the Poorhouse." *Cleburne County Historical Journal* 6, no. 4 (1980).

Ball, Donald B. "Further Observations on Gravehouse Origins in the Upland South." *Tennessee Folklore Society Bulletin* 61, no. 2 (2005).

Banes, Marian Tebbetts. *The Journal of Marian Tebbetts Banes.* Fayetteville, AR: Washington County Historical Society, 1977.

———. "Tebbetts Family History." *Flashback* (Washington County Historical Society) 21, no. 1 (1971).

Barker, Catherine S. *Yesterday Today; Life in the Ozarks.* Caldwell, ID: Caxton Printers, 1941.

"Batesville, Arkansas Crystalline Oolitic Marble, 'Arkansas White.'" (Brochure), Pfeiffer Stone Co., n.d.

Baxter County. Unpublished county history, no author, Mountain Home Public Library (Baxter County).

Baxter, William, Rev. "The Battle of Prairie Grove and Its Aftermath." Originally published 1864, reprinted in *Flashback* (Washington County Historical Society) 2, no. 6 (1952).

Bayliss, Garland E. "The Arkansas State Penitentiary Under Democratic Control, 1874–1896." *Arkansas Historical Quarterly* 34, no. 3 (1975).

Bearden, Robert E. L. "The Romance of Arkansas Methodism." *Flashback* (Washington County Historical Society) 7, no. 2 (1957).

Berry, Evalena. *Sugar Loaf Springs: Heber's Elegant Watering Place*. Conway, AR: River Road Press, 1985.

"Better Birth Registration." *Arkansas Health Bulletin* (State Board of Health) 3, no. 1 (1946).

Biggs, A., M.D. *The Botanico Medical Reference Book*. Memphis, TN: Wells & Carr, 1847. Shiloh Museum of Ozarks History collection.

Birnie [Brothers] Funeral Home records, Fort Smith (Sebastian County), 14 January 1882–14 September 1904. Special Collections, Fort Smith Public Library.

"'Black Friday': The Lee Mills Hanging." *Van Buren County Historical Society Journal* 22, no. 86 (2007).

Black, J. Dickson. *History of Benton County*. Little Rock, AR: n.p., 1975.

Bland, Jim. "The Poor Farm." *Lawrence County Historical Journal* 4, no. 1 (1999).

Blevins, Brooks. *Hill Folks: A History of Arkansas Ozarkers and Their Image*. Chapel Hill: University of North Carolina Press, 2002.

———. "'In the Land of a Million Smiles': Twentieth-Century America Discovers the Arkansas Ozarks." *Arkansas Historical Quarterly* 61, no. 1 (2002).

"Blister sign of death." *Journal of the Arkansas Medical Society* 4, no. 10 (1907–1908).

Boise, Bob. "A Pioneer Tragedy." *Van Buren County Historical Society Journal* 17, no. 67 (2002).

Boles, Clementine Watson. Letter to "Aunt Sarah," Fayetteville, 19 September 1889, Shiloh Museum of Ozark History collection.

Bolton, S. Charles. *Arkansas, 1800–1860, Remote and Restless*. Fayetteville: University of Arkansas Press, 1998.

Bondeson, Jan. *Buried Alive: The Terrifying History of Our Most Primal Fear*. New York: W. W. Norton & Company, 2001.

Boulden, Ben. David Matlock interview, 6 May 2004. Fort Smith Historical Society, at http://fortsmithhistory.com.

Bowen, Ruth McCarson. *Yea! I'm an Orphan*. Atlanta, GA: Wright Publishing Company, 1985.

Bowling, Inez Rogers. "William Sherman Rogers M.D." *Van Buren County Historical Journal* 2, no. 26 (1991).

Boyertown Burial Casket Company revised price list. Boyertown, Pennsylvania and Columbus, OH, 1926. Museum of Funeral Customs, Springfield, Illinois, collection.

Bradstreet, John M. *Bradstreet's Book of Commercial Ratings of Bankers, Merchants, Manufacturers, etc., in the United States and the Dominion of Canada*. New York: Bradstreet Co., 1893. In the private collection of Bob Besom.

Brelowski, Doris. "Gone But Not Forgotten." *Bittersweet* 3, no. 1 (1975).

Britton, Nancy, ed. *Independence Pioneers, 1836–1986, A Collection of Historical Sketches of Some Early Families of the Original Independence County Region*, vol. 2. Batesville, AR: Independence Pioneers Committee, 1986.

Britton, Nancy, and Nancy Griffith, eds. "The Elvena Maxfield Journals, 1861–1866, Vol. 1." *Independence County Chronicle* 44, nos. 1 & 2 (October 2002–January 2003).

———. "The Elvena Maxfield Journals, Vol. 2." *Independence County Chronicle* 44, nos. 3 & 4 (April–July 2003).

Brotherton, Velda. "The Train Whistle Cries for Them." *Ozarks Mountaineer* 48, no. 6 (2000).

Brown, Connell J. *Hard Times in God's Country*. [No location:] Blurb, 2010.

Brown, Frank C. *The Frank C. Brown Collection of North Carolina Folklore*, vol. 7. "Popular Beliefs and Superstitions from North Carolina," ed. Wayland D. Hand. Durham, NC: Duke University Press, 1964.

Bryant Hardware Company records, Rogers (Benton County), 1899–1906 and 1912–1914, Rogers Historical Museum collection.

Buckelew, Richard A. "Racial Violence in Arkansas: Lynchings and Mob Rule, 1860–1930." Ph.D. dissertation, University of Arkansas, 1999.

Burgess, W. A. "Building the Frisco Roadbed in Northwest Arkansas." *Arkansas Historical Quarterly* 10, no. 4 (1951).

Burleson, Floyd, comp. *History of Cedar Grove Methodist Church, 1859–1985*. N.p., n.d.

Burnett, Abby. "No Pompous Marble to Thy Name We Raise." *Flashback* (Washington County Historical Society) 58, no. 3 (2008).

Burnett, E. E. "John J. Hunter Dies." *Van Buren County Historical Society Journal* 20, no. 81 (Winter 2005).

Butler, Steven Ray. "The Forgotten Soldiers: Deceased U.S. Military Personnel in the War With Mexico." M.A. thesis, University of Texas at Arlington, 1999.

Bynum, John. "Russellville Lynching in 1912; Lynch Law in Russellville: The Hanging of Moses Franklin." *Pope County Historical Association Quarterly* 28, no. 3 (1994).

Campbell, Treva Pauline Barham. "Growing Up in Zinc." *Boone County Historian/Oak Leaves* 1, no. 2 (2003).

"Captain E. G. Miller: His War." *Flashback* (Washington County Historical Society) 10, no. 4 (1960).

Carreiro, Anna Lee Burge. "Burge Family Reminiscences." In *A History of Cave City, Arkansas*. Cave City History Committee, 2001.

Carter, Deane G. "Brother Sherman and His Words of Comfort." *Flashback* (Washington County Historical Society) 14, no. 3 (July 1964).

Carter, James Byars, M.D. "Disease and Death in the Nineteenth Century: A Genealogical Perspective." *National Geographic Society Quarterly* 76, no. 4 (1988).

Cavender, Anthony P. *Folk Medicine in Southern Appalachia*. Chapel Hill: University of North Carolina Press, 2003.

Cave Springs Library Board. *Cave Springs Memories*. N.p., n.d. [not paginated].

Chalk, Shirley Roten. "Coy Cleveland Roten." In *Biographies of Van Buren County, Arkansas*. Clinton, AR: Van Buren County Historical Society, 1996.

Clark, Ruby Neal, Mae Shull Holloway, Eleanor Bowling Ryman, and Alma Dean Stroud, eds. *A History of Van Buren County, Arkansas*. Conway, AR: River Road Press, 1976.

Clark, Wayne, comp. *The Letters and Diaries of Isaac A. Clarke, Innovative Educator in Post Civil War Arkansas*. Victoria, Canada: Trafford Publishing, 2006.

Coffin, Maude K. "Pioneer Days." Maude K. Coffin and Fairy Coffin Lynd papers, Special Collections, University of Arkansas Libraries, Fayetteville.

Coger, Samuel Robert. "Memories of Kingston." *Carroll County Historical Quarterly* 46, no. 2 (2001).

Cohn, David L., Sinclair Lewis, and James Harvey Young. *The Good Old Days—A History of American Morals and Manners as Seen Through the Sears, Roebuck Catalogs, 1905 to Present*. New York: Simon & Schuster, 1940.

Cole, Charlotte. *"Back in the Olden Days," A Stone Cutter and His Trade*. Student paper, Arkansas College (now Lyon College), Regional Studies Center, Lyon College, Batesville, Arkansas, 1979.

———, and Cassie Creighton, taped interview with P. E. Stone, 4 May 1979, Batesville, AR. Transcribed by Abby Burnett, 2011, Regional Studies Center, Lyon College, Batesville, Arkansas.

Conner, Jennifer. "Moving Forward and Gaining Character." Undated student folklore paper, Special Collections, University of Arkansas Libraries, Fayetteville.

Cook, Roxie Smith. Interviewed by Susan Young, 6 September 1996. Shiloh Museum of Ozark History, Springdale, Arkansas, Oral History Collection.

Counts, Gladys. "Gladys Counts' Life Story." *Madison County Musings* 28, no. 3 (2009).

Crabtree, Freida, Jackie Crabtree, and Mary Rogers Durand, eds. *Pea Ridge 1850–2000: Anchored to the Past . . . Rising to the Future*. N.p. [2000].

Craig, Marion Stark. "Death of Dr. Daniel J. Chapman: 1857." *Independence County Chronicle* 20, no. 1 (1978).

Craig, Robert D. *A History of Newark, Arkansas: The Story of a Town, The Personality of a People*. [No location:] Craig Printing Co., 1999.

———. "The Magnesses: Pioneers of Big Bottom." In *Independence Pioneers, 1836–1986, A Collection of Historical Sketches of Some Early Families of the Original Independence County Region*, vol. 2, ed. Nancy Britton. Batesville, AR: Independence Pioneers Committee, 1986.

Cralle, Eva Lee. *A Part of All She Touched*. Westport, CT: PPC Books, 2000.

Crane & Breed Mfg. Co. history, www.coachbuilt.com.

Crawford, Sybil F. *Jubilee: Mount Holly Cemetery, Little Rock, Arkansas: Its First 150 Years*. Little Rock, AR: Mount Holly Cemetery Association, 1993.

Crowder, Hope. "Stumptoe School." *Van Buren County Historical Journal* 2, no. 24 (Winter 1991).

Curry, Melvin Elmo. "The History of Melvin Elmo Curry." Unpublished memoir transcribed by, and courtesy of, Wilson family descendants.

"Daguerreotypes on Tombstones." *Hutchings' California Magazine*, November 1857.

Dawson, Dr. *Daybook of Dr. Dawson*. Manuscript billing ledger, Van Buren County Museum and Historical Society, Clinton, Arkansas.

"Death of Newborn Leads to Murder Trial." *Pope County Historical Association Quarterly* 36, no. 4 (December 2002).

Downs, William D., Jr. *Stories of Survival: Arkansas Farmers during the Great Depression.* Fayetteville, AR: Phoenix International, 2011.

"Dr. I. Harmon Pavatt." *Van Buren County Historical Journal* 2, no. 21 (1990).

Duck, Fannie, interviewed by Elise Upton, about 1954. "This is Newton County," vol. 3 (on CD). Jasper, AR: Newton County Library, 2002.

Dunn Funeral Home records, W. W. Dunn and Son, Sulphur Springs (1893–1923), genealogy collection, Bentonville Public Library (Benton County).

Dunn Funeral Home records, John T. Dunn, Sulphur Springs (1923–1942), genealogy collection, Bentonville Public Library (Benton County).

Dunn, R. G. *The Mercantile Agency Reference Book (and Key).* New York: R. G. Dunn & Co., 1902.

Duvall, Harold (Joe Bill). *Hoopsnakes and Horseshoes: The Memoirs of Moreland.* N.p., 1993.

Edge, Maryanne, comp. *Was It Murder? The Dark Side of Baxter County History.* Mountain Home, AR: Baxter County Historical & Genealogical Society, 2005.

Edmiston Store Day Book, 1882, Washington County, Arkansas. Typescript, genealogy collection, Fayetteville Public Library (Washington County).

"Electrocution Replaces Hanging." *Flashback* (Washington County Historical Society) 6, no. 1 (1956).

Encyclopedia of Arkansas History and Culture. Guy Lancaster, ed., online: www.encyclo pediaofarkansas.net.

    Burnett, Abby, "Lucy J. Daniel," 2013.

    Burnett, Abby, "Nick Miller," 2009.

    Dougan, Michael B., "Archibald Yell," 2012.

    Dougan, Michael B., "Health and Medicine," 2010.

    Haden, Rebecca, "Hookworm Eradication," 2010.

    Harris, Francis R., "Arkansas Medical, Dental, and Pharmaceutical Association," 2011.

    Howard, J. Michael, "Dimension Stone Mining," 2010.

    Lancaster, Guy, "Smallpox," 2010.

    McDowell, Linda, "Frank Barbour Coffin," 2011.

    Moneyhon, Carl H., "Slavery," 2011.

    Puryear, Jerry, "University of Arkansas Medical Sciences (UAMS)," 2012.

    Rickard, David L., "Capital Punishment," 2011.

    Riffel, Brent E., "Lynching," 2011.

    Wilcox, Ralph S., "Poor Houses," 2008.

    Wintory, Blake, "Mosaic Templars of America," 2012.

Encyclopedia of Southern Culture. Charles Reagan Wilson and William Ferris, eds. Chapel Hill: University of North Carolina Press, 1989.

    Dougherty, Molly C., "Healers, Women."

    Frate, Dennis A., "Dirt Eating."

    Jeane, D. Gregory, "Cemeteries."

    Patterson, Daniel, "Grave Markers."

    Wilson, Charles Reagan, "Funerals."

Encyclopedia of Southern History. David C. Roller and Robert W. Twyman, eds. Baton Rouge: Louisiana State University Press, 1979.

   Roller and Twyman, "Clay Eaters."

   Shapiro, Herbert, "Lynching."

Estes, Thomas Jerome. *Early Days and War Times in Northern Arkansas.* (Pamphlet, originally published 1914), Yellville, AR: Historical and Genealogical Society of Marion County, revised and republished 1928.

Eureka Springs Centennial Commission. *Eureka Springs: A Post Card History, 1879–1979.* N.p.

Evans, Doris, and Jimmie Dewberry, comps. *Evans, Oark, Patterson Springs, and Yale Cemeteries: Johnson County, Arkansas.* Conway, AR: Arkansas Research, 2002.

Ewing, Mary Sue. "Chronicle of John Guin Bledsoe (Part 1)." *Pope County Historical Association Quarterly* 28, no. 2 (1994).

"Execution of Bushwhackers." Fort Smith Historical Society archive accessed at: http://www.fortsmithhistory.org, 2011.

"Extracts From the Marble City Highlander." *Newton County Homestead* (Newton County Historical Society) 6, no. 2 (1961).

Faris, Paul. *Ozark Log Cabin Folks: The Way They Were.* N.p., 1983.

Farmer, Fayrene Stafford. *The Home Place: Meditations on an Ozark Life.* [No location:] Litho Printers & Bindery, 1997.

Fayetteville Evergreen Cemetery Association Records, minutes, correspondence, property records, maps and other papers, 1885–1988. Special Collections, University of Arkansas Libraries, Fayetteville.

Ferguson, John L., and J. H. Atkinson. *Historic Arkansas.* Little Rock: Arkansas History Commission, 1966.

Ferguson, Mayme. *Hangman's Harvest.* (Pamphlet), n.p., n.d.

Fischer, David Hackett. *Albion's Seed: Four British Folkways in America.* New York: Oxford University Press, 1989.

Fisk Metallic Burial Case Co., untitled catalog, W. M. Raymond and Co., New York, Museum of Funeral Customs, Springfield, Illinois collection.

Forbes, Thomas R. "The Madstone." In *American Folk Medicine: A Symposium*, ed. Wayland D. Hand. Berkeley: University of California Press, 1979.

Fountain, Sarah M., ed. *Sisters, Seeds, and Cedars: Rediscovering Nineteenth-Century Life Through Correspondence from Rural Arkansas and Alabama.* Conway: University of Central Arkansas Press, 1995.

Freemasons. *Masonic Monitor of the Degrees of Entered Apprentice, Fellow Craft and Master Mason Together with the Ceremony of Receiving Visitors, Instituting and Constituting Lodges, Installation, Laying Corner Stones, Dedications, Masonic Burials, and Lodge of Sorrow.* Little Rock: Masons of Arkansas, 1993. [Adopted by the Most Worshipful Grand Lodge Free & Accepted Masons of Arkansas, 16 November 1954.]

Frigid Fluid Company, Embalmers, Undertakers and Cemetery Supplies. Chicago, IL: n.p., 1934, The Museum of Funeral Customs, Springfield, Illinois, collection.

Garner Hardware inventory ledger (1925–1927), Calico Rock Museum (Izard County).

Gatewood, Willard B., Jr. "Arkansas Negroes in the 1890s." *Arkansas Historical Quarterly* 33, no. 4 (1974).

Gibson, Lanny. "Mabel Wilson: Rural School Teacher 1923–33." *Carroll County Historical Quarterly* 50, no. 2 (2005).

"The Gift Book." Springdale, AR: The Missionary Society of the Methodist Church, South, 1924. (Pamphlet), Arkansas Cookbook Collection, Special Collections, University of Arkansas Libraries, Fayetteville.

Gillespie, Thomas. "The Chronicle." *Pope County Historical Association Quarterly* 5, no. 3 (1971).

Godbey Funeral Record Book, vol. 1, Atkins (Pope County), 23 January 1927–20 March 1935. Genealogy collection, Pope County Library, Russellville.

Goodspeed Publishing Company. *Goodspeed's 1889 History of Benton County, Arkansas: Benton County Section of Goodspeed's Benton, Washington, Carroll, Madison, Crawford, Franklin and Sebastian Counties, Arkansas*. Reprint, Bentonville, AR: Benton County Historical Society, 1999, originally published Chicago: Goodspeed Publishing Co., 1889.

Gordon, Fon Louise. *Caste and Class: The Black Experience in Arkansas, 1880–1920*. Athens: University of Georgia Press, 1995.

Goss, Lisa, and Melinda Steward. "Rockabye Baby: Raising Babies in the Early 1900s." *Bittersweet* 10, no. 3 (1983).

Grand, Stella, and Nancy Grimes. "Graves and Graveyards," student report, Fall 1958. Mary Celestia Parler manuscript collection, Special Collections, University of Arkansas Libraries, Fayetteville.

"Graves Registration; Quartermaster Review—May/June 1946." Fort Lee, VA: U.S. Army Quartermaster Foundation; accessed online: http://www.qmfound.com/graves_regis tration.htm.

"Green Kuykendall: Gone But Not Forgotten." *Franklin County Historical Association Observer* 6, no. 1 (July 1985).

Grigg, Jeanetta Richardson. *Dear Jean: The History of a Family, and the Story of One Girl's Life Growing up in the Ozark Mountains of Northern Arkansas*. Springdale, AR: Seven Hills Publications, 1993.

Gunn, John G. *Gunn's Domestic Medicine, or Poor Man's Friend*. Facsimile first edition, 1830, Knoxville: University of Tennessee Press, 1986.

Haberstein, Robert W., and William M. Lamers. *The History of American Funeral Directing*. Milwaukee, WI: Bulfin Printers, 1955.

———. *Funeral Customs the World Over*. Milwaukee, WI: Bulfin Printers, 1960.

Halbrook, William Erwin. *A School Man of the Ozarks*. Van Buren, AR: Press-Argus, 1959.

Hansen, Bert. "America's First Medical Breakthrough: How Popular Excitement about a French Rabies Cure in 1885 Raised New Expectations for Medical Progress." *American Historical Review* 103, no. 2 (1998).

Harral, Rex. "Pioneer Funerals." Typescript of a column written for Heber Springs' *Sun Times* (probably 2007).

Harrell, Mary Francis, ed. *History and Folklore of Searcy County, Arkansas, Source Book*. Harrison, AR: New Leaf Press, 1977.

Hasson, Janet S. *Widows, Weepers and Wakes: Mourning in Middle Tennessee*. Nashville, TN: Belle Meade Plantation, 1995.

Hatfield, Geraldine. "Old Time Burials." In *A History of Alabam*. Huntsville, AR: Theta Mu Epsilon, 1980.

Hatfield, Kevin. *The Huntsville Massacre*. Huntsville, AR: Madison County Genealogical & Historical Society, 2007.

Hearn, Bea. "The Ingram Cemetery." In *History of Randolph County, Arkansas*, ed. Regina Cook. Dallas, TX: Curtis Media Corporation, 1992.

Hefley, James C. *Way Back When*. [No location:] Lithocolor Press, 1992.

Henker, Fred O. "The Evolution of Mental Health Care in Arkansas." *Arkansas Historical Quarterly* 38, no. 3 (1978).

Henning, (Mrs.) W. J. "My Grandfather, Willis Taylor Inman." *Independence County Chronicle* 10, no. 4 (1962).

Hensley, John R. "The Arkansas Commemorative Stone for the Washington National Monument." *Ozarks Mountaineer* 60, no. 4 (2012).

Hetrick, Joyce. *Plumerville Foundations: Early Conway and Yell County, Arkansas, History from 1851 to 1927*. Conway: Arkansas Research, 2001.

Hill, John Robert. *I Remember St. Paul: Hill Roots Grow Deep in Arkansas History*. N.p., n.d.

"History of Patent Medicine," Hagley Museum and Library, Wilmington, Delaware, accessed at http://www.hagley.org/library/exhibits/patentmed/history/history.html, 2013.

"History of the Pottsville Circuit," facsimile of Pottsville Methodist Episcopal Church's 1913 dedication service program. *Pope County Historical Association Quarterly* 38, no. 2 (June 2004).

Hodges, Mary Frances, transcriber. *Johnson County, Arkansas Funeral Book, 1911–1914*. [No location:] Angel Creek Press, 2001 [not paginated].

Hogue, Wayman. *Back Yonder: An Ozark Chronicle*. New York: Minton, Balch & Co., 1932.

———. "The Cat and the Corpse." *Arkansas Folklore* (Arkansas Folklore Society) 4, no. 1 (1953).

Holloway, Karla. *Passed On: African American Mourning Stories*. Durham, NC: Duke University Press, 2002.

Holmes, Louise, R.N. "Home Care for Patients with Tuberculosis." *American Journal of Nursing* 48, no. 8 (1948).

Hopkins, T. C. "Marbles and Other Limestones." In *Annual Report of the Geological Survey of Arkansas for 1890*, vol. 4, ed. Dr. John C. Banner. Little Rock, AR: Brown Printing Company, 1893.

Horne, Ronald William. *Forgotten Faces—A Window Into Our Immigrant Past*. San Francisco: Personal Genesis Publishing, 2004.

"How Pasteur Antirabic Vaccine is Supplied." *Therapeutic Notes* 19, no. 1 Detroit, MI: Parke, Davis & Co., 1912.

How To Beautify Your Cemetery Plot. New York State Association of Cemeteries, and Memorial Extension Commission, 1934. (Pamphlet), Springdale/Emerson Monument Company papers, 1930–1995, Shiloh Museum of Ozark History, Springdale.

How To Make Crepe Paper Flowers. Framingham, MA: Dennison Manufacturing Co., 1922 (pamphlet).

Huhn, H. G. "The B. F. Hobbs Account Book." *Benton County Pioneer* 10, no. 3 (1965).

Hunter, Carl G. *Trees, Shrubs, and Vines of Arkansas*. Little Rock, AR: Ozark Society Foundation, 1989.

Interstate Directory Company's Fayetteville, Arkansas, City Directory, 1927–1928. Springfield, MO: Interstate Directory Company, 1927.

Interstate Directory Company's Fayetteville, Arkansas, City Directory, 1932–1933. Springfield, MO: Interstate Directory Company, 1932.

Iserson, Kenneth V., M.D. *Death to Dust: What Happens to Dead Bodies?* Tucson, AZ: Galen Press, 1994.

Jabbour, Alan, and Karen Singer Jabbour. *Decoration Day in the Mountains: Traditions of Cemetery Decoration in the Southern Appalachians*. Chapel Hill: University of North Carolina Press, 2010.

Jamieson, Ross W. "Material Culture and Social Death: African-American Burial Practices." *Historical Archaeology* (Journal of the Society for Historical Archaeology) 29, no. 4, 1995.

Jeane, D. Gregory. "The Upland South Folk Cemetery Complex: Some Suggestions of Origin." In *Cemeteries and Gravemarkers: Voices of American Culture*, ed. Richard E. Meyer. Ann Arbor, MI: UMI Research Press, 1989.

Jenkins, Mildred. "The Montgomery Family of Lower Wharton, As Told to Mildred Jenkins by Ida Montgomery-Dotson." *Madison County Musings* 26, no. 3 (2007).

Jines, Billie. "Bushwhackers Lose Head, Arm to Walker's Broadax." *Morning News* [no date given], in *Pea Ridge, 1850–2000: Anchored in the Past . . . Rising to the Future*, ed. Freida Crabtree, Jackie Crabtree, and Mary Rogers Durand. N.p., n.d.

Johnson, Claude E. *The Humorous History of White County, Arkansas*. N.p.: 1975.

Johnson, Edward C. "Civil War Embalming." [Chicago, IL?]: *Funeral Director's Review*, three-part article, June, July, and August 1965.

Johnson, Glenn. "Annual Decoration of Cemeteries." In *History of Marion County*, Silver Anniversary Edition, ed. Earl Berry. Yellville, AR: Historic [sic] Genealogical Society of Marion County, 2002.

Jones, Creo. "*I Remember When*": Memoirs of an Ozark Hill Boy. N.p., 1988.

Jones, W. R. *Gleanings of Pioneer History*. Yellville, AR: Historic [sic] Genealogical Society of Marion County, 2001, pamphlet reprinted from the *[Yellville] Mountain Echo*, 1929–1930.

Jordan-Bychkov, Terry G. *The Upland South: The Making of an American Folk Region and Landscape*. Santa Fe, NM: Center for American Places, in association with Charlottesville: University of Virginia Press, 2003.

Journal of the American Medical Association. Untitled response to a query, 49, no. 1 (July 1907).

Journal of the Arkansas Medical Society. "Personals," 9, no. 3 (August 1912).

———. "Personals," 9, no. 7 (December 1912).

———. "Personals," 11, no. 4 (September 1914).

———. "Arkansas in Vital Statistics Area," 23, no. 10 (October 1927).

Journal of Proceedings, Grand Lodge I.O.O.F., State of Arkansas, Special Session, Little Rock, June 8, 1931. N.p., genealogy collection, Old Independence Regional Museum, Batesville, Arkansas.

Kalklosch, L. J. *The Healing Fountain, Eureka Springs, Ark., A Complete History.* Eureka Springs, AR: L. J. Kalklosch, 1881.

Kammen, Michael. *Digging Up the Dead: A History of Notable American Reburials.* Chicago, IL: University of Chicago Press, 2010.

Karns, Brooxie. "Uncle Fate." *Searcy County Ancestor Information Exchange* 13, no. 4 (2003).

Keister, Douglas. *Stories in Stone: A Field Guide to Cemetery Symbolism and Iconography.* Salt Lake City, UT: Gibbs Smith, 2004.

Kenevich, Tanya. "Cremation: Old Idea, New Options." *American Cemetery* 82, no. 5 (2010).

Kephart, Horace. *Our Southern Highlanders.* Knoxville: University of Tennessee Press, 1984, originally published in 1913.

Key, Vera. "History of the Blackburn Family." *Benton County Pioneer* (Benton County Historical Society) 1, no. 1 (1955).

———. "Some Early Business Men of Rogers." *Benton County Pioneer* 18, no. 4 (1973).

King, John E., Sr. *The Dunlap Opera House, 1906–1937, A History of the Theatres in Johnson County with News and Trivia.* N.p., n.d., typescript, genealogy collection, Johnson County Public Library, Clarksville, Arkansas.

Kirby, Leonidas, M.D. Manuscript copy of 1878–1879 billing ledger, Boone County Heritage Museum, Harrison, Arkansas.

Knotts, Burton Ray. *Death Notices in Pocahontas, Randolph County, Arkansas, Newspapers, 1911–1920.* Conway: Arkansas Research, 2007.

Kregel Casket Co. *Illustrated Catalogue.* St. Louis, MO: The Company, [1895?].

Kunhardt, Dorothy Meserve, and Philip B. Kunhardt Jr. *Twenty Days: A Narrative in Text and Pictures of the Assassination of Abraham Lincoln.* New York: Harper and Row, 1965.

Laderman, Gary. *The Sacred Remains: American Attitudes toward Death, 1799–1883.* New Haven, CT: Yale University Press, 1996.

Lang, Kathryn Ann. "Coffins and Caskets: Their Contribution to the Archaeological Record." M.A. thesis, University of Idaho, 1984.

Lankford, George E., ed. *Bearing Witness: Memories of Arkansas Slavery, Narratives from the 1930s WPA Collections.* Fayetteville: University of Arkansas Press, 2006.

Leach, Ina. "Happenings In and Near Floyd, Arkansas." *White County Heritage* (White County Historical Society) 14, no. 11 (1976).

Leland, Anne, and Mari-Jana "M-J" Oboroceanu. *American War and Military Operations Casualties: Lists and Statistics.* Congressional Research Service, 7-5700, CSR Report for Congress, 26 February 2010, accessed at www.crs.gov.

Lemke, W. J. "The Account Books of W. H. Rhea, 1855–1868." *Flashback* (Washington County Historical Association) 6, no. 4 (1956).

———. "Come All You Sons of Ioway." *Flashback* 12, no. 4 (1962).

———. "Judge Sebron Graham Sneed." *Flashback* 8, no. 4 (1958).

——. "Rare Old Collection of Correspondence Includes Letters from Prominent Fayetteville Men." *Flashback*, unnumbered first vol. (March 1951).

——. "An Unusual Execution in Fayetteville." *Flashback* 2, no. 3 (1952).

——. "Violent History or Historical Violence." *Flashback* 6, no. 1 (1956).

——. *Early Colleges and Academies of Washington County, Arkansas*. Fayetteville, AR: Washington County Historical Society, 1954 [Bulletin No. 6].

Lemley, J. B. "Business Houses of Russellville." *Pope County History Articles, Book #1*. N.p., n.d.

Lesh, Ruth Ellis, M.D. "A Century of Medicine in Northwest Arkansas." Paper presented at the 100th meeting of the Arkansas Medical Society, Hot Springs, Arkansas, April 1975, accessed at http://www.drmuseum.net/lesh/document28.pdf, 2013.

"Letter of General Moore, Who Settled Colonel Yell's Estate." *Flashback* (Washington County Historical Society) 2, no. 4 (1952).

Longfellow, Henry Wadsworth. "Resignation." *The Seaside and the Fireside*. Boston, MA: Ticknor, Reed, and Fields, 1850.

Lyon, Marguerite. *Hurrah For Arkansas! From Razorbacks to Diamonds*. Indianapolis: Bobbs-Merrill Company, 1947.

Maddox, William S. "Calling Central." *Van Buren County Historical Journal* 2, no. 27 (1991).

Mainfort, Robert C., Jr., and James M. Davidson, eds. *Two Historic Cemeteries in Crawford County, Arkansas*. Fayetteville: Arkansas Archeological Survey, 2006 [Research Series No. 62].

Martin, Edith Simmons. "A History of the Rushing Community: 1830–1930." Student paper, College of the Ozarks, Point Lookout, Missouri, 1980.

Martin, Edward A. *Psychology of the Funeral Service*. N.p., 1945.

Martin, Wayne. *Pettigrew, Arkansas: The Hardwood Capital of the World*. Springdale, AR: Shiloh Museum of Ozark History, 2010.

Massey, Ellen Gray, ed. *Bittersweet Country*. Garden City, NY: Anchor Books, 1978.

May, Trevor. *The Victorian Undertaker* (pamphlet). Great Britain: Shire Publications, 2003.

Mayer, Robert G. *Embalming: History, Theory, and Practice*. Norwalk, CT: Appleton & Lance, 1990.

McChristian, Gladys. *Bits and Pieces for Joan*. Unpublished memoir, written 1986–1987, private collection of John D. Little, Kingston, Arkansas.

McColloch, Etta. "The Doctors of Old Cane Hill." *Flashback* (Washington County Historical Society) 13, no. 2 (1963).

McCollum, Betty Guthrie, and Sue Shell Chrisco. *Down Memory Lane*. N.p., 1999, unnumbered first volume in series of oral histories.

——. Vol. 2, N.p., 2000.

——. Vol. 3, N.p., 2001.

——. Vol. 4, N.p., 2002.

——. Vol. 5, N.p., 2003.

——. Vol. 6, N.p., 2005.

——. Vol. 7, N.p., 2006.

——. Vol. 8, N.p., 2008.

McConnell, F. M. "History of the Middle Fork." *Flashback* (Washington County Historical Society) 15, no. 2 (1965).

McDonough, Nancy. *Garden Sass: A Catalog of Arkansas Folkways*. New York: Coward, McCann & Geoghegan, 1975.

McGrew, Marian Ray. "Memories of Grandfather and Grandmother King." *Madison County Musings* 26, no. 4 (2007).

"McKinney Cemetery." *Franklin County Historical Association Observer* 7, no. 1 (1988).

McLane, Bobbie Jones, Charles Williams Cunning, and Wendy Bradley Richter, comps. *Observations of Arkansas: The 1824–1863 Letters of Hiram Abiff Whittington*. Hot Springs, AR: Garland County Historical Society, 1997.

McMurry, Neva Barnes. *Mama's Trunk of Memories*. Las Vegas, NV: Yellow Ribbon Company, 1996.

Mecklin, Robert W. *The Mecklin Letters: Written in 1862–64 at Mount Comfort*, ed. W. J. Lemke. Fayetteville, AR: Washington County Historical Society, 1955 [Bulletin #10].

Meyer, Lotte Larsen. "Mourning in a Distant Land: Gold Star Pilgrimages to American Military Cemeteries in Europe, 1930–33." *Markers* (Journal of the Association for Gravestone Studies) 20 (2003).

"Midwife Practice in Arkansas—1940–1961." *Journal of the Arkansas Medical Society* 59, no. 4 (1962).

Miller, C. L. *Postmortem Collectibles*. Atglen, PA: Schiffer Publishing, 2001.

Miller, Conrow R. *The Cane Hill Story, 1825–1969*. Cane Hill, AR: ARC Press of Cane Hill, 1989, reprint [originally published 1969?].

"Miscellany." *Flashback* (Washington County Historical Society) 28, no. 1 (1978).

Montague, Margaret. "Growing Up With the Century." *Franklin County Historical Association Observer* 4, no. 2 (1980).

Montell, William Lynwood. *Ghosts Along the Cumberland: Deathlore in the Kentucky Foothills*. Knoxville: University of Tennessee Press, 1975.

The Monumental News, Chicago, Illinois, accessed at http://quarriesandbeyond.org.

Monuments[,] Tombstones and Markers, catalog. Montgomery Ward & Co. 1929, accessed at http://quarriesandbeyond.org.

Mooney, Walter. *Mrs. Lola Brown Diary, Dec. 26, 1923–Nov. 29, 1930*. Women's Studies manuscript collection, Special Collections, University of Arkansas Libraries, Fayetteville.

Moore, Mrs. T. "Diary of Mrs. T. Moore." *Franklin County Historical Association Observer* 1, no. 2 (1976–1977).

Morton Mortuary Funeral Home records, in the private collection of David Zimmerman, Eureka Springs, Arkansas.

Moshinskie, Jim. *Early Arkansas Undertakers and Embalmers, Survey Book 1*. Little Rock, AR: n.p., 1978 [not paginated].

Moss, Henry Beecher. *Beecher Moss's Turn of the Century Coming of Age Memoir: A Story of Family Fragility and Strength*. Jasper, AR: Newton County Historical Society, n.d. [originally published 1999].

"Mountain View Telephone Company Directories." *Heritage of Stone* (Stone County Historical Society) 27, no. 2 (2003).

Moyers, David M. "From Quackery to Qualification: Arkansas Medical and Drug Legislation, 1881–1909." *Arkansas Historical Quarterly* 35, no. 1 (1976).

Mullen, Margaret. *An Arkansas Childhood: Growing Up in the Athens of the Ozarks.* Fayetteville, AR: M & M Press, 1989.

Mumey, Nolie. *University of Arkansas School of Medicine, With an Early History of the State, its Natural Resources, and the Founding of the University: Reminiscences of the Years 1912–1916.* Denver, CO: Range Press, 1975.

Muncy, Raymond Lee. *Searcy, Arkansas: A Frontier Town Grows Up With America.* Searcy, AR: Harding Press, 1976.

Murphy, Altha. *Naked Ears: A Child's-Eye View of the Great Depression.* [no location:] 1st Books Library, 2002 [not paginated].

Nabors, Michael. "Elmwood: Early Settlement of Boone County." *Boone County Historian* 3, no. 2 (1980) [not paginated].

Neal, Avon. "Gravestone Carving, an Historical Overview of a New England Art Form." *Newsletter of the Association for Gravestone Studies* 10, no. 1 (1985–1986).

Neal, James P. "The Memoirs of Col. James P. Neal." *Flashback* (Washington County Historical Society) 5, no. 4 (August 1955).

"News From the Rural Districts." *Franklin County Historical Association Observer* 4, no. 1 (1980).

Noll, John J. "Crosses." *American Legion Monthly*, September 1930.

Norton, Diane, and Linda Matthews. "More Independence County Pioneers: Royal Fugatt and Margaret Emeline Penland Fugatt." *Independence County Chronicle* 46, no. 2 (July 2005).

Ober, K. Patrick. *Mark Twain and Medicine: "Any Mummery Will Cure."* Columbia: University of Missouri Press, 2003.

"The Ocker/Byars Family Heritage and History in Crawford County." *Panning For Nuggets of Old* (Crawford County Genealogical Society) 28, no. 1 (2007).

Ocker Funeral Home records, Fort Smith (Sebastian County), 1918–1971, Special Collections, Fort Smith Public Library.

O'Neal, Leonard. "The Canaan Cemetery." *Searcy County, Arkansas; A History of Searcy County, Arkansas, and Its People.* Marshall, AR: Searcy County Retired Teachers Association, 1987.

Opie, Iona, and Moira Tatem. *A Dictionary of Superstitions.* Oxford: Oxford University Press, 1989.

"Oral History Concerning the Hurricane Creek Area of Newton County with Russell & Mildred Heffley." *Newton County Historical Society Newsletter* 18, no. 3 (2002).

Page, Tate C. *The Voices of Moccasin Creek.* Point Lookout, MO: School of the Ozarks Press, 1972.

Parker, Milbra Eaton, interviewed by Bob Besom, 20 February 2004, unpublished, in the private collection of Bob Besom.

Parler, Mary Celestia, ed. *Folk Beliefs from Arkansas Collected by University Students,* vol. 1, Birth, Childhood (bound typescript, 1962), University of Arkansas Libraries, Fayetteville.

———. *Folk Beliefs from Arkansas Collected by University Students*, vol. 2, Human Body, Folk Medicine (bound typescript, 1962), University of Arkansas Libraries, Fayetteville.

———. *Folk Beliefs from Arkansas Collected by University Students*, vol. 3, Folk Medicine (bound typescript, 1962), University of Arkansas Libraries, Fayetteville.

———. *Folk Beliefs from Arkansas Collected by University Students*, vol. 8, Death and Funereal Customs (bound typescript, 1962), University of Arkansas Libraries, Fayetteville.

Pasteur Foundation website: http://www.pasteurfoundation.org.

Patterson, Nancy-Lou. "United Above Though Parted Below: The Hand as Symbol on Nineteenth-Century Southwest Ontario Gravestones." *Markers* (Journal of the Association for Gravestone Studies) 6 (1989).

Payne, Ruth Holt. "The Cincinnati Story." *Flashback* (Washington County Historical Society) 11, no. 1 (1961).

Peacock, Nancy C. "Turpentine: A [*sic*] Intriguing Element of Southern Folk Medicine." *Tennessee Anthropologist* 18, no. 2 (Fall 1993).

Peel, Zillah Cross. "Gold Star Mother Returns From France," n.d., no source. [Peel wrote regular columns for both Fayetteville and Fort Smith newspapers.] Susan Walker Shelton scrapbook, Reagan papers, Special Collections, University of Arkansas Libraries, Fayetteville.

The People's Home Library: A Library of Three Practical Books. Cleveland, OH: R. C. Barnum Co., 1916.

Percefull, Janis. "A Public Health Response: 1895 Spa City Smallpox Epidemic." *The Record* (Journal of the Garland County Historical Society) 51, 2010.

Phillips, Bud. *The New Ozark Cousins*. Jasper, AR: Newton County Historical Society, 1984.

Phillips, Jewell Willey. "Liberty Hill Cemetery." *Johnson County Historical Society Journal* 3, no. 1 (1977).

Phillips, Samuel R., ed. *Loyalties Divided: Civil War Years 1862–1865, Batesville, Arkansas: The Journal of Young Mary Adelia Byers*. N.p., 2005–2010.

Pierce, R. V., M.D. *The People's Common Sense Medical Adviser in Plain English; or, Medicine Simplified*. Buffalo, NY: World's Dispensary Medical Association, 1918.

Pile, John David. "Decoration Day at Lowes Creek." In *Remembering the Small Communities of South Franklin County*, ed. Mayme Vest. N.p., 1993.

"Pioneer Woman Embalmer: Lina D. Odou, 1853–19[?]." (Pamphlet), n.p., n.d., Museum of Funeral Customs, Springfield, Illinois.

Pipes, Gerald H. *Strange Customs of the Ozark Hillbilly*. (Pamphlet), n.p., 1956, Special Collections, University of Arkansas Libraries, Fayetteville.

"Poem Written 80 Years Ago Found Behind Picture Frame." *Hermitage* (Crawford County Historical Society) 5, no. 4 (1962).

Polk, R. L. *Arkansas State Gazetteer and Business Directory*, vol. 1. St. Louis, MO: R. L. Polk, 1884.

———. *Arkansas State Gazetteer and Business Directory*, vol. 3. Detroit, MI: R. L. Polk, 1892.

Pollan, Carolyn, ed. "Diary." *Journal* (Fort Smith Historical Society) 1, no. 2 (1977).

Poteet, Rena Bean. "Our Country Cemeteries." *Johnson County Historical Society Journal* 6, no. 1 (April 1980).

Powell, Wilson. "Independence Lodge No. 4 and the I.O.O.F. Home." *Independence County Chronicle* (Independence County Historical Society) 8, no. 3 (1967).

———. "The Kruegers of the Pfeiffer Stone Company." *Independence County Chronicle* (Independence County Historical Society) 15, no. 4 (1974).

Poyner, Martha. "Early Medicine." *Carroll County Historical Quarterly* 43, no. 4 (December 1998).

Puckett, Newbell Niles. *Folk Beliefs of the Southern Negro*. Chapel Hill: University of North Carolina Press, 1926.

Putnam Funeral Home records (Sebastian County), Special Collections, Fort Smith Public Library.

Pye, Jeremy W. "Where Death Sows Rotting Seeds: GIS Assessment of Cemetery Placement in Crawford County, Arkansas." Term paper prepared for ANTH 4553 (Raster GIS), Dept. of Anthropology, University of Arkansas, Fayetteville, 2006.

Quinn, Seabury. *A Syllabus of Mortuary Jurisprudence*. Kansas City, KS: Clement Williams, 1933.

Rafferty, Milton D. *The Ozarks: Land and Life*. Fayetteville: University of Arkansas Press, 2001.

Rahm, Betty Crumrine. "The Crumrine Family of Mountain Home." *Johnson County Historical Society Journal* 21, no. 2 (1995).

Randolph, Vance. *Ozark Folksongs*, ed. Norm Cohen. Urbana: University of Illinois Press, 1982.

———. *Ozark Magic and Folklore*. Mineola, NY: Dover Publications, 1964, reprint. Originally titled *Ozark Superstitions*. New York: Columbia University Press, 1947.

Rayburn, Otto Ernest. *Ozark Country*. New York: Duell, Sloan and Pearce, 1941.

———. *Ozark Folk Encyclopedia*, vol. D-2, unpublished collection of letters, clippings, and photos arranged by subject, Otto Ernest Rayburn papers, Special Collections, University of Arkansas Libraries, Fayetteville:

Cazort, W. S., Mount Ida, Arkansas, undated letter to Rayburn.

France, Isabel. "The Hills of Home: Familiar Custom of Cemetery Decoration is Hallowed Ceremony of Ozark Residents," no source or date.

McCord, May Kennedy. "Hillbilly Heartbeats," newspaper columns, no source or date. McCord published in Missouri's *Springfield Daily News* and the *Springfield Leader* in the 1940s.

Shannon, Karr. "Run of the News: Remember 'Way Back When People Sat Up With Dead?" [*sic*], no source or date.

Unsigned. "A Backwoods Buryin'," no source.

———. Vol. F-2, "'Feather Crown' Omen of Death?" possibly May Kennedy McCord, "Hillbilly Heartbeats" column, no source given.

———. Vol. M-1, Masnor, Lucile, "Keeps Madstone In Bank Vault," undated newspaper clipping datelined Van Buren (either Missouri or Arkansas, probably 1953 or 1954).

———. "Ozark Cyclopedia." *Rayburn's Ozark Guide* 41 (Summer 1954).

———. "Ozark Fact and Folklore: An Encyclopedic Treatment of Things Ozarkian." *Rayburn's Ozark Guide* 42 (Autumn 1954).

——. "Folklore By Mail." *Rayburn's Ozark Guide* 48 (Spring 1956).

——. "Ozark Folk-Ways." *Will-O'-The-Wisp: Madison County Folklore.* Huntsville, Arkansas, Middle School: Theta Mu Epsilon, n.d. [not paginated].

Remsberg, Virginnia Russell. "From Coffin-Making to Undertaking: The Rise of the Funeral Directing Industry in the 1880s." M.A. thesis, University of Delaware, 1992.

Richardson, Ellen Earle. *Early Settlers of Cane Hill.* Fayetteville, AR: Washington County Historical Society, 1955 [Bulletin #9].

Richardson, Eudora Ramsay, and Sherman Allan. *Quartermaster Supply in the European Theater of Operations in World War II, Vol. VII, Graves Registration.* Camp Lee, VA: Quartermaster School, 1948.

Roach, Mary. *Gulp, Adventures on the Alimentary Canal.* New York: W. W. Norton and Company, 2013.

Robinson, Grace. "Mothers Remember: An Account of the Gold Star Pilgrimage to American Cemeteries in France." *Liberty Magazine,* 19 July 1930.

Robinson, Ray. "The Legend of Frank James." *Ozark Trails.* Winona, MN: Apollo Books, 1984.

Rose, Jerome C., ed. *Gone to a Better Land: A Biohistory of a Rural Black Cemetery in the Post-Reconstruction South.* Fayetteville: Arkansas Archeological Survey, 1985 [Research Series No. 25].

Rothman, Sheila M. *Living in the Shadow of Death: Tuberculosis and the Social Experience of Illness in American History.* Baltimore: Johns Hopkins University Press, 1994.

Rothrock, Thomas. "Sarah Elizabeth Banks Recalled the Old Days." *Flashback* (Washington County Historical Society) 6, no. 4 (1956).

Rotundo, Barbara. "Monumental Bronze." In *Cemeteries and Gravemarkers: Voices of American Culture,* ed. Richard E. Meyer. Ann Arbor, MI: UMI Research Press, 1989.

Russell, Joy. *Pre-1920 Obituaries of Madison County, Arkansas, Residents.* Huntsville, AR: Madison County Genealogical & Historical Society, 2011.

——. *Stepping Back Into Time: St. Paul, Arkansas, 1886–1937.* Huntsville, AR: Madison County Genealogical & Historical Society, 2005.

Russell, Joy, and Christy Russell, comps. *History of Hindsville, Arkansas: The Town, the Area, and the People.* Huntsville, AR: Madison County Genealogical & Historical Society, 2001.

Sandels, L. P., and Joseph M. Hill. *A Digest of the Statutes of Arkansas Embracing All Laws of a General Nature in Force at the Close of the Session of the General Assembly of One Thousand Eight Hundred and Ninety-Three.* Columbia, MO: Press of E. W. Stephens, 1894.

Sargent, L. M. *Dealings with the Dead, by a Sexton of the Old School.* Boston: Dutton and Wentworth, 1856.

Saxbe, William B., Jr. "Nineteenth-Century Death Records: How Dependable Are They?" *National Genealogical Society Quarterly* 87, no. 1 (1999).

Schaefer, Susan. *Signs of the Past From Eureka Springs.* Eureka Springs, AR: Ozark Mountain Press, 1994 [not paginated].

Scholle, Sarah Hudson. *The Pain in Prevention, A History of Public Health in Arkansas.* Little Rock: Arkansas Department of Health, 1990.

Scroggins, Louise Taylor. *Old Obituaries, Crawford County Arkansas 1824–1874*. N.p.: 1986 [not paginated].

Searcy County Obituaries, Vol. 1, 1891–1905. Marshall, AR: Jim G. Ferguson Searcy County Library, 2000.

Sears, Roebuck and Co. Incorporated: Consumers Guide, Fall 1900. facsimile edition. Northfield, IL: DBI Books, 1970.

Sears, Roebuck and Co. *Catalogue No. 117*. [N.p.:] Chicago, Illinois, 1908.

Sebastian County Medical Society, and Amelia Whitaker Martin. *Physicians and Medicine: Crawford and Sebastian Counties, Arkansas 1817–1976*. [No location]: Sebastian County Medical Society, 1977.

"Sebern J. Davis' Funeral." *Franklin County Historical Association Observer* 6, no. 1 (July 1985).

Shelton, Susan Walker, undated scrapbook. Reagan papers, Special Collections, University of Arkansas Libraries, Fayetteville.

Sherman, William. *A Brief Account of the Life of William Sherman (An Autobiography)*, ed. W. J. Lemke. Fayetteville, AR: Washington County Historical Society, 1955 [Bulletin No. 18; not paginated].

———. "Funeral Notes, 1930–1958." Microfilm, University of Arkansas Libraries, Fayetteville.

Shull, Laura L. "The Forgotten of Pope County: The Paupers—Part 2." *Pope County Historical Association Quarterly* 36, no. 1 (2002).

———. "Who Is Mandy?" *Pope County Historical Association Quarterly* 38, no. 3 (2004).

Shults, Steve, and Joe Martin. *Randolph County, Arkansas: A Pictorial History*. Morley, MO: Acclaim Press, 2006.

Skelton, Alan Gordon, comp. "The William and John Thaddeus Skelton Families." *Flashback* (Washington County Historical Society) 10, no. 3 (1960).

Sledge, Michael. *Soldier Dead: How We Recover, Identify, Bury and Honor Our Military Fallen*. New York: Columbia University Press, 2005.

Slocum, Linda L. "Customs and Beliefs Surrounding Marriages and Funerals of Negroes in Pine Bluff, Arkansas." Student paper, Parler Folklore Collection, Special Collections, University of Arkansas Libraries, Fayetteville.

"Smallpox in Russellville." *Pope County Historical Association Quarterly* 42, no. 2 (2008).

Smiley, Harold P. "Buried Twice." *Backtracker* (Northwest Arkansas Genealogical Society) 21, no. 1 (1992).

Smith, Flossie Cook, interviewed by Susan Young, 9 September 1997, transcribed by Abby Burnett, Oral History Collection, Shiloh Museum of Ozark History, Springdale, Arkansas.

Smith, Joe E., ed. *Sexton's Record for Van Buren Cemetery (Fairview Cemetery)*. Unpublished typescript, Van Buren (Crawford County) City Archives.

Smith, Louel Collard, comp. *Descendants of Elijah Collard, 1765*. Typescript, 1983, Cleburne County Historical Society, Heber Springs, Arkansas.

Smith, Watson. "Madstone—Medicine or Myth?" *Van Buren County Historical Society Journal* 18, no. 73 (2003).

Sparks, Charldene. *Walking the Wagon Road: Fiction, Fact and Fantasy*. Freeman, SD: Pine Hill Press, 1993.

Standlee, Nora L. Davis. "Life as It Was in Early Carroll County." *Carroll County Historical Quarterly* 43, no. 3 (1988).

Stanley, Mack, and Bess Stanley, comps. *Fort Smith Well Remembered*. N.p., n.d.

Starck, Nigel. *Life After Death: The Art of the Obituary*. Victoria, Australia: Melbourne University Press, 2006.

Starr, Fred. *Climb the Highest Mountain*. Boston: Christopher Publishing House, 1964.

Steele, Pauline Davis. *Hill Country Sayin's and Ozark Folklore*. West Fork, AR: Hutcheson Press, n.d. [not paginated].

Steele, Phillip W. *Two Longs and a Short: An Ozark Boyhood Remembered*. Gretna, LA: Pelican Publishing Co., 2002.

Stephan, A. Stephen. "Changes in the Status of Negroes in Arkansas, 1948–50." *Arkansas Historical Quarterly* 9, no. 1 (1950).

Sterling, R. A. *R. A. Sterling's Rogers, Arkansas, City Directory, 1943*. [No location:] Shofner's Printing, 1943.

Stott, Annette. "The Woodmen of the World Monument Program." *Markers* (Journal of the Association for Gravestone Studies) 20 (2003).

"Sulphur Rock Described as Health Resort With Bright Future in 1903." *Independence County Chronicle* 1, no. 4 (1960).

Swedlund, Alan C. *Shadows in the Valley: A Cultural History of Illness, Death, and Loss in New England, 1840–1916*. Amherst: University of Massachusetts Press, 2010.

Swinburn, Susan Stevenson, and Doris Stevenson West. *History in Headstones: A Complete Listing of All Marked Graves in Known Cemeteries of Crawford County, Arkansas*. Van Buren, AR: Press Argus, 1970.

Szedegin, Estella Wright. *As I Remember Piney*. N.p. [Crawford County Genealogical Society?], 1979.

——— [Mrs. Andrew]. *I'm Thinking About That Tree Yet*. Fort Smith, AR: Calvert McBride, 1992.

———. "Early Medical Practice in the Ozarks." In *Rear View Mirror*, ed. Edwin and Evelyn Hicks. Fort Smith, AR: Westark Community College, 1976.

Taylor, Opal Lee Arnold. *Medicine Time in the Hills of Home*. (Pamphlet), n.p., n.d., Special Collections, University of Arkansas Libraries, Fayetteville.

Taylor, Opal Arnold, unknown interviewer; Searcy County oral history project. Undated videotape (made prior to 1994), transcribed by Abby Burnett, Ozark Heritage Arts Center and Museum, Leslie, Arkansas.

Taylor, Tessie Phillips. "James Willis Phillips: History of James Willis and Tina Whitlow Phillips." *Searcy County Ancestor Information Exchange* 16, no. 3 (2006).

Tharp, Brent Warren. "Preserving Their Form and Features: The Role of Coffins in the American Understanding of Death, 1607–1870." Ph.D. dissertation, College of William and Mary, 1996.

Theta Mu Epsilon. *Will-O'-The-Wisp: Madison County Folklore*. Huntsville, Arkansas, Middle School: N.d. [not paginated].

Thielemier, Susan Moore. *The Making of Catholic Hill*. Corning, AR: J. V. Rockwell Co., 1999.

Thomas, David Y., ed. *Arkansas and Its People, A History, 1541–1930*, vol. 2. New York: American Historical Society, 1930.

Torian, Sarah Hodgson, ed. "Ante-Bellum and War Memories of Mrs. Telfair Hodgson." *Georgia Historical Quarterly* 27, no. 4 (1943).

"The Tracy Family of Fulton and Baxter Counties." *Fulton County Chronicles* 14, no. 1 (1999).

Turnbo, Silas Claiborne. "More Killing in War Days." Springfield–Greene County, Missouri, Library, http://thelibrary.org/lochist/turnbo/toc.html, vol. 2.

———. "Shocking Scenes Enacted at Yellville," vol. 2.

———. "Visiting the Grave of Her Affiance," vol. 3.

———. "The Old Pioneer Joe Magness and His Family," vol. 17.

———. "Brief Sketch of Early History of the Grave Yard in the South West Corner of Ozark County, Missouri," vol. 18.

———. "Died at an Extreme Old Age," vol. 18.

———. "A Part of an Account of the Coker Family Biographical and Historical," vol. 18.

———. "A Death Stricken Family," vol. 19.

———. "Several Old Time Items Worthy of Interest," vol. 19.

———. "Among the Dead," vol. 20.

———. "Bewildered in the Wild Woods," vol. 23.

———. "A Dying Man Tells How He Is Haunted," vol. 24.

———. "In the Midst of Death," vol. 26.

———. "The Prayers of a Devoted Wife Saves Her Sick Husband From Death," vol. 26.

———. "Disinterment of a Young Lady After She had been Dead 12 or 13 Years," vol. 27.

———. "She Did Not Want to be Dead as Bad as She Pretended," vol. 27.

Turpentine, G. R. "Reminiscences." *Pope County Historical Association Quarterly* 6, no. 2 (1971).

U.S. Bureau of the Census. *Mortality Schedules, Arkansas* 1850, 1860, 1870, 1880. Microfilm. [7th U.S. Census—10th U.S. Census].

———. *Tenth Census of the United States, Census of the Blind, Deaf, and Senile.* Washington, DC: United States Census Office, 1880.

———. *Twelfth Census of the United States—1900, Census Reports Vol. 2—Population, Part 2.* Washington, DC: United States Census Office, 1902. Accessed at: http://www.census .gov/prod/www/decennial.html.

Varno, Susan. "Trimble Campground Cemetery (Part II)." *Izard County Historian* 27, no. 1 (2002).

———, and Dan Tyree. "One Dead as Result of Stabbing Affray: The Fight at Deweytown School." *Izard County Historian* 30, no. 1 (2005).

Vaughan, Bruce. *Growing Up Rich, Though Dirt Poor.* [No location:] Farmhouse Books, 2010.

———. *Shiloh Recollections: Historical Facts, Stories, and Tales of Our Entrance, Sometimes Reluctantly, Into the 20th Century.* Springdale, AR: Shiloh Museum of Ozark History, 1997.

Vaughn, Columbus. *Heartbeats of Home.* N.p., 1987. [Note: A *Newton County Times* article, having the same title and author, is cited in the notes for chapter 6.]

Walden, James A. *The Journals of James A. Walden, Part 2, Methodist Minister*, ed. W. J. Lemke. Fayetteville, AR: Washington County Historical Society, 1954 [Bulletin #5].

Walker, Fannie. "Some Items From Mrs. Walker's Collection of Historical Mementoes." *Flashback* (Washington County Historical Society) 11, no. 4 (1961).

Warren, Luther E. *Truth Twisters: Ozark Humor, History, and Political Commentaries.* Conway, AR: Penny Pincher Printing, 1999.

Wassell, Mrs. Sam S. "Negro Folklore," written 1919, in *Folklore of Romantic Arkansas*, vol. 2, by Fred W. Allsopp. Boston, MA: Grolier Society, 1931.

Wasserman, Emily. *Gravestone Designs: Rubbings and Photographs From Early New York and New Jersey.* Mineola, NY: Dover Publications, 1973.

Watts, Isaac. *Hymns and Spiritual Songs, in Three Books*, Book 1. London, England: Printed for W. Strahan, J. and F. Rivington, J. Buckland, G. Keith, L. Hawes, W. Clarke and B. Collins, T. Longman, T. Field, and E. and C. Dilly, 1773.

Wayland, Paul T. "Batesville's Memorial Park Cemetery." *Independence County Chronicle* 15, no. 4 (1974).

Webster, Roy. *Under a Buttermilk Moon, A Country Memoir.* Little Rock, AR: August House, 1984.

Westphal, June, and Catharine Osterhage. *A Fame Not Easily Forgotten: An Autobiography of Eureka Springs.* Conway, AR: River Road Press, 1970.

Whittemore, Carol. *Fading Memories, A History of the Lives and Times of Madison County People*, vol. 1. N.p., 1989.

———. *Fading Memories*, vol. 2. N.p., 1992.

———. *Fading Memories*, vol. 3. N.p., 1999.

Wiggins, Jack. "Remembering Annie Eliza Acord Eubanks: An Arkansas Pioneer." *Johnson County Historical Society Journal* 29, no. 4 (2002).

Wilder, Jeremy H. "Thirty-Seventh Illinois at Prairie Grove." *Arkansas Historical Quarterly* 49, no. 1 (1990)

Wilhoit, Ed. "A Doctor's Saddle-Bags of Cures." *Izard County Historian* 19, no. 1 (1988).

Williams, Mollie E. *A Thrilling Romance of The Civil War; The History of Mrs. Mollie E. Williams; Written by Herself; Forty-Two Days in Search of a Missing Husband; A Lesson of Woman's Fidelity, Fortitude and Affection.* N.p.: Chicago, 1902, reprinted by the Jim G. Ferguson Searcy County Library, Marshall, Arkansas.

Williams, Pearl Thomas. "Something Good to Say about Everybody." In *Come Go With Me: Old-Timer Stories from the Southern Mountains.* comp. Roy Edwin Thomas. New York: Farrar, Straus, Giroux, 1994.

Williams, [Vester ?]. "The Pioneer Coffin Makers, Native Coffin Making in the Days of Ozark Pioneers." In *Compilation of Articles on Fulton County and Salem, Ark.* Noah Cain, Dorothy Brinker, Tom W. Campbell, and Vester Williams, compilers. N.p., 1972.

Wilson, Jaunita. *Cincinnati, Arkansas, 1838–1986, Illinois Township.* N.p., Siloam Springs Printing, 1986.

Winn, Robert G. "A Smallpox Epidemic." *Flashback* (Washington County Historical Society) 26, no. 3 (1976).

———. *The Story of Winslow's Maud Duncan.* Fayetteville, AR: Washington County Historical Society, 1992.

Winslow Centennial Book Committee. *Winslow, Arkansas: Past and Present, 1905–2005.*
    [Winslow, AR]: The Committee, 2005.

Wise, Ruth. "Burials, Back When." *Carroll County Historical Quarterly* 44, no. 3 (1999).

Witherspoon, Birdie Parks. *Pioneer Life In Rural Missouri: Personal Reflections.* (Pamphlet),
    n.p., [1970?].

Wolfe, Joseph M. *Album of Odd Fellows Homes.* Minneapolis, MN: n.p., n.d. Genealogy
    library, Old Independence Regional Museum, Batesville, Arkansas.

Wolf, John Quincy. *Life in the Leatherwoods: An Ozark Boyhood Remembered.* Little Rock,
    AR: August House, 1988.

Woodmen of the World Life Insurance Co. *Ritual of the Woodmen of the World, Containing
    the Opening Ceremony, Protection Degree, Closing Ceremony, Installation and Instituting
    Services, Unveiling of Monuments, Funeral, Burial, Dedication and Corner Stone Ser-
    vices.* Omaha, NE: Beacon Press Print, 1903.

Wooley, Capt. Richard W. "A Short History of Identification Tags." Quartermaster Profes-
    sional Bulletin, December 1988, U.S. Army Quartermaster Foundation, accessed at
    www.qmfound.com/short_history_of_identification_tags.htm.

Works Progress Administration. Historical Records Survey, Special Collections, University
    of Arkansas Libraries, Fayetteville.

———. Early Settlers' Personal History Questionnaires.

———. "Coroners." Unsigned typescript dated 19 December 1938, Benton County Health
    Unit.

———. "Midwife Pledge Card." Arkansas State Board of Health, Bureau of Child Hygiene,
    in cooperation with the U.S. Department of Labor, Children's Bureau, Baxter County
    Health Unit, 1938.

Wright, Sewell Peaslee. *Ethical Advertising for Funeral Directors.* Chicago: Trade Periodical
    Company, 1924.

Wright, Roberta Hughes, Wilbur B. Hughes III, and Barbara K. Hughes Smith, eds. *The
    Death Care Industry: African American Cemeteries and Funeral Homes.* N.p., 2007.

Young, Susan. "*So Big, This Little Place*": The Founding of Tontitown, Arkansas, 1898–1917.
    Tontitown, AR: Tontitown Historical Museum, 2009.

Oral Histories

When the subjects, listed below, are quoted in the text, they are identified by their county
and dates, but these interviews are not cited in the notes. There are, however, six exceptions:
Connell Brown, Rex Harral, Wayne Martin, David Matlock, Tom Olmstead, and Bruce
Vaughan, who published memoirs, were interviewed by others and may also have corresponded with me via e-mail, so when they are quoted the notes reflect these varied sources.

In five instances I had access to oral histories, conducted by others, that are not readily
available to the public. These are interviews with Fannie Duck, Roxie Smith Cook, Milbra
Eaton Parker, Flossie Cook Smith, and Opal Arnold Taylor; when these women are quoted
the oral history sources are identified in the notes.

Agee, Frank. Hasty (Newton). January 2006.

Boyd, Vernon. Wesley (Madison). June 2007.

Bradshaw, Gladys. Kingston (Madison). January 2011.

Brashears, Sumner, and Lucina. Huntsville (Madison). March 2011.

Brown, Connell. Everton (Boone). March 2011.

Bryant, Jessie. Fayetteville (Washington). June 2006.

Burnett, Imodell Price. Bergman (Boone). September 2007.

Burnett, Shirley. Upper Campground (Madison). February 2013.

Cain, Phillip. Kingston (Madison). October 2006.

Carnahan, Hester. Fayetteville (Washington). August 2006.

Clark, Eul Dean Casey. Boxley Valley (Newton). January 2007.

Collins, Ruth. Wesley (Madison). June 2007.

Cotton, Joy. Wickes (Polk). June 2006.

Fancher, Burr. Kingston (Madison). September 2005.

Ferguson, Roberta Watts. Landis (Searcy). October 2007

Ford, Coy. Crossroads/Stoverville (Newton). August 2010.

Gallagher, Mary Maude. Clarksville (Johnson). October 2007.

Grigg, Charlene Cook. Kingston (Madison). March 2006.

Grubbs, Charles K. Huntsville (Madison). April 2007.

Gurley, Truman. Osage (Newton). July 2006.

Hall, Joe, M.D. Lincoln (Washington). March 2007.

Harral, Rex. Wilburn (Cleburne). June 2007.

Hatfield, Kevin. Forum/Alabam (Madison). April 2010.

Hefley, Howard. Sam's Throne (Newton). March 2006.

Horton, Kathryn. St. Joe (Searcy). June 2006.

Larimer, Ted. Green Forest (Carroll). August 2005.

Leister, Mira. Clarksville (Johnson). April 2010.

Lindsay, Ruby Holland. Alabam (Madison). February 1998.

Little, John D. Kingston (Madison). December 1994, January 2006, December 2007.

Marquess, Mary. Rogers/Bentonville (Benton). April 2007.

Martin, Wayne, and June (Baker). Pettigrew (Madison). November 2005.

Matlock, David. Fort Smith (Sebastian). January 2008.

McConnell, Grace. Huntsville (Madison). April 2006.

Mhoon, Bernice. Morrow (Washington). June 2007.

Mills, Reva. Fayetteville (Washington). November 2010.

Mitchell, Charles. Pinnacle Mt. (Madison). January 2006.

Mooney, Tommie Hoskins. Spoke Plant (Madison). December 2005.

Morrison, Ulis Warren. Campbell's Valley (Searcy). June 2005.

Newton, Robert. Harrison (Boone). September 2011.

Olmstead, Tom. Heber Springs (Cleburne). January 2006, May 2007.

Ott, Lou Ann Clough. Rush (Marion). February 2007.

Parish, Rev. A. J. Fort Smith (Sebastian). January 2006.

Pearson, Wilson Bud. Lamar (Johnson). October 2005.

Phillips, Emma. Marshall (Searcy). June 2006.

Phillips, Virgil. Coal Hill (Johnson). June 2012.

Powell, Norman. Ozark (Franklin). August 2005.

Ragan, Glenna. Harrison (Boone). September 2011.

Reed, Pauline. Ball Creek/Japton (Madison). March 2006.

Russell, Joy. Huntsville (Madison). August 2000.

Rutherford, James. Batesville (Independence). May 2007.

Scott, James C., Jr. Russellville (Pope). May 2007.

Sparks, Alene Hattabaugh. Coal Hill (Johnson). December 2005.

Spurlock, Darby. Whorton Creek (Madison). April 2012.

Stepp, Artist. Spoke Plant (Madison). October 2005.

Stepp, Peggy Harmon. Oak Grove (Johnson). January 2006.

Stockton, Charles. Kingston (Madison). September 2004.

Tassey, Veda McElhaney. Witter (Madison). December 2005.

Terherst, Nellie Peden. Enon (Boone). September 2005.

Tomkins, Ethel. Post Oak (Jackson). July 2011.

Vaughan, Bruce. Spring Valley (Washington). August 2005.

Vaughan, Mary Maestri. Tontitown (Washington). September 2005.

Williams, Kathleen Miller. Winslow (Washington). September 2005.

Williams, Viola. Alpena (Boone/Carroll). July 2005.

Wyatt, Ray, and Orphea Sparks. Fallsville, Cave Mt. (Newton). July 2007.

INDEX